LESBIAN TEXTS AND CONTEXTS

FEMINIST CROSSCURRENTS

EDITED BY KATHLEEN BARRY

American Feminism: A Contemporary History
GINETTE CASTRO
Translated from the French by Elizabeth Loverde-Bagwell

Lesbian Texts and Contexts: Radical Revisions
EDITED BY KARLA JAY AND JOANNE GLASGOW

LESBIAN TEXTS AND CONTEXTS: RADICAL REVISIONS

**Edited by
Karla Jay and Joanne Glasgow**

NEW YORK UNIVERSITY PRESS

NEW YORK AND LONDON

Library of Congress Cataloging-in-Publication Data

Lesbian texts and contexts : radical revisions /
edited by Karla Jay and Joanne Glasgow.
p.   cm. — (Feminist crosscurrents)
Includes bibliographical references.
ISBN 0-8147-4175-4 (alk. paper) — ISBN 0-8147-4177-0 (pbk. : alk. paper)
1. Lesbians' writings, American—History and criticism.
2. Lesbians' writings, English—History and criticism.
3. Lesbianism in literature.   4. Feminism and literature.
5. Lesbians in literature.   6. Women and literature.
I. Jay, Karla.   II. Glasgow, Joanne, 1943–   .   III. Series.
PS153.L46L46   1990   810.9'353—dc20   90-30567
                                            CIP

New York University Press books are printed on acid-free paper,
and their binding materials are chosen for strength and durability.

Contents

Foreword

The current women's movement of the 1990s is more vigorous than ever.
But despite all of its creative energy and political determinism, for the last
twenty years the prophets of doom in the media have continually proclaimed
it dead while academicians designate our demise in terms such as *postfem-
inism*. Yet feminism has expanded to encompass the global dimensions of
patriarchal oppression with theories and actions that reveal a sharpened
politics and deeper analysis of sex class conditions. Racial, cultural, national diversities among women make the work of international feminism
all the more profound as it carves out and celebrates that which women
share in common and politically unifies us against patriarchal domination.

Since the late 1960s the women's movement has proven itself to be the
most viable social movement of the 1970s and the most urgently necessary
of the 1980s and now is one of our strongest hopes in the 1990s. Feminism
has refused conservative-fundamentalist efforts to reduce women to their
reproductive functions and contested the liberal ideal of women as pornographic sexual objects. Feminist scholarship, at its best, is charting its own
course and emerging from women's lives to define theory and shape research
around the globe.

The Feminist Crosscurrents series is committed to emphasizing the
critical links between scholarly research and theory and feminist politics
and practice. This series recognizes that radicalism is critical to any movement of feminist thought, and that women's oppression constitutes a class
condition. We are concerned with theory and analysis that enlightens
research and activism on how sex class, gender stratification, and race
interface in the lives of women, yet we do not invalidate white middle-class
women's experience by reducing it, as many have tried, to "privileged" or
"bourgeois." And, we do not avoid works that may be considered "too
hostile" because they expose systems of male privileges and awards as class
conditions of domination over women. We seek to present works from a
diverse, international community of feminist scholars in a broad range of
academic disciplines that speaks to the fullest dimensions of the condition
of women. Our series has been launched with a range of works that reflect
this goal and include works on women, sexuality, and war in the Middle

East, a legal history of U.S. women, a French study of the American women's movement, and an anthropology of fraternity gang rape.

Joanne Glasgow's and Karla Jay's anthology, *Lesbian Texts and Contexts: Radical Revisions,* breaks ground in literary criticism by offering the first collection that definitively marks off lesbian/feminist literary criticism as its own distinctive field of study. While scholarly in its scope, by invoking author, reader, and text, this work vividly reminds us of the significance of lesbian novels, plays, and poetry in locating personal experience in literary text. By exploring gendered readings of text and giving voice to lesbianism in literature through a myriad of perspectives from scholars in this field, this work reveals the text, not as a distanced objectified entity, but rather as a highly political and cultural instrument of our society.

KATHLEEN BARRY
Pennsylvania State University

Acknowledgments

There are many people who have helped us to create a book of this scope. First, we are grateful to Kathleen Barry for encouraging us to develop an anthology of lesbian literary criticism, and to Kitty Moore of New York University Press for her enthusiasm for the project. We would also like to thank Elizabeth Meese for providing several good suggestions for a title, one of which we finally chose; Valerie Miner, whose essay generated the first section of this collection; Minnie Bruce Pratt, who tried to connect us with a variety of writers; Jane Marcus, Ruth Johnston, and Yvonne M. Klein for their advice on various essays; Barbara Grier of Naiad Press, Vivian Scheinmann of Pandora Book Peddlers, the Lesbian Herstory Archives, and A Different Light Bookshop (New York) for their help with bibliographic references.

Grateful acknowledgment is made to Daphne Marlatt, Nicole Brossard, and nbj for permission to reproduce passages from Daphne Marlatt and Nicole Brossard, *Character/Jeu de Lettres* (copyright © 1986, by Daphne Marlatt, Nicole Brossard, and nbj.

Grateful acknowledgment is made to Little, Brown and Company for permission to quote from *The Complete Poems of Emily Dickinson*, edited by Thomas H. Johnson. Copyright 1914, 1929, 1942 by Martha Dickinson Bianchi; copyright © renewed 1957 by Mary L. Hampson. By permission of Little, Brown and Company.

Grateful acknowledgment is made to the publishers and Trustees of Amherst College for permission to quote from *The Poems of Emily Dickinson*, Thomas H. Johnson, ed., Cambridge, Mass.: The Belknap Press of Harvard University Press. Copyright 1951, © 1955, 1979, 1983 by the President and Fellows of Harvard College.

Grateful acknowledgment is made to New Directions Publishing Corporation for permission to quote from H. D., *HERmione*, copyright © 1981 by The Estate of Hilda Doolittle; and from previously unpublished material by H. D., copyright © 1989 by Perdita Schaffner. Used by permission of New Directions Publishing Corporation, Agents.

Grateful acknowledgment is made to Editions Quinze, Montreal, and to Nicole Brossard for permission to quote from *Amantes*.

Grateful acknowledgment is made to Editions Quinze, Montreal, to Guernica Editions, to Nicole Brossard, and to Barbara Godard for permission to quote from *Lovhers*.

Grateful acknowledgment is made to Nancy Rawls for permission to quote from her work.

Contributors

KATE ADAMS has a master's degree in English from San Jose State University and is completing a Ph.D. in the American Civilization Program at the University of Texas, Austin. Her dissertation, "Economies of Poetry," is a study of post–World War II U.S. poetry and American cultural politics inside and outside the academy.

PAULA BENNETT has taught at University College, Northeastern University, for the past thirteen years. A former editor of *Focus: A Journal for Lesbians,* she is the author of *My Life a Loaded Gun: Female Creativity and Feminist Poetics,* a biographical study of Dickinson, Plath, and Rich. She has also written *Emily Dickinson,* the first full-length interpretation of Dickinson's poetry by a lesbian/feminist. She is now at work on a biography of Dickinson based on the poet's letters. When not writing criticism, she is trying to learn how to write science fiction/fantasy.

SHARI BENSTOCK is Professor of English and Director of Women's Studies at the University of Miami. She is author of *Women of the Left Bank, Textualizing the Feminine: Essays on the Limits of Genre,* and editor of *Feminist Issues in Literary Scholarship* and *The Private Self: Theory and Practice of Women's Autobiographical Writings,* in addition to books on James Joyce. She is coeditor of *Reading Women Writing,* a feminist book series at Cornell University Press. She is the former editor of *Tulsa Studies in Women's Literature.*

SDIANE A. BOGUS, poet, writer, publisher, teacher, and scholar, has published in such journals and magazines as *Black Thought, The Sack Butt Review, Sinister Wisdom, CLA Journal, Common Lives/Lesbian Lives, The Black American Literature Forum,* and *Black America Magazine.* Her books include *I'm Off to See the Goddamn Wizard, Alright! Woman in the Moon, Her Poems,* and *Sapphire Sampler.* She lives in Turlock, California, where she teaches Composition, Literature, Black Studies, and Women's Studies at California State University, Stanislaus.

MAUREEN BRADY, author of the novels *Give Me Your Good Ear* and *Folly,* and the collection of short stories, *The Question She Put to Herself,* has been awarded grants from Creative Artists in Public Service, New York State Council on the Arts writer-in-residence program, and Money for

Women/Barbara Deming Memorial Fund. Currently, she teaches writing workshops and is at work on a novel. Her essay began as a talk, "Writing Ourselves Whole," which was presented at the Third International Feminist Book Fair in Montreal in 1988.

ROSEMARY CURB is Professor of English and Women's Studies at Rollins College in Florida where she initiated and coordinates the Women's Studies program and teaches many women's studies and gay studies courses. She has published numerous articles on African-American playwrights and feminist theater. She has been an activist for lesbian rights in professional organizations, recently serving as Cochair of the Lesbian and Gay Caucus of the Modern Language Association and Chair of the Lesbian Caucus of the National Women's Studies Association. With Nancy Manahan she is coeditor of *Lesbian Nuns: Breaking Silence*.

MARILYN R. FARWELL is Associate Professor of English at the University of Oregon. Her current research focuses on the relationship between contemporary lesbian literary theory and women's literature. She has published essays on Adrienne Rich, Virginia Woolf, Milton, and more recently on lesbian literary theory. She is currently working on a collection of essays which defines ways in which lesbian literary theory can offer new readings of literature by women.

JUDITH FETTERLEY is Professor of English and Women's Studies and Director of Graduate Studies for the Department of English at SUNY, Albany. She is the author of *The Resisting Reader: A Feminist Approach to American Fiction* and *Provisions: A Reader from Nineteenth Century American Women*, as well as of numerous articles on a variety of nineteenth- and twentieth-century American writers. With Joanne Dobson and Elaine Showalter, she founded the Rutgers University Press American Women Writers series. For this series, she edited a volume of the short fiction of Alice Cary. She is currently coauthoring, with Marjorie Pryse, a forthcoming anthology of American women regionalist writers. She lives in Albany, New York, with her lover, her lover's two children, and her very own car.

NOEL RILEY FITCH is the author of *Sylvia Beach and the Lost Generation: A History of Literary Paris in the Twenties and Thirties* (now in its ninth printing), *Literary Cafés*, and *Hemingway in Paris*. Fitch teaches at the University of Southern California and lives in Los Angeles.

JOANNE GLASGOW is Professor of English and Women's Studies at Bergen Community College, New Jersey, and Past President of the Women's Caucus for the Modern Languages. She has written many articles and reviews for *New Directions for Women* and is currently working on a biographical and literary study of Radclyffe Hall.

KARLA JAY is the coeditor (with Allen Young) of three anthologies on gay liberation: *Out of the Closets: Voices of Gay Liberation, After You're Out,* and *Lavender Culture,* all published by Pyramid/Jove. With Young, she also coauthored *The Gay Report.* Her most recent book is *The Amazon and the Page: Natalie Clifford Barney and Renée Vivien,* which was nominated for a Lambda Book Award. She is an Associate Professor of English and Women's Studies at Pace University in New York.

YVONNE M. KLEIN was born in New York City and emigrated to Montreal in 1969, where she teaches English and Women's Literature at Dawson College. She has published a number of translations from French, including (with Karla Jay) Renée Vivien's *The Woman of the Wolf* and Jovette Marchessault's *Lesbian Triptych, Like a Child of the Earth,* and *Mother of the Grass,* as well as numerous book reviews and critical articles. Her translation of the *Triptych* won the Canada Council's prize for best translation in 1986.

CASSANDRA LAITY is Assistant Professor of English at the University of Oregon. She is presently completing a book on H. D. and Decadent-Romantic influence entitled *H. D. and the Turn of the Century: Gender, Modernism and Romantic Influence.* She is also editor of the forthcoming collection on the New Woman, *The New Woman, 1880–1940: Images and Realities.*

LEE LYNCH is the author of three novels, two collections of short stories, and a collection of her syndicated columns. Her most recent novel is *Sue Slate, Private Eye,* whose protagonist is lesbian, cat, and detective. Her reviews, columns, and feature articles appear in gay and lesbian periodicals nationwide. She lives in Southern Oregon where she earns her living in the social services.

JANE MARCUS is the author of *Virginia Woolf and the Languages of Patriarchy* and *Art and Anger,* and she is the editor of three volumes of feminist Woolf criticism and the *Young Rebecca West.* She wrote the Afterword for the 1989 Feminist Press reprint of June Arnold's *Sister Gin.* She is Professor of English at the City University of New York Graduate Center and the City College of New York.

ELIZABETH MEESE is Professor of English and Adjunct Professor of Women's Studies at the University of Alabama. She has written two books, *Crossing the Double-Cross: The Practice of Feminist Literary Criticism* and the forthcoming *(Ex)Tensions: Re-Figuring Feminist Criticism,* and has coedited (with Alice Parker) two volumes of feminist critical scholarship—*The Difference Within: Feminism and Critical Theory* and the forthcoming *Feminist Critical Negotiations.* The essay included here is the first chapter of her new work, entitled *(Sem)erotics: Theorizing Lesbian Writing.*

MARY MEIGS was born in Philadelphia in 1917, graduated from Bryn Mawr College in 1939, studied painting after World War II and had one-woman shows in Boston, New York, Cape Cod, and Paris. She moved to Quebec in 1975. Her first book, *Lily Briscoe: A Self-Portrait,* published in 1981, was followed by *The Medusa Head* and *The Box Closet,* all published by Talonbooks, Vancouver. She is currently writing about her experience with six other women over sixty-five in a National Film Board semidocumentary, "The Bus," filmed in summer 1988.

VALERIE MINER'S novels are *All Good Women, Winter's Edge, Movement, Blood Sisters,* and *Murder in the English Department* and her new short story collection is called *Trespassing.* Her collaborative efforts include coauthoring *Her Own Woman, Tales I Tell My Mother,* and *Competition: A Feminist Taboo?* She has taught at the University of California, Berkeley, for eleven years. She also travels widely, giving readings and lectures.

ALICE PARKER is Associate Professor of French and Humanities at the University of Alabama. She has published articles on eighteenth-century and twentieth-century feminist and lesbian writers, has coedited two volumes of theoretical essays, and is currently writing a book on Nicole Brossard.

NAMASCAR SHAKTINI'S articles on *The Lesbian Body* by Monique Wittig have appeared in the United States, England, and France. As a student in Paris, she witnessed the events of May 1968, studied with Roland Barthes at the Ecole Pratique des Hautes Etudes, and was arrested in the first public action on the Mouvement de Libération des Femmes on 26 August 1970 at the Arc de Triomphe. An Assistant Professor of French at Florida Atlantic University, she is currently writing a book on Monique Wittig's revolutionary signifier.

CATHARINE R. STIMPSON is Professor of English, Dean of the Graduate School, and Vice-Provost for Graduate Education at Rutgers, The State University of New Jersey (New Brunswick). Now the editor of a book series for the University of Chicago Press, she was the founding editor of *Signs.* The author of a novel, *Class Notes,* and the editor of seven books, she has also published over 115 monographs, essays, stories, and reviews.

A selection of essays, *Where the Meanings Are,* appeared in 1988. She is currently completing a book on Gertrude Stein.

ANNETTE VAN DYKE is the Associate Director of the Center for Women's Studies, University of Cincinnati, Ohio. She has a Ph.D. in American Studies from the University of Minnesota and is currently revising her dissertation, "Feminist Curing Ceremonies: The Goddess in Contemporary Spiritual Traditions," for publication. She lives with her partner of fifteen years and their three cats.

BONNIE ZIMMERMAN is Professor of Women's Studies at San Diego State University. She has published articles on George Eliot and on lesbian literature and theory. This is her first attempt to bring the two together. She is the author of the forthcoming *The Safe Sea of Women: Lesbian Fiction 1969–1988.*

Introduction

Joanne Glasgow and Karla Jay

This collection of essays grew out of a perceived need that we both articu-lated in the summer of 1987. We had each been teaching women's studies and literature courses which included work by significant numbers of lesbian writers. Together and separately we had been searching for the best lesbian/feminist critical essays to assign our students and to sharpen our own critical insights. And there were some very fine articles to choose from, some widely available, some hardly accessible at all. As members of the Division of Gay Studies in Language and Literature of the Modern Lan-guage Association, we both knew how much excellent lesbian scholarship was being produced. But when we looked for critical collections reflecting this burgeoning scholarship, we discovered that there were none. We had no convenient place to send students to, no volume which contained an overview of recent trends, methodologies, theories, and new research on lesbian writers. Such a collection as the one we have assembled here seemed overdue and sorely needed.

At about the same time, Kathleen Barry had begun to edit a feminist series for New York University Press, entitled "Feminist Crosscurrents," and she recognized the need for a collection such as ours. When we began assembling essays for inclusion in the book, we were approached by Valerie Miner and later by several other lesbian writers who thought we should include essays about reader-writer interaction, the question of audience for the lesbian writer, the question of audience for the nonlesbian writing about lesbians, for the lesbian writing about nonlesbians or researching women and/or developing characters who represented diverse classes, races, religions, or values. This opened exciting new possibilities for an anthology, one which could examine the complex entanglements of identity, voice, intersubjectivity, textualities, and sexualities.

As we began work, we envisioned a collection that was original and that would significantly add to the body of lesbian criticism available to our colleagues, but we also wanted one that could be read by most lesbians and by our gay and straight students as well. We also wanted essays that would illustrate the wide variety of approaches and methodologies that characterize lesbian scholarship in the 1990s.

The subtitle *Radical Revisions* consciously echoes one of the earliest (1971) and best lesbian/feminist essays, Adrienne Rich's "When We Dead Awaken: Writing as Re-Vision." In that essay Rich defines re-vision as "the act of looking back, of seeing with fresh eyes, of entering an old text from a new critical direction" (90). This revision, she argues, is not merely self-reflexive nor self-affirming, but an "act of survival" (90). For almost twenty years, Rich and other pioneering lesbian/feminist writers and readers have been constructing, deconstructing, reconstructing, and exploding the language of experience and the experience of language. Sometimes the act of re-visioning becomes abstract and theoretical; sometimes it is personal and narrative. Often it draws upon the current theoretical bases of 1980s' literary criticism: Lacanian psychoanalytical theory, Bakhtinian discourse analysis, semiotics, poststructuralism, reader-response theory, or the gynocriticism advocated and practiced by Showalter and Gilbert and Gubar, among others. Occasionally it uses the techniques of the new historicism or harks back to the old "New Criticism." But whatever the theoretical stance and whatever the methodology employed, lesbian criticism never loses sight of Rich's early activist assumption—unless we see with fresh eyes, unless we find our own language and inscribe our own experience, we will be again silenced or erased. We cannot survive without our words. It is a criticism about and for our lives, what Sandra Gilbert, in another context, has called "Life Studies" (Auerbach 151).

Despite this rich diversity of approach there is a common feminist literary principle, one that clearly marks any feminist critical project as different from the (assumed) neutral or gender-free or (impossibly) universalist position once so widespread and unquestioningly held by the male-dominated academy. Simply stated, for feminists, every text is written from a gendered consciousness, just as every reading is a gendered experience.

Gynocriticism, to use Elaine Showalter's term, is an exploration of these gendered texts inspired by the search for the special qualities of "woman's writing." And much exciting and challenging criticism has come from this woman-centered approach to reading. But all too often there are unexamined race, class, and sexual preference assumptions in the simple term *woman*. As Barbara Christian has pointed out in *Black Feminist Criticism*, the term itself in the nineteenth century was reserved for white privileged females (161). Nor is this exclusionary labeling a thing of the past. Elizabeth Fox-Genovese asserts in a 1987 essay that "[f]or white American women, the self comes wrapped in gender, or rather, gender constitutes the invisible, seamless wrapping of the self. Such is the point of gender in a stable society" (168). Fox-Genovese goes on to argue that the dominant gender system has "powerfully influenced the ways in which most American women have written about themselves and their lives, and has especially influenced their sense of their readers" (168), even when those writers are black.

These observations seem indisputably true, and they help us to recognize the problematic nature of feminist criticism that fails to deal with racial, class, ethnic, and religious diversity. But even Fox-Genovese fails to recognize the heterosexist assumptions of her critique. For her, gender is structured exclusively through male-female interaction. "How to be a woman," she writes, "is defined in relation to how to be a man and the reverse. Neither maleness nor femaleness exists as an absolute" (168). While Fox-Genovese states that gender constructions can "come unstuck" from sexuality, she never acknowledges that gender is different from biological maleness and femaleness. This kind of language knot is at the heart of the language problem of gender that we must explore.

Lesbian/feminist criticism, therefore, must subject this principle of gendered reading/writing to further analysis. Gendered experience is simply not the same for lesbians as for nonlesbians. Women's experience of gendered culture and gendered texts is filtered by sexual preference and sexual behavior. Language, always problematic for women in a phallologocentric world, is more problematic still for the lesbian, who finds that common assumptions built into the gendered language are heterosexist. What does it mean to view "woman" or "woman's experience" as Other when the object of desire is not differentiated by either sex or gender? How does one view common feminist assumptions about gender that posit "wife" and/or "mother" as primary predicates, or that erase the existence of lesbian mothers or presume the term to be oxymoronic? What does one say about gender, *in the first place,* if gender is constructed only and exclusively according to heterosexual norms? And thus, what is one to make of the language, limited as it is to heterosexist assumptions, which we nevertheless all must use to express gender? How to use this heterosexist gender language and how to read it when others use it become questions of increasing complexity as lesbian writers and readers grapple with texts, subtexts, contexts. As Teresa de Lauretis explains, lesbian writers and artists have attempted to solve these dilemmas through attempts "variously to escape gender, to deny it, transcend it, or perform it in excess, and to inscribe the erotic in cryptic, allegorical, realistic, camp, or other modes of representation, pursuing diverse strategies of writing and of reading the intransitive and yet obdurate relation of reference to meaning, of flesh to language" (159). In one way or another, using one or another of many different theories and methodologies, each contributor to this volume addresses those complex questions.

Central to these explorations is an awareness of the interaction of author/text/reader, at least one of which is identified as lesbian. Such identification is, of course, problematic, because the language itself remains problematic. Even in 1990, a generation after the debate began, thoughtful and concerned feminists do not, perhaps *cannot,* agree about just who *is* a lesbian. Is she a woman whose erotic desires are for other women, or is she a "woman-identified woman"? Is she a woman at all, if *woman* is a heterosexist language construct?[1] And if this term is so problematic, how can one ever hope to define or label a lesbian text? Who is the lesbian writer or the lesbian reader? Are lesbian texts, readers, and writers so hopelessly unknowable that we can only shout each other off the page?

Without arguing for a definitive answer to any of these questions, we do offer our belief that reader-response theory can help to extricate us from the apparent impasse and help to explain as well one aspect of the dynamic we call (paraphrasing Jonathan Culler) "Reading as a Lesbian."[2]

It will be obvious, even from the Table of Contents and from the varied positions of the contributors, that we do believe that one can read as a lesbian even if one is not thus self-identified. As Culler argues in "Reading as a Woman," for generations women have been encouraged, trained, and rewarded academically for "reading as men" (43), despite the high price exacted by this identification *against* ourselves.[3] Moreover, according to Culler, men as well as women can "read as women" if by that phrase we mean "to avoid reading as a man, to identify the specific defenses and distortions of male readings and provide corrections" (54). The task of the reader is to "investigate whether the procedures, assumptions, and goals of current criticism are in complicity with the preservation of male authority, and to explore alternatives" (61). Reading, thus, is an exercise in interpretive strategies and is not, nor should it be, bound to specific, shared life experiences.

When Culler uses *woman*, we would substitute *lesbian*, and where he uses *male* we would substitute *heterosexual*. We would then argue for interpretive strategies that enable us to deconstruct the category of the Lesbian Other. That this is a feasible reading strategy is demonstrated by the authors, texts, and readers included in this collection. Moreover, being teachers as well as critics, we know experientially that it is indeed possible to "read as a lesbian," to read "with fresh eyes," whether one is lesbian or straight, female or male. Otherwise, all reading is solipsistic and all texts hermeneutically inaccessible except to those already inside the closed circle.

At the same time, however, reader-response theory also affirms that self-identification and lived experience can and often do create significantly different readings of texts. As Jane Marcus points out in the introduction to her collection *Art and Anger: Reading Like a Woman,* the "vulgarism" of *like* "signals an inside 'natural,' though not biologically essentialist, woman's reading position" (xxi). Who we are matters in creating the text we read. de Lauretis echoes this view: ". . . each reading is a rewriting of the text, each writing a rereading of (one's) experience" (161). Reading with a lesbian consciousness, thus, can make us alert to "coded" texts and enable us to read them in radically altered ways, as Paula Bennett demonstrates in her reading of Emily Dickinson. Reading as lesbians can also enable us to deconstruct the heterosexual surfaces of seemingly "straight" forward texts, as both Marilyn R. Farwell and Bonnie Zimmerman illustrate. The lesbian reading is not identical with the straight reading.

Nevertheless, we must beware of collapsing difference even as we "read" difference. As Biddy Martin writes in a recent essay, the lesbian reading experience offers dynamic possibilities we have only begun to explore:

If we lend credence to the lesbian reader's sensitivity to the ways in which lesbianism is encoded in only apparently "straight" . . . accounts, the obsession with the author's identity, the text's mimetic function and the reader's necessary identification, if we then consider the reader's pleasure, the ways in which she feels addressed, her desire engaged, then the question of what is lesbian about a life or an account of a life shifts much more dramatically. (77)

Martin's essay challenges us, however, to avoid the homogeneity trap and to beware universalizing the term *lesbian*. Reading as a lesbian is not the same for women of color as for whites, for the old as for the young, for the poor as for the privileged, for the physically challenged as for the able-bodied. For Martin, as for many of us, the word *lesbian* is not an "identity with a predictable content, [constituting] a total political and self-identification" (113). Rather, lesbianism is "a position from which to speak" (113). Lesbian readings, different as they are and as they ought to be, are neither universal nor universally the same. What they share, their common "position from which to speak," is a sensitivity to and an analysis of the "discontinuities between biological sex, gender identity, and sexuality" (Martin 85).

There is, of course, another dynamic in the author/text/reader continuum, that between the author and the text, or more properly, as the writers here attest, between author and reader through the text. This dynamic in its lesbian context is to our knowledge explored in these pages for the first time. Six writers, some lesbians, others not, discuss issues of authorship and readership. Whether it is Lee Lynch describing her deprivation as a young reader or Noel Riley Fitch wrestling with the obligations and limitations of self-definition, all the writers in this section engage us in the politics of inclusion. And they refuse the easy liberalism of tolerance. What they read and what they write matters on the front lines, not always as starkly and poignantly as the battle Maureen Brady describes in "Insider/Outsider," but always passionately.

We have tried to provide a cross-section of interests and a variety of viewpoints and writing styles. These issues of authorship and readership are crucial to the writing of texts, as Lee Lynch, Mary Meigs, Valerie Miner, and Maureen Brady demonstrate. Often these authors show as well that their own responses as readers shape and inform their texts. We have concluded this section with what we think is a brilliant example of one kind of lesbian writing practiced today, Elizabeth Meese's "Theorizing Lesbian: Writing—A Love Letter." In the tradition of current deconstructionist lesbian writing and criticism, this essay both analyzes language designed to escape the self-silencing inherent in the voices and words of heterosexist patriarchy and is itself an illustration of that very language, at once both theory and praxis.

The second part of the book gathers together literary criticism that analyzes such language from the point of view of the reader. This section begins with a challenging reading of all kinds of texts, including heterosexual and lesbian. In what we hope will be a growing number of new theoretical explorations, Marilyn R. Farwell offers a definition of lesbian reading that goes beyond encoding and decoding and explodes the narrative confines of heterosexual texts. But problems of "encoded" language remain and make especially difficult the analysis of all those texts written from a lesbian sensibility that was covered over, masked, or hidden from disapproving or simply uncomprehending eyes. Some of these authors, Willa Cather and Virginia Woolf, for example, have become household names on the lists of lesbian authors, often more because of their lives than their works. Judith Fetterley uses a careful reading of both language and narrative structure to decode the lesbian plot in *My Ántonia,* while Jane Marcus, in a revision of her essay "Sapphistry: Narration as Lesbian Seduction in *A Room of One's Own,*" situates the lesbianism in the reader's response to Woolf's text. More startling to many readers, however, is the inclusion of authors almost never read as lesbian, encoded or not. Paula Bennett in "The Pea That Duty Locks" applies just such a focus to Emily Dickinson, with astonishing results. Bonnie Zimmerman examines another aspect of lesbian encoding in the heterosexual plots of George Eliot and offers, as well, a careful historical reading of Eliot's letters to reveal her growing awareness of the dilemma of lesbian consciousness.

The final section of reader analysis explores more overtly lesbian texts and contexts. After Renée Vivien and Natalie Clifford Barney, and certainly after Radclyffe Hall, many, though certainly not all, lesbian writers began to claim their own voice, to challenge heterosexist assumptions, to create "a literature of their own." The chapters exploring this distinctive literature have been, for the most part, arranged chronologically, from the expatriates of the 1920s and 1930s, Radclyffe Hall, H. D., and Djuna Barnes, to contemporary American and French poets, novelists, and dramatists.

The writers of these eleven chapters use very different methodologies and theories. (In effect, they illustrate the very diversity of approach we have noted as a characteristic of contemporary lesbian/feminist criticism.) Some chapters, like Shari Benstock's "Expatriate Sapphic Modernism," Yvonne M. Klein's "Myth and Community in Recent Lesbian Autobiographical Fiction," and Rosemary Curb's "Core of the Apple,'" provide syntheses of trends and issues. Many others focus on a single author. Some employ historical critical techniques, others Lacanian analysis, or close textual readings. Some analyze the relationship of author to community, whether religious or cultural. There is, however, a common purpose in all these chapters, to heed Adrienne Rich's call to see with "fresh eyes," to begin unraveling all those knotty questions of language and gender and reality, to open up the dialogue on what it means to write as a lesbian, to read as a lesbian.

We have attempted in this volume to bring together examples of some of the best unpublished lesbian/feminist criticism being produced today. It must be acknowledged, however, that there is much that is not included, partly because no one anthology can contain the growing body of work being done today. As a result, many readers will find their own favorite authors or texts missing from the discussions here. We have therefore included an extensive Bibliography to direct readers to many of the fine essays and books already published on well-known authors.

A more serious issue is the underrepresentation of lesbians of color. Because we believe that differences are crucial to our understanding of lesbian identities and of our diverse literature, we made a very serious effort to solicit essays from as many races, classes, and ethnic groups as possible. We wrote to more than forty lesbian writers and critics whose work on race and class issues provides important and challenging insights. Many of these women wished us well, but were overcommitted at the time. Others did not respond. Four essays by black lesbians and two by Hispanic lesbians were promised, but did not materialize. Our difficulties reflect a larger problem in the academic world. Those who speak from a vantage point outside the dominant, white, heterosexual "center" are all too often overworked and overcommitted, asked repeatedly to participate in projects and activities not their own, made to bear the burden of speaking as and for "Others."

The real solution to this dilemma lies in institutional strategies that encourage true diversity among scholars and teachers, that abandon the gatekeeping functions in favor of genuine inclusiveness so that there are many more lesbian/feminist scholars and teachers of all races, classes, and ethnic backgrounds. Until that millennium, however, we must acknowledge the shortcomings and try to foster a wide and thorough appreciation of the work being done by all lesbians. We hope that the Bibliography included in this volume will present readers with valuable sources and provide testimony as well to the fine and serious work being done by and about lesbians of color. We can do more, however. Perhaps it is time that we all, regardless of background, heed Audre Lorde's words in *Sister/Outsider* and hold ourselves accountable for all the diverse truths of lesbians. If we can read (and teach and write about) Shakespeare, Lorde argues, surely we can read (and teach and write about) each other.

Yet even as we acknowledge these gaps in the present volume, we find ourselves also celebrating the wealth of lesbian reading and writing that makes such gaps inevitable. We believe that this collection of essays is the first of its kind, the first to bring together writers and readers and texts that illuminate and challenge what we mean by lesbian writing and reading. The work represented here is only a beginning. The dialogue between writers and readers will continue. We hope that this collection will contribute to that necessary dialogue—for all our lives.

NOTES

1. For an overview of these conflicting positions, see Zimmerman's "What Has Never Been" and Marcus's "Under Review." The specific positions about lesbian definition can be found in Stimpson's "Zero Degree Deviancy"; Rich's "Compulsory Heterosexuality and Lesbian Existence"; Wittig's "The Straight Mind"; and de Lauretis's "Sexual Indifference and Lesbian Representation."
2. See Culler's "Reading as a Woman," in his *On Deconstruction*.
3. For a cogent analysis of this reading dilemma, see Fetterley's *The Resisting Reader*.

WORKS CITED

Auerbach, Nina. "Engorging the Patriarchy." In *Feminist Issues in Literary Scholarship*. Ed. Shari Benstock. Bloomington: Indiana Univ. Press, 1987. 150–60.

Christian, Barbara. *Black Feminist Criticism: Perspectives on Black Women Writers*. New York: Pergamon, 1985.

Culler, Jonathan. *On Deconstruction: Theory and Criticism after Structuralism*. Ithaca: Cornell Univ. Press, 1982.

de Lauretis, Teresa. "Sexual Indifference and Lesbian Representation." *Theatre Journal* 40 (May 1988): 155–77.

Fetterley, Judith. *The Resisting Reader*. Bloomington: Indiana Univ. Press, 1978.

Fox-Genovese, Elizabeth. "To Write My Self: The Autobiographies of Afro-American Women." In *Feminist Issues in Literary Scholarship*. Ed. Shari Benstock. Bloomington: Indiana Univ. Press, 1987. 161–80.

Lorde, Audre. *Sister/Outsider: Essays and Speeches by Audre Lorde*. Trumansburg, N.Y.: Crossing Press, 1984.

Marcus, Jane. *Art and Anger: Reading Like a Woman*. Columbus: Ohio State Univ. Press, 1988.

———. "Under Review: How to Read a Hot Flash." Afterword to June Arnold's *Sister Gin*. New York: Feminist, 1989.

Martin, Biddy. "Lesbian Identity and Autobiographical Difference(s)." In *Life/*

Lines. Ed. Bella Brodski and Celeste Schenck. Ithaca: Cornell Univ. Press, 1988. 77–103.

Rich, Adrienne. "Compulsory Heterosexuality and Lesbian Existence." In *Powers of Desire: The Politics of Sexuality*. Ed. Ann Snitow, Christine Stansell, and Sharon Thompson. New York: Monthly Review, 1983. 177–205.

———. "When We Dead Awaken: Writing as Re-Vision." *Adrienne Rich's Poetry*. Ed. Barbara Charlesworth Gelpi and Albert Gelpi. 1971. Rpt. New York: Norton, 1975. 90–8.

Stimpson, Catharine R. "Zero Degree Deviancy: The Lesbian Novel in English." In *Writing and Sexual Difference*. Ed. Elizabeth Abel. Chicago: Univ. of Chicago Press, 1982. 243–59.

Wittig, Monique. "The Straight Mind." *Feminist Issues* 1, no. 1 (Summer 1980): 102–10.

Zimmerman, Bonnie. "What Has Never Been: An Overview of Lesbian Feminist Literary Criticism." In *The New Feminist Criticism: Women, Literature and Theory*. Ed. Elaine Showalter. New York: Pantheon, 1985. 200–24.

PART I

Writers on Their Work

ONE

An Imaginative Collectivity of Writers and Readers

Valerie Miner

Recently I dreamt that my two lesbian neighbors had been raped and beaten. In my dream I was wakened by the ambulance. I ran out to the driveway but it was too late to be of use. Each woman lay on a stretcher with wounds on her face and terror in her eyes. I felt this had been my fault. If only I hadn't been sleeping when the man broke in. If only I had heard the noises in time. Then I woke to what we sometimes call reality. All day I fought the impulse to tell the neighbors my story, their story, to warn them to watch out. Instead I went to my desk and finished the first draft of this essay.

Perhaps the dream is a transparent metaphor for my work as a lesbian novelist. Every day I sit at a desk sifting through experience, drawing from common memory and imagination, sometimes issuing warnings. Just as readers may enter my novels through dreams, I hope to enter readers' dreams occasionally through my books.

The nightmare about my neighbors also represents the fears I have writing this essay. Although I have "come out" many times in print and in person, it still feels dangerous. At first I try to dismiss my writer's block as personal homophobia, and perhaps that is part of the cause. But while we confront the shadow of our own internalized biases, we need to keep our eyes open for very real outside threats. Our books get censored by publishing houses, review journals, bookshops, libraries, schools. Even in liberal environments where people support one's right to perversion, our lesbianism—which for some of us is a political choice—is still only temporarily tolerated. It *is not safe* to be a lesbian writer or reader today; we need our collective wits to survive.

I write as a lesbian. I write as someone who grew up in an immigrant, working-class household. I write as a feminist who found my voice—as well as my mind—in the women's movement. I write as a reluctant American who has lived abroad for many years. These various identities all enrich my work, yet sometimes they seem to contradict each other and readers who align with separate camps. Not all lesbians are feminists and not all feminists are lesbians, but for me the two identities are inextricable because I became a lesbian through the feminist worldview I developed in the women's movement. Thus while I present my ideas here about the relationship between *lesbian writers and readers,* my voice emerges in different registers, drawing on class background, cultural identity, international experience, and, particularly, feminist politics, highlighting the multidimensionality of lesbian fiction.

To claim a strong bond between writer and reader is to transgress much that is sacred in Western criticism. Scholars charge that only those scribblers afflicted with commercial motives or exhortatory messages have a direct, conscious relationship with readers. This artificial isolation of storyteller from audience is characterized by most Americans' distinction between art (which is rewarded) and work (which is paid). Writing brings "royalties" or awards or prizes, but *never wages.* The perception of writers as supernatural beings who create through singular genesis and the segregation between artist and audience is at the core of a crisis facing American fiction. So many contemporary novels lack imagination, depth, conscience, and vitality because they are dissociated from society. I notice myself continually turning back to feminist writing for aesthetic pleasure and intellectual provocation.

Like many feminist writers, I cannot insulate my art from my politics. My feminism is nurtured by other women on the streets where we all work and live. Many stories would not be written without such inspiration. They would not be published without feminist editors. They would not be visible without feminist reviewers, booksellers, librarians, and teachers. They would not endure without word-of-mouth campaigns among feminist readers. I call this vital web an "imaginative collectivity of writers and readers." Feminists have made profound contributions to my novels as well as to my life. Conversely, I try to engage audience actively in the *process* of my fiction.

GENRE

To begin at the beginning, audience provokes the work itself. Feminists have influenced my very choice of genre.

I started writing as a journalist. During my twenties, I worked as a reporter in Great Britain, Canada, Tanzania, and other countries. In those days, my primary impulse was "to help other people communicate with each other." The motivations were varied. As a woman I was drawn to the traditional role as cipher (for the opinions of my mainly male interview subjects). As a young radical, I was eager to leave this country, to go out and find other people's answers. Essentially my movement was outward, toward more information, toward patriarchal wisdom, toward external union and reunion.

Yet the articles I wrote about *women* always made me pause and reflect inward. Consistently I was forced back to my personal experience as I reported about Native Canadian wives fighting for land rights; sexual stereotyping in high schools; beauty pageants; suburban housewives; women farming in Ujamaa villages. Likewise, I was encouraged to examine my own life in consciousness-raising groups and in organizations affected by feminist process. Gradually, I found the nerve to speak and write in a different way.

First, I was given voice to ask questions about my own life, my mother's life, my grandmother's life. My grandmother, Mae Campbell, died from an abortion on the kitchen table in an Edinburgh tenement during World War I. My mother, Mary McKenzie, orphaned at age twelve, quit school and began to work at a coffee shop. She immigrated to the United States at the age of twenty, and last year at seventy-seven, she was laid off her job at a San Francisco coffee shop. Feminism helped me see the lives of these women as more than individual cases of suffering and courage, but as part of a daily, international history. Moreover, feminism provided survival strategies for my own life. When I was vomiting every morning and convinced I was pregnant although my doctor kept denying this, it was through the women's movement that I found someone who told me the truth and was willing to perform an illegal abortion. It was feminist friends who listened to my quandaries about a marriage which was keeping me mute. And it was in the women's movement that I learned to speak a new language as a lesbian.

I began to read more women novelists in the early 1970s. Doris Lessing and Toni Morrison and Jane Rule and Margaret Atwood inspired me to write my own words. I wanted to move from journalism to the deeper communication—emotionally, psychologically, sensually, intellectually—that I personally found in fiction. I wanted a more substantial relationship with readers. In an article, one is lucky if readers spend an hour with one's work. In a novel, readers are involved for days or weeks at a time. The book becomes a companion in all sorts of unlikely places. Consequently, the characters and issues remain alive between readings and have a longer afterlife.

Thus, from the beginning, I was conscious of my art emerging from a world of women. I have received considerable flack from mainstream critics for this self-identification, as well as stimulating support from readers. In recent years I have been disturbed by the growth of "postfeminist discourse" —not only because I disagree with much of it, but because just as the women's movement gave me and others permission to write, this line of criticism silences us by denying our continuing existence. Sometimes when I hear people discussing "postfeminist" literature, I am amused, imagining telephone poles along the highway, each with a dead book nailed to it. But more often I am terrified by the censorship that can result when such codes are absorbed into the cultural psyche. Before we say that the second wave of feminist writing is over, let us distinguish between the writing and the publishing. Let us look at the marketplace. Literary fashion is not designed by fate but by a homogeneous, incestuous network of editors, reviewers, academics, and foundation people. Many books are written; comparatively few are published—particularly those which don't have the proper credentials for the primarily white, male, middle-class, Eastern seaboard publishers. For instance, Doubleday receives 10,000 unsolicited manuscripts a year, of which they publish three or four (Coser, Kadushin, and Powell 130).

Inevitably at this stage in the argument someone points to a few books by black women or Indian lesbians and impoverished Appalachian mothers, asking, "What do you mean, censorship?" I call these the "despite" books. They get published *despite* their demographical demerits, *despite* the conventional judgments of editors and they are published in small enough quantities to be unthreatening. They are also the "because" books. They surface and thrive *because* they have something to say, *because* they shake things up. However, the American publishing industry, monopolized by media conglomerates, is not in the business of triggering earthquakes. God knows what would happen to those profitable canonical backlists so assiduously organized along the faultlines of capitalist taste and value if we had more aesthetic tremblors.

Feminist books *are* being written. A few are getting published by mainstream houses. A few, particularly the more radical and lesbian books, are produced by independents such as Kitchen Table/Women of Color Press, Alyson, Spinsters/Aunt Lute and Crossing. But what chance do these books have if they are shunned even in our most liberal of environments? At the University of California, 36 percent of faculty surveyed on the nine campuses said they refrained from doing research on lesbian and gay topics for fear of negative response from colleagues. As many as 41 percent decided against including such material in their courses (University of California Lesbian and Gay Intercampus Network Appendix A). Yes, a few lesbian novels are being published and taught. A lot are stuffed with heavy hearts into drawers and sometimes closets and sometimes graves.

It is hard to keep publishing—indeed, writing—while the contemporary women's movement is being eroded from without and within. How do we write in a world where vocabulary has been transformed—where "solidarity" has dissolved into "community"; "comrades" have metamorphosed into "colleagues"; women's studies has lost momentum and funding as it is subsumed into "gender studies"; "right" has been transformed into "choice" and "choice" is now read as "preference"? Some of us feel great pressure to cash in social goals to mortgage our houses. Others have discovered spirituality as a substitute for (rather than a supplement to) political action. All around us the culture invites women to trade sisterhood for motherhood. Too often these former sisters wind up battling each other for their children's places in exclusive schools. Rhetoric of the family has become the reflexive language. Dreams of mass movement are lost in cloistered, privatized routines. Yet is is not only dangerous but inaccurate to brand this time as an era of postfeminist literature, for many women do continue to imagine and fight and create and march and organize as feminists; many do continue to write with the old words and the spirit of change.

FORM AND STYLE

Feminist discourse has encouraged me to view the "canon" from different perspectives and to play with new approaches to fictional form. The conventional novel has become an endurance test in which the writer and reader begin at the beginning and pursue the end relentlessly without pause, in form, for reflection, consideration, question, or argument. The writer's role is paternalistic as he provides a catharsis—raising a dilemma, presenting a set of variables, stringing the reader along a line of tension and insinuating a resolution.

My vision of feminist fiction is storytelling which so deeply involves the reader in feelings, issues, and ideas that she asks, "How does this apply to my own life?" Good feminist fiction is not policy statement, although some women's writing, in an urgency to be politically correct, tries to protect the audience from contradictions. I think stories are most effective not when they are didactic, but quite the opposite, when they empower readers by raising a range of possibilities and the momentum to deal with them. And, partially because of my working-class family, I try for a clarity of language which makes my fiction accessible to a broad audience. Perhaps the best way to explain this philosophy is to articulate some of the strategies behind my different books.

Blood Sisters, my first novel, is about three generations of women in an Irish-American family, how they relate to each other, and how questions of sexuality, nationalism, and feminism affect them. I want readers to stand in the middle of arguments between Liz, a lesbian feminist, and Beth, a member of the Provisional Wing of the IRA. I hope they will hear the voices of the mothers as well as of the daughters. I present various images of Ireland—as a romantic state of mind, a war-wrenched country, a metaphor for international politics. The book is a feminist reinterpretation of *Hamlet* and, as such, ends more in provocation than in cataclysm. Survival, not sacrifice, is the act of courage in all its continuing complexity.

My second book, *Movement,* is both a novel and a collection of stories, a book which explores the territory between as well as beyond these forms. Readers accompany the protagonist, Susan, through ten years of spiritual, political, emotional, and geographical movement. In contrast with linear novels which can distance the reader through a forced march forward, *Movement* can be read in any order. Life, or "movement," is experienced as fantasy, memory, premonition, and this fiction is layered to express the intricacies. Most chapters follow one another in a chronological sequence, yet they are also self-contained stories. Susan's chapters are introduced by short-short pieces about women from different races, classes, ages, and cultures who are experiencing similar kinds of movement. I write these short-shorts to break through the isolationism and individualism of the

Bildungsroman. Susan does not know, and may never meet, any of these women. Their stories are told as shadows and illuminations of our mutual momentum. The book begins and ends in the same restaurant, completing a circle, surrounding readers with questions about Susan's unsettled choices regarding sexuality, motherhood, and political allegiance.

Next, I wrote *Murder in the English Department,* a novel of ideas suspended against an untraditional mystery. In this alternative to the genre detective story, readers are told "who done it" and who was "done" near the beginning of the book. They, like the protagonist Nan, are peripheral to the death, yet intensely caught up in subsequent moral issues. When Nan, a middle-aged college professor, risks her life in defense of a student, they are embroiled together in quandaries about innocence, loyalty, and love. The quicksand between private feeling and public action is the setting of this book as well as of *Winter's Edge,* which depicts the friendship between two old women who live and work in San Francisco's Tenderloin district. Their relationship is sparked by the differences between Chrissie's radical causes and Margaret's more discreet kind of social responsibility. The violence of a local political campaign gets turned on them, threatening their neighborhood, their friendship, and their lives. I leave it to readers to consider who is right or whether they are both right.

All Good Women, the most recent novel, examines the friendship among four young working-class women during World War II, tracing the impact on women's feeling of possibility. Many war women, like the suffragists and more recent feminists, were pioneers. For many, war was a time without men. What did this do to their sense of self and community?

My new book of stories is called *Trespassing.* I feel as if I am always trespassing—as a working-class woman in a middle-class world; as a frequently expatriate American; as an artist who doesn't quite fit into the university where I earn my living; as a political person indulging in art; as a novelist who writes about social issues; as a formerly obedient Catholic girl who grew up to pierce my ears, have an abortion, get divorced, and become a lesbian.

Some people complain about the questions and contradictions in my books. Some demand answers. Who speaks the truth, Beth or Liz? Will Nan continue teaching? Has Chrissie convinced Margaret or has Margaret convinced Chrissie? A couple of reviewers have complained about my "neglect" of resolution, while others have insisted that I speak for various (mutually exclusive) sides of a point. Still, I persist with my open endings because we live in a world where literary answers are cheap and eminently forgettable in the face of real life. Concluding fiction with stimulating contradictions pays more respect to the text and to the reader. The contradictions serve as lumpy bookmarks which make the novel, and hopefully the reader's mind, harder to close, thus leaving the questions reverberating in "real life."

For the lesbian writer, questions and contradictions about sexuality are especially problematic. When she chooses a heterosexual protagonist, she is often charged with being "inauthentic" or "selling out." This is a problem not just in the gay press. When May Sarton published *Anger,* a heterosexual reviewer in the *New York Times* criticized her for not making the main character a lesbian. Likewise, I have had people ask why Chrissie and Margaret in *Winter's Edge* are not lesbians and why Nan in *Murder in the English Department* is still making up her mind about sexuality. One answer is that I am particularly engaged by relationships among women which cross cultures, classes, and sexual choices. It's far more interesting to make connections between lesbians and heterosexual women than simply to write about a particular group all the time. One of my strategies is to incite readers' consciousness about choice. What decision will Susan make in *Movement?* The cathartic solution might inhibit the reader from considering what choice she, herself, is making.

This raises the touchy question: What is a lesbian novel? I think that the definition proceeds from the term *woman-identified.* For example, I'd say what makes *All Good Women* a lesbian novel is as much the deep bonds among the four protagonists as the explicit lesbianism of one of them. Moreover, I wonder why critics refuse to recognize a lesbian unless she is wearing a lavender T-shirt. Why do some people presume Chrissie MacInnes is heterosexual?

Occasionally lesbian readers warn writers not to "betray the community." Because homophobic harassment is so pervasive, some say that we shouldn't portray lesbians in a negative light—that we shouldn't show women battering, or drinking to excess, or being exploitative—lest we feed harmful stereotypes. Others say not to share lesbian secrets with the general public because that information can be used against us. Still others protest that lesbian erotica can be abused by men. All these concerns are real, yet as a writer I think the dangers of silence are always greater than the dangers of exposure. As Nadine Gordimer declares in *The Essential*

Gesture, "Censorship may have to do with literature; but literature has nothing whatever to do with censorship" (260).

REACHING OUT

The imaginative collectivity of writers and readers is not always in agreement. I picture a quilting bee where women are arguing, gossiping, challenging, recollecting, and envisioning. The "women's writing group" is a good metaphor and model. Writing has long been glorified as virtuoso performance; therefore working together provides significant feminist testimony. These writing groups can create environments where our voices will be heard and our languages understood. They provide forums for analytical argument and artistic support where the writer is reader.

During the early 1970s in Toronto, I met regularly with a group of women journalists. Eventually we published a joint collection of essays, *Her Own Woman.* Later, in London, I worked with four women to create a fictional documentary of the British women's movement. For five months in a row, *Spare Rib* published a story by each of us. In 1978, Journeyman Press published *Tales I Tell My Mother.* Back in this country, I have participated in several groups in which women concentrated on their own books. From these very direct reader reactions I have learned to weather editors' rejections and reviewers' biases and impossibly low wages, which, too often, lead me to the edge of despair. These writing groups have given me the spirit to continue writing.

On a large scale, the writing circle includes other women writers and readers. When I read *Zami: A New Spelling of My Name,* Audre Lorde provokes me toward new possibilities for the lesbian novel. When I read Sandy Boucher's *The Notebooks of Leni Clare* or Tess Gallagher's *Instructions to the Double,* my awareness of working-class feminists is deepened. "For books continue each other in spite of our habit of judging them separately," as Virginia Woolf observed. Later Sylvia Plath was to say of Woolf, "Her novels make mine possible." [1] Gertrude Stein, Mary Daly, and Kathleen Fraser have all taught me to be more playful with words. Adrienne Rich gives me hope for communication with her *Dream of a Common Language.* Paula Gunn Allen teaches me about fiction as ritual in *The Woman Who Owned the Shadows.* Again, the writer is reader.

Everyone asks, "Whom do you write for?" Ursula Le Guin explained in a recent issue of *Women's Review of Books* (Le Guin 4) that we create our own audience. I imagine different readers at each stage in a novel. In the beginning, I write to myself. I follow a story, hoping to make a discovery. During the first draft I am "reading" the text in my brain as I transfer it to paper—the mirror image of my audience's ultimate experience. During the many subsequent drafts, I am more conscious of "communicating" than of "expressing" and I think of members of that imaginative collectivity— hoping to recycle the inspiration they have given me.

As my books have become more widely available, I've had many different kinds of feedback from my own readers. The encounters are often provocative in surprising ways. Let me offer four examples.

In 1987, a woman told me that after hearing me read an erotic lesbian scene from *All Good Women* at the convention of the Modern Language Association, she and her partner went back to their hotel room and made love, forgetting the conference for the rest of the day.

A few years ago I was standing in Giovanni's Room Bookstore in Philadelphia when a young woman entered and asked the manager, "Do you have any good new lesbian trash?" "No," the clerk said, then nodded to me by way of introduction, "but you might want to read Valerie Miner's new book. It's a very good lesbian novel." The young dyke eyed me suspiciously, nodded semipolitely, and disappeared toward the back of the bookshop.

One summer evening, after a panel in Bristol, a woman spoke to me in the bathroom. With tears in her eyes, she told me how much she appreciated my coming out as a lesbian and how she hoped to come out one day herself.

Last spring I received a letter from a woman in Tasmania who had admired my work until she reached a certain point. She wrote, "'Let me remind you of the fate of homosexuals in Sodom and Gommorah. Genesis 18, 19. I appreciate your struggle in life and your upward mobility but I hope and pray you'll find your way out of the course of Lesbianism before you delay too long and are beyond redemption." The only thing that puzzled me about the letter was what she meant by upward mobility.

Public presentations are direct, dynamic ways to widen the circle. Audre Lorde noted in a recent issue of *Coda,* "A poem is not finished until I feel the flavor of the audience reaction rising to me. Reading is part of the creative process" (8). These presentations also alert audiences to forthcoming books and give writers sustenance (sometimes financial) to complete a work. I have read to gatherings ranging from four women in the back of a

Brooklyn bookstore, to hundreds of academics at a California conference, to loudly cheerful patrons at a Sydney pub. Sometimes the individual feedback is quite helpful. Sometimes readings have more of a symbolic value, reminding us of the continuing trial of making female voices heard. I'll never forget the afternoon Marge Piercy read at an outdoor cafe in San Francisco. She had to stand on top of a chair which was on top of a table, shouting her poetry against the fierce Bay winds.

THE MOVING MOVEMENT

Movements, of course, move. Varying readerships develop according to race, culture, sexuality, and language, creating a vigorous exchange about the definition of feminism and lesbianism. Authors tend to have distinct relationships with their constituencies, with the larger feminist audience, and with readers in general.

At a recent literary conference, I heard a lesbian critic disparage gay novels which cross class or cultural lines and "get overinvolved in external issues." And this year at a progressive bookstore, I heard critics on the Left advising writers not to complicate their writing with marginal sexual identities to which working people "can't relate." Meanwhile, astute publishers explain they may be able to market one of the above, but combination plates (books about working-class, lesbian feminists, for example) do not sell.

On the contrary, I think sexual marginality offers a valuable lens through which to appreciate other marginalities—national, ethnic, linguistic, economic—and to learn about uniqueness and commonality. We can't create solidarity by denying difference. We can relish individual identity and cultural distinctiveness while observing the similarities within the differences.

The lesson is that one continues to cross borders. Life is movement. Or, as Gloria Anzaldúa says in *Borderlands/La Frontera*, "you must live *sin fronteras*" (194–95). Among lesbians and gay men, the early, unitary notions of gay identity are more and more frequently set aside for a richer understanding about our multicultural interactions. Few of us any longer can afford romantic dreams about simple homosexual loyalty. Diversity does not dilute gay culture, but rather strengthens it. "We are everywhere," proclaimed the lavender balloons we released at the National Women's Conference in Houston in 1977. The "we" is a kaleidoscope through which to consider a complex daily reality rather than a telescope into an idealized future order. The experience of being sexually marginalized informs our appreciation for other identities within ourselves and within each other. We live *in* a world which pretends to segregate us. The popular imagination insists that we are one thing or another—"flamingoes or bears" to borrow a poem from Jewelle Gomez. But the only way to survive as lesbian writers is to refuse narrow definition, by insisting on claiming all our identities, creating a communal arcade from separate roots, and reaching into our histories for visions.

Can we write about cultures other than our own? (Is it permissible to? Are we able to?) My life has been immeasurably enriched by the powerful fiction and poetry of contemporary women of color. My own writing has been invigorated by Barbara Burford, Linda Hogan, Joy Kogawa, and a number of authors already mentioned. Thanks to their voices as well as to the consciousness of race in the fiction of white women like Grace Paley, feminist literature is becoming increasingly multicultural. In my early books, I was tentative about describing nonwhite characters, always placing them in minor parts. My reluctance was based in timidity as well as in politics. I didn't want to "get a character wrong"—to slip on a reference or a dialect or to expose my racism inadvertently. For years I also felt it was impertinent for me to portray Asians or blacks or Latinas or Native Americans. As a white person who already took up a lot of space in the world, I wanted to leave room for them to write about themselves. Now more and more fiction by women of color is published, indeed heralded. They have hardly needed me to make room for them. And I have recovered somewhat from my timidity. In *Winter's Edge*, a black and a Chicana play pivotal roles. In *All Good Women*, one of the four protagonists is nisei. No doubt each characterization has its faults, but over the years I've developed several practices to mitigate against inauthenticity and stereotype. I write many drafts of each book and after each draft, several people read the manuscript. I make sure to invite readers from my characters' cultural backgrounds to help me catch errors. I have learned that the scrupulous omission of nonwhite characters perpetuates invisibility as well as seriously limits the heart of the fiction itself. I believe we must integrate our art if we hope to integrate our imaginations and the societies our imaginations create.

In 1983 I attended a party in Beijing where Chinese and American women writers stood in a circle holding hands while Alice Walker led us singing a song Ding Ling had requested, "We Shall Overcome." This scene illustrates for me the rich spirit of international feminism. Simply living abroad for seven years allowed me to look past the blinders of American provincialism. (Perhaps this has worked too well in some regard because I find it harder to publish my books in this country. American editors have an allergy to social or political literature. Five of my six books of fiction and two other collaborative collections of stories were published in Great Britain before they appeared in the United States.) It's easy in this country to be persuaded that feminism and even lesbianism are American phenomena. I try to keep perspective through international journals and translated books. Of course, U.S. presses have a long way to go in publishing foreign literature, particularly from third world countries. When our small writers' delegation returned from China, we were loaded with books. But one does not have to get on a plane to take the journey.

WRITER AS WORKER

Tensions arise between audience and author when we confuse the writing with the writer herself. Most Americans romanticize art as magic. We perceive literature as the result of "creativity" rather than "creative labor," forgetting that writers are workers.[2] We invest the writer with special powers, in part because we want to experience the romance vicariously. And lesbians, perhaps because we often identify with a subculture, expect women writers to perform miracles at public events or to solve readers' romantic problems (since "it was just like you wrote in the book"). Sometimes a sadomasochistic struggle develops in which readers want the author to be addicted or psychotic or impoverished or dead as proof of or penance for her art. When we confuse the writing with the writer, we often expect her to be a stronger or more sensitive or more developed human being. Denise Levertov insists on a different perspective in *Light Up the Cave,* "My own belief . . . is that a poet is only a poet when engaged in making poems, and has no rightful claim to *feeling* more than others, but only to being able to *articulate* feeling through the medium of language" (117).

Writers like myself from working-class families find the act of writing a complicated form of disenfranchisement. For whom are we writing when over sixty million adult Americans are illiterate or functionally illiterate? Certain cultures emphasize reading more than others, but for many working-class people, becoming a writer is an irrevocable immigration to a country beyond the family's imagination. For years I've kept a comment from Simone Weil over my desk, "This domination of those who know how to handle words over those who know how to handle things is rediscovered at every stage of human history. It is necessary to add that, as a group, these manipulators of words, whether priests or intellectuals, have always been on the side of the ruling class, on the side of the exploiters against the producers" (Petrement 207).

Acknowledging writing as work might have pervasive consequences. It might result in a less neurotic relationship between writers and readers. It might encourage better wages and working conditions for artists. It might inspire a clearer portrayal of working-class people in our books. It might open a light on how art can emerge from and contribute to an impulse for social change.

THE—OPEN—END

My fiction has developed through the women's movement. I am conscious, while writing, of involving readers in the process of a story. Meanwhile, readers have influenced my themes, styles, and forms and have provided me with courage to continue. As Gertrude Stein declared in *The Making of Americans*:

It is a very strange feeling when . . . you write a book and while you write it you are ashamed for every one must think you are a silly or a crazy one and yet you write it and you are ashamed, you know you will be laughed at or pitied by everyone and you have a queer feeling and you are not very certain and you go on writing. Then someone says yes to it, to something you are liking or doing or making and then never again can you have completely such a feeling of being afraid and ashamed that you had then when you were writing or liking the thing and not anyone had said yes about the thing. (304)

I cannot predict the ways feminist readers will continue to affect me. Yet I do know that because of this imaginative collectivity, I am not alone.

NOTES

Parts of this essay were delivered in my talk at a forum, "Living Afresh: Women as Authors and Scholars Reflect on Writing and Research," at the Conference of the Modern Language Association in New Orleans on 28 December 1989. The forum was sponsored by the Division of Women's Studies in Language and Literature of the Modern Language Association. Parts also appeared in an essay ("Reader Is Writer Is Reader") I wrote for *Hurricane Alice* (Winter/Spring 1984).

1. Virginia Woolf, *A Room of One's Own* (1929; rpt. New York: Harcourt, 1957), 84. Sylvia Plath, *The Journals of Sylvia Plath*, ed. Ted Hughes and Frances McCullough (New York: Dial, 1982), 168. I am grateful to Sandra M. Gilbert for directing me to the quotes from Plath and Woolf in her essay, "In Yeats's House: The Death and Resurrection of Sylvia Plath." The essay is published in *Coming to Light*, ed. Diane Wood Middlebrook and Marilyn Yalom (Ann Arbor: Univ. of Michigan Press, 1985), 145–66.

2. For a fuller discussion of these issues, see *Competition: A Feminist Taboo?* ed. Valerie Miner and Helen E. Longino (New York: Feminist, 1987).

WORKS CITED

Anzaldúa, Gloria. "To Live in the Borderlands Means You." In *Borderlands/La Frontera*. San Francisco: Spinsters/Aunt Lute, 1987.

Coser, Lewis A., Charles Kadushin, and Walter W. Power. *Books: The Culture and Commerce of Publishing*. New York: Basic, 1982.

Fairbairns, Zoë. *More Tales I Tell My Mother: Feminist Short Stories*. London: Journeyman, 1987.

———. *Tales I Tell My Mother: A Collection of Feminist Short Stories*. London: Journeyman, 1978.

Gordimer, Nadine. *The Essential Gesture*. New York: Knopf, 1988.

Kostash, Myrna. *Her Own Woman: Profiles of Ten Canadian Women*. Toronto: Macmillan, 1975.

Le Guin, Ursula K. Letter. *Women's Review of Books* (September 1988): 4.

Levertov, Denise. "On the Edge of Darkness: What Is Political Poetry?" In *Light Up the Cave*. New York: New Directions, 1981, 115–29.

Lorde, Audre. *Coda* (November/December 1983): 8–9.

Miner, Valerie. *All Good Women*. Freedom, Calif.: Crossing Press, 1987.

———. *Blood Sisters: An Examination of Conscience*. New York: St. Martin's, 1982.

———. *Movement, A Novel in Stories*. Trumansburg, N.Y.: Crossing Press, 1982.

———. *Murder in the English Department*. New York: St. Martin's, 1983.

———. *Winter's Edge*. Trumansburg, N.Y.: Crossing Press, 1985.

Miner, Valerie, and Helen E. Longino, eds. *Competition: A Feminist Taboo?* New York: Feminist, 1987.

Petrement, Simone. *Simone Weil*. New York: Pantheon, 1976.

Stein, Gertrude. *The Making of Americans*. In *Selected Writings of Gertrude Stein*. Ed. Carl Van Vechten. New York: Vintage, 1972.

University of California Lesbian and Gay Intercampus Network. Report to the Regents of the University of California, 16 June 1983. Appendix A.

TWO

Falling between the Cracks

Mary Meigs

"For whom are you writing?" This question has always surprised me, for it implies an intention directed outward, rather than the autonomous intention to write what one wants to say. It implies that a writer chooses a suitable group of readers, people of like mind, but unless one's books are addressed to a specific category of readers—children, scholars, nature-lovers, people who like to cook—the writer of a first book has no idea of who will be of like mind. It may be that autobiography is a genre of writing which is not aimed at anyone in particular. With my first book, *Lily Briscoe: A Self-Portrait,* (my coming out both as a writer and a lesbian) the audience cut across sexual, class, and gender differences and included heterosexual men and women, working-class women, lesbians, and gay men. Above all, I was surprised that parts of my experience as a white, privileged lesbian could be shared by people whose lives had been very different from mine, so my definition of the ideal reader for me became someone willing to enter my experience and listen to what I have to say. Of course, I immediately discovered that there are readers (particularly critics) who feel it their duty to tell a writer how she should have written and how her experience is flawed. The writer should never make an appeal for understanding to any category of readers, for it is certain that this will be misunderstood. Without seeking readers, she will find them in unexpected places; she must patiently wait for the ideal reader to find *her*.

Inevitably after a first book, discrete audiences, pro and con, coalesce, and become more precise with every subsequent book. My work has been disliked by readers from the same groups who liked it, in particular those who feel threatened by it: closeted lesbians, daughters who have always lived in harmony with their mothers, privileged women who have had happily married lives, and all those who believe in the ideal of "privacy." The last shudder at close analysis of any human being *except in fiction*. Later

I will discuss the peculiarly vulnerable position of the lesbian autobiographer, and how the decision to write autobiographical fiction might be an understandable form of passing. The range of reactions to my books stems directly from the fact that I chose to come out as a lesbian. Certain critics seem to be angrily holding up a germ-infected rag with a pair of tongs and warning readers away. They are offended by my very presence, even more by the fact that I presume to have ideas that question patriarchal institutions, and state them without apology. The writer of fiction can say exactly the same things, but she does not stand in full view as a tempting target.

"When gay people in a homophobic society come out," says Eve Kosofsky Sedgwick, "it is with the consciousness of a potential for serious injury that is likely to go in each direction" (51). She makes a parallel with Racine's *Esther*, based on the biblical story of Queen Esther, who came out as a Jew to her husband, King Ahasueras, and because she was loved by him, succeeded in saving her threatened people, but not herself. Later Sedgwick humorously scolds herself for her "sentimentality" in identifying with the noble queen. "At this moment," she says (meaning the moment when Esther is about to come out), "the particular operation of suspense around her would be recognizable to any gay person who has inched toward coming out to homophobic parents" (46). Or suspected homophobic siblings or friends, I should add. The entire future of a lesbian, or any gay person, lies in the few seconds of coming out, and the freedom one gains comes with a new experience of unforeseen penalties.

At the beginning of "Epistemology of the Closet," Sedgwick quotes Proust: "The lie, the perfect lie about people we know, about the relations we have had with them . . . the lie as to what we are, whom we love . . . —that lie is one of the few things in the world that can open windows for us on to what is new and unknown" (39). Yet even a great novelist's definition of fiction cannot protect him or her from being hounded by critics or interviewers who are determined to find the writer in the work. "Writing as a novelist who is routinely asked at every interview, 'Is your work autobiographical?' I know that looking to the writer's personality and history for one-to-one correlations with the writing is absurdly reductionist." This is Lisa Alther in "The Writer and Her Critics," a review of two books about Doris Lessing (11). "Such over-simplification relegates fiction to autobiography and/or neurosis, leaving little room for the predictive and prescriptive function of fiction, and granting insufficient credit to the power of imagination and craft" (Alther 11).

Well, the novelist may feel reduced and "relegated" to autobiography when she is plagued by the question, "Is your work autobiographical?" but she can always find legitimate refuge in Proust's "perfect lie." Even in a novel which can be called fictional autobiography, which sticks closely to the facts of the writer's life, the writer has enjoyed the freedom of the "perfect lie." "The lie," Proust continues, "can awaken in us sleeping senses for the contemplation of universes that otherwise we would never have known" (Sedgwick 39). The novelist, when asked if her work is autobiographical, can reply, "Of course I'm somewhere in it, but try to find me." The perfect lie has enabled her to be everywhere at once and to be nowhere in her own person. She knows that lurking in the question ("Is your work autobiographical?") is the accusation: if it is, it is less creative, it has been easier to write; it is suspect because it is supposedly subjective and the subjective view is assumed to be less truthful rather than more so. The reader of an autobiography accepts it much less readily as truth than she/he accepts fiction as truth, because many people believe (and I have heard several novelists say this) that fiction is "truer" than autobiography. Thus, the simple statement that an autobiography is fiction will, paradoxically, make it more believable. My autobiographical writing feels "truer" to *me* than any fiction I could write; for a novelist like Lisa Alther, a more complex truth than that of autobiography lies in the freedom fiction gives for "imagination and craft" (11). If the novelist is a lesbian who has chosen not to come out she benefits, as Proust did, from two perfect lies, one of fiction and the other of the closet. Her choice not to come out is understandable because it allows her a freer use of her creative energies. The perfect lie does not entirely protect her from the animus of interviewers and critics, but it allows her to elude direct charges against her, for she can refuse to fit definitions or to feel responsible for her characters (they are free spirits, after all).

The autobiographer who has come out is called upon to answer both for her own truth and for that of all the other people in the book. Sometimes they are seen as her victims, and the reader wishes to protect them from the writer's intrusiveness. "I feel as though I'm looking through a keyhole," said one of my readers about *The Medusa Head*, my second book, published in 1983. The keyhole image describes a particular kind of squeamishness which focuses on the lesbian autobiographer and spreads to her entire subject matter; she does not have the novelist's freedom to speculate on people's lives. Of course the lesbian autobiographer's own scruples have exercised a kind of censorship while she was writing the book; she is never as free as the novelist, and is responsible to her subjects whether they are alive or dead. But a homophobic reader will further narrow the lesbian autobiographer's freedom by presuming that her entire view of life is biased. If she attempts an interpretation of her subjects as she knew them, even if they give their own evidence in letters and diaries, she will be seen (because she is a lesbian) as an unreliable interpreter, particularly of heterosexual lives. A woman reviewer says of my recent book, *The Box Closet*, "In the end *The Box Closet* turns out to be a portrait of two people painted not as a faithful likeness but as a reflection of the author's view of her own subjects" (Barclay 9). She apparently believes that my book should have been composed *only* of letters and journals (she seems not to have noticed that the book contains portraits of more than two people), that I should have let them "tell their own story." I wonder how this critic arrived at her conclusion that my portraits are *not* faithful likenesses. Did she know my subjects? And how would she guarantee that a selection of letters, unless it was made by lottery, would not reflect a view of some kind? The choice of letters necessarily forms part of the work of interpretation and adds another dimension to the portrait. A book composed only of my family letters would have been criticized on the ground that it was not interesting, but, as we see from another review, even extensive cutting did not obviate this danger: "Meigs tries to present objective lifelike portraits of people very near and dear to her . . . but her family is not as interesting to the reader as it is to the writer" (McGrath 124).

This critic then goes on to say, in effect, that the only interest in my book lies "in the temptation it offers to the reader to trace the influences that helped to shape the character of the author and may have played a part in making her one of the respected voices of the gay community of today" (124). I was struck by the mixture of kindliness and concealed sternness in this last sentence, which so firmly puts me in my place, and it confirms my view that a writer who has come out as a lesbian, no matter what the subject of a subsequent book or its percentage of lesbian content (about 1 percent in *The Box Closet*) is forever sealed in her lesbian identity like an insect in plexiglass.

Perhaps every lesbian has the secret hope that her book will dissolve homophobia, even in those straight people who, before they read the book, were unable to say the word *lesbian* without an overtone of disgust. Having read the book, they are now able to associate the word with a "respectable" woman of over sixty. But though amnesty is granted to this one lesbian writer, the homophobia is still intact and is ready to sound the alarm. The same readers who have granted me amnesty are as afraid as ever of having a lesbian daughter, or even an apparently straight daughter who might want to go to a women's college where there are said to be lesbian students or teachers. To me it is remarkable if a few college students have managed to slip through the net of homophobia in the school system. Eve Kosofsky Sedgwick speaks of the "unaccustomed perhaps impossible responsibilities that devolve on college faculty as a result of the homophobia uniformly enjoined on teachers throughout the primary and secondary levels of public school—where teachers are subject to being fired, not only for being visibly gay, but, whatever their sexuality, for providing any intimation that homosexual desires, identities, cultures, adults, children, or adolescents have a right to expression or existence" (10).

Many parents of both sexes see "contagious" lesbianism as a greater threat to their daughters than the danger of rape, alcoholism, drugs, or Communism. Their fear and ignorance are illustrated by the question a straight friend asked when I told her that a lesbian friend had been sexually abused by her cousin for ten years: "By a boy or a girl?" Lesbians are seen to be as dangerous for women as men are; we are also working from within, like the Communists; if we are allowed any power, we "take over."

To us lesbians, it is natural to enjoy the little power we have in an overwhelmingly heterosexual world. But the lesbian who comes out in a book finds that along with the euphoria of sisterhood comes the gradual knowledge that she has been sealed in. She discovers that she has done straight people a favor by coming out; now, whether they are mildly or violently homophobic, they know what to expect. If they once found it difficult to say the word *lesbian,* they are now unable *not* to say it. "You wanted to be known as a lesbian, didn't you?" The prejudicial stereotype in these readers' minds will from now on color everything I write. In every subsequent book I will be assumed to be writing from a lesbian viewpoint, primarily for lesbian readers. *"The Medusa Head* merits a 'For Lesbians Only' sticker," wrote Alan Twigg about my second book (6). For just as books by feminists are considered both by many men and by certain women to be propaganda, so books by avowed lesbians are seen as not worthy of attention or belief because they are based on false premises (that women can really love other women, and, above all, that they do not need men).

Belittling words about lesbian relationships have the power to hurt even established writers, now dead, who never come out of the closet. The caution of writers like Willa Cather, Virginia Woolf, or Elizabeth Bishop protected them during their lifetimes from the contamination of loaded words. They were also protected from open speculation about whether a relationship with another woman was sexual or not, since sexual activity between women is considered a proof of lesbianism, unless it is seen as an aberration in an otherwise heterosexual life. Proof of it releases the homophobic poison which has been held in suspension. A lesbian in the closet is preternaturally aware of herself as a substance which can release this poison, which may contaminate her relationships and affect future judgments of her work. She is also aware of unspoken thoughts, of facial expressions, covert put-downs, and of the slightest sign of uneasiness or fear—fear by association. Still closeted, she feels this fear herself. She hopes that coming out will banish this fear, and indeed, after coming out, she feels the exhilaration of her victory. But she discovers to her surprise that each coming out to straight people, now expected of her because she has become a spokeswoman for her lesbian sisters, is almost as difficult as the first. The first seemed like an affirmation; in those that follow she confronts straight people who are bored with the subject and may perceive it as irrelevant and gratuitous.

It is perhaps because I belong to an older generation of lesbians, for whom coming out was (and still is, for many of us) unthinkable, that I still quake when I have to make yet another public avowal. Let us call it *post-euphoria,* the state in which the joy has seeped out of avowal, and the nagging question, "Is it really necessary?" has taken its place. This past summer, I was the only lesbian member of the cast of *The Bus,* a semidocumentary film made by the National Film Board of Canada, about seven women, all over sixty-five. In one scene I was supposed to talk to Constance (aged eighty-eight), who in real life had read my first book, about coming out as a lesbian. But she did not want to give me the cue that would lead to my coming out on camera. "I don't see why we have to talk about all those things," she said. Constance had voiced a common view of straight people who hope that lesbian subject matter will disappear from the work of a lesbian writer. Yet they cannot forget that the lesbian is lurking behind everything she writes, and they comb each book for the reassurance that she is still there and can be judged accordingly. I am not talking here about readers who like my work, those who were responsible for the joyful aspect of coming out, but about those who reject it for the prejudicial reason that

I am a "lesbian writer." The lesbian writer who comes out is squeezed between those who want less (or no) lesbian content in subsequent books, and those (other lesbians) who want more. In the interval between the appearance of my first book (1981) and my third (1987), the idea of the audience a lesbian writer is supposed to seek has become narrowed and politicized, and an implicit accusation hangs in the air, "You aren't writing for me (or for us)."

Even as powerful a novelist as Jane Rule, who writes, one might say, for any intelligent reader, is harried from both sides. Lesbians may say, "There isn't enough about *us*," yet I have heard, after the publication of *Memory Board* in 1987, the question addressed to her by a man in her audience at McGill University, "Do you call yourself a lesbian writer?" This question, which is legitimate when posed by a lesbian, was in this case intended to be a trap similar to, "Do you still beat your wife?" Everybody knows that Rule had the courage to come out many years ago and is, strictly speaking, a lesbian writer. I would argue that by coming out she renounced the protection of the second perfect lie in her novels, and, in spite of her stature as a novelist, is still the victim of homophobia. "Jane Rule . . . is known as a lesbian writer—a label she encourages rather than resists," writes John Godard in the Montreal *Gazette*. He adds, "She officially launched *Memory Board* at l'Androgyne Bookstore in Montreal . . . where her books can be found under 'Lesbian Literature,' and where she drew an almost exclusively female crowd" (12). Rule, perceiving the trap, replied, in effect, that she does not write exclusively about (or for) lesbians but about life as she sees it. She *resists the label*, rather than encouraging it, for the intention of the labeler is to cast suspicion on her vision of the world.

Lesbian writers who are proud of the label in its positive meaning know immediately if it is being used negatively, to express homophobia. After the publication of *Sexual Politics* in 1970, when Kate Millett was still in the closet, reporters anxious to pin the label on her closed in like sharks that have smelt blood. Perhaps people are more polite now, but they can sometimes barely conceal their interest in the lesbian as prey that must be run down and kept apart from heterosexual writers, and even from writers who have stayed in the closet. The writer (a lesbian) can be thankful for the continuing freedom which the "perfect lie" has given her. In its largest meaning, it is the discreet silence which protects all lesbians still in the closet from their parents and employers, and, if they are writers, from the hostility of straight readers. It is, in the story of Alice and the Fawn in

Through the Looking-Glass, "the wood where things have no name" (Carroll 64). As they emerge from the wood, the Fawn, who has been walking close to Alice, sees that she is a "human child" and runs away in terror. It is a perfect parable of coming out; the person who is named ceases to be herself and immediately embodies the fear-inspiring name, and she can never return to the sheltering wood. The writer who stays in the wood has the freedom to say everything except, *"I* am a lesbian." She can say, "My heroine is a lesbian," or, "in my book there are women who love women"; she can suggest that this is natural, that it can be beautiful, that these women are happy in their love, and she will still not be labeled a "lesbian writer."

The writer-lesbian, or indeed any lesbian who has come out of the closet, must learn to live with the role of scapegoat; she must develop special gills for breathing homophobic air, special muscles for a robust sense of humor. The lesbian writer suffers less from the charge contained in the word *lesbian* than the teacher or editor who wants the word to work positively in her students or readers and who runs the risk of being seen as subversive. Lisa Weil, the editor of *Trivia,* in a talk she gave in Montreal in March 1988, discussed the difficulties of giving a course at Hamilton College, which was listed in the course catalog as "Lesbian Literature." "Students, mostly lesbians," said Weil, "began coming into my office saying that they really wanted to take the course—but they couldn't have 'that word' on their transcripts. . . . With parents paying for their education, it was hard enough for some of them to get away with 'Women's Studies.' " Weil discovered that "no one had ever offered such a course. And for this very reason . . . it was too threatening . . . and teachers didn't want it on their résumés any more than students did. . . . So, at the last minute, I changed the title of the course, which is now officially called 'Female Voices: Reclaiming the Monster' " (2). In the same way, the title of a course in lesbian literature to be given by Yvonne M. Klein at Concordia University in Montreal, was changed by the administration to "Women's Sexuality," with the result that the first lecture attracted a horde of curious male students, who dropped out when they discovered the real subject of the course.

Under cover of her new course name, Lisa Weil was able to keep the focus entirely on lesbian writers of poetry, fiction, and nonfiction. Her reading list, particularly of contemporary writers (Broumas, Gidlow, Grahn, Lorde, Marchessault, Morgan, Rich, and Rule, among others) gives one a sense of the richness of lesbian writing. Weil succeeded in getting her students to think about what the words *lesbian writing* meant to them and to air both their positive and negative reactions. She interested them in the possibility of reclaiming the "Monster," a conventionally negative and threatening image of the lesbian, as a source of lesbian power. "I chose a group of books and poems," she said in her Montreal talk, "that exhibited . . . a distinctively lesbian quality, in the way that Bertha Harris uses *lesbian*—that is, *monstrous,* in some significant way, unassimilable, awesome, dangerous, outrageous, different, distinguished" (4).

Weil belongs in spirit with the Quebec feminists who have been developing a theory of language supple enough to express the whole being of each writer. In *La Théorie, un dimanche,* six of these writers who have experimented with "unassimilable, dangerous, or outrageous" language (that is, outside the patriarchal mainstream) discuss their theories of language. "A feminist consciousness is essential to the creation of a subject," says Louise Cotnoir, "because it permits the re-creation of a self-image which corresponds integrally with what I know I am" (155). "So where . . . and *how,*" asks Gail Scott, "might my subject, denied her full existence in any patriarchal paradigm . . . *be* a subject-in-the-feminine? . . . If she . . . cannot be expressed in any established form, she needs to find another place where the words she speaks will fit her gestures" (Scott 20–21). And she continues, "The subject's resistance to drawing rigid boundaries around herself . . . *makes her incomprehensible to the male modernist . . .* and embarrassing" (22–23). All these writers are "unassimilable," that is, they refuse to conform to patriarchal expectations, and are viewed with the "embarrassment" that monsters provoke. Scott's heroine (her subject-in-the-feminine) also refuses to conform to feminist or lesbian expectations: she refuses to be "correct." She is "suspicious of transcendence," including that of feminist utopias, "a suspicion that has led me to place myself (in writing)," she says, "between certain expectations of my feminist community and my desire to be excessive" (25–26). She wants, like Persephone, to descend into the Underworld: "the areas of repression in the mind, the darkest corners, that if worked through, lead to fascinating places" (26). In my own view, Persephone, who was kidnapped by the patriarchy (Pluto) and forced into the bondage of marriage, is not a model for the freedom to be excessive, but Scott likes to think of her in her triple aspect: "Diana in the leaves, Luna, shining brightly, Persephone in the Underworld" (22). The Luna aspect means brightness in darkness, like the humor which is so much a part of

Quebec life, "the laughter that in the same breath assures transgression" (20).

Humor is often overlooked by readers, perhaps because they perceive that its true purpose is to mock covertly their most cherished beliefs. A tragicomic novel is seen by some readers to be unremitting tragedy, and the lesbian writer who has intended to be funny at times (I am one of these) can actually provoke anger. Yet humor is part of the language of defiance that enables feminists to live in a repressive climate. For Gail Scott it is a carnival mask, which is "a comment on her current grasp of meaning" (30). A mask, like the perfect lie, enables the wearer to see without being seen; in the same way, the play of laughter conceals a serious intent. Mary Daly and Jane Caputi have "conjured" a whole new language of mockery in their *Wickedary (Webster's First New Intergalactic Wickedary of the English Language)*. In the last fifteen years, lesbian laughter has broken out in a language revolution. "In search of woman-identity: dictionaries were blown wide open, words uprooted, neologisms coined, punctuation upset or willfully ignored, codes, genders and syntax fissured, personal pronouns mixed around" (Cotnoir, "Quebec Women's Writing," 13). Cotnoir continues, "This subversive revolt takes the form of texts where fiction and theory overlap" (14). The "space-in-between theory and fiction" (15) is the space of the "imaginaire," a word coined by the lesbian/feminist translator, Susanne de Lotbinière-Harwood, to convey "the sense of an inner landscape, a territory of possibilities" (16). Lesbian writers have found freedom by enlarging *spaces-in-between,* including the space between the cracks. I have found my own freedom in the territory where theory and autobiography overlap, in defiance of patriarchal rules that a piece of writing be one thing or the other. And I've come to think that defiance is the only answer a lesbian writer can make to the exigencies of *all* expectations, and that each of us must learn to free-fall in our almost unlimited space of possibilities.

WORKS CITED

Alther, Lisa. "The Writer and Her Critics." *Women's Review of Books* (October 1988): 11.
Barclay, Pat. "Memoir." *Books in Canada* (October 1988): 9.
Carroll, Lewis. *Alice Through the Looking-Glass.* New York: Macmillan, 1906.
Cotnoir, Louise. "Quebec Women's Writing." Trans. Susanne de Lotbinière-Harwood. *Trivia* 13, no. 3 (1988): 13–16.

————. *La Théorie, un dimanche*. Paris: Les Editions du Rémue-ménage, 1988.

Daly, Mary, and Jane Caputi. *Webster's First New Intergalactic Wickedary of the English Language*. Boston: Beacon, 1987.

Godard, John. "Books." *The* [Montreal] *Gazette,* 14 November 1987.

McGrath, Joan. "Collected Essays." *Colliers* 4 (July 1988): 124.

Meigs, Mary. *The Box Closet*. Vancouver: Talonbooks, 1987.

————. *Lily Briscoe: A Self-Portrait*. Vancouver: Talonbooks, 1981.

————. *The Medusa Head*. Vancouver: Talonbooks, 1983.

Scott, Gail. "A Feminist at the Carnival." *Trivia* 13, no. 3 (1988): 17.

Sedgwick, Eve Kosofsky. "The Closet, the Canon, and Allan Bloom." *Gay Studies Newsletter* (Nov. 1988): 1, 8–10.

————. "Epistemology of the Closet." *Raritan* 7 (1988): 39–51.

Twigg, Alan. "Books." *The Magazine,* 15 January 1984, 6.

Weil, Lisa. "Reclaiming the Monster: Lesbians in Academe." Public lecture. Montreal, 13 March 1988.

THREE

Cruising the Libraries

Lee Lynch

Little Ms. Muffet? Phooey. Cinderella? You have to be kidding. *Maybe* Prince Charming, but he was pretty innocuous, as well as male. Certainly no one in Grimm and Anderson. As a matter of fact, all those nursery rhymes and fairy tales, where the women were stolen or disappeared in a puff of smoke, where animals were hurt and men were not just powerful, but superhuman, frightened me.

Nancy Drew? Now, she had promise. Dr. Doolittle? Absolutely. Young dykes are often more comfortable with animals than with humans—except who could identify with a bumbling, middle-aged man? Wasn't there anyone in literature like little Lee? I felt a real affinity with the fairies of Ireland, but all the available stories had them stealing babies, like queers corrupting Anita Bryant's children. Besides, they'd been shrunk to less than life size and I felt diminutive enough, lost enough in the crowd of rapacious, rough-necking boys and primping girls who were my peers.

Where were the stories of tomboys? Of little kids growing up with same sex or single parents? Why did Nancy Drew have to have a boyfriend? Why couldn't a writer portray puppy love between best girlfriends? Why wouldn't a librarian order such books? Wasn't there one picture book, when I was five, of a little girl fighting to the death the horror of being skirted-up for a first day at school—and winning? Did Jill never save Jack? Or Jane, Jill?

At about the age of thirteen I stumbled across Carson McCullers's *The Member of the Wedding.* I totally understood Frankie Addams. Her anguish at not belonging in the world was mine. Her aborted attempts to relate to the wedding couple, to the femmy little girlfriend, and to the sailor who picked her up were so like my own search. When I found *The Heart Is a Lonely Hunter,* Carson McCullers gifted me with hope. Wasn't Mick in this situation just like me?

"Are you just going to tramp around the room all day? It makes me sick to see you in those silly boys' clothes. Somebody ought to clamp down on you, Mick Kelly, and make you behave," Etta said.

"Shut up," said Mick. "I wear shorts because I don't want to wear your old hand-me-downs. I don't want to look like either of you. And I won't. That's why I wear shorts. I'd rather be a boy any day." (35)

Still, Mick and all McCullers characters seemed to live in a twisted place nearly as frightening as a fairy tale. In *The Member of the Wedding*, Frankie feared that her own difference would trap her in a world of "freaks" like the ones she'd seen at the circus.

Throughout childhood and adolescence, I searched and searched for images of myself in literature, on television, in movies. I identified not with Scarlett, but with Rhett. At fourteen I thought Thomas Wolfe's passion was my own; I began to pour my heart onto paper just like him. Jean-Paul Sartre described exactly my feelings of discomfort in the world; I despaired and grew cynical.

At fifteen I came out. I accepted my Rhettness, but no one else did. My feeling of exclusion only deepened. I grew more fairylike, lost in the dells of my ire-land.

I found Radclyffe Hall's *The Well of Loneliness*, Ann Bannon's books, Vin Packer and her other pseudonym, Ann Aldrich. At last, lesbians! I devoured the books, loved the characters, identified completely. This was a mistake. These books, while validating because they acknowledged the existence of lesbians by portraying us, destroyed any incipient pride I might have had in my true fairy self. Titles like *Queer Patterns, The Evil Friendship*, and *The Sex Between* were instant signals of gay books. The characters were more miserable than Sartre's, and despised as well.

Ann Aldrich's *Take a Lesbian to Lunch*, while not released until 1971, illustrates the tone of books I read in the early sixties, her heyday. (I suspect this was written then and only published when the women's movement began to take hold, as if it reflected that spirit!) Aldrich purports to interview a straight male "host" in a Mafia-run lesbian bar. He declaims:

"The pretty ones who come in here—they're twisted somewhere in their heads. I'm better buddies with the butches. I know what they're about. No man would want them in the first place. As females they're mistakes, pukes. Half of them got faces like little midgets—I've observed that about them—something about their faces, baby faces—they didn't develop right. Something in their genes . . . But the goodlooking ones who could pass for my wife or daughter . . . They become gay to spit in men's eyes." (95)

I had found models of lesbians in literature at last, but inside them lurked Frankie Addams without her innocence. Radclyffe Hall's Stephen Gordon asserts in *The Well of Loneliness* what we homosexuals "must realize more clearly than ever, that love is only permissible to those who are cut in every respect to life's pattern" (188). These lessons were hard, but I took them with pride, a sexual rebel.

So I joined the underground of my own supposedly tormented kind, rejecting the far from baby-faced butches and the occasional spitting-mad femme, even as I followed them around New York City and learned their ways. I fell in love with many young women, some of whom wanted to come out, some of whom I refused in order to spare them my fate. At the same time I exulted in my lot, celebrated it with the girls (and boys) who were either of it already or who proved more persistent than my scruples. I felt as torn as the lovers in Valerie Taylor's 1957 novel, *Whisper Their Love*.

"I don't care. I'd like to tell everybody." "I care," Edith said sharply. "I like my job, apart from having to earn a living. You don't know how they crucify people like us, tear us limb from limb and laugh when we suffer. . . . Everybody hates us." (56)

Although I read every one of these mass-market paperbacks I could get my hands on, always hungry for my life in literature, I yearned for more substance. I started to search the libraries and used bookstores to discover more authors like McCullers, who hinted at lives behind the heterosexual stories they wrote. It is amazing how unerring a kid with a variant eye can be, like a musical child prodigy with a perfect ear. Katherine Hume wasn't uncloseted for years, nor were Edna St. Vincent Millay, Mary Renault, or Virginia Woolf, but they felt variant to me. I even checked Cecil Beaton's photographs out of the library, and stared at the work of Louise Nevelson at the Museum of Modern Art, fascinated by the variance I sensed in their images.

Sherwood Anderson became my new hero when I found his *Beyond Desire*. John O'Hara was obviously fascinated by lesbians in work like his novel *The Ewings*. I found poets, Charlotte Mew and H.D., for example, before the gay scholars had at them. I could have taught a course in gay lit. by the time I hit college.

For the next several years, even into the start of women's and gay liberation, I continued the activity I came to call "cruising the libraries." Identifying variant books was as subtle, frustrating, and exciting a process as spotting lesbians on the street. Success depended on a vigilant desperation. I *had* to find reflections of myself to be assured that I was a valuable human being and not alone in the world.

This slightly tinged lavender culture was all I had, this and, later, the liquid solace of the bars. From fifteen to twenty-five, when the revolution finally reached me personally, I was driven, searching for my nourishment like a starveling, grabbing at any crumb that looked, tasted, or smelled digestible. Often wrong, always hopeful, my gay antennae never rested. Most of the passages quoted here I have taken from a yellowing collection of index cards I began to gather at age fifteen. These are the words which taught me who and what I was, which frightened and comforted me, which gave me my own life's work.

It's hard to reconstruct that literary cruising process. My tools were few and crude. There was the obvious one: the card catalog, though it yielded little enough. I can remember poring through it at my local library in Queens, N.Y., fruitlessly searching for other books by Radclyffe Hall. I was shaken by the intellectual thrill of finding, at Manhattan's 42nd Street library, a cross-reference to Una Troubridge and a book called *The Life and Death of Radclyffe Hall*. Until then, I hadn't been certain that Hall was anything more than a straight writer who'd written a chance novel about lesbians, but Troubridge's book, its cover, and photographs were fairly convincing evidence—and I took this evidence, hoarding it like a lone jewel in an otherwise empty case. Not only had I found lesbian characters, but a definitely lesbian writer, as I wanted to be.

How, though, had I first located *The Well of Loneliness?* I recall that moment, too. These were, after all, not simply formative, but decisive episodes at the start of a career I would dedicate to lesbians and lesbian words. There were no bookstores in my city, but next to the Paramount Theater in Manhattan was a stationery store. I must have drifted out of a Doris Day feature and into the stationery store to browse through the books. I'd already discovered paperback racks in the corner drugstore. My brother had bought me my first adult book there: *The Hunchback of Notre Dame*. Now *there's* a story of an outcast, and a love that dared not speak its name. But on this newly discovered rack I found *The Well of Loneliness*. The title had a provocative ring to it. Hadn't I fallen into just such a well? I peered inside. Imagine the effect of this passage on a gay, sixteen-year-old, would-be writer:

"You're neither unnatural, nor abominable, nor mad; you're as much a part of what people call nature as anyone else; only you're unexplained as yet—you've not got your niche in creation. But some day that will come, and meanwhile don't shrink from yourself, but just face yourself calmly and bravely. Have courage; do the best you can with your burden. For their sakes show the world that people like you and they can be quite as selfless and kind as the rest of mankind. Let your life go to prove this—it would be a really great life-work, Stephen." (154)

These words, spoken by Puddle in the novel, still move and inspire me.

Other racks over the years would yield further rewards. I found Gore Vidal on a shelf in a little bookshop at Grand Central Station. On Main Street in Bridgeport, Connecticut, there was a newspaper store where regular vigilance turned up books I was petrified to take to the cashier. Their ludicrous and blatantly sensational cover copy were both my signals and my shame. Valerie Taylor's *The Girls in Three-B* and Randy Salem's *Man among Women*: these books I would savor alone, heart pounding from both lust and terror of discovery, poised to plunge the tainted tome into hiding.

From *Spring Fire* by Vin Packer: "her hands found Leda's body. Then for the first time she was the aggressor. The strength that was sleeping in her awakened. A powerful compulsion welled up inside Mitch as she felt the pliant curves of Leda's body. Then they lay together, breathless and filled with a new peace . . ." (78). I recognized this compulsion that heterosexuals called passion; I knew the peace "normal" people called love.

Just as other gays dotted the street populations of my young world, turning it into an endless exciting cruising ground, so a few of these compatriots led me, by word of mouth, to more precious books. This is how I originally heard of Ann Aldrich and Vin Packer, whom I was to learn years later are one and the same. Ann Bannon's books were so well loved I never even read one until much later. Some treasures were so priceless no one would lend them.

The other gay kids acted as a grapevine. (The word *grapevine* itself would tip me off to Jess Stern's work of the same name, an exploitative exposé of lesbians.) We had an oral *Who's Who* which included not only peers, movie stars, and pop singers, but authors. How did the famous names—Somerset Maugham, for example, or Marianne Moore—filter down to the sticky tables of Pam Pam's, the baby gays' ice-cream parlor on Sixth Avenue? It could be a hint as small as one I recently ran across in a movie review about a male character who wore nail polish to work. Immediately my feelers twitched and I was searching for more. A long, deeply ingrained habit—or has it become an instinct for survival?

Traditionally, Clue Number One would always be marital status. A wedding ring in our circle did not mean quite the same thing that it would to a young het stalking husbands. Single was suspect and sometimes proof. Of course, married people were not safe either. We knew all about marriages of convenience. Someone always knew someone who was married because of her parents. Cover photographs were scrutinized for short hair on women, a pinky ring, and the indefinable "look" we sought on everyone: that dyke or faggot stamp that is utterly indefinable. These tactics did not always work. Françoise Sagan finally disappointed me. She'd had the short hair, the right face, and it was so easy to assume that she'd changed the pronouns in her slightly decadent love stories.

Also indefinable was variant content. McCullers was obvious, with her tomboys and otherly characters. I sought writers like her in the style I would later learn was Southern Gothic. Though Flannery O'Connor and William Faulkner proved worthless for my cause, Truman Capote, with his sissified young men, was as obvious as McCullers. My first taste of Tennessee Williams was through the mysterious but undeniably homosexual Sebastian in *Suddenly Last Summer*.

What did I find in these and other books which made the *New York Times Book Review*? Everything from shadows of my life to reflections of my mind—seldom out front, mostly nuance, never certain, always terribly exciting. Why was this so important? Simply, I suspected that all of these authors might be queer like me. Yet they belonged, truly had a place in the world, were valued. Even the fact that those who were gay were closeted thrilled me because I was part of their secret society. Someday I, too, might be valued *even though I was gay*.

Still, the words I neeeded to see in print remained invisible. It was all guesswork on my part: a photograph of no-frills Willa Cather; the literary whisper of a close friendship between Virginia Woolf and Vita Sackville-West; the frank, unabashed eyes and crew cut of Gertrude Stein; certain themes like the idyllic childhood scenes of Louisa May Alcott and Mazo de la Roche. The latter panned out much later, though I could not have named the attraction of the Jaina novels when I read them. I only remember being hooked, completely. Was Rennie really a woman in de la Roche's mind? Alcott, of course, married, but having recently visited her home, and stood in those tiny rooms where privacy was obviously unheard of, I can understand why she would not come out. Even the desk where she wrote was totally exposed.

And the words, the lovely discriminating words of the poets, non–gender specific like Emily Dickinson and Louise Bogan, or full of Christina Rossetti's fiery passion, or of imagery which suggested variance.

Other tip-offs, as unreliable as short hair, were androgynous names. This was my original route to Carson McCullers. It also led me to Djuna Barnes. Although her lesbians were remote to me—as disturbed as Randy Salem's and as distant in terms of class as Radclyffe Hall's—Barnes's writing was brilliant. If I couldn't imagine knowing her characters, or creating a world like hers when I became a writer, I could at least dream, in adolescence, of writing as poetically. Though Barnes was later to deny her lesbian sexuality, at least I had someone to idolize when it counted. I visited Patchin Place, where she lived, like a shrine.

What is this love we have for the invert, boy or girl? It was they who were spoken of in every romance that we ever read. The girl lost, what is she but the prince found? The prince on the white horse that we have always been seeking. And the pretty lad who is a girl, what but the prince-princess in pointlace—neither one and half the other, the painting on the fan! . . . for in the girl it is the prince, and in the boy it is the girl that makes a prince a prince—and not a man. (Barnes, Nightwood 136–37)

Then, in a magazine shop in Greenwich Village, I found The Ladder. This small, rough periodical was not full of unhappy endings. I sensed that its very existence proclaimed a kind of healthy survival I hadn't imagined possible. There were stories and poems and articles, advertisements and letters and editorials, just like in a real magazine. To a sadsack little kid who'd been badly beaten by blows dealt her from the hands of literary gays and straights alike, blows of persuasion to hide and mourn her very being, The Ladder allowed entry into a legitimate universe.

I was too young. I've told this tale on myself many times, about my disappointment when, reading the subscription blank, it said I had to be twenty-one to subscribe. Not that I had any place where I could have received the priceless journals by mail. Not that I would have had the price of a subscription.

But I now knew The Ladder existed, a magazine for me when I grew up. Most importantly, I had something, as a young writer, to which I could aspire.

Oh, I'm not saying that as a teenager my whole goal in life was to write lesbian materials for lesbians and to be published in a lesbian periodical and to be part of a growing gay publishing empire. No, I wanted to be Wolfe still, and Kerouac and Dreiser. Little by little, though, I began to wonder what a lesbian Wolfe would sound like.

Much later Jane Rule's work came into my life. *The Desert of the Heart,* first published in 1964, put together good writing with healthy, respectable lesbians. Rule had the magical ability to treat her gay characters as if they could function normally in a world large enough to hold them. No longer did I just want to write for *The Ladder,* which I was, by then, doing. Now I wanted to write like Jane Rule. The only words I could put to this yearning were the ones I use still: I wanted to make gay people feel as good about themselves as Jane Rule made me feel.

Evelyn saw Ann. It had not been her intention at first. It had not been her intention ever. And it was not her intention now, but it was her desire to be here or anywhere with Ann, a desire which all her intentions denied. (Rule 221)

Now when I read from the vast selection of lesbian and gay literature, I am looking for that same uplifting experience. I don't want the tormented complaints of our past abuse, unless they're turned around into hope and acceptance. I don't want melodramatic stories of desolation. I want our protagonists and heroes to be rounded people living in the world. I want our literature to project our own new-found or newly acknowledged health and I don't care if it's in mysteries and romances, or heady intellectual novels and perfect short stories. I want us thriving through our words.

I do care who writes the words. Straight authors writing gay characters are likely to fall as flat as I now realize John O'Hara did when creating those stiff, sexless lesbians of his. I'm not that hungry anymore. Though straight writers are not the only ones who carry homophobia like an illness in the blood (especially if they want to make a buck), they have little motivation to practice safe writing: writing that's not dangerous to the gay psyche.

I want gay characters to be as honestly passionate as gay people are. To throb with love and greed and hunger and all the driving forces of life which make for a common humanity. Gay characters do not have to thrash around obsessed with sexuality, though as long as it's an issue in the world at large it will be part of our literary thrashings.

I don't believe in prettying up our world for readers. Like heterosexuals, some of us are sick, or mean, or criminal. I don't believe in pretending happy endings when they aren't appropriate. On the other hand, there's a whole world of people who think they have no stake in our future and who continue to perpetuate the negative stereotypes of gays that heterosexual fear has invented. Vin Packer's bar host Arty was ignorant; he need be no longer.

I have been through years of self-destructive behavior, therapy, and recovery. I've experienced the damage of all that negativity. I want to create an alternative literature; to embrace where we were, but to deliberately flood our culture with the positive images which will make a better future; to create real characters with all their foibles, but to let them loose into a universe which will support them.

Writing about Radclyffe Hall, Una Troubridge asserted:

She had long wanted to write a book on sexual inversion. . . . It was her absolute conviction that such a book could only be written by a sexual invert, who alone could be qualified by personal knowledge and experience to speak on behalf of a misjudged and misunderstood minority. (81–82)

There is no way Little Miss Muffet or Cinderella was gay, but Judy Grahn in *Another Mother Tongue* has traced a gay connection to the Fairy people. And I was fervently grateful when I stumbled across Hall who had achieved her aim and made possible every bit of lesbian literature which has followed.

Jane Rule's *Desert* wasn't there for me then, but it's pushed back even further the walls which squeezed us, sometimes to death. The young dyke writers growing up will be stronger for Hall and for Rule, and will create a literature ever freer of doom because of their foremothers. There is no way the constantly expanded freedoms of the press won't affect everyone who reads our work. Where it will evolve I can't imagine, as I once could not imagine our current culture. My interest is that no little Lee ever suffer alone again.

WORKS CITED

Aldrich, Ann. *Take a Lesbian to Lunch*. New York: Macfadden-Bartell, 1972.
Barnes, Djuna. *Nightwood*. 1937. Rpt. New York: New Directions, 1961.
Grahn, Judy. *Another Mother Tongue: Gay Words, Gay Worlds*. Boston: Beacon, 1984.
Hall, Radclyffe. *The Well of Loneliness*. 1928. Rpt. New York: Pocket, 1950.
McCullers, Carson. *The Heart Is a Lonely Hunter*. 1940. Rpt. New York: Bantam, 1953.
———. *The Member of the Wedding*. Boston: Houghton, 1946.

Packer, Vin. *Spring Fire*. Greenwich, Conn.: Fawcett, 1952.
Rule, Jane. *The Desert of the Heart*. Cleveland: World, 1964.
Salem, Randy. *Man among Women*. Boston: Beacon, 1960.
Taylor, Valerie. *The Girls in Three-B*. New York: Crest, 1959.
———. *Whisper Their Love*. New York: Crest, 1957.
Troubridge, Una. *The Life and Death of Radclyffe Hall*. London: Hammond, 1961.

FOUR

Insider/Outsider Coming of Age

Maureen Brady

I hadn't anticipated that my forty-fifth birthday would serve as a deadline to move me along. However, mid-life as the age was, I found myself wondering could it bring me to a more mature state as a writer? Or did such a thing even exist? I wasn't at all sure. But as I began to peer around, trying to see outside my shadow like a groundhog in February, I perceived I had been acting always against the constraint of an eking out model, that I had always written as if I were on a word allowance. Also, I was on an allowance for both how much success and how much failure could be tolerated in any given period. And suddenly it seemed time to face the knowledge that this model was not going to sustain me for a lifetime, nor would I want it to. There was too much miserliness to it.

What mid-life seems to require of me is greater discrimination about where to direct my energy. Having nourished and validated contact with my muse, I no longer have the problem of needing to "think up" what to write next. There seem to be an ever-increasing number of novels or stories which would choose me to write them. The problem is *when*. The conflict is accentuated by my still having to earn a living with work outside of writing, of course. In my twenties I remember thinking how criminal it was of our society not to support young writers (when they really needed it); now that I've aged, it seems even more outrageous that we don't support the mid-life writer.

But while I have little or no control over the economics of being a writer (and one who has chosen to write openly as a lesbian), I realized I was free to explore why the work had so often felt eked out in the way one squeezes the last of the toothpaste out of the nearly empty tube. I need not settle magnanimously for accepting myself as simply a slow writer who would always take at least five years to write a novel, while becoming fiercely envious whenever I heard of someone knocking out a draft of a novel in

49

three or four or six months. Here's a literal bank-type account from Virginia Woolf's *A Writer's Diary*, an example of something that set off my envy:

> . . . my Waves account runs, I think, as follows: —
> I began it, seriously about September 10, 1929.
> I finished the first version on April 10th, 1930.
> I began the second version on May 1, 1930.
> I finished the second version on February 7th, 1931.
> I began to correct the second version on May 1, 1931, finished 22nd June 1931.
> I began to correct the typescript on 25th June 1931.
> Shall finish (I hope) 18th July 1931. (Woolf 168)

She actually records finishing on 17 July 1931.

Just as salivating can lead me to identify hunger, I've noticed that this sort of envy can steer me to awareness of what I want and am missing. In the case of reading Woolf, I identified a yearning for a freer, fuller flow to my work. I did not want in the years ahead always to have to push through that feeling that there was a kink in the hose.

I can recall still fairly vividly my coming out in the mid-seventies after years of keeping my inklings of a lesbian sexuality in a straitjacket. I took my time working up to it, but the final declaration came with the release of a great flow of energy and inward entitlement, at the same time that, ironically, I was crossing a fence which made me less acceptable in outer realms. I couldn't have guessed then that this gust of joy was not the be-all and end-all of abundance, but would serve in part to blow me down the road of my journey.

I remember at eleven or twelve scuffing along the shelves in my small town library, believing if I concentrated hard enough, I could follow my nose to a good book. Who knows what I missed that I might have devoured, given a bit of parental or teacher guidance? But the upside of this method was that it made room for intuition to be honorably respected and has lasted as one of my primary ways to cope when feeling lost and undirected amidst life's mysterious forces. I still wander through a bookstore or a library, intuition channel open, until I'm led to the right book. It was in this way I believe I was led to read, back to back, Ruby Redinger's *George Eliot: The Emergent Self*, and Sharon O'Brien's *Willa Cather: The Emerging Voice*. No accident the repetition of "emerge" in the titles, these biographies each focus on a woman coming to maturity as a writer. That these writers did seem to reach a point of flowering inspired greater faith in my exploration of the notion that there might be such a thing as a proliferation of generative energy. I pictured bulbs planted a few years back hitting the year when they came into their own. A writer who'd sat poised many years might ripen; a writer who'd eked things out might find another way to go.

Of course the development of any writer cannot be reduced to any one simple deed or turn or resolution, and even if it could, the crossing for another wouldn't necessarily have reference to my own. Still, if not through modeling, how else do we make the leaps we often need to make? So I read these (for me) pathfinder books carefully, looking for the forces that had seemed to check these women and for how they had overcome them to emerge.

George Eliot's energetic and highly creative self seemed to emerge as she released herself from a particular childhood relationship to her brother, Isaac, who held her somewhat psychically captive. He was angered when she moved into her imagination (Redinger 61). In adulthood, though he was not physically present, Isaac held the purse strings to her inheritance until she arranged to deposit her money into George Lewes's account, only a couple of years after she'd begun her late flowering to fiction at nearly forty (Redinger 340). Redinger surmises that Isaac was Eliot first imagined audience and as such he would have been at worst disapproving and at best wholly indifferent (Redinger 345). Lewes served as an alternate male authority but one strongly supportive of her writing, and Mary Anne Evans became George Eliot, a move far more significant than the taking of a pseudonym. It was the taking of a persona with the authority to write fiction (Redinger 336). The taking of authority, perceived as being "male," was actually the owning of her power.

It seems significant that while Mary Anne became George, Willa Cather became Willie for a period of her life. In the O'Brien biography the pictures of Willie the cross-dresser make a strong impression of "coming out." I wonder if lesbian writers, freer to come out today (it seemed as if when Willa tried to do it, no one was willing to notice), find some ritual equivalent in that emergence to claiming powers traditionally granted the masculine world, which earlier women writers did with naming. Willa had no given middle name and so gave herself one (Love) in childhood, which she later changed to Sibert, absorbing the identity of an uncle. She published her work until 1920 using Willa Sibert Cather (O'Brien 107–10). Probably more important to her coming of age as a writer were leaving a job in which she had siphoned her creative energy into the works of others as an editor at McClures, and finding her way to a woman's literary tradition which she had largely shunned as sentimental but which she eventually embraced via Sarah Orne Jewett (O'Brien 339). She had to stop using the values of the male literary establishment (trying to write like Henry James and believing the only stories people would want to read would be written about Bostonian drawing rooms and their inhabitants). In Sarah Orne Jewett, she acquired the grace of a loving female mentor, a grace many of us lack. Simply reading precious kernels quoted from the letters made me recognize my deep desire for this sort of mentor. Imagine receiving a letter that says, "Do not hurry too fast in these early winter days, — a quiet hour is worth more to you than anything you can do in it" (O'Brien 336). Jewett encouraged Cather to "find a quiet place near the best companions (not those who admire and wonder at everything one does, but those who know the good things with delight!)." She ended this letter by reassuring Cather she had been "growing" even when she felt "most hindered" and reminded her she was not alone: "I have been full of thought about you" (O'Brien 346).

Here is a relationship full of the mentoring of "the Good Mother": validation of the imagination, validation of the struggle. It is extraordinary to be reminded that a quiet hour is worth more than anything one can do in it. I remember in childhood how I stayed in bed late on weekends to gain a quiet hour, covers over my head to gain privacy from my sister.

Back then it seemed that every quiet hour I took for myself was punishable by mockery. Perhaps this is why I still need to hear the refrain chimed so lyrically by Sara Orne Jewett not to be so parsimonious with the taking. For it is in the quiet hours we glimpse our hidden aspects, both the ones we want to claim and the ones we wish were not ours at all. It was in those hours I came to understand I was a survivor of incest, and that my own coming to maturity as a writer would have to center on divesting myself of the unchosen, unwelcome bond of incest with a female primary perpetrator. I know *incest* is a charged word, so much so that some people shut down as soon as they hear it. I've had the humbling experience of having been one of them until a few years ago. Or they want to know the details so they can stop trying to imagine them and fit the incident inside or outside of their definition. But specific details aren't necessary to understand that, just as ultraviolet is only a segment on the light spectrum, incest has a place on the continuum of power as we know it in patriarchy. One doesn't have to be an incest survivor to identify with this particular struggle or to have a similar relationship to power. *Author-ity:* the incest survivor is not supposed to have it. The pen is the power of the writer. So the conflict arises; there's a kink in the hose.

The first knowledge of power for me was the experience of childhood, of someone larger and in charge having power over me, deciding how much privacy and how much autonomy I would be afforded. This someone utilized the inequities of size and vulnerability to express her unconscious needs upon me. Perhaps I was stuck with someone who unknowingly needed to retaliate for whatever was committed upon her in her powerlessness. For a child in this situation there is a contamination of both love and power. Trust is impossibly betrayed. And loyalty is demanded without being merited. While incest isn't about sex but about power, it's no accident that it moves in the realm of sexuality, because sexuality is closely akin to spirituality and instinctual expression. And it is this, the spirit, the true self of the child, which a perpetrator needs to overwhelm in order to experience possession, a taking of power against his or her own powerlessness. It sounds sinister and malicious. It is, regardless of whether the perpetrator had deliberate intent to injure or was unconsciously acting out of unowned wounds, counting somehow upon the idea that the child's memory (really the child's separate life) would not start until some later age.

Silence in the face of powerlessness is primal. So, too, is breaking silence, which brings with it both the power to heal and the threat of terror. That is why I always had the feeling I was given a hose with a kink in it. There was actually no kink in the hose; there was someone stepping on it.

Taking back, repossessing, making whole, creating autonomy where none was respected, how does this occur? Creating an autonomous character in my writing is one way I've been able to do this. The spirit of the character, born of its creator, becomes itself and goes out to enter the universe in a birth—nurture—release cycle. Love does not possess but fosters a cycle of abundance instead.

I remember the difficult time I had letting go of Folly (the protagonist of my second novel, *Folly*) who I felt had become a real fantasy friend to me. I resisted finishing the book and entering the changes which came in my life when I did complete it. The typesetter wrote me a note saying, "I hope you'll write a sequel and I'll be able to typeset it," and for a minute, overwhelmed by the compliment, I thought, "My God, I'll have to spend the next five years writing a sequel." But I didn't. A couple of years later, in a somewhat lean writing period for me, Folly put in an appearance in a dream. She was with Martha (her cohort in the novel) and we were on a working-class porch much like the place where she had first come to me, and they had brought lasagna. Many people were coming but they said, "Don't worry, we'll be able to feed them all." It was a dream which warmed me with the impression of being provided for.

When imagination has been developed as a survival tool, how does one wield it without having to do so always as a defense? When the going got grim in my childhood, I made up stories and whole worlds. The imagination can be an amazing resource for the preservation of dignity in the face of someone's attempts to extinguish or overwhelm one's true self. And while it's surely a constructive defense used in this way, can the same gift be transformed into the power to consciously manipulate material into literature without being fettered to the status of victim, to defense? George Eliot wrote that the genuine imagination "is always based on a keen vision, a keen consciousness of what is, and carries the store of definite knowledge as material for the construction of its inward visions" (Redinger 91). I take this statement to mean that my imagination has its own reality, its own truth. I have my own store and if I enter into it, I will find all the materials already present for the construction of a novel. I believe it. To believe it is to have the power that is mine. But then the voices come saying that to make something up is incongruent with the truth, is to cheat, is to lie. I have to identify these voices as perpetrators, invested in having my point of view if not buried or discredited, at least spoken too quietly or confusedly to be heard.

Adrienne Rich, in a poem called "Power," noting how Marie Curie's radiation sickness came from her purification of uranium, pointed out that wounds come from the same source as power. This recognition is a declaration of wholeness. So is the reverse: her power came from the same source as her wounds.

What I envision as *my* coming of age as a writer (at least for this moment, this age) is not that the imagination should forget its origins, but that its power grow independent from them. The gift given in relation to a wound is not meant to be static and does not have to be used up in the healing. The eking out model has a lot to do with power and with the ways women have been discouraged from taking their truest power seriously or fully. I've not been exempt, but have done my share of bargaining and negotiating to see just how much I could take, how much I could say before disturbing others. Now I would like to be able to invite Folly back to serve up the lasagna.

Unfortunately this brings me to the next question: who wants the lasagna?

Being a lesbian writer with or without a history of incest is a constant lesson in breaking silences. I live in a space fraught with tension between the desire to write what must be written because it is true to my experience, and the desire to be part of a group, whether that group is the lesbian community, the lesbian literary subculture, or mainstream society. The presence of a lesbian literary community and its burgeoning publications in the seventies and early eighties provided for me both nurturance and malnutrition at different junctures. I'd been writing stories and a novel for about five years before coming out (in fact I was writing my way out), and though I sent my work out diligently, the most consistent word which came back in my mailbox was "no." I collected many a rejection slip, not a single acceptance. I took heart from the excitement of the work itself, the way it sounded to me and the few others who heard it in my various writing workshops or groups, and from hearing Muriel Rukeyser give a talk in which she said she'd once lined a trash can with rejection letters, and then she added, "As long as you're getting your no, you know you're doing something right."

Acceptance came first from *Letters,* a journal edited in Saratoga Springs (where I then resided), and was rapidly followed by an acceptance in *So's Your Old Lady* and another in *Conditions.* Those were boom years for the lesbian-feminist movement, and I am grateful to have been published frequently from 1977 and through the next several years as a part of that movement. But by around 1982 I began to experience being an insider in this community as restrictive; while it was buoying me in some aspects, it seemed to suffocate me in others. I wanted wider recognition, not less recognition from the lesbian reader, but a greater validation in the literary world. I wanted my work to range further; for instance, I wanted fathers and daughters to be just as good a subject for my writing as mothers and daughters. Within the mother-daughter subject, I needed hatred and alienation (working up to incest) to be as legitimate a focus as love and connection. Because I was an incest survivor, I was particularly sensitive to underlying messages communicating that love was conditional. The messages were and are there. I notice them in the reviewing of lesbian fiction (including my own) in which the nearly exclusive focus of the review is the content and consciousness of the material, while virtually no attention is paid to the literary effectiveness or construction of the work. Is this not a deprivation of the lesbian writer, who needs a garden to grow in as much as anyone else, a responsiveness, a recognition given to what is skillful and what is not? As Sarah Orne Jewett implied, the best companions are not those who admire and wonder at everything one does, but those who know and recognize the good things distinctly (O'Brien 346).

Perhaps there is a coming of age issue for the community at work in what I am describing. Development of a community begins with forming an identity, which implores of its writers: show us who we are (we who have been invisible). This clear need seems to have created something of a genre lesbian novel in which women brave the odds to be able to love one another —indeed no easy street—but does one have to be a hero to do it? The characters who emerge seem to be the archetypal lesbian hero, the adventurer, the monster. When a community is bonded by identity (this is who *we* are, what *we* believe in), how does it hold its bonds when individuation becomes the next developmental stage? And how do its writers thrive when they move to that terrain in their own interests?

In my own experience this is where the malnutrition came in. There was a time when I was deeply involved with the lesbian literary community. It became for me more and more closed as a unit, similar to the incestuous or alcoholic family, where blurring of separate boundaries is a requirement for protecting the system, not its individual people. There were two tracks. On the outer one, which was given visibility, we made ourselves so good, so positive, so powerful (really so grandiose we might as well be goddesses), became judges and, not very humbly, began judging each other; on the secret track we hid in our shadow the feelings legislated out (such as competition, envy, jealousy). I myself contributed to writing about lesbians in a way that tended to idealize us out of the human race, and I believe the drive to do so grew out of the need to redress the balance of history, a past in which lesbians were portrayed as sick or pathetic or grotesque. When I began to feel community claustrophobia, I sensed that to continue to develop as a writer and an honest human being, I would have to make an effort to integrate the secret shadow track both of myself and my community. This work demanded breaking ranks and trespassing boundaries. My writing continued to be about lesbians but in what seemed to me a more holistic telling of individual character. I was interested in allowing the character to be less heroic, to have greater vulnerability, to be more graphi-cally sexual (because that too seemed to me to have been held in check in my writing). Then began the experience of repeated rejections by the same lesbian and feminist journals that had once eagerly published me, rejection by some of my writer peers and mentors—I was not fit for the "in group." It has been another five years of the "no," with the exception of publishing my stories in a collection and one in a West Coast feminist journal. Not being a total masochist, I stopped submitting to those lesbian-feminist journals after a while and directed my submissions to mainstream literary journals. I've collected many more rejections on that count.

When reading to a lesbian audience, I'm often still introduced as "one of *our* best." What gives me a queasy feeling is the notion that I am a known commodity, one with some feature of belongingness to the introducer and the audience. While I appreciate the pride in the introduction and have a deep yearning for the belonging, what is wrong with this picture is that it does not at all contain the truth that for at least five years I've felt outcast from the lesbian literary community.

I've often gone back to that statement of Muriel Rukeyser's about the "no's." I wish I could ask her how many no's she thinks are enough, because while every writer must encounter his or her share, "no" can also be deadly as a silencer. And having no community puts lesbians and gay men in greater danger, fear, and isolation than they already contend with. We have a history which demonstrates this fact to us. Also, I am weary. My endurance has bottomed out and I think of submitting to the message of the "no": Stop writing. If I can't imagine making that choice, when for so many years I have relied upon this resource to bring me into proper alignment with myself, I can at least admit here, and hope that it will touch someone else's isolation, that it is no gravy life, being a lesbian writer. There are plenty of unmet needs, plenty of places to fall down and not be picked up. We need foundations and grants that single out and support our work and provide some compensation for the frequency with which it is discriminated against in the traditional grants' world. (Goddess bless the one or two that we have.) We need laws that would legitimize our status so that we can even seek protection against discrimination. We need matrons and gentle mentors. We need thorough, serious, and respectful criticism.

Incest survivors face the question early in life: who will care for me if not that person who was meant to care for me? In the healing, one must hear the mournful howl of the child, like a wolf-cub abandoned by its parent. It is that child who holds on to the knowledge of her innocence and must seek consolation for the damages. It is often that child too, underneath a pyre of shame, who keeps alive the ember of caring.

It's easy to tap into feeling victimized as a lesbian writer. I am neither impervious to internalized homophobia nor to the judgment of my lesbian sisters. It is the child who howls then with that same refrain: Who will care for me if not those who were meant to? I've learned through incest recovery that it's essential not to turn rejection into shame, feeling and acting as if there is something wrong with me when there is not.

It is the lot of the writer both to reflect the inner life and to stand outside in order to do that. No easy task. I'm grateful Sarah Orne Jewett told Willa Cather she was growing even when she felt most hindered. I take heart from this both for myself and for my community.

WORKS CITED

Brady, Maureen. *Folly.* Trumansburg, N.Y.: Crossing Press, 1982.
O'Brien, Sharon. *Willa Cather: The Emerging Voice.* New York: Ballantine, 1988.
Redinger, Ruby V. *George Eliot: The Emergent Self.* New York: Knopf, 1975.
Rich, Adrienne. *The Dream of a Common Language.* New York: Norton, 1978.
Woolf, Virginia. *A Writer's Diary.* New York: Harcourt, 1953.

FIVE

The Elusive "Seamless Whole": A Biographer Treats (or Fails to Treat) Lesbianism

Noel Riley Fitch

To Virginia Woolf the central problem of biography was how "to weld . . . into one seamless whole" the "granite-like solidarity" of truth and the "rainbow-like intangibility" of personality ("Biography," 229). It is an impossible task, as she herself seemed to conclude. Complicating this "steep grind" and "appalling grind" (*Diary* 235, 155), to use Woolf's description of biographical writing, is the biographer's awareness of her own relationship to her subject and the challenges of modern psychoanalysis and feminism.

Friends and readers have frequently suggested that I may have devoted fifteen years to research and writing about Sylvia Beach and her Shakespeare and Company bookshop in Paris because we share a similar background. Like Beach, I am one of three daughters of a Protestant minister: she grew up in a Presbyterian parsonage, I in a Nazarene parsonage (though for generations the Rileys were Presbyterian). This seemingly unusual correspondence in no way explains, in part or in whole, my long and complicated fascination with literary modernism and Paris exile. In fact, I do not believe that I even cared about this parsonage and sibling similarity until, after more than a decade of research, I began writing chapter 2 of what I then called the history of Shakespeare and Company. Because the history of this bookshop, lending library, and publishing house is inexorably linked to the woman who created and nurtured it, my history also became a biography. It happened after the brief opening chapter, which recreates that moment on 2 February 1922 when Beach collected the first copy of James Joyce's *Ulysses* from her printer at the Gare de Lyon. In chapter 2 I began the life of Beach and her family—the years that led to the opening of the bookshop. As I was explaining her family life in the parsonage and the relationship of three girls in their birth order and place in the family, I understood the personal knowledge that I was bringing to this story. I was probably not one of those biographers (Freud did not accuse them all) who, he believed, "fixated on their heroes in a quite special way" (Freud 80). I did not think then nor do I think now that I was telling her story out of some deep psychological need to probe my parsonage life.

By contrast, friends and readers did not question me about how I related to, perceived, or understood Beach's sexuality. There were a few questions about whether she was, in fact, a lesbian (I was surprised that I had not made this clear) and why I did not give more detail about her private physical/sexual life, but with one exception (out of dozens of interviews and a hundred reviews), I was not asked about my personal response to her homosexuality. The exception was a journalist in San Diego, then my hometown, who asked pointedly if I had any "trouble" or "uneasiness" writing a history about so many homosexuals.[1] She asked in part because she "knew" that I was not lesbian and in part because I was then teaching at a church-related college, which she assumed would be hostile to homosexuality. I shrugged off the question, saying something about feeling at ease with both straight and gay artists, and then, on second thought, and with an awareness of the campus setting of the interview, I added that I merely told their story: I did not determine with whom they could sleep. In an otherwise laudatory review in this newspaper the week before, it was suggested that I was prudish in my handling of sex—"tact and discretion are carried to the point of prudishness" (Dexter 4)—because I did not detail the lesbian relationship of Sylvia Beach and Adrienne Monnier, who owned the French bookshop and lending library La Maison des Amis des Livres.

I would like to take these challenges as a springboard toward grappling with several important questions concerning the place of sex in biography and the relationship between this heterosexual biographer and her lesbian subject. The implications in the questions go to the very heart of three sins that can snare or entrap the biographer: suppression, invention, and sitting in judgment. In dealing with these philosophical questions, I must burden the reader with my personal experience. The discussion of biography, like the biography itself, involves the writer, for biography has two subjects, the life being recreated and the person who recreates it.

Can the absence of a full disclosure or exploration of a subject's sex life be considered suppression? Leon Edel, one of our preeminent biographers, has warned against the demand on modern literary biography to "know intimately the 'sex-life' of his subject (particularly whether he was hetero- or homosexual!) as if this were the essence of the matter" (Clifford 227). Some lives do demand a focus on their sex life; others do not. Sex can be overemphasized in modern biography. It is possible both to question this occasional overemphasis upon sexual psychology and also to welcome the freedom to explore and discuss all aspects of an artist's life. Beach and Monnier kept their sexuality private. While accepting sexual freedom and diversity, they were critical of public displays—whether Gide's homosexual advertisements or James Farrell's heterosexual posings. Their sense of privacy was typical of the time, of Beach's parsonage upbringing, and of the French sense of privacy and discretion. Because she kept her sexuality private, Beach left me little, if any, historical evidence. It was not just my own parsonage discretion—I had not yet heard the warning that "discretion is not the better part of biography"—but my academic training that kept me from indulging in speculative detail, a contemporary indulgence that in its extreme Joyce Carol Oates calls "pathology" (Quoted by Atlas, 40). I acknowledged Beach's lesbian relationship with Monnier because the little evidence available confirmed it, but I went no further. The only serious struggle that I had with revealing intimate details was my decision to reveal the suicide of Beach's mother, which had been kept even from her own family. In this case I had concrete information, including the suicide note of Mrs. Beach, and I believed that her suicide was one of the first steps in Beach's withdrawal from Joyce's demands and, therefore, relevant to the history.

A subject's sexuality is not, I would hasten to add, irrelevant to one's creative and social life. George Barnard Shaw mistakenly asserted in a letter to his biographer Frank Harris that sex plays a negligible role in biography: "If I were to tell you every such adventure that I have enjoyed, you would be none the wiser as to my personal, not even to my sexual, history" (Shaw 234). Perhaps Shaw was guarding himself against this particular biographer, for Frank Harris's own *My Lives and Loves* certainly established his interest in sexual adventure. (Hemingway once remarked to Beach that it also revealed his fictional talents.[2] Perhaps it was more caution in the face of an aggressive biographer, for Shaw revealingly adds, "I found sex hopeless as a basis for permanent relations, and never dreamt of marriage in connection with it" (Shaw 236). Such a startling view certainly suggests some bearing on Shaw's relations with others and on his fictional recreation of sexual relations. Ailments affecting the sex life of a subject, like Martin Luther's hemorrhoids, like Proust's asthma, or Woolf's melancholia, may indeed have a direct bearing on his/her creative and social life.

Beach's relationship with Monnier, whether sexual or not, was vital to her social and professional life. Through Monnier, Beach was the only American member of several closed French groups of artists: Jules Romains's *copains*, Gide's circle, and the Valéry Larbaud/Léon-Paul Fargue group. These associations enabled Beach to translate and publish works by many American and English writers in France. She and Monnier translated T. S. Eliot's "The Love Song of J. Alfred Prufrock" for the first time and were on the editorial boards of several French publications, including *Commerce, Mésures,* and Monnier's *Le navire d'argent.* Beach published the English editions of Joyce's *Ulysses,* Monnier the French. Together they made the rue de l'Odéon a crossroads of international modernism. Because their professional loyalty was unwavering and each participated in the other's artistic projects, I assume that their sexual relationship strengthened and enriched their public union.

Because this union freed Beach for her literary career and eventually nurtured two generations of modernist writers, I believed it was integral to the life of Beach and Shakespeare and Company. Thus, I began the book with the following words:

"My loves were Adrienne Monnier and James Joyce and Shakespeare and Company," proclaims Sylvia Beach. This . . . is the story of these three loves. The first is the story of the love between two women. The details were and still are little known. (Fitch 11)

No bedroom scenes follow and the word *lesbian* does not appear for seventy-two pages, and then in connection with Natalie Barney. This emphasis on the "love," not the sex, of the Beach-Monnier union was deliberate. Later I note that in 1936, after Gisèle Freund moved into their apartment when Beach was visiting the United States, "these intimate years with Adrienne ended" for Sylvia, who upon her return, moved into an apartment in the building where her shop was located. Nevertheless, the Beach-Monnier friendship remained "fast until 1955 when Adrienne committed suicide after a long illness. The thirty-eight years' devotion of these women is similar in its duration and character to the fifty-three-year friendship of Bryher and H.D. and the thirty-nine-year friendship of Stein and Toklas.

Eros channeled into sorority yielded both personal and literary fruits" (Fitch 367–68). The only other direct comment I make on their personal relationship is at the death of Monnier, who had suggested that Beach join her in death: "Sometimes you wish you had left with her as she suggested—she knew what living without her was going to be like," wrote Beach in a note left among her papers. To this I add: "Personal happiness went with the death of Adrienne, who for thirty-eight years had been a sister, lover, mother, and mentor. The rest of Sylvia's life, as one friend notes, was marked by mere honorary awards" (Fitch 411). This direct statement carries power that further speculation would weaken.

A biographer must be careful to distinguish between a truth that is established in fact and a truth that is suggested by circumstantial evidence. I always assumed that Beach and Monnier were lesbian lovers. The question I sought to answer was whether their love was physically expressed. I interviewed as many of their friends who swore that they had a physical relationship as swore that they did not. Beach's own sister Cyprian would have been among the latter, for she and her lover, Helen Eddy, with whom I talked at length, believed that the Parisian couple, in contrast to their own California standards, were too "up-tight" for physical expression. As a biographer who listens and weighs all the evidence, I concluded otherwise. Richard McDougall, the translator and interpreter of Monnier, has established the passionate nature of Monnier and her earlier lesbian affair with her former classmate Suzanne Bonnierre in his *The Very Rich Hours of Adrienne Monnier*. I also had the testimony of Myrsine Moschos, Beach's assistant during the 1920s, that Mrs. Sylvester Beach had misgivings about the relationship of her daughter to Monnier. Because Moschos refused to discuss any intimate details, I could not conclude whether Mrs. Beach's hostility was directed at the undue influence of Monnier on Beach or at the nature of their intimate relations.

One source of evidence in establishing truth can be the words of the subject herself: I had little such evidence. I had few letters of Beach to Monnier, and her statement in her memoirs that she loved Monnier was coupled with an expression of her love for Joyce. I did have an unpublished essay by Beach entitled "Those Unfortunate Creatures: My Life and Loves" —the subtitle consciously echoing her friend Frank Harris. In this brief one-page essay, she indirectly discusses her sexuality, probably prompted by a friend's remark that any autobiography had to have some sex. She mentions those persons who thought they "knew" she was James Joyce's lover and those who took for granted that she was a lesbian. Though she claims that her "strictly tailored costume . . . seemed quite indicative of tendencies inverted," she states that the costume was "adopted for convenience in a business life." She neither affirms nor denies her association with lesbians. She fondly, perhaps with amusement, describes the many homosexual "couples who stood with their arms around each other" before the "shrine" of pictures of Oscar Wilde and Lord Alfred Douglas. "Lesbians flocked to contemplate my person and to mark their unmistakable sympathy for me and my bookshop," she adds. Then she gently mocks those visitors who inquire in whispers about "queer books" and ask if she has "anything more about those unfortunate people" (Beach). Also, she was enthusiastic about Radclyffe Hall's *The Well of Loneliness* and recommended it to one of her young married assistants (Herrick). She defended her cousin's wife when the wife left him for a woman and fled to Europe from California. And finally, in an unpublished portion of her memoirs, Beach states that she was "always afraid of men":

> I think Gide was very much disappointed in me one summer when he joined Adrienne and me at Hyeres and nothing funny ever happened.
> A lady who attended the American Church and used to know my respectable father told someone she would not set foot in my shop where she had heard dreadful things went on.
> My "loves", as any lists may have perceived, were Adrienne Monnier [,] James Joyce and Shakespeare and Company. And once I felt so drawn to Robert McAlmon that I wrote and told him so, in what must have seemed like the awed tones of a young wife announcing that she thinks she may be expecting the happy event. He was, I am sure, quite alarmed and didn't turn up for some time. But by the time he did my thirteen generations of clergymen had regained their ascendance and to McAlmon's evident relief, we talked only of the weather. Adrienne used to call me *Fleur de Presbytère*—"Flower of the Parsonage." Whether from my puritan ancestry or puritanical upbringing—once when I was in my early teens my mother told me "never to let a man touch me"—I was always physically afraid of men. That is probably why I lived happily so many years with Adrienne.[3]

This passage suggests that she may have been bisexual, and that her mother, who fled her marriage bed after the birth of her third daughter, may have tipped the balance.

I had a number of these clues, but no single one conclusive. More importantly, I had lived in spirit with Beach long enough to get an impression of her character. Therefore, when I found an "unauthorized biography" of Drew Pearson alleging that he had impregnated one of the Beach sisters (Holly or Sylvia) during their service with the Red Cross in Serbia in 1919, I rejected this gossip (after unsuccessfully attempting to confirm it) as out of character for Sylvia, and probably for Holly as well.

A biographer is a "[witness] upon oath," to use the words of André Maurois (Clifford 168), or "an artist upon oath," in the words of Desmond MacCarthy (Quoted by Oates, iv). She cannot put conversation into the mouth of her subject any more than she can mention the weather without evidence. There are times, however, when facts do not speak for themselves. At these times, the duty to record only the facts—Strachey called it "laying bare the facts of the case" (vii)—does not accord with the burden to tell the truth. In the case of Beach's sex life—where I have clues but no "witnesses"—I had to establish the truth based on these clues. Had I explained the route I took to find this truth, as I have done here, I might have satisfied the San Diego reviewer. Had I elaborated on the private actions of Beach, I might have told what could have happened or what must have happened, but not what did happen.

Though the biographer must strive to tell the whole truth, she knows that nobody can tell the entire truth about a full and busy life in one book. Nor is the biographer a computer or court record. She is a human being and thus subjective and individual, with her own interests (mine was the bookshop), her own history, her own vision and frame of reference. This human individuality affects the selection of details because not all details can or should be presented—though all must be considered. She is a human being and, as a writer once pointed out, leans in a particular direction, for no one is born perpendicular.

As Jacques Barzun so eloquently explains, brute facts cannot grasp a life or history: "The complexity of life, taken both quantitatively and qualitatively, is greater than our documentary, chronological, and critical schemes allow for. . . . The Ariadne's thread is missing. It is found in no letter, no archive, no encyclopedia." Thus, he concludes, "It must be spun from one's inner consciousness. . . . Hence the need for *a priori* sympathy, in the exact meaning of that term: *feeling with*" (80). André Maurois suggests that the biographer "cultivate reactions similar" to her subject. Subsuming one's own emotional identity can be "very dangerous," he warns, but "there is no other method" (133).

A biographer must "feel with," thus "live with," her subject on intimate terms. The relationship has often been described, by Strachey, Jacques Barzun, and others, as a symbiotic one in which the biographer transcends personal limits in order to comprehend and "illuminate" the subject from within. Otherwise, how can the biographer reexperience her subject's feelings, trials, joys, or thoughts? Otherwise, how can she see through the eyes of or over the shoulder of her subject? This symbiosis or empathy can be facilitated in part by the curiosity and imagination of the life-writer. A certain amount of shared experience also seems necessary. Similar sexual experience, national origin, gender, or occupation can give the writer insight. Maurois claims that anyone who has "had various love affairs . . . understands Liszt and Wagner much better than would a Puritan, or a home-secluded scholar" (Quoted in Clifford 170). Because no biographer shares all the experiences of her subject, all biography presents, to one degree or another, a limited image. One way to avoid making too many mistakes is by writing only about those things with which one has a clear affinity. A century ago, Renan, the biographer and historian said, "one should write only about what one loves" (Quoted by Bowen, 65). Whether the modern biographer is motivated by "love" or money, she should, according to Sir Harold Nicolson, select a subject within the area of her "general knowledge" and within the range of her "sympathy" (157). It would be a mistake for a writer unfamiliar with the rudiments of music to undertake a biography of Chopin or a writer ignorant of the humanities to start a life of Erasmus.

To say that a biographer must share the gender or race or sexual preference of her subject is erroneous. By this criterion, a man could not write a biography of a woman, a woman could not write a biography of a man, a German could not tell the story of an American, a heterosexual could not interpret the life and times of a homosexual. The key lies in having some shared experiences as well as a sympathy for those not shared. If she does not share her subject's sexual history—whether it be chastity, promiscuity, homosexuality, heterosexuality, or bisexuality—she must try to suspend her own experience and "walk with" her subject. I could not have "lived with" Beach had I felt estranged from her lesbianism. As the one who would tell her story, I had to see the world over her shoulder. Though we did not have sexual preference or historical time in common, nor did I have experience in handling the suicides of loved ones, I did share gender, nationality, parsonage childhood, a respect for service to others (to a cause larger than one's self), feminism, and a love of Paris and literature —even the tendency to migraine headaches. In a larger sense I also share companionship and support of women—a gift that gives me a sense of sisterhood with both gay and straight women. I also had the understanding of Beach's deviation from orthodoxy and her conservative religious background, the need to leave her homeland in order to live her own life, even perhaps the guilt or the anxiety that resulted from her leaving church and family. On a smaller scale, I too have experienced this sexual break for freedom. Conceivably, I have perhaps a greater empathy for this early parsonage feminist than a contemporary secular feminist would.

These common experiences potentially offer a unique opportunity for understanding; they do not, however, guarantee wisdom and insight into human mind and character. These common experiences may, in fact, even endanger objectivity and tempt the biographer to project her own experience into the life she is writing.

The reverse may also occur, for the subject may infect the tone of the biographer, either consciously, as in the case of Mark Shorer who adopted the tone of voice of Sinclair Lewis for his biography, or less consciously, as in the reticence of the biographer of a discreet and private subject. I was probably influenced by the discretion of Beach's life. Had she been an active advocate of lesbianism—had it been one of the "main themes" of her life— it would have been imperative that I discuss, justify, and explain her sexuality at length, and I may not have been the best biographer for this. However, she would not have wanted her sexuality analyzed, and her sensibilities infected me. She was indeed an open advocate of what we, but not she, call feminism, and from this perspective I was able to discuss all the evidence from her letters and associations.

Undoubtedly all biographers write from the perspective of their own time and country, and thus speak to the readers of their own country. But in a more specific sense, a biographer is usually aware of those who await her story. This audience may be the family and friends of the subject, the colleagues of the biographer, the potential reviewers and professional critics, and the readers of the book. This latter group may include special interest groups such as lesbians, sailors, writers, preachers, mothers, or the physically challenged. In my situation, I was fleetingly aware of, but not preoccupied by, the audience awaiting the Sylvia Beach story: librarians, bookshop owners, lovers of Paris, professors of literature, feminists, lesbians, Joyceans, and others. Frankly, only the Joyceans worried me because I was dealing with ignoble aspects of his character. But I consciously chose an audience before I began writing. I selected an educated and well-traveled neighbor of mine named William Price, who reads voraciously but has no special interest in a particular modernist writer. That is, I deliberately wrote to the widest possible (educated) audience, knowing that my sympathy for Beach and her love of Monnier would be understood by lesbian readers and that Beach's discretion would protect her from any homophobic reader.

Biographers writing for this wider audience should beware of a double-edged problem: the projection of modern standards and principles on past lives and customs and, directly related to this, the use of special language, whether that be the psychoanalysis of the clinician or the terminology of feminism or Marxism. Though a verbal shorthand for a small professional audience, special language is not understood by a larger readership and fosters the projection of today's customs and sensibilities onto another time and place. One who does not use contemporary analytical techniques and languages, however, risks the charge of omission and suppression. In my fear of inventing something that was not true, I erred in the direction of understatement, just short, some accused me, of suppression. The biographer balances many scales, including the temptations of suppression and invention. She must be both participant and observer—the one who through empathy and perception arrives at an intimate identification with her subject, but also the "objective" truth-teller. The biographer of a lesbian must transcend her own limitations and identify with her subject, show understanding, and, in the words of Strachey, "lay bare the facts . . . dispassionately, impartially, and without ulterior intentions" (vii).

NOTES

1. This question was asked by Noel Osment in the interview for her story "Getting Close to Beach in Paris," *San Diego Union*, 20 July 1983, D1, D3.
2. "Frank Harris is trying to get Sylvia Beach, who published Ulysses, to publish his autobiography. She doesn't want to although I tell her it will be the finest fiction ever written," wrote Ernest Hemingway to Harriet Monroe, 16 November 1922 (72).
3. This early and unpublished portion of Beach's memoirs is typed, except for the second sentence, which is written in Beach's hand (Sylvia Beach Papers).

WORKS CITED

Atlas, James. "Speaking Ill of the Dead." *New York Times*, 6 Nov. 1988, sec. 6, 40ff.

Barzun, Jacques. "Truth in Biography: Berlioz." *University Review: A Journal of the University of Kansas* 5 (1939): 80.

Beach Sylvia. Sylvia Beach Papers. Firestone Library. Princeton Univ. Library, Princeton, N.J.

Bowen, Catherine Drinker. *Biography: The Craft and the Calling.* Boston: Little, 1968.

Clifford, James L., ed. *Biography as an Art: Selected Criticism 1560–1960.* New York: Oxford Univ. Press, 1962.

Dexter, Bruce. "Literary Paris Is Given Life." *San Diego Union,* Book Review, 10 July 1983, 14.

Fitch, Noel Riley. *Sylvia Beach and the Lost Generation: A History of Literary Paris in the Twenties and Thirties.* New York: Norton, 1983.

Freud, Sigmund. *Leonardo da Vinci and a Memory of His Childhood.* Trans. Alan Tyson. New York: Norton, 1964.

Hemingway, Ernest. *Selected Letters.* Ed. Carlos Baker. New York: Scribners, 1981.

Herrick, Eleanor Oldenberger. Interview with the author. January 1979, San Diego, Calif.

Maurois, André. *Aspects of Biography.* Trans. Sydney Castle Roberts. New York: Appleton, 1929.

Monnier, Adrienne. *The Very Rich Hours of Adrienne Monnier.* Trans. with Intro. and Commentaries Richard McDougall. New York: Scribners, 1976.

Nicolson, Harold. "The Practice of Biography." *American Scholar* 23, no. 2 (1954): 153–61.

Oates, Stephen B., ed. With Prologue. *Biography as High Adventure: Life-Writers Speak on Their Art.* Amherst: Univ. of Massachussetts Press, 1986.

Osment, Noel. "Getting Close to Beach in Paris." *San Diego Union* 20 July 1983, D1, D3.

Shaw, George Bernard, and Frank Harris. *The Playwright and the Pirate: Bernard Shaw and Frank Harris, A Correspondence.* Ed. Stanley Weintraub. University Park: Pennsylvania Univ. Press, 1982.

Strachey, Lytton. *Eminent Victorians.* New York: Harcourt, 1918.

Woolf, Virginia. *The Diary of Virginia Woolf: Volume Five, 1936–1941.* Ed. Anne Olivier Bell. New York: Harcourt, 1984.

———. "The New Biography." In *Collected Essays: Volume Four.* New York: Harcourt, 1967. 229–35.

SIX

Theorizing Lesbian : Writing—
A Love Letter

Elizabeth Meese

> . . . *reality begins with the intention of you*
> —Nicole Brossard, *Lovhers*

> It is always a matter of waking up, but never of some first awakening. My own presence to myself has been preceded by a language. Older than consciousness, older than the spectator, prior to any attendance, a sentence awaits "you": looks at you, observes you, watches over you, and regards you from every side. There is always a sentence that has already been sealed somewhere waiting for you where you think you are opening up some virgin territory. . . .
> —Jacques Derrida, *Dissemination*

> Analysis is a womanly word. It means that they discover there are laws.
> —Gertrude Stein, *How to Write*

Why is it that the lesbian seems like a shadow—a shadow with/in woman, with/in writing? A contrastive shape in a shadow play, slightly formless, the edges blurred by the turns of the field, the sheets on which a drama is projected. The lesbian subject is not all I am and it is in all I am. A shadow of who I am that attests to my being there, I am never with/out this lesbian. And we are always turning, this way and that, in one place and another. The shadows alone, never mind the body, make such a complex choreography in our struggle to make sense. An architechtonics of light and shade, moving, converging and I have only begun to describe the body in its shadow state, in two dimensions, in the equally shadowy medium of words. What could be the auto-bio-graph-y of this figure, of this writing "lesbian"? The word, the letter *L*, and the lesbian of this auto-biography, this auto-graph?

I like the letter *L* which contains its own shadow, makes and is made up of shadow, so that I cannot de-cipher the thing from its reflection. Does the horizontal stroke throw itself upward? Or is it the vertical stroke which casts its long shadow on the ground? The question of which is thing and what is shadow depends upon where I stand, or how I regard the letter. And is it the case that the body is always more substantial than the shadow it casts? I used to think so, but now this question appears familiar, like the old conundrums of figure and ground, content and form, body and mind. How then to begin to say what lesbian : writing is, to write its story, to speak of the letter of the letter?

In "Zero Degree Deviancy," Catharine Stimpson defines "the lesbian" in a "conservative and severely literal" way: "She is a woman who finds other women erotically attractive and gratifying" (364). Her definition, she says, holds to the "literal," or we might say, the "letteral"—to the body, which seems like the lesbian body, or perhaps to the word as the em-bodied inscription of lesbian : writing: "That carnality distinguishes it from gestures of political sympathy with homosexuals and from affectionate friendships in which women enjoy each other, support each other, and commingle a sense of identity, and well-being. Lesbianism represents a commitment of skin, blood, breast, and bone" (364). But the literal body, powerfully evoked, is a referential one, the "skin" and "bone" of textuality's absent lesbian, "there," and, literally speaking, not there at all, whose "being" depends on the word's evocation. She is called forth, in the way that I see your figure on the page, make you present for me as I write my letter to you. Your body is only as "literal" as the letter, the shade and angle of the marks on a page, the course of associations or forms in the mind, an/other instance of some mysterious relation between the word and the flesh. What, then, does it mean to claim, as Stimpson does, that lesbian writing springs from some other "physical presence in the world" (364)?

Writing the lesbian means writing someone who does not yet exist. This is not a project I take lightly, for as Brossard reminds us, "A lesbian who does not reinvent the word is a lesbian in the process of disappearing" (*Aerial* 122). Writing demands that I bring a "self" (I could say myself) into existence. A self I create as I write, as I say "I" and "lesbian," searching for the words, syntax, and grammar that can articulate the body, my body, and perhaps yours. When I write my love letter to you, I want to bring myself to you, hand myself over. When I write about lesbian : writing, I take my life in my hands, as my text. Or is it that I take my text as my life in my search for a language capable of expressing what those words—lesbian : writing—mean when our fingers, soft and electric, just meet, pulled together by their own magnetically charged engagement as (though) they have a life, a movement, of their own. Or when my tongue slides over the osmotic, lively breathing surface of your skin like words in the more elusive *glissement,* gliding like waves, one just over the other, enveloping their letters, as, in their representational capacity, they produce signification which we take as meanings. Or as the pen makes its tracks across the body of the page, its friction and its struggle to mark the course faithfully, our passions inscribed energetically in the body of language in the mind: a love letter.

THE LETTER OF THE LAW

Lesbian : writing takes (its) place in a semantic field subject to, that is, ordering itself and us, around the phallus (the prick of the phallo-logo-centric system). According to its rule, all subjects are subject to the law of the phallus if we are to found ourselves as speakers, in other words, to (pro)claim an identity. Luce Irigaray suggests in this respect that "we might suspect the *phallus* (Phallus) of being the *contemporary figure of a god jealous of his prerogatives;* we might suspect it of claiming, on this basis, to be the ultimate meaning of all discourse, the standard of truth and propriety, in particular as regards sex, the signifier and/or the ultimate signified of all desire, in addition to continuing, as emblem and agent of the patriarchal system, to shore up the name of the father" ("Father," *This Sex Which Is Not One,* 67). This phallic reign, in the interest of perpetuating and replicating itself, writes itself as the law of representation and representationality. But the law hides itself, a condition, we might suspect, of its effectiveness. This is what Lacan means when he says that the phallus "can play its role only when veiled" (288).

The law—like reason, its regulatory agent—drives a system, polices it, while pretending that it is not itself written in it. It refuses to appear, representing itself as being above the law. Derrida offers a variation on this theme in "Sending": "Perhaps law itself outreaches any representation, perhaps it is never before us, as what posits itself in a figure or composes a figure for itself" (325). We read the effects of the Law but never the Law-itself. By hiding, it escapes revision and protects its autocratic rule. As speaking subjects, we are positioned before it. Thus, Derrida observes in the terms of Kafka's parable, "The guardian of the law and the man from the country are 'before the law,' *Vor dem Gesetz,* says Kafka's title, only at the cost of never coming to see it, never being able to arrive at it. It is neither presentable nor representable, and the 'entry' into it, according to an order which the man from the country interiorizes and gives himself, is put off until death" ("Sending" 325). Such is the subject's double-bind: were we to arrive "there," we would no longer be "before" the law, that is, subject to it. It saves itself, perpetuates our subjugation, by its refusal to (re)present itself to us, to show its face, to allow itself to be seen, except through its effects, which we frequently apprehend with difficulty and (mis)take for the Law-itself. We read it as we read a dream which writes us and is written by us. Brossard describes its operation and effects as follows: "as soon as we speak of culture, we necessarily speak of codes, signs, exchanges, communication, and recognition. Likewise, we must speak of a system of values which, on the one hand, determines what makes sense or non-sense and which, on the other, normalizes sense so that eccentricity, marginality, and transgression can be readily identified as such, in order to control them if need be" (*Aerial* 103). In language, as we take on "selves," we offer ourselves up for regulation. The sentence awaits us. The paradoxical condition of being "before," which we have accepted in order to speak, remains in effect/affect until death.

The issue here for the feminist and lesbian reader/writer is to consider what it means to be "there" (even if "there" is "nowhere"), like it or not, standing before the law as that which regulates "the acquisition of an interpretive fiction" we call knowledge (Causse, "L'Interloquée" 79). Our task is to discover ways to challenge and to subvert the law before death, to risk inciting it through unthinkable forms of resistance. What, after all, do I have to lose by breaking the law? There is a special sense in which Derrida's comments concerning the law's refusal to be represented pertain to women; that is, we have a particular investment in its application. He writes, "The law has often been considered as that which puts things in place, posits itself and gathers itself up in composition (thesis, *Gesetz,* in other words what governs the order of representation), and autonomy in this respect always presupposes representation, as thematization, becoming-theme" ("Sending" 325–26). Does woman, as she author-izes her "own" discourse, represent herself as "herself," or is she merely an effect of the law at work? What law operates at the borderline of life and text in her work of "self"-composition? Can she, in Causse's words, set up some woman-ordered regulative technology (gynolect) and/or take over his language ("androlect," an idiolect masquerading as the only "sexolect") and, with it, his "place" ("L'Interloquée" 80–82)?

Causse responds to these questions by proposing a shocking, scandalous shift in the sex/gender system (sexualization, she points out elsewhere, "plays like segregation" ["Le Monde" 14]) which involves the rewriting of man (presumably defined, like woman, by "conceptual capacities" rather than "biological properties" [L'Interloquée" 88]) as sole occupant of the subject position and his relegation to the place of "second" person (the [no]"place" of the second sex?)—"hey, *you* (over) there." As Causse puts it, the "adress(h)er" "creates the scandal of a male 'we' shifted onto the site of the 'you' " ("L'Interloquée" 86–87). Her strategy achieves the startling effect of the deconstructive reversal where relations of power are exchanged, and she moves us toward the ultimately desired displacement which might trans-form the structure of relations. The reversal can only be satisfying for the lesbian whose *personal* stake/investment rests in the domination of men, and not particularly in the liberation of "women" and "men." This poses problems of definition—who is that man and this woman/lesbian?—and of solidarity with "brothers," who, like homosexual and third world men, may have more (and less) ambiguous relations to phallic authority and masculine privilege.

What if I want to address, as I do now, a beautiful woman, to you about us, you and me? When, in my letter, I write "I love you," what am I writing? Who am "I" then, and who are "you"? (Isn't this always our problem?)

Both Causse and Wittig locate the preliminary work of a revolution in lesbian : writing in the subject of writing, as writing: *Je* (Causse "Le Monde," 15). It is as though, through a properly improper writing, the contract with the father's law, which constitutes the female (subject) as object, can be shattered. The letters composing the subject are broken apart: j/e. Wittig describes the radical violence of lesbian : writing when she says, in her prefatory note to *The Lesbian Body*, " 'I' *[Je]* as a generic feminine subject can *only* enter by force into a language which is foreign to it, for all that is human (masculine) is foreign to it, the human not being feminine grammatically speaking but he *[il]* or they *[ils]*. . . . 'I' *[Je]* obliterates the fact that *elle* or *elles* are submerged in *il* or *ils,* i.e., that all the feminine persons are complementary to the masculine persons" (*Lesbian Body* 10). This is the condition of woman writing who "cannot be '*un* écrivain' " (10). We do not dare forget that, as Irigaray puts it in *Speculum of the Other Woman,* "any theory of the 'subject' has always been appropriated by the 'masculine' " (133). Thus Wittig inscribes her alienation and resistance in the body of the word: "*J/e* is the symbol of the lived, rending experience which is m/y writing, of this cutting in two which throughout literature is the exercise of a language which does not constitute m/e as subject. *J/e* poses the ideological and historic question of feminine subjects" (*Lesbian Body* 10–11). A mutilation of the word that slashes the subject's presumptive unicity, J/e, like the mark of the hysterical symptom, stands (in) as the inscription of violence on the body of the (female) subject. Lesbian : writing, in this sense, turns on the Father as phallus, the big prick who regulates the construction of woman. It turns him into the figure that he is—a linguistic site in which substitutions can occur, a rhetorical trope which is subject to revision and re-motivation in a re-writing where woman attempts "the conquest of an *I [Je]*" (Causse, "Le Monde" 15).

Unlike the symptom, the body's inscription of its unconscious conflict with the world, this broken sign, j/e, marks a certain willful triumph. It signals a response to the problem of acquiring lesbianism as my sign, how to take it on as part of me: I-lesbian, the sign that stands for me when I say "I." Language, the letter, stands in for me when I am away, not there. I can only enter language as a subject by speaking myself. I construct myself, make myself a lesbian subject, by giving myself a sign, which also means a signification and a value, and by addressing myself to a woman I want to (be) like me. The subject is the "first" person, not the second (the problem we always have as we love each other), and certainly not the third, the object or "thing" spoken of. This j/e that I take on says, "look at me, look what you have made of me, look at what I must now do to (re)present myself."

THE LAW OF THE LETTER

To write lesbianism is to enter a rhetorical, that is a metaphorical, field —a scene of "transposition . . . [involving] the *figure as such*" and a scene of *"resemblance"* (Ricoeur 17). In other words, when I write (of) the lesbian, I engage the problem of speaking metaphorically about metaphor, or representationally of representation. Through resemblances, I write "in other words" of the "woman" and her "lesbian"/shadow, or the "lesbian" and her "woman"/shadow, of "me" and "you." Metaphor speaks a language of deviation, the quality of something attributed to something else (its transposition), as well as meaning both anchored (materialized in the figure) and adrift (transferring from figure to figure) from some always unknown origin. Ricoeur explains that metaphor as a "categorical transgression" can be "understood as a deviation in relation to a pre-existing logical order, as a dis-ordering in a scheme of classification. This transgression is interesting only because it creates meaning . . . should we not say that metaphor destroys an order only to invent a new one; and that the category-mistake is nothing but the complement of a logic of discovery?" (Ricoeur 22). In addition, the order destroyed or supplanted by metaphor is itself an/other metaphorical representation. Lesbian : writing creates a curious case where the metaphoric language of deviation (of substitution, drift, and transposition) is put in the service of writing what culture has historically regarded as deviation (as aberration and perversion). Claudie Lesselier puts this in slightly different terms when she describes the tension inhabiting the lesbian subject as both included in and standing against the social discourse which produces it, the effect of the letter of the law in tension with the law of the letter. The lesbian subject exhibits a "tension between, on the one hand, *claiming a category* (by giving it another meaning) and, on the other hand, *subverting the whole system of categorization*" (93). Creation/ destruction. It is precisely this project of subversion as aberration and as trans-position which preoccupies lesbian : writing.

Lesbian theorizing is always at once theoretical and "pre"-theoretical: the writer behaves as though she knows what the lesbian is, what theorizing lesbianism entails, despite what Mary Daly and Jane Caputi term its "wildness," what is "not accounted for by any known theories" (100). The "pre"-theoretical of lesbian theorizing is and is not a "pre"- on its way to becoming something in itself, is and is not a stage of anticipation before the letter—a "pre"-, waiting to be "post"-. The lesbian writer presents her subject as (the) One in the absence of others. Her lesbian, the lesbian in her, is made "present" in language, standing as representative for and representation of the one(s) not here. Her words contend with the polysemy and polyvocality of an unlimited field, striking (down) limits with every word she writes in a signifying system which prefers dimorphic binarism to polymorphic abundance, feigning presence when every word stands in for some one or some thing else/where. *L.* It cannot be denied that there is something of *capital* importance here, a capital investment in/of the letter

—a remainder, a sentence, a matter of principal importance, counting on a return.

When I write "I love you," I act as though I know who I am and what it means to love. And who you are, and that you will understand what it means to me to tell you. I have to write as though we are together in this.

If language/text, in its metaphorical activity, always comes back to itself, defers and refers to itself in uncanny ways, what keeps woman within the system of its control when its ability to control is failed, incomplete, deficient? As such, one law of language—definition/signification (the need for woman as the "other" of the symbolic system) is at odds with another—language's inability to control and to determine itself perfectly or completely: (the lesbian slips in). She will always escape, slide in and/or out through the bar(s), and, like it or not, so will some of her fugitive and rebellious sisters and brothers. In her description of the slippery imperfection of language, Brossard suggests how this might occur: "It doesn't take much for *god* to become *dog,* and it takes nothing, in French, for 'she is named' [Elle est comme on nomme] to be heard as 'she is like a man' [Elle est comme un homme]. The magic of words is also this way with which, and this 'what' with which we can transform reality or the sense we give it" (*Aerial* 107). In the gaps, the "holes," or the "spaces," by a willful (though erratic/erotic) trajectory, comes desire, excess. Woman comes. I could say, then, that our tasks involve learning to be an "escape artist," and making an art, by perfecting our techniques, of such a criminal behavior. The love letter is a secret letter, making its way out.

The need for these trans-formative arts grows apparent as we begin to write. Almost with the first word, we encounter the Rule of contemporary theorizing: it is forbidden "to essentialize" woman or lesbian, to claim an essence, a nature, or some particular properties for woman as woman-in-herself. On balance (what the rule is about), this is not a bad proscription since such a speaking of woman-as-woman and lesbian-as-lesbian has produced the problem we struggle against now. In a sense, we are always, after our detours, returning to it, can't help but return to this place even when we think we are discussing the way in which the social text writes woman-as-woman. There is a sense in which phallocentrism, heterosexism, feminism, and lesbianism (homosexuality as well) are, paradoxically, effects of the Law of the Same. As Derrida suggests to Christie McDonald, "phallocentrism and homosexuality can go, so to speak, hand in hand, and I take these terms, whether it is a question of feminine or masculine homosexuality, in a very broad and radical sense" (72). Surely, we want to say, this odd coupling, phallocentrism and lesbianism, shows the phallocratic philosopher for what he is. But this is the very trap Wittig and others seek to escape by positioning the word "lesbian" outside of the sex-gender con/figuration, outside the opposition man/woman and heterosexual/homosexual, the terms of which present themselves to us, have their differences founded, in just these essential ways (Wittig, "Mark" 7–11; "Paradigm" 118–21).

Nonetheless, we must admit that there is a certain terror in the notion of sexuality set out by Derrida, and in another way, Wittig and Deleuze/Guattari: Gone "the woman." Unlike Derrida, Wittig has an investment in wanting to claim something special for the lesbian as not-"woman," not-"man." But what can lesbianism be without "woman" as sex or gender? Man/woman: lesbian. Wittig wants to make "lesbian" a third "place"—the site of a gap, a space or a rupture in the oppositional rule-driven system of signification. Wittig maintains, "The designation 'woman' will disappear no doubt just as the designation 'man' with the oppression/exploitation of women as a class by men as a class. Humankind must find another name for itself and another system of grammar that will do away with genders, the linguistic indicator of political oppression" ("Paradigm" 121). A threat declares itself in multiple, polymorphous sexuality, where there is difference but not the two: man/woman. Derrida offers us an/other representation: "a chorus, for a choreographic text with polysexual signatures" which "goes beyond known or coded marks, beyond the grammar and spelling, shall we say (metaphorically) of sexuality." Finally, he arrives at the most provocative question: "what if we were to approach here (for one does not arrive at this as one would at a determined location) the area of a relationship to the other where the code of sexual marks would no longer be discriminating? The relationship would not be a-sexual, far from it, but would be sexual otherwise: beyond the binary difference that governs the decorum of all codes, beyond the opposition feminine/masculine, beyond bisexuality as well, beyond homosexuality and heterosexuality which come to the same thing" ("Choreographies" 76).

What is this "sexual otherwise," the "beyond" of sexuality, "beyond" lesbianism, as we name them today? The elaboration Derrida offers elsewhere is richly suggestive: "At that point there would be no more sexes . . . there would be one sex for each time. One sex for each gift. A sexual difference for each gift. That can be produced within the situation of a man and a woman, a man and a man, a woman and a woman, three men and a woman, etc. By definition, one cannot calculate the gift. We are in the order of the incalculable, of undecidability which is a strategic undecidability where one says 'it is undecidable because it is not this term of the opposition or the other.' This is sexual difference. It is absolutely heterogeneous" (Derrida, "Women" 199). Similarly, Wittig notes that "For us there are, it seems, not one or two sexes but many (cf. Deleuze/Guattari), as many sexes as there are individuals" ("Paradigm" 119). This is the step away from "the true sex" constructed in the interest of guaranteeing heterosexuality/reproduction. The play of sexes recalls Christiane Rochefort's discovery through writing that she also had homosexual fantasies: "I didn't have them 'consciously,' but it was something in me nonetheless. . . . But something that, all things considered, I would have liked. Had I been a man I would have been homosexual too. Both. Another triumph. Be all four sexes. All four. Yes" (112–13). She counts to four, the easy multiplication of male/female, homosexual/heterosexual. Another reckoning, one of a "lesbian" abundance, might yield up more. Where, then, in this wide field of play, this wildness of heterogeneous sexual difference and of theorizing, is the "woman," the "lesbian" and "lesbianism"? What does it mean to insist, as Brossard repeatedly does, "To write *I am a woman* is full of consequence" ["Ecrire *je suis une femme* est plein de conséquences"] (*L'Amer* 53)? What's in the name?[1]

Because we do not know, or in order to know, we answer anyway. We write, just as I am writing my love letters to you, in the belief that we can say something theoretical or philosophical (or personal and intimate) about "lesbianism," *as if* "experience" and "self-definition," in opposition to philosophical argument, were distinct from metaphoric turns. We might even say that writing compels us to behave this way. Or at least we write out of a belief in the value of seeking an answer. We write (or want to, can't help but write) as though lesbianism were an already there of/in the real, a direct ontology, because "language," as Monique Wittig points out, "casts sheaves of reality upon the social body, stamping it and violently shaping it" ("Mark," 4). What is it, after all, to be a (lesbian) without the word, without writing l-e-s-b-i-a-n or something like it? It seems like nothing. So I write, and in doing so, I enter metaphor, or metaphor enters me. I take up my grammatical place: the lesbian subject. Though it seems to provide a ready-made structure, metaphor allows the writer to defy the tidy organization of container and contained. In this regard, Cixous explains how figures dislocate language: "metaphor breaks free; all that belongs to the realm of fantasmatic production *(la production fantasmatique)*, all that belongs to the imaginary and smashes language from all sides represents a force that cannot be controlled. Metaphors are what drive language mad" (71). Like description, figuration works on the principle of likeness, resemblances of one thing to another ("the lesbian is . . ."; "lesbianism is . . ."). Slippages enter even as this writing wants to answer what it is we want and even need to know. "L." Additionally, or further, in the resemblance of one thing to another, there is always an absence. Absence is "further" (beyond); absence is "added" to what the figure stands for. There is resemblance but not identity—likeness to the thing but never the thing or the thing-in-itself ("The mimeme is neither the thing itself nor something totally other," Derrida, *Margins* 240 fn 43). So that at the heart of the very description which is supposed to give us lesbian presence, lesbian identity, this absence lingers. You and I, as lesbian women, are not there in the sentence. We speak as though we can re-invent language to write a new identity, to make us present (Daly and Caputi).

It may be more appropriate to say that lesbian : writing wants to evacuate patriarchal discourse in order to re-write writing. The vacancy, the absence on/in which I dwell, (re)presents the space for writing which writers like Brossard want to create, the break in the semiotic surface the lesbian/ woman slips through: "Unconsciously, and for all time, the knowing body opposes itself to the learned letter. But everybody knows, what counts is the letter. I write in self-defense. If I can find the lost stream, writing interests me" (*Aerial* 39–40). The lesbian writer seeks to intervene in language, reinvent, or better, re-work its texture, to produce an exploratory language through which we can find ourselves as subject and (of) desire.

DEAR "L,"

I miss you. I've been working very hard on the first chapter of my book. There's always a rush at the start of a new project, like the point where a runner glides into overdrive (I've been watching the Olympics too). It's reassuring to know that I'm not finished. But this project is the best one yet because, when I write about lesbianism, it is easy to imagine that I am writing to you. We are together on the page. Sometimes I hear you saying the words just ahead of me, as if you were writing me writing.

And that word, "lesbian." Can you tell me whose word it is? When, and under what circumstances, did you first hear it? Or did you initially read it on a page somewhere, since it more often goes unspoken? Does it come from "within" or from "without"? It is a double word (play): the turn of the tongue on the letter tells me what it means, whether one way or the other. "Lesbian" is applied to me in a system I do not control, that cannot control itself. Yet it is a word I want to embrace, re-write and re-claim, not to install it but to explode its meaning in the shuttle motion from the pejorative (mis)understandings of the "outside" of lesbianism to what I want to create as an energetic, affectionate designation of the "inside" lesbianism. How we speak of it to one another. Through the dynamic interaction I present the site of the word, a "beyond" lesbianism that is neither the fixed place of the damned nor the (ec)static transcendental position of the saved —those polarities Stimpson calls "the dying fall, a narrative of damnation" and the "enabling escape, a narrative of reversal" (364). Language is not "outside" me, except in the way that skin is "outside" the body. No skin, no body. The body is already in(side) language. Lesbian is the word/name a given woman chooses for her idea of herself, to represent her idea (representation) of herself. I am/you are/she is that place where wor(l)ds of meaning collide.

It is hard for me to believe that the question of "lesbian being" should be exempt from the Derridean critique of being in general (*Grammatology* ch. 1)—something we presume and assume, attributing to it some essential or transcendental status, in order to speak about it. So it is both before and after the letter, before and after what I write about it. How else could I ever say "I love you"? "Lesbian being" is something which is "there," when "there" shifts and ex-changes itself to suit the speaker, who also ex-changes herself (making more of us.) The critiques of identity and presence suggest that we "leave open the question of this energetic absence" (Derrida, *Margins* 240), the means by which I am always describing lesbianism. Thus, I am always writing, describing "the lesbian" as an il-licit (unreadable, *illisible,* or unwritable) woman, whose meaning I am constantly called upon to (re)produce:

she has no character meaning
indissoluble boundaries
   s/he:
s plural in excess of he

(Marlatt, Brossard)

What can be said about this difference in the letter: the *s/* of *s/he?* What difference does (the) difference make? The supplement of excess. Why is it an extra, a difference, in the first place? The extra, extrinsic quality is precisely the problem: the problem of "firstness," of the first place.

I would like to think that lesbianism, like feminism, could position itself "outside." There's a comfort in the tidiness offered by the absence of complicity and the certainty of an absolute difference. But lesbianism, as an attack on hetero-relations, takes (its) place within the structure of the institution of heterosexuality. The lesbian is born of/in it. We know the condition(ing) is not fatal, just as we mark its torturous limits. It might even afford a strategic value to be "there," if Derrida is right that attacks occur from within, because attacks "are not possible and effective, nor can they take accurate aim, except by inhabiting those structures. Inhabiting them *in a certain way,* because one always inhabits, and all the more when one does not suspect it." But, as Derrida continues, danger lurks in this structural relation: "Operating necessarily from the inside, borrowing all the strategic and economic resources of subversion from the old structure, borrowing them structurally . . . the enterprise of deconstruction always in a certain way falls prey to its own work" (*Grammatology* 24). The illusionary and visionary project (it must be both of these) of lesbianism is to be writing the "beyond" of heterosexual phallologocentrism, even though this is also what is always recuperating us, claiming to (re)produce us as one of its effects. I am in writing and writing is in me. I am no different from what I say about it, no better, no worse. When I speak of its structures, I speak of myself, even in resistance. Language over/takes me, and I am over/come. I say again and again "I love you."

Some kind of terror disguises itself when an excess is pronounced, like the terror of Derrida's speculation on sex, his "no" to lesbianism and feminism. Because it goes "beyond" us, we do not know what "it" is in this unsettling economy of excess. The step beyond. Step, no step, two step; Derrida's *pas de thèse* (*Postcard* 293) leaves me without a position, a place that I can count on, or on the basis of which I can calculate the gains. A specter presents itself in the fear of speculation. Yes, this shadow asks for identification, differentiation. Is it me? Or not me, but you? Is it there at all, an effect of speculation's own fear? What path can lead us to the "yes" of "the lesbian" beyond the male-female opposition of hetero-relational feminism (Raymond 4), "the lesbian" beyond the Derridean refusal of lesbianism as homosexuality's opposition to heterosexuality (terms he also refuses)?

When you look at me, what do you see? I try to read the signs of it in your eyes. On the street, I see only the women; and more, when I look at a particular woman, I see only the lesbian(s) in her, the woman to whom I want to address my letter, the pleasure we could have together. When I look at you, I never want to see myself without you. I want to see the woman/lesbian you are and what you see in me. None of this is easy. It requires an effort of mind for which there are no certain signs.

In lesbianism we exchange our bodies and their properties in an economy where woman places woman (herself) in circulation. Lesbianism installs an un-utterable difference of difference—"I"/"me" and "my lover," "she"/"me"—in the woman, as a double woman, a double subject: "she" and "she." It provides for the breaking open of the phallocratically constructed "woman," passed from hand to hand, always a "woman" who knows herself only as a "man's woman" in a series of "hetero"sexual contracts. The lesbian goes and comes, a departure and a return. Hers is a profitable absence, produces "more" writing, the undecidability of which permits, indeed, requires us to produce other writings, other likenesses, diversity, change. My not-knowing produces this speculation, and in the interest of future speculation, something in me does not want to know. In/completion motivates our compulsion, our obsession, and, better still, our passion for the return, the repetition as reappearance of the lesbian-in-writing, who, in coming *again,* comes a second and a third time as though recalling that illusory, shadowy first time, and, of course, the first (mythically originary) Lesbian—the narrative of her appearance before. In telling this story, I come again and again. How will you know if I am a c(o)unterfeit or the "real" thing, if "it" is really happening, if this letter is authentic or a forgery? Whether or not it is really you and I and love that I mean when I write "I love you"?

"Lesbian" is a word written in invisible ink, readable when held up to a flame and self-consuming, a disappearing trick before my eyes where the letters appear and fade into the paper on which they are written, like a field which inscribes them. An unwriting goes on as quickly as the inscription takes (its) place. Not the erasure of time's vast conspiratorial silence, that invisibility censoriously imposed on us, but an un-writing as carefully prepared and enacted as the act of lesbian : composition itself. Lesbian. This word which, like us, threatens to disappear is one we must demand, say over and over again, re-calling it. Lesbian, les-bian, -bian, *bien,* "L," *lesbienne:* a word that won't stay put. Rich explains the stakes we understand so well: "The word *lesbian* must be affirmed because to discard it is to collaborate with silence and lying about our very existence; with the closet-game, the creation of the *unspeakable" (On Lies* 202). In the interest of staging a resistance, I want to re-write writing, write (it) over again, returning, coming again.

I want this word to be a place where my story is not known to myself, to anyone; where the story of the other remains also a mystery, always being solved or written—made and unmade every day like Penelope's handwork. A place between the ecstasy of desire and passion, and of arrest, silence, not knowing. A space where both occur. The danger of love always inhabits the other. The bar, lesbian life, the bedroom where passion is found and made, but also dangerous places of discovery, exchange, and loss. "There is," Brossard writes," consistency in wanting all orgasmic bliss clandestine even though it might happen openly" (*These* 76). The passion is not in the repetition of a pattern, a way, but in a going (off), in anticipation and confrontation with the danger and/in the prospect. The pattern wants to enforce itself, imprint itself beyond interrogation, beyond the energizing forces of not knowing, discovering, and creating. Against arrest which is more (*arrêt*) than it seems. I am still amazed by the way the smallest stroke can occasion an extraordinary moment of surprise.

Some encounters mark a turning point. Picking up the book, a love gift, I turn away from solitary speculation into the course of words, articulations of pleasure that ask for a response. The pleasure in/of writing as engagement stands in for other pleasures—a kiss or an embrace; perhaps just a touch. Not the thing itself, which a photo might pretend to show, but the feeling or fusion of passion in a few simple strokes which might always only, even by choice or circumstance, remain in the regard—the glance, the slight correction or connection of the eyes with a letter on the page. So when her lover is no longer or not ever there, the writer returns to writing, the engagement I can produce when the lover and my love for her are nothing other than a memory but are at least no less than a memory.

I approach the white body of the page—stroke its surface as I would your skin—inscribing on it the literal signs of my affection, sometimes with an animated passion, sometimes with a thoughtfully gentle contemplation.[2] Surface to surface which, like all inscriptions, connect beyond to some deeper, more powerful significances. Something happens as well in the mind where love is an inventive gesture.

After writing, after reading, we no longer make love the same way. The words are no longer ours, as we (re)write how "Chloe loved Olivia" but not for the first time in English letters; certainly not only in English, and perhaps beyond the letter. We cannot make love alone. The other lesbian, the writer-lover, produces our amazement at how words, joy and play, passion come together; the body, memory, the language of the writer compels us in a synergystic field of circulating energies, but without the closure such a systemic metaphor suggests. Instead, there is incompletion where energy jumps the synapses, from the word of one to the word of another, experiences translated, language transmuting in an engagement with the word as hot as when the writer and her electric lover-reader meet, as though when the hands touch, or when the finger turns the page, passion sparks. Trans-literation.

No, we are far from alone. There are three or four, maybe five of us, the other('s) words encircling kaleidoscopically—"conch-shell" and "coral," "the seacarved pip" (Causse, *Lesbiana* 25–26,), "the little pearl" (Brossard, *Sous la langue*), the "little scallop" in its moist, warm bed. Others participate as I consider "that small rose-coloured anemone dredged from the depths of the sea opening out under my exploring fingers. A moon-like spectre emerged from that innocent sea-flower and made my heart throb" (Maraini 35). Leaf after leaf, an explosive f(r)iction as one lover then the next or several, five works together, go off—an explosion in the seme (seem). At this moment, it is easier to think of the body than the letter, its pulsations—regular and then not so regular. It is more difficult to say what this f(r)iction means to the delicate anemone, the seaflower whose tendrils g(r)asp and a-spire toward orgasm, the f(r)iction of the pen, of the letter in a revolutionary play becoming lesbian : writing in a spark(l)ing, glistening chain. One word always in the company of another and another. Did we find these words or did they find us? Did the "real" scene write the text or did the text compose the scene? The words of love multiply, acquire color and form, powerful descriptions, yes even determinants, of what we are doing in our lesbian silence. This is what I mean when I say that the lesbian-writer (re)writes us as "ourselves." Words are never alone. But for me, reading and writing are not enough. Without you, or at least my narrative memory of you, with just me and these words, mine and/or yours, hers, theirs, the ecstasy of/ with the letter eventually fades.

Love,
"L"

P.S. Sorry about my wandering, unruly letter. Try to wait up for me. I'll return by evening on Friday; perhaps I'll even come before my letter.

NOTES

1. The question of the similarities and differences between Derrida, Wittig, Brossard, and Deleuze/Guattari with respect to polysexuality, "woman," and "lesbian" affords such a complex field of convergence and divergence that it deserves an extended essay devoted to its exploration.
2. See Annie Leclerc's "La Lettre d'amour," in Cixous, Gagnon, and Leclerc, *La Venue à l'écriture*, 117–52.

WORKS CITED

Brossard, Nicole. *The Aerial Letter*. Trans. Marlene Wildeman. Toronto: Women's Press, 1988.
———. *L'Amer ou le chapître effrité: théorie fiction*. Montreal: L'Hexagone, 1977.
———. *Lovhers*. Trans. Barbara Godard. Montreal: Guernica, 1986.
———. *Sous la langue/Under Tongue*. Montreal: Gynergy, 1987.
———. *These Our Mothers: Or: The Disintegrating Chapter*. Trans. Barbara Godard. Quebec: Coach House Quebec Translations, 1983.
Causse, Michèle. "L'Interloquée." *Trivia* 13 (1988):79–90.
———. "Le Monde comme volonté et comme représentation." *Vlasta* 1 (1983): 10–25.
———. *Lesbiana: Seven Portraits*. Paris: Le Nouveau Commerce, 1980.
Cixous, Hélène. "Rethinking Differences: An Interview." Trans. Isabelle de Courtivron. In *Homosexualities and French Literature: Cultural Contexts/Critical Texts*. Ed. George Stambolian and Elaine Marks. Ithaca: Cornell Univ. Press, 1979. 70–86.
Cixous, Hélène, Madeleine Gagnon, and Annie Leclerc. *La Venue à l'écriture*. Paris: Union Générale d'Editions, 1977.
Daly, Mary, and Jane Caputi. *Websters' First New Intergalactic Wickedary of the English Language*. Boston: Beacon, 1987.
Deleuze, Gilles, and Felix Guattari. *Anti-Oedipus: Capitalism and Schizophrenia*. Trans. Robert Hurley et al. New York: Viking, 1972.

Derrida, Jacques. *Dissemination*. Trans. Barbara Johnson. Chicago: Univ. of Chicago Press, 1981.

———. *Margins of Philosophy*. Trans. Alan Bass. Chicago: Univ. of Chicago Press, 1982.

———. *Of Grammatology*. Trans. Gayatri Chakovorty Spivak. Baltimore: The Johns Hopkins Univ. Press, 1976.

———. *The Postcard: From Socrates to Freud and Beyond*. Trans. Alan Bass. Chicago: Univ. of Chicago Press, 1987.

———. "Sending: On Representation." *Social Research* 49 (1982): 294–326.

———. "Women in the Beehive: A Seminar with Jacques Derrida." In *Men in Feminism*. Ed. Alice Jardine and Paul Smith. New York: Methuen, 1987. 189–203.

Derrida, Jacques, and Christie V. McDonald. "Choreographies." *Diacritics* 12 (1982): 66–76.

Irigaray, Luce. *Speculum of the Other Women*. Trans. Gillian C. Gill. Ithaca: Cornell Univ. Press, 1985.

———. *This Sex Which Is Not One*. Trans. Catherine Porter. Ithaca: Cornell Univ. Press, 1985.

Lacan, Jacques. *Ecrits: A Selection*. Trans. Alan Sheridan. New York: Norton, 1977.

Lesselier, Claudie. "Social Categorizations and Construction of a Lesbian Subject." Trans. Mary Jo Lakeland. *Feminist Issues* 7, no. 1 (1987): 89–94.

Maraini, Dacia. *Letters to Marina*. Trans. Dick Kitto and Elspeth Spottiswood. Freedom, Calif.: Crossing Press, 1987.

Marlatt, Daphne, and Nicole Brossard. *Characters/Jeu de Lettres*. Montreal: abj writing, 1986.

Raymond, Janice G. *A Passion for Friends: Toward a Philosophy of Female Affection*. Boston: Beacon, 1986.

Rich, Adrienne. *On Lies, Secrets and Silence: Selected Prose 1966–1978*. New York: Norton, 1979.

Ricoeur, Paul. *The Rule of Metaphor: Multi-disciplinary Studies of the Creation of Meaning in Language*. Trans. Robert Czerny. Toronto: Univ. of Toronto Press, 1977.

Rochefort, Christiane. "The Privilege of Consciousness: An Interview by Cecile Arsene." Trans. Marilyn Schuster. In *Homosexualities and French Literature: Cultural Contexts/Critical Texts*. Ed. George Stambolian and Elaine Marks. Ithaca: Cornell Univ. Press, 1979. 101–13.

Stein, Gertrude. *How to Write*. West Glover, Vt.: Something Else Press, 1973.

Stimpson, Catharine R. "Zero Degree Deviancy: The Lesbian Novel in English." *Critical Inquiry* 8 (1981): 363–79.

Wittig, Monique. *The Lesbian Body*. Trans. David Le Vay. New York: Morrow, 1975.

———. "The Mark of Gender." *Feminist Issues* 5, no. 2 (1985) 3–12.

———. "Paradigm." Trans. George Stambolian. In *Homosexualities and French Literature: Cultural Contexts/Critical Texts*. Ed. George Stambolian and Elaine Marks. Ithaca: Cornell Univ. Press, 1979. 114–21.

PART II

Lesbian Encodings, Decodings

Heterosexual Plots and Lesbian Subtexts: Toward a Theory of Lesbian Narrative Space

Marilyn R. Farwell

Nearly two-thirds of the way into Marion Zimmer Bradley's *The Mists of Avalon,* the central character, Morgaine of the Fairies, now an old woman, returns to her home in Avalon after years of exile. She brings with her a younger self, Lancelot and Elaine's child, Nimue, to become a priestess of the goddess, and she encounters a former self in Raven, the woman sworn to serve the goddess with her silence. In the dark of the night, Raven enters Morgaine's sleeping quarters and awakens her. With ritualistic fervor, Raven removes her own cloak, takes Morgaine in her arms and touches "her slowly, with ritual silence and significance" (639). Raven quietly gives Morgaine the silver crescent, the ritual ornament of the priestess, and Viviane's ritual knife, items that Morgaine left behind when she fled in anger from Avalon and her Aunt Viviane's control. Then, in an act of bonding, each pierces herself: "from the breastbone she [Raven] pricked a single drop of blood, and Morgaine, bowing her head, took the knife and made a slight cut over her heart" (639). In an already sexually charged scene, the tension becomes stronger in their next exchange: "Raven bent to her and licked the blood away from the small cut; Morgaine bent and touched her lips to the small, welling stain at Raven's breast, knowing that this was a sealing long past the vows she had taken when she came to womanhood. Then Raven drew her again into her arms" (639–40). In the italicized words in this passage, which indicate her thoughts as they often do throughout the book, Morgaine recounts her heterosexual passions, Lancelot and Accolon, *"Yet Never,"* she says of this reunion with Raven, *"have I known what it was to be received simply in love"* (639–40).

While this short scene, two pages in a book of 876 pages, does not contain the romantic tension that Bradley lavishes on the great heterosexual affairs of the text—Igraine and Uther Pendragon, Morgaine and Lancelot, Morgaine and Accolon—it is an unmistakably charged lesbian scene. Only three other hints of lesbianism are apparent in this text, each one centering on Morgaine and each a short interlude in Morgaine's heterosexual life. Yet because this scene represents Morgaine's return to her home, to her mother, the goddess, and, of course, a return to herself and the old powers of priestess which she forswore earlier in the novel, it is a pivotal scene. From this powerful experience she also gains the strength and courage to attempt the difficult mission which occupies the rest of her journey. But how in a basically heterosexual text are we to read this short but erotic and undeniably lesbian section? We could read it as an innocent but intense religious ritual devoid of real sexuality or as a curiosity in a long book that might need curiosities to sustain itself. We could also excuse the lesbian proclivities, as often happens in life and in literary criticism, with the insistence that one encounter does not make either character a "real" lesbian, in effect denying or ignoring what happened. The problems with both attempts to minimize the importance of this scene are the facts: it is an intensely erotic scene, and it is a crucial if not *the* crucial scene of the book. What we must ask instead is how the strong lesbian overtones function in the text as a whole, especially in a novel which cannot, without violence, be called lesbian.

I believe that current feminist discussions of narrative theory are relevant in reading the lesbian content of this text. Twentieth-century narrative theory has taught us that heroic stories, of which *Mists* is a feminist version, are replete with codes and patterns repeated endlessly; feminist critical theory has taught us that these codes are decidedly patriarchal. Feminist literary theory has been eager to recognize the possibility of disruptive plots and spaces that position women as subjects of their own stories. In this search, theorists have, at times, acknowledged the importance of women's relationships, erotic and otherwise, and at other times have minimized their importance. In current continental theory, on which many contemporary feminist theorists depend, male thinkers like Derrida and Foucault have sought a new space for the worn-out (male) subjectivity which has structured the Western narrative. They have described that space of "alterity" or otherness as female, but not as lesbian. In her analysis of continental male thinking, Alice Jardine states that:

Not only are the abstract spaces of alterity in contemporary thought gendered female (Freud-Lacan's "unconscious," Derrida's "écriture," Deleuze's "machines," Foucault's "madness"), but so too are the main characters of its theoretical fiction. Evidence for this ranges from the privileging by psychoanalysis of the focus on female hysterics to the emphasis by contemporary philosophy on those bodies which have escaped Western society's definition of "the normal male": the insane, the criminal, the male homosexual. (115)

In some ways it is a relief not to have lesbian included on that list, but many feminist theorists, whatever their theoretical allegiances, have explored the importance of women's bonding, often termed lesbian whatever the sexuality of the women, as a powerful tool for breaking narrative codes.

In her lucid account of new themes that are emerging for biographers of women, Carolyn G. Heilbrun points to the importance of the almost hidden realm of women's friendships, "from passionate bodily love to friendships between women married or living with men" (108). But Heilbrun stops far short of connecting heterosexuality with the old narrative script as other theorists have done. Rachel Blau DuPlessis, for example, has argued that "the erotic and emotional intensity of women's friendship cuts the Gordian knots of both heterosexuality and narrative convention" (149). In a comparable book on women writers' transgression of male heroic stories, Lee R. Edwards attacks the stranglehold that heterosexuality has exercised on heroines because tradition has "derived female identity from an equation linking limited aspiration and circumscribed activity to institutionalized heterosexuality." The female hero must then attempt to nullify "these conjunctions and the conclusions they require" (237). Although she minimizes the potential for women's love to be a disruptive force in the narrative, her original insight coincides with that of DuPlessis: to inscribe female desire in a plot demands a questioning of heterosexuality. Other critics have extended this logic and defined certain metaphoric and structural transgressions of the narrative as lesbian. Barbara Smith opened a new critical category when she suggested that Toni Morrison's *Sula* is a lesbian novel not because Nel and Sula are lesbians—they decidedly are not—but because the novel provides a critique of heterosexual institutions (189). Monique Wittig and Luce Irigaray write of the need to disrupt language and genre by opening new spaces which privilege lesbian as the place of the new alterity. In defining lesbian, they go beyond the sexuality of characters and position lesbian in the revision of the binary structures of male/female, subject/ other, presence/absence of Western narratives. Thus, they provide a basis for my development of the idea of a lesbian narrative space as a disruptive space of sameness as opposed to difference which has structured most Western narratives.[1]

In *Alice Doesn't,* Teresa de Lauretis offers one of the strongest feminist analyses of a narrative structured by gender difference, but, at the same time, she does not imagine the transgression of this narrative structure in a homoerotic space outside of the construction of difference. De Lauretis argues that most of the giants of twentieth-century narrative theory have ignored the gender dimension of narrative structure. The Soviet theorist, Jurij Lotman, is a primary example of someone who identifies different narrative spaces without any consciousness of the gender implications of his divisions. Lotman orders narrative by a simple division, as de Lauretis states:

> Lotman finds a simple chain of two functions, open at both ends and thus endlessly repeatable: "entry into a closed space, and emergence from it." He then adds, "Inasmuch as closed space *can be interpreted* as 'a cave,' 'the grave,' 'a house,' 'woman' (and, correspondingly, be allotted the features of darkness, warmth, dampness), entry into it *is interpreted* on various levels as 'death,' 'conception,' 'return home' and so on; moreover, all these acts *are thought of as mutually identical.*" (118, de Lauretis's emphasis)

In other words, one space is active and mobile, the other passive and inert. De Lauretis adds that these spaces are also coded by gender, for symbolically and psychologically the male is defined by the active principle, the female by the passive. Using Freud's Oedipal paradigm, she interprets the movement of the narrative in terms of sexual desire, and since male desire is the only desire Freud recognized, the active space must be male; the female space must be that which is overcome (the monster) or that which is desired (the princess). The female is either the obstacle or the reward. Moreover, characters do not determine spaces, but spaces the characters, for women can occupy male space and men—although less likely—can occupy female space: "In this mythical-textual mechanics, then, the hero must be male, regardless of the gender of the text-image, because the obstacle, whatever its personification, is morphologically female and indeed, simply, the womb" (118–19). Difference is not only in the gender identities of the characters but in the narrative spaces which they occupy. Rosalind in *As You Like It* is not a feminist in drag when she dons the weeds of a man, but simply an occupant of male space, a situation which reinforces rather than transgresses the master narrative.

Crucial, then, to this heroic narrative is what is crucial to all of the master narratives: the construction of difference according to the dichotomies which structure Western thought, those dualities such as active/

passive, mind/body, presence/absence, which ultimately rely on the gender dualism, male/female. What de Lauretis does not acknowledge nor analyze is the fact that this dualism, this division of narrative space by gender, is also necessarily heterosexual. When Monique Wittig argues that sex differences are based not on nature but on economic, political, and ideological structures, she concludes that these differences construct not only a system of domination but also an "unnatural" system of heterosexuality: "The category of sex is the political category that founds society as heterosexual" ("Category" 66). Thus, the same narrative structure that identifies narrative space in gendered terms, that reinforces gender difference symbolically, also reinforces heterosexuality, for in defining the movement of male desire, the active space, into and through the passive space, morphologically female, we have a narrative reenactment of the heterosexual act. The master plot is not just androcentric or phallocentric, it is also basically heterosexual. The question is how female desire can be encoded in a structure which claims her desire as his desire or more accurately as the end of his desire.

This transgressive act cannot be found, I believe, among some of the popularly accepted "feminist" narratives which rely on the gender identity of certain characters. From de Lauretis's distinction between characters and narrative space we can conclude that a lesbian can occupy heterosexual space and a heterosexual can occupy what I propose to call lesbian narrative space, just as male and female characters can occupy the oppositely gendered narrative space. This distinction allows us to avoid calling a text feminist which in fact reinforces the structurally gendered spaces or naming a text about lesbians transgressive that merely replicates gendered ideas. For example, Sigourney Weaver as Ripley in the movie, *Aliens,* has been hailed as a new feminist hero in the same way that Rosalind in *As You Like It* has often been offered as an example of Shakespeare's feminism. Within the structural view of narrative, neither text can be called disruptive of patriarchal codes. Ripley, the courageous leader and hero of this science fiction movie, is not a female Rambo; she is carefully saved from that fate by the discreet presence of a foil—Vasquez, a woman far too threateningly masculine to be allowed heroic status in a popular film—and by her motherly devotion to the little girl. We cannot, however, ignore some of the tension created by a woman occupying male space. Barbara Creed indicates how conservatism and radicality can exist in the same text, for while the process of birth is depicted in horrid detail, at the same time, the combination of male and female characteristics in Ripley does depict a different kind of hero in "a period of profound social and cultural change" (65). Yet, I believe, conservatism wins out because Ripley does occupy the same narrative space as Rambo. She moves through the female space as obstacle in the form of the planet controlled by the horrible mother who grotesquely gives birth to her eggs. She conquers that space and emerges triumphantly from it; in the process she distances herself from the female by destroying the female insect and by calling her a "bitch." Despite the minor part the romantic interest plays in the movie—if it played a larger part Ripley would automatically be forced into female space—the plot remains heterosexual and patriarchal because the movement of the male space into the female space maintains the old structural codes.

Shakespeare's Rosalind is allowed that brief moment in the Forest of Arden when, by wearing male clothing, she is given male space in the narrative, space to malign women and to control the action. Arden is a magical place which is constructed as female: it is a realm of nature, of the momentary suspension of rigid dichotomies, and of love and intuition. It is also a brief sojourn into homosexual territory, for Rosalind's assumed name, Ganymede, is synonymous in the Renaissance with a male homosexual, and Phoebe's passion for Ganymede/Rosalind is the most direct threat to conventional heterosexuality. But homosexuality is never possible structurally. When difference is threatened by sameness, Shakespeare quickly returns to the comfortable dualism. The momentary gender reversal of Rosalind and Orlando and the seeming suspension of rigid dichotomies are disallowed when the implications include the valorization of sameness, including lesbian passion. Rosalind thus emerges from her sojourn as male moving through female space before any serious reconsideration of the codes can occur and takes her place in the old dichotomies; she returns to marriage, women's weeds, and the "real world."

In this analytical context many lesbian novels cannot be considered radical transgressors of heterosexual codes, for often and with considerable vigor the dualities of the male active and female passive spaces are reconfirmed. Gillian Whitlock's recent essay on Radclyffe Hall's *The Well of Loneliness* has given us a more complex view of this novel; she argues "that the book is a political intervention in which Hall starts the process of producing a 'reverse discourse,' a space for other lesbians to speak for themselves and so move toward self-definition" (560). This space, which includes the deconstruction of many categories of gender and genre, is cut short in the end, for "Stephen finally lacks the courage and the vision to make the break with old orders" (575). But while Stephen does seem to challenge gender dichotomies on one level, the novel depends structurally on the maintenance of gender difference. Stephen is identified with male desire, she moves through female space and almost wins the female as her reward; but her desire, like Rosalind's, cannot ultimately possess male space. The oxymoron, female hero/male desire, must be subverted, for otherwise it would destroy the romance genre of which it is part. Mary is the passive figure with whom we are structurally comfortable and who in the end can become a "real woman" and go with a "real man." As with *Aliens*, the fact that the narrative space contains an oxymoron is potentially deconstructive, but the novel, like the movie, cannot draw out the implications without destroying itself. It cannot validate sameness above difference. Even current popular lesbian novels are structured in a way that reaffirms codes of sexual difference. Anne Cameron's *The Journey* is such an example. Anne and Sarah play out gender roles in their journey through the early West to win a place of their own. Anne hunts, Sarah cooks. Their adventures are replete with the tensions of violence that structure novels built on sexual difference, although unlike the lesbian despair that informs Hall's novel, this one ends triumphantly, making it what Catharine R. Stimpson has called a lesbian novel of "enabling escape" (244). *The Journey* replicates the male adventure story with only slightly different characters occupying the traditional narrative spaces.

The question remains, then, how can the old narrative structure be changed to allow for the existence of female desire? Because female desire within the dichotomous structures of Western thinking is inconceivable—Freud, we will remember, allowed women no desire of their own—I believe that only in the space of sameness can this desire emerge. This space is created when women forge what Adrienne Rich calls a "primary presence" of themselves to one another (*Lies* 250) or exhibit what Rich elsewhere calls a "primary intensity" for one another ("Compulsory" 648), thus defying a world that has defined them only by their relationships to men. Such a concentration of one woman on another disturbs if not destroys Western dualisms. The result is a space defined by fluid instead of rigid boundaries. My use of the word *lesbian* in this context is metaphoric, for while sexuality can be a part of construction of sameness, it is not a necessary part. This metaphoric use is not without its problems, some of which I have addressed in another essay (100–104).[2] But the fact remains that contemporary theorists have often designated that space outside of categories of difference as lesbian, what Elaine Showalter in another context has called the "wild zone" in women's writing and theory (263). Monique Wittig's definition of *lesbian* can serve as the key for this metaphoric definition. *Lesbian,* she has argued, is that space which is "not-woman," which is not dependent on the categorization of difference that resides in the dualisms of man and woman ("One Is Not Born" 150). *Lesbian* is a word that denotes, then, a new positioning of female desire, of the lover and beloved, of the subject and object.

Wittig's *The Lesbian Body* is one of the strongest enactments of this new space and new subjectivity. In this experimental text, the traditional Western dichotomies of lover and beloved become a fluid exchange of subject and object, placing the subjects "outside of the presence/absence and center/margin dichotomies" (Shaktini 39). In the deconstruction of the Western idea of lover and beloved, based on domination and heterosexuality, Wittig refuses characters' identities, linear plots, and simple representation. One of her central devices, a *"j/e,"* enacts the destruction of old language patterns. Wittig describes her own effort: "The *j/e* with a bar in *The Lesbian Body* is not an *I* destroyed. It is an *I* become so powerful that it can attack the order of heterosexuality in texts and assault so-called love, the heroes of love, and lesbianize them, lesbianize the symbols, lesbianize the gods and goddesses, lesbianize men and women" ("Mark" 11). In her lyrical conclusion to *This Sex Which Is Not One,* Luce Irigaray plays with the same fluctuating boundaries between lover and beloved, I and you: "We are luminous. Neither one nor two. I've never known how to count. Up to you. In their calculations, we make two. Really, two? Doesn't that make you laugh? An odd sort of two. And yet not one. Especially not one. Let's leave *one* to them" (207). Her attempts to describe their relationship in a new language mean the destruction of the old lovers' dichotomies and the reinscription of a divisionless economy/text: "You? I? That's still saying too much. Dividing too sharply between us: all" (218). Confusing the boundaries between subject/object and lover/beloved undercuts the heterosexuality which is based on this dualism. The point in the narrative where this deconstruction begins is what I would call lesbian narrative space. It happens most often when two women seek another kind of relationship than that which is prescribed in the patriarchal structures, and when it occurs in the narrative, it can cast a different light on the rest of the novel, even on those portions that seem to affirm heterosexual patterns.

With this definition of a lesbian narrative space we can return to *The*

Mists of Avalon and propose a reading which takes into account the homo-eroticism and the primary presence of women to one another that is portrayed in the central scene between Raven and Morgaine. On the surface, Marion Zimmer Bradley's narrative neatly bifurcates the world between two geographical areas that symbolically and stereotypically represent male and female principles. The male Christian world of Britain is in the process of assuring the sexual dichotomization of a world that had once been ruled by women. As if in punishment for woman's previous ascendancy, the priests and especially a viciously portrayed St. Patrick, insist that women are sinful, weak, unreasonable and, at best, passive helpmates to their husbands. As women have done throughout history, Arthur's wife, Gwenhwyfar, becomes the patriarchal enforcer of Christianity's negative view of women. The women of Camelot dutifully fulfill the roles of giddy onlookers, gossiping while they spin, and ignoring the greater political issues and moral questions of their day. On the other hand, while Avalon is slowly fading into the mists because people no longer believe in its values, it still remains the sanctuary for strong feminist values. It worships the goddess along with the gods, its religious island is peopled by priestesses who guard and develop the powers of the Sight, and ultimate authority is vested in the Lady of the Lake. In one way, Avalon is like the Forest of Arden, full of possibility, intuition, the Sight, and a kind of magic beyond empiricism and beyond what Lancelot calls the place where "the real struggles of life are taking place." (146).

But Avalon also reinforces a sexual division which underscores its basic heterosexuality. Its great religious festival is the marriage of the King Stag to the Goddess to ensure the fertility of the land. "What of the flow of life between their two bodies, male and female, the tides of the Goddess rising and compelling them?" Morgaine seems to ask when the much desired Lancelot retreats from making love to her (324). Morgaine does enact this ceremony twice in her life, once with Arthur, her brother, and once with Accolon, her lover in old age. But because of her upbringing in Avalon, Morgaine firmly believes that a woman's body is her own to give to whom-ever she wishes; she accepts none of the Christian-imposed values of the sinfulness of sex, especially for women outside of marriage. The ritual marriages are ceremonial and unbinding as are the number of affairs that Morgaine has, one with Kevin the Harper and another, under the nose of her husband, Uriens, with Accolon. In one way it could be argued that this female sexual autonomy is a new positioning of female desire, for while in the Christian world dualisms imply hierarchy, in Avalon they do not. But at the same time this heterosexuality points to the importance of difference in structuring Avalon as well as Camelot. The place to look for narrative transgression, I believe, is not in the tension between Avalon and Camelot, or in the idealized feminine world of Avalon, but in the momentary revelation of sameness as the core of Avalon.

Several short passages of homoeroticism ask us to restructure that neat dependence on dualism that orders the rest of the novelistic landscape. Instead of positioning female desire within the dualistic system which fosters our way of thinking, the lesbian scenes position desire outside of that structure and therefore outside of the controlling realm of male desire. While, then, female desire is accorded autonomy in the heterosexual world of Avalon, its true source of autonomy is in the lesbian narrative space constructed by sameness. As a subtext, the lesbian becomes the core of female desire and autonomy. A new story cannot be created by a redefinition of difference, as the world of Avalon attempts to do, but instead must be constituted by the more transgressive sameness.

The relationship of Raven and Morgaine becomes, then, the essence of Avalon, a place of fluctuating boundaries, of no division between self and other, subject and object, a place where sameness thrives. Avalon as a whole depends on the exchange of roles among the women, who are mother, daughter, sister, and goddess to one another and to themselves. These relationships are intensified in Raven and Morgaine's love scene. Early in the text, both Morgaine's and Raven's names are given as other names of the goddess, affirming their interchangeability: " 'She is also the Morrigán, the messenger of strife, the Great Raven' " (136). A fluid exchange of mother-daughter roles seems to attend the central love scene. Bradley describes Morgaine's final feelings in this scene as a meditation on her mother: "It seemed to Morgaine, half in a dream, that she lay in the lap of her mother . . . no, not Igraine, but welcomed back into the arms of the Great Mother . . ." (640). That connection is made in an earlier homoerotic scene when Morgaine, having wandered in the fairy world, describes her sexual encounter with a maiden as a memory: "She remembered that she had lain in the lady's lap and suckled at her breast, and it did not seem strange to her at all that she, a grown woman, should lie in her mother's lap, and be kissed and dandled like an infant" (405). As with Shug and Celie in Alice Walker's *The Color Purple*, the two women become mother and daughter to one another at the same time, with no warped, psychological insights attending the exchange. Of their lovemaking, Celie reports, "Then I feels something real soft and wet on my breast, feel like one of my little lost babies mouth. Way after while, I act like a little lost baby too" (97). In another, much shorter, lesbian scene between Morgaine and Raven, immediately before the great event that will destroy Raven and send Morgaine with the holy relics into hiding, Morgaine becomes the mother, cradling Raven, "like a child" and once again they enact the unity they experienced earlier: "She held Raven against her, touching her, caressing her, their bodies clinging together in something like a frenzy. Neither spoke, but Morgaine felt the world trembling in a strange and sacramental rhythm around them . . . woman to woman, affirming life in the shadow of death" (765).

All of the depictions of women loving women in Avalon are made without negative comment. Only in the Christian world is there any tension or shame about homoerotic desires. In the fairy world, Morgaine, "to her surprise, . . . found the maiden—yes, she looked somewhat like Raven— twining her arms around her neck and kissing her, and she returned the kisses without surprise or shame" (405). It is Lancelot who is tormented by his relationship and attraction to Arthur and whose potential homosexuality is scorned. Mordred recounts a story about Lancelot to the court " 'something of a ballad made when they thrust a harp into his hand and bade him play, and he sang some lay of Rome or the days of Alexander, I know not what, of the love of knightly companions, and they jeered at him for it. Since then, his songs are all of the beauty of our queen, or knightly tales of adventure and dragons' " (713). The only hint of homosexuality in the Christian world that is free from this pain occurs between Raven and Morgaine the night before they enter Camelot for the great Pentecostal feast.

Sameness, then, is in one way not a threat in Avalon; in another way it destroys Avalon's reliance on heterosexuality and on gender difference for meaning. This sameness does not depend on whether or not these characters are lesbian but on the space they create which outlaws difference from its midst. This lesbian space also seems to be the strength and core of Avalon. When Morgaine returns home, she is given the courage to complete her task in the act of love with Raven. And again with the love scene immediately before the great event in Camelot, Raven and Morgaine come together "woman to woman" as in prayer: "priestesses of Avalon together called on the life of the Goddess and in silence she answered them" (766).

Sameness, ironically, undercuts the stark symbolic gender differences which are created in the rest of the text and undercuts the heterosexuality which informs the rest of the narrative. At the center of Avalon is the contradiction which deconstructs its faith in heterosexuality and the novel's symbolic structure. Thus, Morgaine's journey reverses the normal, gender-identified movement of the narrative. Symbolically she moves from the female space of Avalon to and through the male space of Camelot, but the core of that female space—that which gives her power and strength—is sameness, is her connection with another woman. The space of movement in this novel is at its center defined by female desire, the desire of one woman for another, for Morgaine is at home only when she is in the arms of another woman.

I am not arguing that *Mists* is ultimately a more transgressive novel than others mentioned earlier and seemingly dismissed, but rather that in opening a new narrative space the reader can forge a subtext that explores female desire while the main text does not. The subtext gives us the possibility for a transgressive narrative that can be more fully realized in other narratives or that can be part of our readings of other texts that seem to reinforce the bonding between heterosexuality and the narrative. With the recognition of a truly transgressive space, we will no longer have to settle for a few narratives that pass as radical.

NOTES

1. In choosing to use the words *sameness* and *difference* I have been influenced, in part, by Toni A. H. McNaron's paper delivered at the 1988 MLA session, "When Chloe Likes Olivia: Lesbian Literary Theory."
2. Ahistoricism and essentialism are the central problems which have plagued the attempt to define lesbian metaphorically. I believe that some of those problems are eliminated when one speaks of lesbian as a space rather than as an essence.

WORKS CITED

Bradley, Marion Zimmer. *The Mists of Avalon.* New York: Ballantine, 1982.
Cameron, Anne. *The Journey.* San Francisco: Spinsters/Aunt Lute, 1986.
Creed, Barbara. "From Here to Modernity: Feminism and Post Modernism." *Screen* 28, no. 2 (1987): 47–67.
de Lauretis, Teresa. *Alice Doesn't: Feminism, Semiotics, Cinema.* Bloomington: Indiana Univ. Press, 1984.

DuPlessis, Rachel Blau. *Writing beyond the Ending: Narrative Strategies of Twentieth-Century Women Writers*. Bloomington: Indiana Univ. Press, 1985.

Edwards, Lee R. *Psyche as Hero: Female Heroism and Fictional Form*. Middletown, Conn.: Wesleyan Univ. Press, 1984.

Farwell, Marilyn R. "Toward a Definition of Lesbian Literary Imagination." *Signs* 14 (1988): 100–18.

Heilbrun, Carolyn G. *Writing a Woman's Life*. New York: Norton, 1988.

Irigaray, Luce. *This Sex Which Is Not One*. Trans. Catherine Porter. Ithaca: Cornell Univ. Press, 1985.

Jardine, Alice A. *Gynesis: Configurations of Woman and Modernity*. Ithaca: Cornell Univ. Press, 1986.

McNaron, Toni A. H. "Mirrors and Sameness: Lesbian Theory through Imagery." MLA Convention. New Orleans, 29 Dec. 1988.

Rich, Adrienne. "Compulsory Heterosexuality and Lesbian Existence." *Signs* 5 (1980): 631–60.

———. *On Lies, Secrets, and Silence: Selected Prose 1966–1978*. New York: Norton, 1979.

Shaktini, Namascar. "Displacing the Phallic Subject: Wittig's Lesbian Writing." *Signs* 8 (1982): 29–44.

Showalter, Elaine. "Feminist Criticism in the Wilderness." In *The New Feminist Criticism: Essays on Women, Literature, and Theory*. Ed. Elaine Showalter. New York: Pantheon, 1985. 243–70.

Smith, Barbara. "Toward a Black Feminist Criticism." *Women's Studies International Quarterly* 2, no. 2 (1979): 183–94.

Stimpson, Catharine R. "Zero Degree Deviancy: The Lesbian Novel in English." In *Writing and Sexual Difference*. Ed. Elizabeth Abel. Chicago: Univ. of Chicago Press, 1982. 243–59.

Walker, Alice. *The Color Purple*. New York: Harcourt, 1982.

Whitlock, Gillian. " 'Everything is Out of Place': Radclyffe Hall and the Lesbian Literary Tradition." *Feminist Studies* 13 (1987): 555–82.

Wittig, Monique. "The Category of Sex." *Feminist Issues* 2 (1982): 63–68.

———. *The Lesbian Body*. Trans. David Le Vay. New York: Morrow, 1975.

———. "The Mark of Gender." *Feminist Issues* 5, no. 2 (1985): 3–12.

———. "One Is Not Born a Woman." In *Feminist Frameworks: Alternative Theoretical Accounts of Relations between Women and Men*. Ed. Alison M. Jagger and Paula S. Rothenberg. New York: McGraw, 1984. 148–52.

EIGHT

The Pea That Duty Locks: Lesbian and Feminist-Heterosexual Readings of Emily Dickinson's Poetry

Paula Bennett

[The clitoris] is endowed with the most intense erotic sensibility, and is probably the prime seat of that peculiar life power, although not the sole one.
—Charles D. Meigs, *Woman: Her Diseases and Remedies*, 1851

One would have to dig down very deep indeed to discover . . . some clue to woman's sexuality. That extremely ancient civilization would undoubtedly have a different alphabet, a different language. . . . Woman's desire would not be expected to speak the same language as man's.
—Luce Irigaray, *This Sex Which is Not One*, 1985

In a 1985 essay in *Feminist Studies*, Margaret Homans brilliantly analyzes Emily Dickinson's use of vaginal imagery ("lips") as a multivalent figure for female sexual and poetic power (" 'Syllables' " 583–86, 591). Homans quite rightly identifies Dickinson's concept of the volcanic "lips that never lie" in "A still—Volcano—Life" (*The Poems* 461)[1] with the genital/lingual lips from which the hummingbird sucks in "All the letters I can write":

All the letters I can write
Are not fair as this—
Syllables of Velvet—
Sentences of Plush,
Depths of Ruby, undrained,
Hid, Lip, for Thee—
Play it were a Humming Bird—
And just sipped—me—

(#334)

Less happily, Homans treats Dickinson's use of genital imagery entirely within the context of the (male) tradition of the romantic love lyric (that is, as a "subversion" of the "scopic" economy, or visual orientation, of masculinist love poetry). Not only does she fail to discuss the poem's homoerotic or lesbian possibilities, she barely notes them—this despite the fact that the poem's only known variant was originally sent—with a flower—to a woman, Dickinson's cousin, Eudocia (Converse) Flynt, of Monson, Massachusetts. For Homans, text—not sex—is the issue.

As in "A still—Volcano—Life," the imagery in "All the letters I can write" is undoubtedly (if not necessarily, consciously) sexual. The reader-lover-bird is told to sip from the well-hidden "depths" of the poet-vagina-flower: "lip" to lips. But the form of sexual congress which the poet fantasizes in this poem is—as Homans fails to specify—oral; and the sex of the beloved-reader-bird is left deliberately (though, for Dickinson, not atypically), vague. He/she/you is referred to as "it." If this poem overturns the scopic conventions of the male-dominated romantic love lyric, it does so not to critique male "gaze," but to celebrate a kind of sexuality the poet refuses, or is unable, to name.

Because of her ambiguity, which makes variant readings such as the above not only possible but inevitable, Dickinson has become a preeminent example of the splitting of feminist criticism along sexual orientation lines. To those critics who read the poet heterosexually, the central narrative of Dickinson's career is her struggle with the male tradition—whether this tradition is seen as embodied in her lover, father, God, muse, or merely her precursor poets. Critics writing from this perspective (which represents, in effect, a feminist retelling of traditional mainstream narratives of the poet's career) include, in chronological order, Gilbert and Gubar, Margaret Homans, Joanne Feit Diehl, Barbara Antonina Clarke Mossberg, Suzanne Juhasz, Vivian Pollak, Jane Donahue Eberwein, Helen McNeil, Alicia Ostriker, and, most recently, Cynthia Griffin Wolff. Although all of these critics are deeply committed to understanding Dickinson as a woman poet, the framework for their discussion is the poet's relationship to the male tradition. Their concern is with "woman's place in man's world," even when, as in Homans's case, they acknowledge the presence of homoerotic strands in the poet's life and work.

In contrast to these critics are those like Rebecca Patterson, Lillian Faderman, Adalaide Morris, Judy Grahn, Martha Nell Smith, Toni McNaron and myself, who believe that Dickinson's relationships with women are of greater significance than her struggles with men or with the male tradition.

While lesbian critics do not necessarily deny the prominence of certain male figures in Dickinson's life, they have dug beneath the more mythic aspects of the poet's heterosexuality (in particular, her supposed "love affair" with a "Master") to uncover the ways in which Dickinson used her relationships to the female and to individual women such as her sister-in-law Susan Gilbert Dickinson to empower herself as a woman and poet. To these critics, the central struggle in Dickinson's career is not, as Joanne Feit Diehl puts it, "to wrest an independent vision" *from* the male ("Reply" 196),[2] but to find a way to identify and utilize specifically female power in her work.

While both heterosexual and lesbian/feminist readings of Dickinson exemplify what Elaine Showalter calls "gynocritisicm" (128), that is, both focus on the woman as writer, the difference between these two approaches to the poet—one privileging the male, the other the female—results in remarkably different presentations of Dickinson's biography and art. In this essay, I will discuss what happens to our reading of Dickinson's poetry when we give priority to her homoeroticism—and what happens when we do not. In particular, I will focus on the ways in which the privileging of homoeroticism affects our interpretation of Dickinson's erotic poetry as this poetry projects Dickinson's sense of self as a woman and as a woman poet (the two issues raised by Homans's essay).

For "straight" readers of Dickinson's texts, the poet's struggle with the tradition is mediated through her relationship with a man whom history has come to call the "Master," since his biographical identity (if any) has yet to be confirmed. Whoever or whatever this man was to the poet—whether lover, father, God, or muse—Dickinson's relationship to him is, according to this view of her texts, fundamental to her poetic development—the means by which she came to define herself. In response to critiques by Lillian Faderman and Louise Bernikow of her theory of a male muse in Dickinson's poetry, Joanne Feit Diehl articulates the underlying assumptions governing the feminist-heterosexual approach to the Master Phenomenon in Dickinson's work:

Bernikow's and Faderman's remarks offer nothing that would cause me to change my assertion that Dickinson found herself by confronting a male-dominated tradition. My essay acknowledges that she sought inspiration and courage from women poets engaged in similar struggles toward self-definition; however, hundreds of poems attest that her primary confrontations are with the male self. Furthermore, it is Dickinson who enables later women poets to trace a more exclusively female lineage. Refusing to ignore the tradition Bernikow and Faderman would deny her, Dickinson confronts her masculine precursors to wrest an independent vision. No woman poet need ever feel so alone again. ("Reply" 196)

The key word here is "alone." Like a latter-day feminist confronting a totally male-dominated environment (whether home, office, or academic department), Dickinson struggles in isolation to "wrest" vision from a male figure (or "tradition") infinitely more powerful than herself, a figure whom she wishes both to seduce and to defy. Because her Master is superior to her—and, perhaps, because she *does* love him—the form her struggle takes is (as Alicia Ostriker puts it), "subversive" not rebellious (39). Dickinson's tools are traditional female weapons, the "weapons" of those who are subordinate and isolated: play, parody, duplicity, evasion, illogic, silence, role-playing, and renunciation. As Ostriker says of the first five, they are strategies "still practiced by women poets today" (43).

For this particular interpretation of the poet and her plight, "The Daisy follows soft the Sun" has, not surprisingly, become the signature poem, mentioned or analyzed in a striking number of feminist-heterosexual readings:[3]

> The Daisy follows soft the Sun—
> And when his golden walk is done—
> Sits shily at his feet—
> He—waking—finds the flower there—
> Wherefore—Maurauder—art thou here?
> Because, Sir, love is sweet!
>
> We are the Flower—Thou the Sun!
> Forgive us, if as days decline—
> We nearer steal to Thee!
> Enamored of the parting West—
> The peace—the flight—the Amethyst—
> Night's possibility!
>
> (#106)

In light of the above discussion, the reason for this poem's appeal to feminist-heterosexual readers should be obvious. Duplicity and subversion are the Daisy's essence. Cloaking herself in a veil of modesty (sitting "shily" at her Master's "feet"), the speaker claims to "follow" the Sun all simplicity and adoration, when in fact her real aim is to "steal" from him at night what he will not allow her to have by day: call it love, poetry, or power.

The Daisy's reverence for her Master may be sincere, but it is also a cloak for highly disobedient ("Marauder"-like) ambitions, ambitions which only "Night's possibility"—and the Sun's "decline"—can fulfill.

I have no quarrel with this reading of the poem or those like it on which it is based. As Diehl's "hundreds of poems" testify, Dickinson was both attracted to and jealous of male power (from her brother's to God's), and she sought a variety of ways, including duplicity and subversion, seduction and evasion, and maybe even fantasies of madness and necrophilia, to compensate for—or to change the conditions of—her unwanted subordination. Indeed, the poet's need to claim power equal to the male's is the primary theme of most of her heterosexual love poetry. His is the "Shaggier Vest" against which she asserts her smaller "Acorn" size ("One Year ago—jots what?" #296). His is the "crown" or "name" she wants to bear ("The face I carry with me—last," #336), even if she—and he—must die in order for her to have it:

> Think of it Lover! I and Thee
> Permitted—face to face to be—
> After a Life—a Death—We'll say—
> For Death was That—
> And This—is Thee—
> . . .
> Forgive me, if the Grave come slow—
> For Coveting to look at Thee—
> Forgive me, if to stroke thy frost
> Outvisions Paradise!
>
> (from #577)

When writing heterosexually, Dickinson apparently could not imagine achieving equality in any other way. Men had the power. For her to have power equal to her male lover's, she had to take, steal, or seduce it from him—or they both had to be dead. Given nineteenth-century gender arrangements (including the arrangements within the Dickinson household), it is not surprising that the poet thought of heterosexual relationships in this way. But this is not the only kind of "love" poem that Dickinson wrote, nor is this the only kind of love story (or story about power) her poems tell.

As research by feminist historians Carroll Smith-Rosenberg and Lillian Faderman suggests, the rigid separation of the sexes produced by nineteenth-century American gender arrangements did not totally disadvantage women (Smith-Rosenberg 53–76, Faderman, *Surpassing*, 147–230). True, women spoke of themselves typically as "low" or "inferior" in respect to men. These are terms Dickinson herself uses in variants to a poem on Elizabeth Barrett Browning (#593). But nineteenth-century women were not solely reliant on their relationships with men for their sense of personal or sexual power (as heterosexual woman in our society tend to be today). On the contrary, one of the ironies of the doctrine of separate spheres was that it encouraged women to form close affectional bonds with each other. Within these bonds, women were able to affirm themselves and their female power despite their presumably inferior state.

Dickinson's letters and poems indicate that she participated in such relationships with women throughout her life and, as I have discussed elsewhere (*My Life a Loaded Gun* 27–37, 55–63), she drew an enormous amount of comfort, both emotional and sexual, from them. Indeed, a study of Dickinson's erotic poetry suggests that it was precisely the safety and protection offered by her relationships with women—that is, by relationships in which sameness not difference was the dominant factor (Morris in Juhasz 103 and *passim*)—that allowed her full access to her sexual feelings. Unlike unambiguously heterosexual poets such as Plath, Wakoski, and Olds, Dickinson did not find male difference exciting. She was awed, frightened, and, finally, repelled by it. In her often-quoted "man of noon" letter, sent to Susan Gilbert prior to the latter's engagement to Austin, the poet's brother, Dickinson compares male love to a sun that "scorches" and "scathes" women (*The Letters* 210). And in her poetry, she exhibits similar anxieties. Thus, for example, in "In Winter in my Room," she depicts male sexuality as a snake "ringed with Power" from whom her speaker flees in terror:

> I shrank—"How fair you are"!
> Propitiation's claw—
> "Afraid he hissed
> Of me"?
>
> . . .
>
> That time I flew
> Both eyes his way
> Lest he pursue

(from #1670)

And this same response of mingled awe and repulsion is repeated more subtly in other poems as well: "I started Early—Took my Dog," (#520) for instance, and "I had been hungry, all the Years" (#579). In each of these poems, the poet's fear of male sexuality—not the arousal of her desire—is the operative emotion. If she cannot find some way to reduce male power, to bring it under control, then she either loses her appetite for it (as in "I had been hungry, all the Years") or else she pulls back before she is engulfed (as in "I started Early—Took my Dog"). As she says in the latter poem, she feared male desire "would eat me up" (#520).

When relating to women, on the other hand, or when describing female sexuality (her own included), Dickinson's poetry could not be more open, eager, and lush. Permeated with images of beauty, nurturance, and protectiveness, and typically oral in emphasis, this poetry bespeaks the poet's overwhelming physical attraction to her own sex, and her faith in the power of her own sexuality even when, as in the following poem, Dickinson is presumably writing from a heterosexual point of view:

I tend my flowers for thee—
Bright Absentee!
My Fuschzia's Coral Seams
Rip—while the Sower—dreams—
Geraniums—tint—and spot—
Low Daisies—dot—
My Cactus—splits her Beard
To show her throat—

Carnations—tip their spice—
And Bees—pick up—
A Hyacinth—I hid—
Puts out a Ruffled head—
And odors fall
From flasks—so small—
You marvel how they held—

Globe Roses—break their satin flake—
Upon my Garden floor—

(from #339)

At the conclusion of this poem, the speaker vows to "dwell in Calyx—Gray," modestly draping herself while "Her Lord" is away, but the damage, so-to-speak, has already been done. The entire emphasis in the poem lies in the speaker's riotous delight in the sensual joys that female sexuality has to offer. Like a painting by Georgia O'Keeffe or Judy Chicago, "I tend my flowers" takes us into the very heart of the flower: its sight, smell, taste, and feel. It is all coral and satin, spice and rose. In its image of the budding hyacinth coming into bloom, it could well be orgasmic.

As in "The Daisy follows soft the Sun," Dickinson employs a heterosexual context in "I tend my flowers" in order to assert female sexuality subversively, but her focus is obviously on female sexuality itself. It is this (not the charms of her absent male lover) that evokes the poet's intensely colored verse, her sensual reveries. When writing outside a specifically heterosexual context, as in the following poems, Dickinson is able to revel in female sexuality's Edenic pleasures without apology or restraint:

Come slowly—Eden!
Lips unused to Thee—
Bashful—sip thy Jessamines—
As the fainting Bee—

Reaching late his flower,
Round her chamber hums—
Counts his nectars—
Enters—and is lost in Balms.

(#211)

Wild Nights—Wild Nights!
Were I with thee
Wild Nights should be
Our luxury!
. . .
Rowing in Eden—
Ah, the Sea!
Might I but moor—Tonight—
In Thee!

(from #249)

Within that little Hive
Such Hints of Honey lay
As made Reality a Dream
And Dreams, Reality—

(#1607)

As Lillian Faderman first observed of "Wild Nights" ("Homoerotic Poetry" 20), these poems are all written from what we would normally think
of as a male perspective. That is, they are written from the perspective of
one who enters, not one who is entered. Because of this ambiguity, they
effectively exclude the male. ("He" is at most a male bee, and hence, being
small and round, equivocally, as we shall see, a female symbol.) The poems
focus on female sexuality instead. "At sea" with this sexuality, Dickinson's
speaker bathes in bliss and moors herself in wonder, eats hidden honey,
adds up her nectars and is "lost in balms." The undisguised lushness of the
imagery, especially when compared to Dickinson's poems on male sexuality,
speaks for itself. For Dickinson, the dangerous aspects of sexual power lay
with the male—the power to devour, scorch, and awe. The sweetness and
balm (the healing) of sexuality, as well as its abundant pleasures, lay in
women. And it was within this basically homoerotic context (a context
created and sustained by nineteenth-century female bonding) that Dickinson
defines her own desire.

As I discuss in *Emily Dickinson: Woman Poet,* in the poetry in which
Dickinson privileges the clitoris even more than in the poetry in which she
extols the delights of vaginal entry, she puts into words her subjective
awareness of this desire and its paradoxical "little-big" nature. In this
poetry, a poetry characterized by images drawn from the "neighboring life"
—dews, crumbs, berries, and peas—Dickinson (in Irigaray's words) digs
beneath the layers of male civilization to recover the ancient language of
female sexuality itself (25). As Dickinson says in a poem sent to Susan
Gilbert Dickinson in 1858, it is a language that sings a "different tune":

She did not sing as we did—
It was a different tune—
Herself to her a music
As Bumble bee of June

. . .

I split the dew—
But took the morn—
I chose this single star

From out the wide night's numbers—
Sue—forevermore!

(from #14)

In *Literary Women* Ellen Moers observes that women writers—including Dickinson—have a predilection for metaphors of smallness which Moers relates to their small physical size. "Littleness," she writes, "is inescapably associated with the female body, and as long as writers describe women they will all make use of the diminutive in language and the miniature in imagery" (244). Even though Moers summarizes these metaphors suggestively as "the little hard nut, the living stone, something precious . . . to be fondled with the hand or cast away in wrath" (244), she does not identify such images as clitoral. However, I believe that we should. Indeed, I believe that we must if we are to understand how a great many women—not just Dickinson—have traditionally (if, perhaps, unconsciously) chosen to represent their difference to themselves.

As nineteenth-century gynecologists such as Charles D. Meigs recognized over a hundred and forty years ago (a recognition "lost" later in the century), the clitoris is the "prime seat" of erotic sensibility in woman just as its homologue, the penis, is the prime seat in man (130).[4] It is reasonable to assume, therefore, that the clitoris's size, shape, and function contribute as much to a woman's sense of self—her inner perception of her power— as does her vagina or womb—the sexual organs on which psychoanalytic critics since Freud have chosen to concentrate.[5] Images of smallness in women's writing unquestionably relate to woman's body size and to her social position. But like phallic images (which also serve these other purposes), such images have a sexual base, and so does the power women so paradoxically attribute to them. In identifying their "little hard nut[s]" with "something precious," women are expressing through their symbolism their body's subjective consciousness of itself. That is, they are expressing their conscious or unconscious awareness of the organic foundation of their (oxymoronic) sexual power.

The existence of a pattern of imagery involving small, round objects in Dickinson's writing cannot be disputed. Whether identified as male or female, bees alone appear 125 times in her poetry. Dews, crumbs, pearls, and berries occur 111 times, and with peas, pebbles, pellets, beads, and nuts, the total number of such images comes to 261. In the context of the poems in which they appear, many of these images are neutral, that is, they seem to have no sexual significance. But their repetitiveness is another matter. So is the way in which they are given primacy in many poems. Analysis of the latter suggests that on the deepest psychological level, these images represented to the poet her subjective awareness of her female sexual self, both its "littleness" (when compared to male sex) and the tremendous force nevertheless contained within it. In privileging this imagery, consciously or unconsciously, Dickinson was replacing the hierarchies of male-dominated heterosexual discourse—hierarchies that disempowered her as woman and poet—with a (paradoxical) clitorocentrism of her own, affirming her specifically female power.

Over and over clitoral images appear in Dickinson's poetry as symbols of an indeterminate good in which she delights, yet which she views as contradictory in one way or another. It is small yet great, modest yet vain, not enough yet all she needs. The following poem brings together many of these motifs:

God gave a Loaf to every Bird—
But just a Crumb—to Me—
I dare not eat it—tho' I starve—
My poignant luxury—

To own it—touch it—
Prove the feat—that made the Pellet mine—
Too happy—for my Sparrow's chance—
For Ampler Coveting—

It might be Famine—all around—
I could not miss an Ear—
Such Plenty smiles upon my Board—
My Garner shows so fair—

I wonder how the Rich—may feel—
An Indiaman—An Earl—
I deem that I—with but a Crumb—
Am Sovreign of them all—

(#791)

There are a number of things to note here. First, the poet is undecided whether the crumb in her possession satisfies her physical or her material appetite. In the first three stanzas it takes care of her hunger (albeit, by touching). In the fourth stanza it makes her wealthy, an "Indiaman" or

"Earl." She also cannot decide whether she is starving or not. For while she can touch and feel the crumb, she cannot eat it. Owning it is, therefore, a paradoxical business. It is a "poignant luxury," that is, a deeply affecting, possibly hurtful, sumptuousness that has archaic overtones of lust. Finally, poor though she is, the crumb makes this sparrow a "Sovereign," that is, it gives her power. She prefers it to "an Ear," presumably an ear of corn, and hence, given the poem's erotic suggestiveness, a phallus.

From one point of view, this poem is, obviously, a stunning example of Dickinson's ambiguity. Despite the many terms whose status as erotic signifiers can be established by reference to passages elsewhere in her work (loaf, bird, eat, luxury, sparrow, famine, plenty, Indiaman, earl, sovereign), there is no way to "know" what the poem is about. Not only do masturbation and cunnilingus fit but so do having a male or female lover, having some other unnamed good instead, sharing communion with God, and being content with her small/great lot as poet.

But whatever reading one adopts, what matters is that Dickinson has used imagery based upon her body as the primary vehicle through which to make her point. Whether or not she intended this poem to be about the clitoris, the clitoris is the one physical item in a woman's possession that pulls together the poem's disparate and conflicting parts. What other *single* crumb satisfies a woman's appetite even though she cannot eat it, and gives her the power of a "Sovereign" (potent male) whoever she is? In trying to represent her sense of self and the paradoxes of her female situation, consciously or unconsciously, Dickinson was drawn to what she loved most: the body she inhabited, the body she shared with other women. And it is the specific and extraordinary power of this body, its sovereign littleness, that she celebrates in this poem. As she says in another poem, this was the "crumb" for which she sang. As figure and fact, it was the source, motivation, and substance of her song:

> The Robin for the Crumb
> Returns no syllable
> But long records the Lady's name
> In Silver Chronicle.

> (#864)

By giving primacy to a clitoral image in this poem, Dickinson is asserting a form of female textuality and female sexuality that falls explicitly *outside* the male tradition. The song this "Robin" sings is "Silver," not golden like the sun/son. It is a "chronicle" that records "the Lady's," not her Master's, "name." And because it is female, it is written in different "syllables" from those of male verse, syllables drawn from the backyard life to which Dickinson's "lot" as a woman had consigned her—the life of robins, bees, and, above all, *crumbs*. From this life comes the "alphabet" in which female desire is reco(r)ded, an alphabet suited to the very different "Pleasure" loving women (as opposed to loving men) gives rise:

> There is an arid Pleasure—
> As different from Joy—
> As Frost is different from Dew—
> Like element—are they—
>
> Yet one—rejoices Flowers—
> And one—the Flowers abhor—
> The finest Honey—curdled—-
> Is worthless—to the Bee—
>
> (#782)[6]

For Dickinson, devoting oneself to this homoerotic pleasure inevitably meant writing a different kind of verse:

> As the Starved Maelstrom laps the Navies
> As the Vulture teazed
> Forces the Broods in lonely Valleys
> As the Tiger eased
>
> By but a Crumb of Blood, fasts Scarlet
> Till he meet a Man
> Dainty adorned with Veins and Tissues
> And partakes—his Tongue
>
> Cooled by the Morsel for a moment
> Grows a fiercer thing
> Till he esteem his Dates and Cocoa
> A Nutrition mean
>
> I, of a finer Famine
> Deem my Supper dry

For but a Berry of Domingo
And a Torrid Eye.

(#872)

In the first three stanzas of this poem, Dickinson compares the "male-storm"[7] created by male appetite sequentially—and hyperbolically—to a whirlpool, a vulture, and a man-eating tiger. In the final stanza, she celebrates her own "finer Famine," satisfied with "a Berry of Domingo/And a Torrid Eye." The theater of blood and lust which Dickinson depicts in the first three stanzas of this poem is so blatantly exaggerated it seems meant to be humorous. Male appetite is so voracious, the speaker claims, it will consume anything, including, finally, itself. (I read both "Crumb of Blood" and "Dates and Cocoa" as references to women.) In the final stanza, the speaker proudly asserts her own "limited" appetite by way of comparison. It is this appetite which defines her, making her the woman and poet she is: "I, of a finer Famine."

For Dickinson this "finer Famine" was a "sumptuous Destitution" (#1382), a paradoxical source of power and poetry, that nourished her throughout her life. In 1864, the same year in which she wrote "As the Starved Maelstrom laps the Navies," she sent Susan the following poem.

The luxury to apprehend
The luxury 'twould be
To look at Thee a single time
An Epicure of Me
In whatsoever Presence makes
Till for a further food
I scarcely recollect to starve
So first am I supplied—
The luxury to meditate
The luxury it was
To banquet on thy Countenance
A Sumptuousness bestows
On plainer Days,
Whose Table, far
As Certainty—can see—
Is laden with a single Crumb—
The Consciousness of Thee.

(#815 Version to Sue)

And in a letter written to Susan in 1883, she declared: "To be Susan is Imagination,/To have been Susan, a Dream—/What depths of Domingo in that torrid Spirit!" (*The Letters* 791). Over the twenty years that intervened between these poems and this letter, Dickinson's patterns of female sexual imagery and the homoerotic values these patterns encoded did not substantially change. Taken together, they were the "berries," "crumbs," and "dews" that—in imagination and in reality—nourished and sustained her as male love (and the male literary tradition) never could.

The importance of Dickinson's commitment to a woman-centered sexuality and textuality seems hard to dispute. But why then have so many feminist critics found it difficult to acknowledge the centrality of Dickinson's homoeroticism to her writing? Put another way, why have so many of them insisted on depicting her, in Diehl's terms, as "alone," even when (given her bonds to other women), she was not? What follows is not meant as a personal attack on these critics, but rather as an exploration of what I believe to be one of the most difficult issues confronting feminist-heterosexual women today—an issue whose political and sexual nature Dickinson was not only aware of but which she addressed in her poetry.

In *This Sex Which Is Not One,* Luce Irigaray makes the following comments on the (heterosexual) woman's place in the "dominant phallic economy," that is, in male-dominated culture:

> Woman, in this sexual imaginary, is only a more or less obliging prop for the enactment of man's fantasies. That she may find pleasure there in that role, by proxy, is possible, even certain. But such pleasure is above all a masochistic prostitution of her body to a desire that is not her own, and it leaves her in a familiar state of dependency upon man. Not knowing what she wants, ready for anything, even asking for more, so long as he will "take" her as his "object" when he seeks his own pleasure. (25).

Women, Irigaray argues, have been "enveloped in the needs/desires/fantasies of . . . men" (134). As such, they have been cut off from their own sexuality. In Irigaray's terms, they have learned to "masquerade" (133–34), assuming the sexual roles men have imposed upon them, while devaluing their own capacity for autonomous sexual response. As "conceptualized" within the phallic economy, Irigaray writes, "woman's erogenous zones never amount to anything but a clitoris-sex that is not comparable to the noble phallic organ, or a hole-envelope that serves to sheathe and massage the penis in intercourse: a non-sex . . ." (23). That women can be sexually equal to men (agents, as it were, of their own desire) is an idea both men and (many) women resist.

The historical appropriation and devaluation of female sexuality by men is hardly news; women in the nineteenth century were also aware of it. But in "The Malay—took the Pearl," Dickinson gives this perception a twist by addressing it from a homoerotic perspective, that is, from a perspective shaped by the poet's (homoerotic) awareness of the role the clitoris plays in autonomous woman-centered sex:

> The Malay—took the Pearl—
> Not—I—the Earl—
> I—feared the Sea—too much
> Unsanctified—to touch—
>
> Praying that I might be
> Worthy—the Destiny—
> The Swarthy fellow swam—
> And bore my Jewel—Home—
>
> Home to the Hut! What lot
> Had I—the Jewel—got—
> Borne on a Dusky Breast—
> I had not a deemed Vest
> Of Amber—fit—
>
> The Negro never knew
> I—wooed it—too
> To gain, or be undone—
> Alike to Him—One—

(#452)

Whether the "Pearl" in this poem stands synecdochically for the woman Dickinson loved or metonymically for the sexual and poetic powers which the poet believed were hers,[8] or, as is probable, for both, the poem's main point is clear. The "Jewel" that the Malay takes and then devalues (brings "Home" to his "hut") is an object of desire not just for the man but the speaker also. Indeed, the speaker (presumably a woman even though she cross-dresses as an "Earl") has far more title to the pearl than the Malay since she appreciates its true worth whereas he does not. (He wears it on a

"Dusky," sun-darkened, "Breast" where she would not deem a "Vest/Of Amber—fit" to bear it.) Nevertheless, she feels she has no right to this prize. She "fears" to touch the sea.

In cross-dressing her speaker in this poem, Dickinson may be expressing some of the awkwardness or perhaps even "unnaturalness" she felt in attributing (active) sexual desire to herself as a woman. As a young woman, Dickinson's problem—as she states in "The Malay—took the Pearl"—had been to gather the courage to appropriate female power for herself, to see herself as equally "sanctified"—and sanctioned—to "dive" (or "climb") into forbidden territories, whether erotic or poetic. In maturity, she lashes out again and again at the damage done women psychologically by such self-serving (masculine) prohibitions, prohibitions that not only prevent women from maturing fully, but turn them into the passive objects of male desire (and male art). Not permitted to act on their own needs or in their own stead, women inevitably become the victims of the men who "envelop" them (or eat them up):

> Over the fence—
> Strawberries—grow—
> Over the fence—
> I could climb—if I tried, I know—
> Berries are nice!
>
> But—if I stained my Apron
> God would certainly scold!
> Oh, dear,—I guess if He were a Boy—
> He'd—climb—if He could!
>
> (#251)

The little girl voice Dickinson adopts in this poem is deliberate and calculated. Boys have a right to "forbidden" fruits, but women (those whose sexual maturation is tied to—and "tied down" by—apron strings) do not. Yet, as this poem's symbolism makes clear, it is precisely women who are the "Berries" that boys so eagerly pick. Hence men's desire to guard their access to this fruit by divine interdiction. The God men worship (or create) protects male right.

What Dickinson is alluding to in this poem is—and has historically been —the paradox (and tragedy) of female sexuality: that its power is something women themselves have been forbidden to enjoy. It is a paradox Dickinson gives brilliant expression to in one of her most teasing yet trenchant epigrams:

> Forbidden Fruit a flavor has
> That lawful Orchards mocks—
> How luscious lies within the Pod
> The Pea that Duty locks—
>
> (#1377)

Whether this poem is about cunnilingus, masturbation, or something else altogether, the sexual implications of its final line are hard to evade. "Duty," that is, women's sense of obligation to a male-dominated culture's self-serving prohibitions, has made women's sexuality inaccessible to them. Women's loss of their sexuality occurred literally during the nineteenth century as they were propagandized to believe that they did not have orgasms. As we now know, in the space of less than fifty years, the physiological importance of the clitoris was expunged from the record and apparently from many women's conscious awareness as well (Laqueur 1–41).

Symbolically, this silencing of female sexual power continues to occur today in the writing of those critics, including those feminist critics, who ignore the significance of the homoerotic (and autoerotic) elements in poetry like Dickinson's. Indeed, feminist-heterosexual interpretations of Dickinson's poetry testify all too vividly to the degree to which, as Irigaray says, female sexuality remains "enveloped" in the needs and desires of men, despite the woman-centeredness of feminist vision. Committed to a heterosexual perspective (a perspective that makes women sexually as well as emotionally and intellectually dependent on men, no matter how much they may compete with them for power), these critics cannot see the centrality of Dickinson's homoeroticism even when—as in her clitoral poetry—it is obviously there. They cannot decode the "alphabet" in which these poems are written. Dickinson's relationship to the Master (a paradigm, perhaps, for these critics' own relationship to what Diehl calls "the male self") overwhelms ("envelopes") their eyes.

No one understood the magnitude of the task involved in women's reappropriation of their sexual power better than Dickinson and there were times when she questioned whether her "Pebble" was adequate to the task.

It was a struggle of epic proportion in which she was David (indeed, less than David) to her culture's Goliath:

> I took my Power in my Hand—
> And went against the World—
> 'Twas not so much as David—had—
> But I—was twice as bold—
>
> I aimed my Pebble—but Myself
> Was all the one that fell—
> Was it Goliath—was too large—
> Or was myself—too small?

(from #540)

But there were other times when she was able to assert without reservation her absolute right to the "Crown" she knew was hers:

> I'm ceded—I've stopped being Their's—
> The name They dropped upon my face
> With water, in the country church
> Is finished using, now . . .
>
> My second Rank—too small the first—
> Crowned—Crowing—on my Father's breast—
> A half unconscious Queen—
> But this time—Adequate—Erect,
> With Will to choose, or to reject,
> And I choose, just a Crown

(from #508)

The full impact of these lines can only be appreciated when they are read against those poems in which the speaker yearns pathetically for her Master's "Crown." In this poem, she stands masculinely "Erect" and crowns herself. Doing so, she takes back the symbol of her womanhood that men have usurped. In baptizing their daughters (as in wedding their wives), men give their names to women, making them "half unconscious Queens" —Queens who are not in full possession of their power (their "Crown"). In "I'm ceded," these rights (and rites) of male possession come to an end. The woman's vagina-ring-crown is hers. So presumably is the personal (creative) power—the "crumb"—that goes with it.

As I have asserted in *Emily Dickinson: Woman Poet,* Dickinson's ability to pose female sexuality and textuality as valid, autonomous *alternatives* to male sexuality and textuality derives from her romantic commitment to women and from her willingness to see in women sources of love, power, and pleasure independent of what Mary Lyon calls "the other sex" (Quoted by Hitchcock, 301). Her use of female sexual imagery suggests, therefore, not the "subversion" of an existing male tradition—but rather the assertion of a concept of female sexuality and female textuality that renders male sexuality and the poetic discourse around male sexuality irrelevant. In privileging the clitoris over the vagina, Dickinson privileged the female sexual organ whose pleasure was clearly independent of the male. She also privileged the sole organ in either sex whose *only* function is pleasure. For Dickinson, her "crumb" was "small" but it was also "plenty." It was "enough."

NOTES

This essay deals with issues which troubled me during the writing of *Emily Dickinson: Woman Poet.* In the book, I argue the case for Dickinson's homo-eroticism (and autoeroticism) much more fully. Here I wish to look at what feminist-heterosexual critics have—or, rather, have not—made of this material—and why.

1. All subsequent citations to Dickinson's poems will appear parenthetically in the text as the # symbol, followed by the Johnson number of the poem. In quoting from Dickinson's poetry and letters, I have retained her idiosyncratic spelling and punctuation.
2. Diehl's original essay has been republished in her *Dickinson and the Romantic Imagination* (13–33).
3. Analyses of "The Daisy follows soft the Sun" may be found in Gilbert and Gubar (600–601), Homans (203–4), and the essays by Gilbert, Keller, Mossberg, Morris, Homans, and Miller published in *Feminist Critics Read Emily Dickinson,* edited by Suzanne Juhasz.
4. The knowledge which Meigs states so definitively was "lost" in the course of the nineteenth century as part of a general (politically motivated) redefining of female sexuality. See Laqueur (1–41).
5. Naomi Schor is the only critic with whom I am familiar who has treated the subject of clitoral imagery and she discusses it only in relation to the use of synecdoche (detail) in male writing ("Female Paranoia" 204–19). In her full-length study of detail in male writing (*Reading in Detail: Aesthetics and the Feminine*), she drops the idea altogether.

The *locus classicus* for a discussion of uterine imagery in women's "art" is

Erik Erikson's influential essay "Womanhood and the Inner Space" (Erikson 261–94). In *Through the Flower,* Judy Chicago discusses her development of vaginal imagery and the empowering effect working with this imagery had on her (especially 51–58).

6. Dickinson identifies two kinds of sexual pleasure in this poem: one that gives the flowers joy and one that dries up *or* freezes them ("arid," "Frost"). If my reading is correct, this latter "pleasure" is the product of male sexuality which Dickinson depicts in some poems as a "sun," and in others as "frost." See for example, "A Visitor in Marl" (#391), and "The Frost of Death was on the Pane" (#1136). In either case, of course, male sexuality's ultimate effect on the women-flowers is the same: death.

7. I am indebted to Ms. Deborah Pfeiffer for calling my attention to this anagram.

8. I have discussed the biographical elements of this poem in *My Life a Loaded Gun* (52–53).

WORKS CITED

Bennett, Paula. *Emily Dickinson.* London: Harvester, 1990.

———. *My Life a Loaded Gun: Female Creativity and Feminist Poetics.* Boston: Beacon, 1986.

Chicago, Judy. *Through the Flower: My Struggle as a Woman Artist.* 1975. Garden City, N.Y.: Anchor-Doubleday, 1982.

Dickinson, Emily. *The Letters of Emily Dickinson.* Ed. Thomas H. Johnson and Theodora Ward. 3 vols. Cambridge, Mass.: Belknap Press of Harvard Univ. Press, 1958.

———. *The Poems of Emily Dickinson.* Ed. Thomas H. Johnson. 3 vols. Cambridge, Mass.: Belknap Press of Harvard Univ. Press, 1958.

Diehl, Joanne Feit. *Dickinson and the Romantic Imagination.* Princeton: Princeton Univ. Press, 1981.

———. "Reply to Faderman and Bernikow." *Signs* 4 (1978): 196.

Erikson, Erik. *Identity: Youth and Crisis.* New York: Norton, 1968.

Faderman, Lillian. "Emily Dickinson's Homoerotic Poetry." *Higginson Journal* 18 (1978): 19–27.

———. *Surpassing the Love of Men: Romantic Friendship and Love between Women from the Renaissance to the Present.* New York: Morrow, 1981.

Gilbert, Sandra M., and Susan Gubar. *The Madwoman in the Attic: The Woman Writer and the Nineteenth-Century Literary Imagination.* New Haven: Yale Univ. Press, 1979.

Hitchcock, Edward, ed., *The Power of Christian Benevolence Illustrated in the Life and Labors of Mary Lyon.* Northampton, Mass.: Hopkins, Bridgman, 1852.

Homans, Margaret. " 'Syllables of Velvet': Dickinson, Rossetti, and the Rhetoric of Sexuality." *Feminist Studies* 11 (1985): 569–93.

———. *Women Writers and Poetic Identity: Dorothy Wordsworth, Emily Brontë, and Emily Dickinson.* Princeton: Princeton Univ. Press, 1980.

Irigaray, Luce. *This Sex Which Is Not One*. Trans. Catherine Porter. Ithaca: Cornell Univ. Press, 1985.

Juhasz, Suzanne, ed. *Feminist Critics Read Emily Dickinson*. Bloomington: Indiana Univ. Press, 1983.

Laqueur, Thomas. "Orgasm, Generation, and the Politics of Reproductive Biology." In *The Making of the Modern Body: Sexuality and Society in the Nineteenth Century*. Ed. Catherine Gallagher and Thomas Laqueur. Berkeley: Univ. of California Press, 1988. 1–41.

Meigs, Charles D. *Woman: Her Diseases and Remedies*. Philadelphia: Lea and Blanchard, 1851.

Moers, Ellen. *Literary Women: The Great Writers*. 1976. Rpt. New York: Oxford Univ. Press, 1985.

Ostriker, Alicia Suskind. *Stealing the Language: The Emergence of Women's Poetry in America*. Boston: Beacon, 1986.

Schor, Naomi. "Female Paranoia: The Case for Psychoanalytical Criticism." *Yale French Studies* 62 (1981):204–19.

———. *Reading in Detail: Aesthetics and the Feminine*. New York: Methuen, 1987.

Showalter, Elaine. "Toward a Feminist Poetics." In *The New Feminist Criticism: Essays on Women, Literature, and Theory*. Ed. Elaine Showalter. New York: Pantheon 1985. 125–43.

Smith-Rosenberg, Carroll. *Disorderly Conduct: Visions of Gender in Victorian America*. New York: Knopf, 1985.

NINE

"The Dark Eye Beaming": Female Friendship in George Eliot's Fictions

Bonnie Zimmerman

Shortly after the publication of *Middlemarch*, George Eliot restated the message of its finale in a letter to Elma Stuart, one of the many younger women who worshipped at the author's shrine. Eliot suggested that modern women might continue the "incalculably diffusive" effect of Dorothea's generous acts:

The influence of one woman's life on the lot of other women is getting greater and greater with the quickening spread of all influences. One likes to think, though, that 2000 years ago Euripides made Iphigenia count it a reason for facing her sacrifice bravely that thereby she might help to save Greek women [from a wrong like Helen's] in the time to come. (*Letters* 5:372)

Eliot, to be sure, did not restrict the influence of a Dorothea to other women alone, as she indicated to her feminist friend, Barbara Bodichon: "Women can do much for the other women (and men) to come" (*Letters* 6:290). Her letters and novels nonetheless convey the impression that a special intimacy exists between women within the domestic sphere, and that woman's influence on man may be in fact parenthetical. As she wrote earlier in her life to Elizabeth Gaskell, "I shall always love to think that one woman wrote another such sweet encouraging words" (*Letters* 3:198).

The record of such "sweet encouraging words" between women affords the contemporary critic, particularly one who casts a lesbian eye on literature, an interesting vantage point from which to survey Eliot's life and fictions. George Eliot was a woman who existed—sometimes comfortably and sometimes uneasily—in an intellectual society populated largely by men as well as in a domestic female subculture. The literary portrayal of this subculture is less dramatic in Eliot's work than in that of her peers, such as Charlotte Brontë and Harriet Beecher Stowe, or in the popular domestic novelists of both England and America. But it exists nonetheless in the portrayals of Mrs. Poyser's dairy and kitchen, of the Dodson sisters, and of Mrs. Transome's incessant needlework. Equally striking are Eliot's fictional recreations of the nurturing, empowering influences exchanged between women.

Carroll Smith-Rosenberg has labeled this bedrock of affection and nurturance upon which many women in the nineteenth century built their lives "the female world of love and ritual" (1). Often this love took the form of intense, emotional "friendships" between two women. For George Eliot, the woman and the author, the most important of such friendships was her youthful passionate involvement with Sara Sophia Hennell. The correspondence between Eliot and Hennell confirms the pattern discerned by Lillian Faderman in nineteenth-century female friendships: "Love between women could be both passionate and spiritually uplifting. It could cast one into a state of euphoria and yet unlock the secrets of life and the intellect" (*Surpassing* 161). Eliot's love for Hennell not only "unlocked" her secret creativity and thus assisted her in becoming one of the greatest writers and intellectuals of the nineteenth century, but the relationships between women that we see in many of George Eliot's novels pay homage to this early "romantic friendship." Curiously, these fictional representations also resemble the feminist idealization of lesbian relationships that developed during the decade of the 1970s. In Eliot's fictions, women bond with each other for protection against male violence and misunderstanding, for aid in finding words through which to articulate their pain and desire, and for the fulfillment found in an encounter based upon equality and mutuality. These relationships, both in literature and in life, are passionate and sensual although not overtly sexual. And, I will argue, late in her life, Eliot grew acutely aware of the difference and danger posed by lesbianism, due in part to the example of a young devotee, Edith Simcox. As a result, Eliot abandoned her vision of the nurturing love extended by one woman to another.

In John Walter Cross's biography of George Eliot, Sara Hennell makes a dramatic entry onto center stage:

In July of this year (1842) Miss Sara Hennell—the gifted sister of Mrs. Bray— came to Rosehill on one of her occasional visits to Coventry, and completed the trio destined to exert the most important influence over the life of George Eliot. . . . To us Miss Sara Hennell is the most important correspondent, for it is to her that Miss Evans mainly turns now for intellectual sympathy; to Mrs. Bray when she is in pain or trouble, and wants affectionate companionship. (57–58)

The division Cross asserts between Sara's "intellectual sympathy" and Cara's "affectionate companionship" is, in fact, artificial, and substantiated only with the help of the extensive editing he performed on the romantic, sensual content of many of Eliot's letters to Sara. Perhaps Cross, in the more sophisticated 1880s, was troubled and embarrassed by his wife's earlier passion. This passion nevertheless had a significant impact on Eliot's life and career. Through her attachment to Sara Hennell, Eliot discovered that women can "light a torch in that vast chamber where nobody has yet been," protecting each other from abuse and alienation in a patriarchal society, and enabling each other to find the words necessary to tell their tales (Woolf, 88).

George Eliot's first letter to Sara Hennell reads like that of a woman in love:

Next to the pleasure of seeing your dark eyes beaming on me was the very unexpected one of having a note from you . . . I shall go on being sentimental and Liebsehnende in defiance of the march of reason and propriety . . . Thank you a thousand times my friend of the dark eye, as the Indians would call you, for destining your Autumn picture for me. . . . All good Angels attend you, my Sarah, love peace and hope, and now and then a thought of your affectionate/Mary Ann. (*Letters* 1:144–45)

Evidence of Eliot's infatuation with her new "friend of the dark eye," as she consistently calls her, abounds in letters written between 1842 and 1849. Early in their friendship she writes, "I have thought of you since receiving your merry kind notes almost as often as a lover of his Geliebte" (*Letters* 1:148). She longs to "one day have the face to kiss again," and reiterates that "I think of you more and love you better than ever, and could almost turn Guebre and worship the sun for giving me a sight of my favourite glance." Celebrating their birthdays (one day apart), she writes, "I am anxious not to let it pass without sending you my love-breathings," and later confesses to Cara Bray that "I have a great longing of heart towards her [Sara] that is my love-fit just now" (*Letters* 1:152, 193). She uses sensual, indeed, erotic, imagery to encode her feelings in an 1845 letter: "O how I shall spread my wings then and caress you with my antennae!" (*Letters* 1:197). Sensuality is also evident in an 1849 letter, written as the romantic phase of their friendship drew to a close: "Your letter, dear love, was brought to me in bed and I managed to read it in spite of unutterable headache. Every scrap of paper . . . is a little winged angel to me, seems to fondle and fan me with its soft dove-like wings" (*Letters* 1:275).

George Eliot wrote in this manner to no one else, male or female, during this period of her life, except on occasion to Cara Bray. In contrast, the Johnsonian sentences in a letter to Martha Jackson render its romantic formulae stiff and detached: "your thoughts of me have not been without something like a corresponding strain of love and sympathy in my mind, of which you, my Patty, have been the object" (*Letters* 1:151). During the same month, she wrote a far different letter, dictated by romantic feeling rather than romantic convention, to Sara: "Your life, mein Liebe, has been all activity and creation and my love longs to crown you with a wreath of the best happiness this sun and moonlit world can give" (*Letters* 1:152). She and Sara apparently consecrated their friendship as a "marriage," since for years Eliot's letters are addressed and signed "Lieber Gemahl," "your true Gemahlinn," "your loving wife," "Liebe Weib," "thine ever affectionate Husband," "dearly beloved spouse," and "Cara Sposa." By 1849, when the friendship had become turbulent, she could still write of their "marriage" in a bantering tone that nevertheless does not diminish the seriousness of their friendship: "I have not been beyond seas long enough to make it lawful for you to take a new husband—therefore I come back to you with all a husband's privileges and command you to love me whether I shew you any love or not, and to be faithful to me though I play you false every day of my life. . . . But in the veriest truth and simplicity, my Sara, thou art very dear to me and I sometimes talk to you in my soul as lovingly as Solomon's Song" (*Letters* 1:279). In addition to being each other's "spouse," Eliot is sometimes Sara's "Beloved Achates" (the inseparable male friend of Aeneas) and Sara is her "Siebenkas" (a character in a novel by Jean Paul Richter who also has a close male companion). Drawing upon Shakespeare for an example of female friendship, she writes to Sara, "Not a word more to throw at a dog. So said Rosalind to Celia and so says one to thee who loves thee as well as Rosalind did her Coz—" (*Letters* 1:203).

Their spiritual marriages did not prevent Eliot from contemplating earthly marriages, for this is the period of her celebrated engagement to an anonymous picture restorer. But however compelling the call of these earthly marriages, her marriage to Sara Hennell remained her deepest emotional attachment before she eloped with George Henry Lewes. Eliot portrayed

Sara as a fairy godmother who entered her dull, secluded life bearing gifts of intellectual stimulation, love, sympathy, and feeling. Sara was "a companion that I love and does me good, body and soul" because they can be "merry and sad, wise and nonsensical, devout and wicked together!" (*Letters* 1:194, 218). Sara offered her high purpose and stimulation: "I am miserable in want of you to stir up my soul and make it shake its wings and begin some kind of flight after something good and noble, for I am in a grovelling slothful condition, and you are the *only* friend I possess who has an animating influence over me" (*Letters* 1:217). At times, Eliot defines their love as strictly intellectual and moral; for example, after the breaking of her engagement, she writes, "So now dear Sara, I am once more your true Gemahlinn, which being interpreted means I have no loves but those that you can share with me—intellectual and religious loves" (*Letters* 1:186). Or, as she wrote late in 1849, "it is your soul to which I am wedded" (*Letters* 1:323). But at other times, she clearly states that their relationship is one of the heart: "Dear Sara—you always know what will give me the most pleasure in the world—I thanked you with delicious happy tears— the only tears almost that I ever shed now. I could hardly believe it was a waking fact that any one loved me well enough to speak to my heart in that sweet way" (*Letters* 1: 281).

Two letters in particular suggest that this friendship between two women, separated by space and joined for long periods of time only by language, unlocked the secrets of George Eliot's life and intellect. In her second letter to Sara (1842), Eliot thanks her for a picture Sara had painted, calling it her "charm," and then asks her "some questions about this same study of magic"—presumably requests for names of art teachers. Does Sara know "any well-disposed respectable genii who can assist gross clay-clothed souls to cheat their fetters and do the deeds that the spirit wills and the flesh denies?" But as painting was never to be George Eliot's art form, she hints at Sara's more direct responsibility to "initiate and introduce" her into her nascent literary powers. Having answered a question of Sara's about the harvest moon, she continues: "The said moon, honey dear, did not call forth any new compliments and invocations from your faithful servant and poetaster, she having like others of her tribe almost exhausted her material in that line, for albeit the *sun* awakened Memnon's harp, it is generally chaste Diana's light that draws the first notes from the young poet's lyre. Tell me another subject and I shall be inspired by your wish though by no other muse" (*Letters* 1: 147). This letter conveys the impression that the young woman has begun to perceive, beneath her "gross clay-clothed" soul, the spirit of a creator as yet a "poetaster" but one who longs to pick up the "poet's lyre." Since moonlight can no longer inspire her transformation, she calls upon her "muse," her romantic friend, Sara Hennell.

This unique reference to the muse in George Eliot's letters is enigmatic, for nowhere else does she suggest a "divine" inspiration for her art. I would interpret Sara Hennell as an *enabling* figure; being a writer and intellectual herself, Sara paid Eliot the compliment of serious attention and reciprocal love and friendship. She thus encouraged her along her initial path toward authorship. If Eliot might never have written novels without Lewes, she might never have written at all without Sara Hennell. In fact, fifteen months after this letter, Eliot initiated her literary career with the translation of Strauss's *Das Leben Jesu*. During the two years devoted to that project, Sara was her inspiration and intellectual mentor. So interchangeable was she as lover and "muse" that exchanges of kisses temporarily were replaced in the letters by exchanges of Greek and German etymology.[1]

Sara inspired and supported Eliot through her translation of Strauss and, more importantly, helped her to think poetically about her own life, always the richest source of her writing. In this way, she may have prompted the eventual emergence of the novelist. Eliot's birthday note of 1848 narrates a fanciful story—a fairy tale of sorts—about "a very young sprite" who presented "Dame Nature" with a "rough though unmistakable sketch of a human baby": herself, the "gross clay-clothed soul," Mary Ann Evans. Mother Nature finds this baby a poor piece of work worthy only of immediate smothering, but the poor sprite's handiwork is saved by his brother genii who remind Mother Nature that they have created other souls to "love and cherish and guard" this "poor rickety" one. The story concludes:

"And see," said one hard-working sprite, "some Novembers ago I brought you a dark-haired maiden and she shall be to this little one as a sister and her dark eye shall beam on the wandering one with love to soothe and grave warning to reclaim." And so Dame Nature heard the intercession and the brother-sprites kept their word. For the poor sketch of a soul was found by the dark eyed maiden and those other bright and good mortals [a reference to Charles and Cara Bray] and they pitied and helped it, so that it grew to think and to love. (*Letters* 1:273)

This story—the first of many fictional retellings of her life—encapsulates that period when Eliot felt isolated in what she perceived to be her "egoism" and "ambition," unable to share the sunlight or find warmth in another human eye, before the dark eyed maiden broke through her reserve and helped her to exchange her solitude for human fellowship and sympathy. Like her alter ego, Latimer in "The Lifted Veil," Eliot felt herself to be tinged with morbid self-absorption, lacking the language to release her passion. And again like Latimer, she is saved from this despair through a same-sex friendship that was both intellectual and emotional, and thus served to enrich her on both counts. Hence, it was one of the crucial experiences of her youth that instilled in her a lifelong commitment to the "community of feeling" (*Essays* 432).

Not long after she wrote her 1848 birthday note, George Eliot began the journey that was to free her from the bondage of the past in order to transform the past artistically. Her relationship with Sara Hennell was a casualty of this journey, for despite numerous protests that Sara is still her sister and beloved friend, Eliot soon found new friends, mostly male, and a new Geliebte more suited to her new life. In response to Sara's complaint that Eliot has grown alienated from her, she responds, "I have as perfect a friendship for you as my imperfect nature can feel—a friendship in which deep respect and admiration are sweetened by a sort of flesh-and-blood sisterly feeling and the happy consciousness that I have your affection, however undeservedly in return" (*Letters* 2:19). Had Sara given this a careful reading, she might have noted the number of qualifying phrases— "my imperfect nature," "a sort of," "however undeservedly"—her Gemahlinn uses. And although Eliot insists that Sara and Cara can never be replaced in her affections, not even by a husband, this is primarily because of the "associations with the past which belong to you" (*Letters* 2:19). Although they maintained an extensive correspondence throughout George Eliot's life, the mismatch of expectations that first becomes evident in 1849 continued throughout the relationship. As late as 1865, Eliot wrote, in an elegiac past tense, "Dear Sara, you do not doubt that I love you? . . . the delight I had in you, and in the hours we spent together and in all your acts of friendship to me, is really part of my life, and can never die out of me" (*Letters* 4:201). Nonetheless, as Sara Hennell retired into deep and unlit closets of philosophical inquiry, she faded in significance to the woman who had once been her "beloved spouse."

Although the "dark eye" of the sister-soul, the "muse," the glowing "sun," the "animating influence," and the bringer of "delicious happy tears" may have faded in Mary Ann Evans's life after 1849, she was reinvoked in George Eliot's novels.[2] Since Eliot drew upon her past freely and fluently, we ought not to be surprised that the image of two women standing "eye to eye" became a key emblem of sisterhood, "sympathetic identification," and storytelling in many of the novels (Bernikow 119; Gilbert and Gubar 517). Because women share a "hard lot" in patriarchy, because they can love each other in a manner free from "temporal" complications, and because they are not inhibited by the structures and strictures of heterosexuality, women function as enabling figures for other women. To adopt Janet Todd's framework, the *sentimental* friendship, "revelling in rapture and romance," that Eliot had experienced with Sara Hennell is transformed by the novelist into a *social* friendship, "a nurturing tie, not pitting women against society but rather smoothing their passage within it" (3–4).

Among the pieces contained in Eliot's earliest published work, is one called "A Little Fable with a Great Moral." The fable concerns two hamadryads who live by a lake, and the moral is one familiar to all readers of George Eliot's novels. One nymph, Idione, "loved to look into the lake because she saw herself there"; the other, Hieria, "cared not to look at herself in the lake; she only cared about watching the heavens as they were reflected in its bosom" (Pinney 21–22). Idione and Hieria are the first examples of the contrasting types of womanhood found throughout Eliot's fictions: the self-absorbed egoist, and the "theoretic" altruist.[3] In several of the novels a meeting between "Idione" and "Hieria," who previously have been separated from each other, climaxes their growth—sometimes fulfilled and sometimes aborted—into sympathy. Each meeting proceeds through a discernible pattern: one woman, who has been cast out by society or feels brutalized and betrayed by men, waits in the darkness, unable to speak or to cry, until the other woman brings light into her darkness by offering love, understanding, and protection. She thus breaks through the egoist's reserve, loosens her tears, and enables her speech. In short, she serves as the letters indicate Sara Hennell once served George Eliot. As a result of this contact, the alienated and isolated woman is able to tell her tale of suffering and the longing for forgiveness and acceptance.

The situation of an Eliot heroine is typically one of oppression and alienation. An extreme case is that of Hetty Sorrel, in *Adam Bede,* whose "shame"—seduction, pregnancy, and abandonment—forces her from the Edenic setting of Hayslope. She becomes a wanderer, an exile in a land that grows progressively darker and more hopeless until, utterly weary, she is tempted by the final alienation of death. She is saved from suicide but not from infanticide by the memory of Dinah Morris, who does not "seem to belong to that world of Hetty's whose glance she dreaded like a scorching fire" (427). Dinah stands apart from the choir of stern rejecting angels—all of whose voices, including the narrator's, are male—that swiftly casts the sinner into a "dark gulf." Condemned as much by her unfeminine "hard immoveability and obstinate silence" as by her "unnatural" crime, Hetty stands alone to hear the verdict of the all-male jury and the death sentence of the judge in his black cap (482).

This pattern of an initially obdurate male world casting out the female sinner is repeated throughout Eliot's novels. Whether its source be psychological, sociological, or literary—that is, found in the recriminations of Eliot's own father and brother, the actual status of Victorian women, or the conventional plots that govern the domestic novel—the pattern necessitates a meeting between the female protagonists in an atmosphere characterized by alienation and isolation. In *The Mill on the Floss,* when Maggie Tulliver goes back on her word to Philip Wakem, and does steal all the love away from the blonde heroine, her rash act alienates her from Lucy and from her community as well. Returning to St. Ogg's, her "natural refuge," she finds the men of her family adamantly turned against her (612). Tom, like Milton's avenging angel, bars her way home; her uncles are "hard in judgment" against her; clever young gentlemen "bow to her with that air of nonchallance which [they] might have bestowed on a friendly barmaid" (630, 623). Although the townswomen are among her harshest critics, it is understandably in the guise of the "world's *wife*" that they cast out their aberrant sister (619). Maggie is supported only by the women of her family and by those men—the minister Kenn and the crippled Philip—who are themselves marginal within the power structure. *Middlemarch*'s Rosamond, as well, retreats further into her ego-bound world when Will Ladislaw, furious with her for compromising him in Dorothea's eyes, "snatch[es] up Rosamond's words again, as if they were reptiles to be throttled and flung off," leaving her "a lonely, bewildered consciousness" (835, 837).

This lonely bewildered consciousness endures a literal "dark night of the soul." Hetty waits for death in her unlit cell, "sinking helpless in a dark gulf" (493). Maggie sits "without a candle in the twilight" searching for Lucy's face in the sad water, only to see it "sink away and be hidden behind a form that thrust itself between and made darkness" (641). Rosamond shuts herself up in her room, like a Victorian invalid, the same dark night Dorothea spends struggling with her soul. Illuminating this darkness is the light brought by the full-spirited woman. As darkness symbolizes the state of egoism, isolation, and despair, so light provides a contrasting symbol of sympathy, often connected to sight or vision. Eliot associated the image of "the dark eye beaming"—an emblem of romantic love in her letters to Sara Hennell—with the conventions that link sight to knowledge and sympathy. In Bernard Paris's formulation, a "sympathetic feeling is one which is excited by the signs of feeling in another person; intelligence, mental vision, is needed to read the signs" (424). As one woman looks another in the eye, compassion is "beamed" between them. Thus eyes in Eliot's philosophy, become a generalized emblem of the love and compassion one woman can extend to another in her passage through a harsh life. Dinah invokes God's aid to bring light into Hetty's dark cell, as into her hard, dark soul, thus opening "the eyes of the blind" (496). When Lucy enters Maggie's dark room, the narrator specifies that "the hazel eyes were there, with their heart-piercing tenderness" (641). In this way, Eliot "rewrote" her youthful infatuation with the dark-eyed Sara Hennell in a manner more appropriate to her mature life.

The connection between eyes and enlightenment is further strengthened by the wash and flood of tears that accompany the visionary light. Ego is eroded by the waters of emotion: "[Rosamond's] eyes met Dorothea's as helplessly as if they had been blue flowers. What was the use of thinking about behaviour after this crying? And Dorothea looked almost as childish, with the neglected trace of a silent tear. Pride was broken down between these two" (854). This sensual imagery of visionary light and emotional floods is further extended by the physical touch that aids in saving the oppressed sinner. Dinah brings Hetty earthly as well as divine contact:

> "I'm come to be with you, Hetty—not to leave you—to stay with you—to be your sister to the last."
> Slowly, while Dinah was speaking, Hetty rose, took a step forward, and was clasped in Dinah's arms. (493)

For Hetty, this physical contact is "something that was come to clasp her now, while she was sinking helpless in a dark gulf"; for Dinah, it is a joyful "first sign that her love was welcomed by the wretched lost soul." Indeed, physical contact is essential to the pattern established in the scene of sisterhood. Maggie and Lucy embrace and hold hands as they make their reconciliation. (In contrast, Philip and Stephen are present to Maggie only through letters.) Finally, Rosamond, whose original handclasp with Will Ladislaw had brought disaster, now "could not avoid putting her small hand into Dorothea's, which clasped it with gentle motherliness" (851). Throughout their emotional interview, Dorothea lays, presses, and rests her hand on Rosamond's, and at its climax, when Rosamond finally speaks, she too "put her lips to Dorothea's forehead, which was very near her and then for a minute the two women clasped each other as if they had been in a ship-wreck" (856).

The importance of physical contact reveals certain limitations to the typical "confessor" relationship between men and women. The priestly confessor is constrained by the inhibiting social conventions that cast sus-picion on all extramarital interactions between men and women. Thus, in *The Mill on the Floss,* Dr. Kenn's hands are tied, as Eliot shows us through his characteristic motion of walking "with his hands behind him" (624, 627). Lucy, on the other hand, need not keep her hands to herself, and while she does not offer Maggie the message of religion and morality, she can offer her the more tangible consolation of reconciliation. Physical contact—prohibited between man and woman but encouraged between two women—creates the literal bridge between two isolated selves that words alone cannot create. The words exchanged in the confession scene may help the sufferer comprehend her situation and the steps necessary to alleviate it (if any steps are possible, which is often not the case). The caresses that are exchanged between women, however, bypass self and rationality, creating an immediate emotional and physical link that banishes separation and alienation. This provides both the solace and comfort essen-tial to the suffering self, and tangible evidence of the possibility of change and growth. One touch is worth a thousand words.

The efficacy of the fatherly confessor is also compromised by the absence of reciprocity between him and the female penitent. Lucy, on the other hand, says to Maggie "in a low voice, that had the solemnity of confession in it, 'you are better than I am. I can't. . . .'" (642–43). Her "confession" illustrates the mutuality that Eliot finds particularly enabling in female-to-female rescue. Consider the diction in two passages already cited:

Slowly, while Dinah was speaking, Hetty rose, took a step forward and was clasped in Dinah's arms.

[Rosamond] could not avoid putting her small hand into Dorothea's, which clasped it with gentle motherliness.

In the first passage, the narrator shifts from active voice ("Hetty rose") to passive ("was clasped"); in the second, the narrator shifts mid-sentence from Rosamond's action to Dorothea's. Both shifts suggest that the relationship between the two women is reciprocal.[4] Hetty and Rosamund must both be saved and save themselves. And, as will be discussed, Dinah and Dorothea, as well as Lucy, are themselves saved through their act of salvation. The source of this reciprocity is the experience of suffering common to all women in a male-ordered world. Bernard Paris summarizes Eliot's philosophy: "Sympathy and vision are both dependent upon experience. Unless we have had an experience much like that which another person is undergoing, we cannot perceive and share the states of feeling signified by his behavior" (424). Men and women all experience pain, which is why many religions imagine a suffering god. But in a patriarchal world, as Eliot knew hers to be, only women share certain aspects of suffering—what Eliot called their "hard lot"—and thus can unite with and intercede for each other.

These scenes of sisterhood also imply that one woman can help another to grow into language through the telling of her sad tale. In each scene, the previously silenced woman finds her words amidst sobs and tears—the language of emotion as appropriate to women (in Eliot's view) as the language of intellect is to men. Convulsed by emotion, Hetty, for the first time in her life, dredges forth words to tell Dinah about killing an unwanted child amidst loneliness, darkness, and despair:

"Dinah," Hetty sobbed out, throwing her arms around Dinah's neck. "I will speak . . . I will tell . . . I won't hide it any more." But the tears and sobs were too violent. . . . It was a long time before the convulsed throat was quiet, and even then they sat some time in stillness and darkness, holding each other's hands. At last Hetty whispered, "I did do it, Dinah." (497)

When Maggie and Lucy meet, the two women embrace and hold hands, but cannot at first find words: "It seemed as if the interview must end without more speech, for speech was very difficult. Each felt that there would be something scorching in the words that would recall the irretrievable wrong. But soon, as Maggie looked, every distinct thought began to be overflowed by a wave of loving penitence, and words burst forth with a sob" (641–42). Maggie is thus able to tell Lucy her story of conflict between passion and duty. Struggling with hysteria at the height of her interview with Rosamond, Dorothea can "only seize her language brokenly," while Rosamond is grappled by the emotional intensity of the moment (855). At last Dorothea, acting as Rosamond's "muse" (as Eliot labeled Sara Hennell), draws forth the crucial words from Rosamond. Mesmerized by Dorothea's touch and animated by her emotion, Rosamond feels for the first time the awful, undefined urge to put another person's well-being before her own.

Previously able only to articulate her own egoistic needs, Rosamond tells Dorothea her brief story of passion and rejection.

Speech is a sign of moral maturity; it is the capacity that distinguishes humans from animals. The woman who is unable to articulate herself—and that is an almost paradigmatic situation in Eliot's novels—is something less than human. She may, like Hetty, remain obstinately mute, or, like Tessa (*Romola*), prattle incessantly and childishly. Only through meaningful speech does she become an adult with a modicum of responsibility. The male-oriented world is inclined to repress her language, especially at a time when women were defined as children by law and public opinion. But through contact with another woman, who shares her disadvantage and dispossession, the silent one awakens to speech. Through that awakening, however momentary it might be, she finds rest, peace, and reconciliation with the male order.

This last point is essential in order to understand the place of female friendship in Eliot's social and literary vision. After saving the poor sinner, the sisterly confessor engineers her reconciliation with or absorption into the male world. Dinah not only assists Hetty's journey from darkness to light, inarticulateness to speech, living death to everlasting life, she also reconciles her to Adam and Arthur Donnithorne the men from whom she has been alienated. As Dinah and "the trembling creature that clung to her as the only visible sign of love and pity" ride toward Hetty's execution, the reader may feel that Dinah, not Arthur, brings Hetty's ultimate reprieve from death, as she released her from silence. So too Maggie not only tells Lucy her own story, but also finds the words that ultimately reunite Lucy with Stephen:

> "Lucy," Maggie began again, "*he* struggled too. He wanted to be true to you. He will come back to you. Forgive him—he will be happy then . . . ."
> These words were wrung forth from Maggie's deepest soul, with an effort like the convulsed clutch of a drowning man. (642)

In reconciling Maggie and Lucy, and restoring the bond between Lucy and Stephen, Eliot also chooses words that suggest the "last conflict," the rescue and drowning that ultimately reconcile Maggie and Tom. Thus, through the love between Lucy and Maggie, both Maggie and the narrator find the words that overcome the alienation between men and women.

These encounters between women not only recover and reconcile the sinner, but also help the rescuer to complete her own story. Judith Kegan

Gardiner has suggested that in twentieth-century novels about female friendships, "the narrator finds herself not by merging with another woman but by *writing* about another woman" (437). In a related manner, Eliot's sympathetic heroine is able to write the conclusion to her own story by drawing out the words of her suffering sister. Dinah's rescue of Hetty draws her closer to the Poysers and to Adam, thus preparing the way for her eventual marriage, a step away from spiritual spinsterhood toward the state of adult wifehood. Lucy asserts her adult selfhood for the first time in her encounter with Maggie—"I shall come to you when I please"—and, many years later, grows up into marriage with Stephen. And in her own curious fashion, Rosamond wishes to reconcile with Will Ladislaw: "now I have told you, and he cannot reproach me any more" (856). Dorothea is thus reassured of Will's fidelity, and Rosamond is left free to make her own uneasy peace with Lydgate, who now enters to end the scene.

Reconciliation *in excelsis* is the goal of these scenes of sisterhood. Woman reconciles with self, with men, and, not insignificantly, with other women. For the mechanics of plot have set these pairs of women into rivalry with each other. Dinah and Hetty, Maggie and Lucy, Dorothea and Rosamond, all compete, however unwillingly or unknowingly, for the same men. Even Esther Lyon and Mrs. Transome (*Felix Holt*) are in some sense rivals for the love of Harold Transome. Tessa and Romola both "marry" Tito Melema, and Mirah exhibits a rare fit of pique over her supposed rival, Gwendolen Harleth (*Daniel Deronda*.) But, contrary to stereotypic notions of female divisiveness, the heroines deny or minimize the effects of their rivalry. The scene of sisterhood serves ultimately to remove and resolve the barriers between women as it does between women and men. Eliot restores the heterosexual imperative of the narrative, but also suggests a ploy in which women might not be friends (and lovers) to men, as Lydgate says about Dorothea, but also to their rivals in love. In this way, the scene of sisterhood serves as a displaced covert climax to the novel. Although the final release of narrative tension conventionally comes with the long-awaited union between Dinah and Adam, Maggie and Tom, or Dorothea and Will, the ground has been prepared by the emotional reconciliations between female protagonists. Only then, in an anti- or postclimactic resolution, are the heterosexual marriages made.

It is a tempting, if idle, fantasy to imagine Rosamond's fate had she been permitted more contact with Dorothea's compassion. Or to ponder whether or not Dinah might have saved Hetty from man's implacable law, or Maggie and Lucy together might have stood up to St. Ogg's. But in George Eliot's fictions, these moments of intensity and love between women are rare and fleeting, corresponding to no deep structure of female bonding that endures beyond the momentary pause of destiny. They enable women to escape from their egoism and alienation, helping them voice perhaps for only one time in their lives the story of their oppression and pain. But women cannot exist alone in George Eliot's fictive worlds and rarely in community with other women. The ultimate purpose of their tears and confessions is to overcome the alienation between men and women, and the isolation of women in a man's world. One would have to say that, for George Eliot, love and compassion between women ultimately serve a heterosexual world order.

So triumphant had become that heterosexual order that in Eliot's final novel, *Daniel Deronda,* the theme of sympathetic identification between women does not even appear. No example of female friendship (other than the sentimental circle of the Meyrick sisters) exists in the novel. Not only are the two primary female figures, Gwendolen and Mirah, denied a reconciliation scene, but the Dinah/Lucy/Dorothea figure becomes instead Gwendolen's quasi-confessor, quasi-lover Daniel, a man whose deepest relationship in the novel, interestingly enough, is with another man.

Why had the dark eye faded so thoroughly? I would suggest that Eliot's consciousness had undergone a radical shift between the 1840s and the 1870s, due in part to her personal commitment to George Henry Lewes and in part to changes in society. For this reason, when another "romantic friend"—the journalist and political activist, Edith Simcox—entered her life, she cast upon her a far more knowing and skeptical eye. Very briefly, Edith Simcox was one of several women who literally fell in love with George Eliot in the last decade of her life.[5] That love was not overtly returned by the author, although Simcox's detailed account shows that they engaged in a rather astonishing amount of flirtation, fondling, and kissing —what K. A. McKenzie fastidiously labels "the more innocent elements of Lesbianism" (102) and what I would identify as coded behavior through which women express their affection and desire for one another. Despite— or because of—this, Eliot was uncomfortable with what she saw as Simcox's man-hating, and repeatedly reminded her of her own creed, that heterosexuality is "a growth and revelation beginning before all history" (*Letters* 4:467–68).

Certain critics—Gordon Haight in particular—claim that Eliot knew Simcox to be a lesbian. Although their views are essentially homophobic and rely upon a simplistic, stereotypical, Freudian model of lesbianism (in which the lesbian is a masculine creature who hates men and loves her mother too well), I do think that Eliot noted a change in women during the 1860s which she (and others) characterized as man-hating, frigidity, and what I will loosely call "neuroticism."[6] In general, the new woman was perceived as neuter, monstrous, "unsexed," or manly—an image that was absorbed into the twentieth-century stereotype of the lesbian. Eliot may have identified Simcox as an unsexed and inappropriately "masculine" woman whose love for other women was suspicious. In this way, Eliot "morbidified" love between women, to use Lillian Faderman's term. Simcox, perhaps influenced by her own feeling of being "half a man" and sexually "inanated" (*Letters* 9:200; McKenzie 7), also seems to have perceived her love as not quite natural, as evidenced in the defensive tone in which she records a conversation with Eliot: "She owned human nature did crave (in reference to our mention before of the dangers of Boxing day) its taste of gin—I said and kissed her crape—was not mine of an innocent sort, and then went away" (*Letters* 9:281).

Is there any basis for linking George Eliot's suspicion of Simcox's "masculinity," her feminism, and her love for women to the modern concept of lesbianism as it developed after the turn of the century? Faderman suggests that female bonding was not condemned until the writings of the sexologists such as Krafft-Ebing (1882) and Ellis (1897). But John Lauritsen and David Thorstad point out that in Germany, "the 1860's saw the beginnings of what could be called scientific interest in homosexual behavior" (8). Karl Heinrich Ulrichs (who was read by Stephen Gordon's father in *The Well of Loneliness*) was widely read in the 1860s. Faderman also refers to an 1870 study of a passing woman reported in a German journal by Dr. Karl Westphal (*Journal of Homosexuality*, 77). During the 1860s and 1870s, George Henry Lewes worked on a monumental philosophical study including the science of knowledge, which he called psychology. (It was finished after his death by Eliot and published as *Problems of Life and Mind*.) His research took them to Germany, where in 1870 he had extensive discussions about psychiatry with a Dr. Westphal. Whether or not this was the same man who authored the pioneering study of female "inversion," Lewes's familiarity with German scholarship (evidenced by their extensive library) suggests that he was well aware of the emerging theory of congenital homosexuality, and passed this information on to Eliot. I therefore conclude that Eliot and Lewes interpreted Edith Simcox's behavior as homosexual—

before the concept became current in England—and for this among other reasons Eliot was reluctant to encourage her romantic friendship.

If my theory is correct, then we can begin to comprehend why Gwendolen Harleth is so isolated. Although the source for the character lies in the popular stereotype of "The Girl of the Period," her strong aversion to male sexuality may have been influenced in part by Eliot's observations of Edith Simcox. Indeed, the ever-vigilant Haight sees traces of lesbianism in Gwendolen as well, although this conclusion is hard to defend given the character's equal dislike for women (496–97). Nevertheless, it is very likely that Eliot's concern over the growing morbidity attached to female friendship, and her anticipatory awareness of the modern concept of lesbianism, caused her at the end of her career to deny the force of female friendship.

After Eliot's death, Edith Simcox recorded in her diary that "Miss Hennell apparently always disapproved of Marian for depending so much on the arm of man" (McKenzie 131). In letters and conversation, Eliot testified that, for her, "the male friends always eclipse the female," and that "the love of men and women for each other must always be more and better than any other" (*Letters* 2:38, 9:299). Nonetheless, George Eliot's women can be sisters and friends, and, ultimately, each other's "muse." Years after having been inspired by the dark-eyed maiden, George Eliot wrote of the restoring love bestowed by Dinah's "pitying eyes," Lucy's "hazel eyes," and Dorothea's "trace of a silent tear." We can see with our own eyes how women helped her find her own words and tell the stories of women's struggles in a harsh and sometimes cruel world. But the fear of lesbianism caused George Eliot, like many other women since, to turn away from that sisterhood. The "dark eye beaming" does not just fade in Eliot's fiction; the author resolutely puts out its light.

NOTES

1. It is also during this period that Eliot may have attempted her first fiction, according to a comment made by Sara Hennell: "we fancy she must be writing her novel." See Haight, 61.
2. Eliot's early essays contain several references to same-sex friendships (see Pinney, 14, 65.) She also read with considerable approval Margaret Fuller's *Memoirs* which chronicle the American author's philosophy and experience of same-sex love (see *Letters* 2:15).

3. Of course, the contrast is not that simple. George Eliot the novelist drew more complex characters than did George Eliot the fabulist. Even the most ardent altruist, such as Dorothea, begins her career submerged in ego.

4. It might be objected that Dorothea acts as a mother to Rosamond (and Dinah to Hetty) and therefore the relationship is not reciprocal. I would argue that although the rescuer has superior moral authority, she does not have social or political power The roles played in these scenes—sister, daughter, mother—are fluid and nonhierarchical. The act of rescue is always mutual.

5. See Zimmerman, "'The Mother's History' in George Eliot's Life, Literature, and Politics."

6. See Zimmerman, "Gwendolen Harleth and 'the Girl of the Period.'"

WORKS CITED

Bernikow, Louise. *Among Women*. New York: Harmony Books, 1980.

Cross, John Walter. *George Eliot's Life and Letters*. New York: The Kelmscott Society Publishers, n.d.

Eliot, George. *Adam Bede*. Harmondsworth: Penguin, 1980.

———. *Middlemarch*. Harmondsworth: Penguin, 1965.

———. *The Mill on the Floss*. Harmondsworth: Penguin, 1979.

———. *Miscellaneous Essays by George Eliot*. Boston: Estes and Lauriat, 1883.

Faderman, Lillian. "The Morbidification of Love between Women by 19th-Century Sexologists." *Journal of Homosexuality* 4, no. 1 (Fall 1978): 73–90.

———. *Surpassing the Love of Men*. New York: Morrow, 1981.

Gardiner, Judith Kegan. "The (US)es of (I)dentity: A Response to Abel on '(E)Merging Identities.'" *Signs* 6, no. 3 (Spring 1981): 436–42.

Gilbert, Sandra M., and Susan Gubar. *The Madwoman in the Attic*. New Haven: Yale Univ. Press, 1979.

Haight, Gordon S. *George Eliot: A Biography*. New York: Oxford Univ. Press, 1968.

———. *The George Eliot Letters*. 7 vols. New Haven: Yale Univ. Press, 1954.

Lauritsen, John, and David Thorstad. *The Early Homosexual Rights Movement*. New York: Times Change Press, 1974.

McKenzie, K. A. *Edith Simcox and George Eliot*. London: Oxford Univ. Press, 1961.

Paris, Bernard J. "George Eliot's Religion of Humanity." *ELH* 29, no. 4 (December 1962): 418–43.

Pinney, Thomas, ed. *The Essays of George Eliot*. New York: Columbia Univ. Press, 1963.

Smith-Rosenberg, Carroll. "The Female World of Love and Ritual." *Signs* 1, no. 1 (Autumn 1975): 1–29.

Todd, Janet. *Women's Friendship in Literature*. New York: Columbia Univ. Press, 1980.

Woolf, Virginia. *A Room of One's Own*. New York: Harcourt, 1928.

Zimmerman, Bonnie. "Gwendolen Harleth and 'the Girl of the Period.'" In *George*

Eliot: Critical Essays. Ed. Anne Smith. Totowa, N.J.: Barnes and Noble, 1980. 196–217.

——. "'The Mother's History' in George Eliot's Life, Literature, and Politics." In *The Lost Tradition: Mothers and Daughters in Literature.* Ed. E. M. Broner and Cathy Davidson. New York: Frederick Ungar, 1980. 81–94.

144 BONNIE ZIMMERMAN

TEN

My Ántonia, Jim Burden, and the Dilemma of the Lesbian Writer

Judith Fetterley

In "To Write 'Like a Woman': Transformations of Identity in Willa Cather," Joanna Russ claims Cather as a lesbian writer and essays to understand the central situation in many of her novels and stories as an indirect expression of a lesbian sensibility. In *Lesbian Images,* Jane Rule explicitly decries a lesbian approach to Cather's work, suggesting that it violates Cather's sense of herself as an artist and a person and fulfills Cather's worst fears of the critical act as merely an effort to "reduce great artists to psychological cripples, explaining away their gifts and visions in neuroses and childhood traumas" (74). Rule shares Cather's fears about the motives of critics; she presents a series of "readings" which she labels "grossly inaccurate" and which she claims "can only be explained by a desire of each of these men to imply that Willa Cather's 'basic psychology,' 'personal failure,' or 'temperament' negatively influenced her vision" (75, 76). Obviously Rule has reason to assume that masculinist critics will seek to find in Cather's lesbianism the "flaw" that explains what is "wrong" with her work. While Rule's anxiety to protect Cather against the masculinist misreadings that result from patriarchal homophobia is both understandable and commendable, her solution is problematic. Reciting the biographical evidence for viewing Cather as a lesbian, she nevertheless severs the life from the work, evidently *unable* to imagine the possibility that Cather's lesbianism might have influenced her art. Labeling *My Ántonia* Cather's "most serene and loving book," she thus demonstrates that, while Cather was emotionally devastated by Isabelle McClung's marriage to Jan Hambourg, her personal torment as a lesbian did not interfere with her ability to write a classic of heterosexual love. While this reading supports her theory, it seems rather out of touch with the text under consideration. Indeed, Rule's theory would appear to require a renunciation of the text Cather actually wrote.

Like many of Cather's readers, I have long thought *My Ántonia* both a remarkably powerful and a remarkably contradictory text and have long suspected that its power was connected with its contradictions.[1] Recently, I have come to suspect that these contradictions are intimately connected to Cather's lesbianism. Seeking like Russ to claim Cather as a lesbian writer and to understand her art in the context of her life, I propose the following reading of *My Ántonia*.[2] As Deborah Lambert has demonstrated, *My Ántonia* was a watershed book for Cather, marking the transition between her ability to write as a woman about women and her decision to write as a "man" about men. In *My Ántonia,* the transition and transformation are still in process and the process is incomplete. What marks *My Ántonia,* then, as a central, if not *the* central Cather text, is not so much the evidence it contains of Cather's capitulation to convention, but rather the evidence it contains of her deep-seated resistance to such capitulation. As such, it defines the nature of Cather's situation as an American writer who was also a lesbian writer and it defines the nature of her solution to the inherent contradiction between American and lesbian.

In Book IV, the Widow Steavens informs Jim of the fate of their Ántonia: "My Ántonia, that had so much good in her, had come home disgraced. And that Lena Lingard, that was always a bad one, say what you will, had turned out so well, and was coming home every summer in her silks and her satins, and doing so much for her mother. I give credit where credit is due, but you know well enough, Jim Burden, that there is a great difference in the principles of those two girls. And here it was the good one that had come to grief!"[3] One might well inquire as to the source of the Widow's certainties, the principles that determine the comfortable clarity of her moral universe. How is she enabled to distinguish so easily the good woman from the bad one? And one might well assume that, for the Widow Steavens, Ántonia's definitive goodness derives from her conventionality; she is all that one could ask for in the way of a traditionally defined woman. She is smart as a whip, but will never attend school; eager and quick to learn the language of her new country, she will always speak broken English with an accent that marks her as foreign and eventually she will speak no English at all; nurturant in the extreme, she saves even the insects, making a nest in her hair for the protection of the sole surviving cricket. Above all, she identifies with men and against women. Passionately devoted to her father, she ennobles him, in a moment of extraordinary disclosure, for having married her mother when he could have bought her off. Since Ántonia herself will recapitulate her mother's experience, her idealization of her father and denigration of her mother are as painful as they are predictable. She pads about after Charley Harling, "fairly panting with eagerness to please him" (155); and she equally "pants" after Jim and his approval, hoping that "maybe I be the kind of girl you like better, now I come to town" (154). With Lena she is cold and distant because Lena "was kind of talked about, out there" (164). Tony is not one to give a sister the same uncritical support she gives men.

In Book II, we learn that Tony is all heart and that this is the source of her power. In Book IV, we learn the limitations of the power of heart: "The trouble with me was," she later explains to Jim, "I never could believe harm of anybody I loved" (344). This radical severance of head from heart leads her directly into the arms of Larry Donovan, for whom she performs the conventional female function of becoming the mirror in which one is seen as large. Against her better judgment, she participates in the mythology of the transforming power of women's love: "I thought if he saw how well I could do for him, he'd want to stay with me" (313). The arms of Larry Donovan open directly onto the realm of the seduced and abandoned and "my" Ántonia is "poor" Ántonia now. Though Jim professes anger at this convention, there is a direct connection between the qualities he values in Ántonia and her abandoned state, between being "good" and being "poor." At the end of Book I, Jim murmurs, "Why aren't you always nice like this, Tony?" (104) Previously, she has not been so nice: "Ántonia ate so noisily now, like a man" (125) and "like a man" she works, competing daily with Ambrosch and boasting of her strength. From the "fate" of acting like a man and losing "all her nice ways," Grandmother Burden "saves" her, getting Ántonia a job in town serving the Harlings. Tony's salvatory tenure at the Harlings is abruptly terminated, however, by another incursion of not-niceness. Forced to choose between working for the Harlings and going dancing, Tony "set[s] her jaw" and leaves. To which Jim responds, "Tony, what's come over you?" (208).

But Jim needn't worry, for Tony's badness is merely a temporary deviation from her path to apotheosis as an earth mother. Book V, fittingly titled "Cuzak's Boys," delivers her to us in this role. Defined not simply as the mother of sons but as the mother of the sons of her husband, Ántonia admits: "That Leo; he's the worst of all. . . . And I love him the best" (335). Obviously, for Ántonia, in boys badness is goodness. Though "a rich mine of life" to others, Ántonia herself appears depleted. A battered woman, her grizzled hair, flat chest, and few remaining teeth reflect the toll exacted of one who plays the role of earth mother.

This is a role that Lena, "coming home here every summer in her silks and satins, and doing so much for her mother," has firmly refused, eliciting thereby the Widow's denunciation of her as "bad." From the moment she first appears at the Harlings' back door, Lena presents a marked contrast to Ántonia. While Tony pants after approval in broken English, Lena moves through the world with perfect composure and perfect English. Unlike Tony, Lena likes town because she sees it as the way up and out, and up and out Lena intends to get. Through with the farm, with family life, and with marriage, Lena wants to be economically and personally independent; she has come to town to learn a profession. Lena puts her clear head in the service of her own self-interest and while she "gave her heart away when she felt like it . . . she kept her head for her business and had got on in the world" (298). Though Lena's success is in itself sufficient to draw the Widow's ire, her definition of "good" requiring an element of failure in which head is submerged in heart and self is deferred to other, perhaps equally upsetting is Lena's desire to extend her success to her mother. To Ántonia's male-identification and glowing commitment to father-right and brother-right, Lena opposes the image of a woman-identified-woman whose hidden agenda is to rescue her mother. Lena resists marriage because she sees it as bad for women—too much work, too many children, too little help, too much danger of physical abuse from cross or sullen husbands. At the same moment that Tony builds a shrine to her father for actually having married a girl he seduced, Lena reveals her hidden agenda: "I'm going to get my mother out of that old sod house where she's lived so many years. The men will never do it" (241). The handkerchiefs Lena wants to buy for her mother carry the letter "B" for Berthe, not "M" for mother.

Though the moral universe of the Widow Steavens is simple, that of the text of My Ántonia is not. At several points and in several ways, My Ántonia fails to confirm or ratify the Widow's easy differentiation. Indeed, My Ántonia visibly confronts the reader with a series of contradictions that force one to raise questions. One such question emerges from Jim's final apotheistic tribute to Ántonia: "It was no wonder that her sons stood tall and straight. She was a rich mine of life, like the founders of early races" (353). But where are these sons? Look at the men in My Ántonia—weak, insubstantial, self-destructive. Emblematic is the nameless tramp whose story Tony recounts in Book II. Arriving out of nowhere, he offers to run the threshing machine and minutes later jumps into it head first. Tony's response emphasizes the peculiar maleness of this behavior: "What would anybody want to kill themselves in summer for? In threshing time, too! It's nice everywhere then." And besides, she adds, "the machine ain't never worked right since" (179, 178). Bewildered Tony may well be as to the cause of this behavior but hardly as to its existence; her own father, in an act which anticipates the demise of Wick Cutter, has blown his head off because life is simply too much for him. He becomes daily less substantial until there remains only enough energy to mark the fact of his existence by the violence of its termination. Are we then to assume that Ántonia herself comprises an entire category, no other earth mother existing, all these other men being the sons of women who are something other than earth mothers? Yet whom has Ántonia nourished? Not her father certainly. Cuzak?—"a crumpled little man" who lifts "one shoulder higher than the other . . . under the burdens of life" (356). Jim, who seems to have no life at all? Where are Ántonia's tall, straight sons?

If there is no evidence of nourishment, there is evidence of poison. Wick Cutter's viciousness, which culminates in his wife's murder and his own suicide, runs on the energy generated by Mrs. Cutter's outrage. Mrs. Harling feeds Mr. Harling, but the result of his feasting is an arrogant imperialism that stops life: "We had jolly evenings at the Harlings' when the father was away" (156). And what are the consequences of Ántonia's whipping up cakes for "Charley"? Charley/Larry doesn't seem to have benefited from her hot lunches. He is last seen disappearing toward Mexico where he may get rich "collecting half-fares off the natives and robbing the company" and where he may just as easily get killed. And Charley/Jim? The most intricate exposure of the problematic nature of female nourishment occurs in a scene that involves Jim, architect of the earth mother image. In Book I, Jim kills a snake, and Ántonia sings the praises of his courage; single-handedly she creates monster and hero, dragon and George, feeding Jim's ego until "I began to think that I had longed for this opportunity, and had hailed it with joy. . . . Her exultation was contagious. The great land had never looked to me so big and free. If the red grass were full of rattlers, I was equal to them all" (47–48). Back at the ranch, Otto, the cowboy, succinctly punctures Ántonia's windy distortion. Later Jim learns how lucky he really was: "A snake of his size, in fighting trim, would be more than any boy could handle. So in reality it was a mock adventure; the game was fixed for me by chance, as it probably was for many a dragon-slayer. I had been adequately armed by Russian Peter; the snake was old and lazy; and I had Ántonia beside me, to appreciate and admire" (49–50). But what if there were no Otto? What if Ántonia's were the only voice Jim heard? Might he not, thus stuffed with heroic imagery, have set off on other adventures where, not so lucky, he would return on his shield rather than with it?

I do not mean to suggest here that *My Ántonia* is an antifeminist text designed to demonstrate how bad women are for men, a position implicit if not explicit in Blanche Gelfant's provocative and insightful essay and a position that finally reinforces the apotheosis of the earth mother. Rather, I wish to suggest that the text of *My Ántonia* radically undercuts the premises of the figure that occupies its center; thus, it calls into question the value of the very conventions it seems to assert. Women are not under attack here for failing to be earth mothers. Nor are earth mothers under attack for failing to fulfill their promises or, more insidiously, for masquerading as nourishers while actually emasculating those they nurture. Rather, it is the apotheosis of the earth mother figure itself that is under seige. The pressure the text resists is the pressure embodied in the voice of the Widow Steavens with her easy assurance of good and bad, and it resists this pressure by undermining the system that supports the earth mother figure. Like a body responding to the implantation of a foreign object, *My Ántonia* surrounds Ántonia with antistories.

One such antistory features Russian Peter and Pavel who, for heroically daring to act out a powerful and radical vision, have suffered banishment and stigmatization. For the Widow Steavens, Lena's badness directly connects to her resistance to marriage; yet *My Ántonia* supports Lena's badness more than Tony's goodness. The significance of the Russians' story may be taken, as Gelfant suggests, from its mode of presentation.[4] Like any highly explosive material, it is carefully contained. Dying, Pavel tells his story to Mr. Shimerda; Ántonia overhears it and, translating first from Russian to Bohemian and then from Bohemian to English, she repeats it to Jim who tells it to us. This highly explosive tale contains a hatred of marriage as pure as the snow onto which the bride and bridegroom are thrown and as intense as the hunger of the wolves who consume them. Pavel's and Peter's priorities are ratified by a text whose hostility to marriage would be hard to exceed. Examples of destructive marriages abound: Cutters, Shimerdas,

Harlings, Crazy Mary and just as crazy Ole, Jim and the woman who "for some reason" wishes to remain Mrs. Burden. Good marriages appear only when their absence would be so notable as to turn the antistory into the story—for example, the marriage of Jim's grandparents and that of Ántonia and Cuzak. Yet even the latter instance proposes a vision of marriage as a structure of mutually conflicting interests: "It did rather seem to me that Cuzak had been made the instrument of Ántonia's special mission. This was a fine life, certainly, but it wasn't the kind of life he had wanted to live. I wondered whether the life that was right for one was ever right for two" (345).

The hatred of marriage embedded in the antistory carries with it an equally negative attitude toward heterosexuality. The positive assertion of Ántonia's extraordinary fecundity finds neither resonance nor reinforcement in a text whose sexual emblems are Crazy Mary, Wick Cutter, and Lena with the reaping hook. The act required to support the "rich mine of life" motif is fraught with danger and repugnance. Mr. Shimerda's dalliance with the servant girl who comes to work for his mother terminates in the gruesome scene in a Nebraska barn with a frozen corpse on the floor and hair stuck to the roof. Like her father's, Ántonia's brief moments of eroticism, those nightly trips to the dancing tent, find an equally painful conclusion in the house attached to the barn. Haunting the landscape of heterosexual passion is the figure of Crazy Mary, whose jealousy of Lena reduces her to a caricature with a corn knife in danger of being recommitted. The pathetic object of her passions has little better luck with his own sexual longing; having married his Mary to keep him steady, he finds the remedy insufficient and himself wandering the prairies looking for Lena.

Though heterosexual desire dooms men as well as women in My Ántonia, a loathing of male, not female, sexuality informs the negative context. Emblematic here is Wick Cutter, whose name reveals at once his phallic identity and the narrative attitude toward it. In Wick, male sexuality emerges as unrestrained, unrestrainable, and rapacious, preying on those women who must serve him to survive. He articulates the hidden and shameful sexual history of Black Hawk, a history of exploitation and abuse which spawns an endless series of pregnant "Marys," some of whom return to town after being "forced to retire from the world for a short time" and some of whom do not return but move on to Omaha and Denver where they are "established in the business" for which they have been "fitted" (203, 210). Though less obvious than the abuse of the hired girls, the anemia, paralysis, and unlived lives of the "white," middle-class town girls must also be laid in part at the door of a sexuality which requires "purity" in wives and mothers and vents its lust on the bodies of servants. Yet *My Ántonia* contains a loathing of male sexuality that transcends the presumably political. The disgust that Wick Cutter's flesh elicits, "his pink, bald head, and his yellow whiskers, always soft and glistening" (210), is adumbrated in the nausea elicited by the extraordinarily phallic snake of Book I: "His abominable masculinity, his loathsome, fluid motion, somehow made me sick. He was as thick as my leg, and looked as if millstones couldn't crush the disgusting vitality out of him. . . . He seemed like the ancient, eldest Evil" (45–47).

Still, even phallic loathing, however much combined with sexual politics, while richly informative of the attitude toward marriage, seems inadequate to explain the aura of fear that encircles sexual experience in *My Ántonia* and creates a radical contradiction within the conventional story between the romanticization of earth mother fecundity and the attribution of "goodness" to her stance of asexuality. Indeed, we must now consider the fact of contradiction within both story and antistory as well as the fact of contradiction between them, and we must consider as well the possibility that the two stories do not simply coexist but coincide, both necessarily present because dynamically related.

The key here rests with the figure of Lena Lingard, whose "badness" is related to her sexuality and whose sexuality reveals the erotic asymmetry at the heart of the novel. If Wick Cutter's flesh elicits loathing and disgust, Lena's elicits desire—in crazy Ole; in the Polish musician who lives across the hall; in old Colonel Raleigh, her landlord; in Jim himself; and in the narrative voice that describes her. The fear Lena arouses can only be understood as a response to the desire she has also and first aroused. And Lena does arouse fear. The landscape of Ántonia's "rich mine of life," the fruit cave whose explosion of life dizzies Jim temporarily, finds no complement in the erotic landscape of Jim's dream life. Rather this landscape is bare, cut and full of shocks. In the dream Jim dreams again and again, Lena appears to him as the grim reaper, armed with the hook that he, at least, never forgets. Though Jim says he wishes he could have this "flattering" dream about Ántonia, it seems clear that his ability to idealize Ántonia, like the Widow's ability to define her as "good," stems directly from her refusal to appear to him as sexual and from her willingness to serve him as an agent of sexual repression and prohibition, reinforcing that part of him which needs to set the erotic in the context of dream and fear. Shortly before Jim tells us about his dream, he records an equally significant exchange between himself and Ántonia. Attempting to kiss Tony as "Lena Lingard lets me kiss her," Jim experiences a sharp rebuff (224). Tony gasps with indignation and snarls protectively, "If she's up to any of her nonsense with you, I'll scratch her eyes out" (224). Looking back on the incident, Jim responded with an outburst of pride in Ántonia and avowed that he now knew "where the real women were, though I was only a boy; and I would not be afraid of them, either!" (225)

It would be quite a job to unravel the contradictions and confusions of this particular bit of textual sequence. But it would be irresponsible to fail to note their existence or to fail to observe that this excessive confusion coincides, precisely with the most overtly sexual moment in the text. Surely, if not answers, questions are being forced upon us. Why is Jim's pride in Ántonia tied to her protecting him from Lena? How can an earth mother, the real woman, be idealized at once for her fecundity and her asexuality? And behind these and all the other questions one might raise is the overriding issue of the source of the imperative against responding to female sexuality. Why can't Jim have erotic dreams about Tony or see Lena without her reaping hook?

In Book III, Jim, accompanied by Lena, attends the theater and on one particular afternoon encounters for the first time the transcendant power of art. *Camille*, the initiating play, has as its theme renunciation. Why is Jim so transfixed by the drama of renunciation and why does this drama enable him to grasp the meaning and function of art? What is being renounced here and who is doing the renouncing?

Jim Burden has presented a problem to many readers of *My Ántonia*. Indeed, Cather's own uneasiness on the subject of her point of view is apparent, not simply in her various explanations/rationalizations of her narrative choice, but also within the text itself.[5] How else can one understand the "Introduction" save as an effort to substantiate Jim Burden, explain his relation to story and character, and make him credible as a narrator? "Unlike the rest of the book," Brown tells us, Cather found the introduction "a labor to write" (Brown and Edel 153). Her difficulty may well suggest something false in the nature of the task, an inability to say what needs to be said, an unwillingness to explain where explanation is essential. Her discomfort was such that for the 1926 reissue of *My Ántonia* she revised the introduction, improving the effect, according to Brown, and most particularly by removing from "the reader's mind a question that could do the book no good—whether in fact it would not have been better told by another woman, the query Miss Jewett had raised about 'On the Gull's Road'" (Brown and Edel 153). Cather's revisions may indeed have improved the introduction, but not because they solved its problems. Rather, her revisions refocus the questions which the introduction will inevitably raise so as to more accurately reflect and engage these problems. The ultimate effect of the revised introduction is to focus the reader's attention on the problematic nature of the narrative voice in the text, for instead of explaining Jim Burden the introduction leaves us wondering who has made the attempt. The "I" who introduces our "eye" is not now Willa Cather who, as a "little girl," had watched Ántonia "come and go" and who has made a feeble attempt to write Ántonia's story herself. Instead, it is a nameless faceless, sexless voice. Three pages into the story, and we itch for definition, crave knowledge of whom we hear. Neither itch nor craving is satisfied here or later and this, I would propose, is precisely the point of Cather's excisions and final "solution." While putatively existing to solve a problem, the introduction in fact serves to identify a problem and to indicate that the problem is the point. Indirect in its strategy, the introduction further reveals that the inability to speak directly is the heart of the problem which is the point.

In revising the introduction, Cather removed all references to herself. Dramatized in the act of revision and embedded thus in the revision itself, palimpsest subtext informing the superimposed surface text, is the renunciation of Cather's own point of view and of the story that could be told from that point of view. To return to the motif of *Camille,* I would suggest that the renunciation at issue is Cather's own. In *My Ántonia* Cather renounces the possibility of writing directly in her own voice, telling her own story, and imagining herself in the pages of her text. Obviously autobiographical, the obvious narrator for *My Ántonia* would have been Cather herself. Yet for Cather to write in a female voice about Ántonia as an object of emotional desire would, in the context of early twentieth-century awareness of sexual "deviance" and thus of the potentially sexual content of "female friendships,"[6] have required her to acknowledge a lesbian sensibility and to feel comfortable with such a self-presentation—a task only slightly easier to do now than then.[7] Indeed, in this context, Jewett's directive to Cather to avoid the "masquerade" of masculine impersonation and write openly in her own voice of women's love for women—("a woman could love her in that same protecting way—a woman could even care enough to wish to take her away from such a life, by some means or other") —seems faintly specious (Fields 247). In fact, it was not "safer" for Cather to write "about him as you did about the others, and not try to be he!" (Fields 246). Her "safety" lay precisely in her masquerade.

Yet *My Ántonia* is not simply "safe." Choosing to transpose her own experience into a masculine key, Cather nonetheless confronts us with a transposition radically incomplete. At the end of Book IV, Jim confesses to Ántonia, "I'd have liked to have you for a sweetheart, or a wife, or my mother or my sister—anything that a woman can be to a man" (321). Why, then, does he not so have her? Cather makes no attempt to answer this question for the contradiction between speech and act cracks open the text and reveals the story within the story, the story that can't be told directly, the essence of whose meaning is the fact that it can't be told.

Though nominally male, Jim behaves in ways that mark him as female. On the farm, he rarely leaves the kitchen; he inhabits women's space: "When grandmother and I went into the Shimerdas' house, we found the women-folk alone. . . . The cold drove the women into the cave-house, and it was soon crowded (114, 115). Yet Cather can't have him doing women's work; thus Jim does virtually nothing, a fact which at once contributes to his insubstantiality and provides a context for understanding its source. Jim's most active moment comes, not surprisingly, when he is left alone. With no one to observe him and with responsibility for all tasks of both sexes, he throws himself into housework and barn work with equal vigor. A point in Book II similarly defines his ambiguity. Realizing he is about to leave Black Hawk, Jim delivers a reminiscent tribute to his life as a Black Hawk boy: "For the first time it occurred to me that I should be homesick for that river after I left it. The sandbars, with their clean white beaches and their little groves of willows and cottonwood seedlings, were a sort of no-man's-land, little newly created worlds that belonged to the Black Hawk boys. Charley Harling and I had hunted through these woods, fished from the fallen logs, until I knew every inch of the river shores and had a friendly feeling for every bar and shallow" (233). To which we can only murmur, "Really?" For we have seen no part of this boys' world. Instead, we have seen Jim hanging out at the Harlings, participating in female-centered family life; Jim playing with the hired girls and getting a reputation for being "sly" and "queer"; Jim studying his books at home alone; Jim walking the streets at night and sneering at the cowardice and hypocrisy of these very Black Hawk boys who are supposedly his fishing and hunting buddies.

Nor does Jim identify with Black Hawk men. How are we to explain Jim's hatred of Mr. Harling, a figure who presumably represents Jim's own possibilities for future gratification? Significantly, Jim's hostility attaches precisely to those features of Mr. Harling's life that most reflect patriarchal privilege—the subservience of his wife and children, their complete catering to his every whim, his ownership of time and space; in short, his "autocratic" and "imperial" ways, the ways of a man "who felt that he had power" (157). Jim's hostility, reminiscent of his earlier contempt for the arbitrary predominance accorded Ambrosch, though unintelligible in a male, makes perfect sense in a female who recognizes in patriarchal privilege both her own future as the object of personal tyranny and a possibility of power from which she is excluded.

Jim's sexual self-presentation equally reveals his gender ambiguity. With Harry Paine, the town boy who loses Tony her job by forcing her to kiss him on the Harlings's back porch, as the Black Hawk norm for adolescent male sexuality, Jim's behavior stands out as "queer" indeed. Attempting to kiss Tony himself and meeting with a similar rebuff, he responds not with force but with petulance and then support. "Lena Lingard lets me kiss her," he weakly asserts, rhetorically disclosing his essential sexual passivity and foreshadowing the postures of his erotic dream. After listening to Tony's lecture on the dangers of playing with Lena, Jim capitulates completely, submerging his dissent in a rush of pride at the "true heart" of his Ántonia. Jim's sympathy for Tony's position, based on her own experience of the dangers of sexuality for women, is worthy of a mother or a sister or a friend, but not of a suitor whose sexual self-interest lies in undermining her perceptions and making her ashamed of her resistance.

Two scenes in *My Ántonia,* both explicitly about sex and gender, unmistakably define the essential femaleness of Jim Burden. In Book I Jim tells us of an incident that made a change in his relationship with Ántonia, a change he claims to have welcomed and enjoyed. By virtue of this experience Ántonia presumably learns that gender means more than age; thus taught, she abandons her tone of superiority and assumes her appropriately subservient place: "Much as I liked Ántonia, I hated a superior tone that she sometimes took with me. She was four years older than I, to be sure, and had seen more of the world; but I was a boy and she was a girl, and I resented her protecting manner. Before the autumn was over, she began to treat me more like an equal and to defer to me in other things than reading lessons. This change came about from an adventure we had together" (43). Jim's sexism here, so unlike anything we know of him before or after, can of course be understood as Cather's attempt to give her "boy" masculine colors. Yet even a cursory glance at the snake episode reveals an agenda very different from the one Jim claims for it, indicating once again Cather's unwillingness to cover the tracks of her narrative transposition and renunciation. Not masculine superiority and the validity of masculine privilege but the fraudulence of male heroics and hence of the feminine worship that accompanies and inspires it are the subjects of this episode. Jim responds to the sudden appearance of the snake with sheer terror, and he kills it by sheer luck. From his experience he learns that a stacked deck makes heroes and a chorus of female praise obscures the sleight of hand. The aura of the impostor colors the scene and explains the absence of any sequel to it. For Jim's experience is far more intelligible as that of a girl, who, while temporarily acting a boy's part, discovers the fraudulence of the premises that support the system of sexism and thus comes to see all men as impostors; but who nevertheless recognizes that, though she may play male roles and sign herself William Cather, her signature is a masquerade and her identity a fake.

The second scene occurs in Book II when Tony, made nervous by the more than usually bizarre behavior of her employer, Wick Cutter, asks Jim to take her place. In theory, Ántonia's request ought to provide Jim with a golden opportunity, a chance to demonstrate that masculine superiority which is the putative lesson of the earlier scene by protecting the woman whom he continually tells us he loves. Further, since Cutter's intention is rape and since the whole town loathes the man, the situation carries with it the additional possibility of becoming a local hero. Knight in shining armor, defender of fair womanhood, Black Hawk avenger—Tom Sawyer would jump at it. Jim Burden turns and runs, straight home to grandmother where he puts his face to the wall and begs, "as I had never begged for anything before," that she allow no one else to see him, not even the doctor (249). To her reiterated note of thankfulness "that I had been there instead of Ántonia," Jim responds with pure hatred: "I felt that I never wanted to see her again. I hated her almost as much as I hated Cutter. She had let me in for all this disgustingness" (250). Surely Jim has literally taken Ántonia's place and experienced the rape intended for her. The physical repulsion, awareness of sexual vulnerability, sense of shame so profound as to demand total isolation—all are intelligible as responses to rape. Jim's identity as "girl" structures the scene, undermining his pretense to masculinity and maleness. Is it not obvious why Jim can't marry Ántonia?

At the end of his story, Jim returns to the landscape of his youth. Setting out, north of town, into "pastures where the land was so rough that it had never been ploughed up," Jim has "the good luck to stumble upon a bit of the first road that went from Black Hawk out to the north country; to my grandfather's farm, then on to the Shimerdas' and to the Norwegian settlement. Everywhere else it had been ploughed under when the highways were surveyed; this half-mile or so within the pasture fence was all that was left of that old road which used to run like a child across the open prairie, clinging to the high places and circling and doubling like a rabbit before the hounds" (369, 370–71). Formless, unploughed, and unsurveyed, with possibilities for wildness, this landscape, so steeped in nostalgia for childhood, reflects a longing for a time before definition, before roads have been marked and set and territories rigidly identified. By the end of the book Jim has returned to a psychological state parallel to that of his beloved landscape. Reunited at last with Ántonia, he is also reunited with a past before the domination of sexual definition when one might be a tomboy and love one's Ántonia to one's heart's content. Not surprisingly, the spirit attendant upon the longing for gender ambiguity is a profound fear like that of a rabbit before hounds. At those moments when gender crossing actually occurs—for example, when Ántonia begins to dress and act like a man and Grandmother Burden determines to "save" her—the text exudes a profound uneasiness. So it is that the tension between impulse and repression, desire and renunciation determines the circlings and doublings described by the text of My Ántonia.

Indeed, the text as a whole recapitulates the burden of narrative choice —a transposition only partially completed; a story, a sensibility, an eroticism only partially renounced. Emblematic of the eroticism Cather can not bring herself to renounce completely is the character of Lena Lingard. If the idealization of Ántonia in "the pioneer woman's story" requires the steady denial of her sexuality,[8] Lena remains convincingly sexual. And significantly, her sexuality is neither conventionally female nor conventionally male but rather identifies an erotic potential possible only outside the patriarchal, heterosexual territory of rigid definitions and polar oppositions. Characterized by a diffused sensuality rooted in a sense of self and neither particularly aggressive nor particularly passive, Lena represents one model of lesbian sexuality. Her presence in the text as a symbol of desire, felt as desirable and allowed to be desired, "flushed like the dawn with a kind of luminous rosiness all about her" (226), provides occasional moments of pure sensual pleasure and indicates the strength of Cather's resistance to renouncing her lesbian sensibility.

In the foreword to his biography of Willa Cather, James Woodress writes: "Although Willa Cather wrote an old friend in 1945 that she never had any ambitions, the truth was just the opposite. Her entire career down to the publication of O Pioneers!, her first important book, shows a very ambitious young woman from the provinces, determined to make good" (13). Certainly that determination to make good must have played a large role in Cather's decision to renounce her own point of view, masquerade as a male, and tell a story that is not her own. As critics from Leslie Fiedler to Carolyn Heilbrun to Nina Baym have demonstrated, American literature as defined by the literary establishment whom Cather intended to impress, is a male preserve; the woman who would make her mark in that territory must perforce write like a man. The pressure that converted Willa Cather into Jim Burden was not simply homophobic; equally powerful was the pressure exerted by the definition of the American "I" as male and the paradigm of American experience as masculine. Yet perhaps the ultimate irony of Cather's career lies in the fact that we remember her best, not for her impersonations of male experience, her masculine masquerades, but rather for the strategies she evolved to maintain her own point of view and tell her own story within the masquerade. In a word, we remember her less for the consequences of her renunciation than for the results of her resistance.

In My Ántonia, Cather reveals the face of that ambition which she later declared the book to have satisfied: "The best thing I've done is My Ántonia. I feel I've made a contribution to American letters with that book" (Bennett 203). It is not surprising that the book in which Cather reveals her artistic ambitions should be her most powerful work. Nor are we surprised to find this book marked by the theme of renunciation and defined by the tension between the pressure to renounce and the equally imperative need to resist this pressure. Nor finally is it surprising that here in this text Cather works out the terms of her compromise with her context—the context of an ambitious American writer who is also female and lesbian.

At the opening of Book III, Jim sits musing on the lines from Virgil's *Georgics*: "'*Primus ego in patriam mecum . . . deducam Musas*'; 'for I shall be the first, if I live, to bring the Muse into my country'" (264). He remembers that his teacher, Gaston Cleric, had explained "that 'patria' here meant, not a nation or even a province, but the little rural neighborhood on the Mincio where the poet was born," and he wonders whether "that particular rocky strip of New England coast about which he had so often told me was Cleric's *patria*" (264, 265). Surely Jim's musings illustrate Cather's ambition—to be, like Virgil, the first to bring the muse into her own country. But if Virgil's country is a *patria*, Cather's Nebraska is ardently female, envisioned and embodied in a lavishly feminine imagery, metaphor, and analogy, that culminates in the identification of the Bohemian girl with the American land.

Equally female is Cather's muse. A knock at the door and the entrance of Lena Lingard interrupts Jim's musings on poets and poetry. After she leaves, "it came to me, as it had never done before, the relation between girls like those and the poetry of Virgil. If there were no girls like them in the world, there would be no poetry" (270). It would be hard to overestimate the significance of this moment for the career of Willa Cather or for the history of the woman artist in America. Locating the source of poetic inspiration in the figure of Lena Lingard—the unconventional, the erotic, the lesbian self retained against all odds—instead of in the figure of Ántonia—the conventional, the desexed, the self distanced and defined as Other (for Ántonia, unlike Lena, could never have written *My Ántonia*), the location one would expect if one read the entire text as "The Pioneer Woman's Story," Cather reverses the transposition that produced Jim Burden, drops her masquerade, defines a woman's love for women as the governing impulse of her art, and places lesbian eroticism at the heart of her concept of artistic creation. Moreover, if muse and country are both female, and if the function of the writer is to bring muse and country together, then in this formulation the textual act itself is equally lesbian. Yet in what sense really does *My Ántonia* bear out this theory of Cather's poetics? Beyond eroticizing Lena Lingard and refusing to make Jim Burden convincingly male, has Cather done anything else in *My Ántonia* to reveal that lesbian eroticism is the governing impulse of her art?

In the introduction to *My Ántonia*, we hear a voice marked neither as male nor female. This voice recurs throughout the text. Often we forget that we are listening to Jim Burden—his maleness, as suggested above, has been made easy to forget—and we assume instead that we are hearing the voice of Willa Cather. This slippage occurs most frequently and most easily when the subject of contemplation is the landscape. A woman's voice making love to a feminine landscape—here, I would suggest, is the key to Cather's genius and achievement. Unable to write directly of her own experience and to tell her own story in her own voice, and thus baffled and inhibited in the development of character and plot, Cather turned her attention elsewhere, bringing the force of her talent to bear on the creation of the land, her country, her *matria*. In the land, Cather created a female figure of heroic proportions, proportions adequate to both her lived experience as woman and to her imaginative reach as a woman writer. In the land, Cather successfully imagined herself; in the land, she imagined a woman who could be safely eroticized and safely loved. Thus the story she could not tell in terms of her characters is told in terms of narrator and country, and the flattening and foreshortening of personality that is the consequence of her renunciation of her own voice has as its corollary a complementary lengthening and enriching of landscape. Cather made her mark in the territory of American literature with her landscape; we remember her *matria* long after we have forgotten her masquerade. Though she may have sold her birthright, the price she got for it was gold.

NOTES

1. See, for example, Brown and Edel, 152–59; Gelfant, 60–82; Stuckey, 473–83.
2. This essay was written before the publication in 1987 of Sharon O'Brien's monumental study of Cather as a lesbian writer, *Willa Cather: The Emerging Voice*. Obviously, O'Brien's book supports my interpretation of *My Ántonia* as the work of a lesbian writer. While reading O'Brien has not materially altered my interpretation of *My Ántonia*, were I to write this essay today I would incorporate O'Brien's perception that Cather's need to separate the maternal and the erotic derived from her complex relationship as a lesbian daughter to her mother. Thus donning a male masquerade protected Cather not only from overtly identifying her erotic sensibility as lesbian; it equally protected her from confronting directly her attraction to a mother at once feared and desired.
3. Willa Cather, *My Ántonia* (Boston: Houghton, 1918; rev. 1926; pb. rpt. 1980),

313. All subsequent references are to the paperback edition and will be included parenthetically within the text.

4. See Gelfant, 74. Gelfant must be credited with first according this scene the attention it deserves. It is, however, interesting that in her interpretation of it as a "grisly acting out of male aversion" to women, she overlooks the fact that the groom as well as the bride gets eaten.

5. See Woodress, 176: "She felt obliged to defend her use of a male point of view, however, when she wrote her old friend and editor Will Jones. Because her knowledge of Annie came mostly from men, she explained, she had to use the male narrator, and then she rationalized that she felt competent to do this because of her experience in writing McClure's autobiography." Or Bennett, 46–47:

One of the people who interested me most as a child was the Bohemian hired girl of one of our neighbors, who was so good to me. She was one of the truest artists I ever knew in the keenness and sensitiveness of her enjoyment, in her love of people and in her willingness to take pains. I did not realize all this as a child, but Annie fascinated me and I always had it in mind to write a story about her. But from what point of view should I write it up? I might give her a lover and write from his standpoint. However, I thought my Ántonia deserved something better than the Saturday Evening Post sort of stuff in her book. Finally, I concluded that I would write from the point of a detached observer, because that was what I had always been. Then I noticed that much of what I knew about Annie came from the talks I had with young men. She had a fascination for them, and they used to be with her whenever they could. They had to manage it on the sly, because she was only a hired girl. But they respected and admired her, and she meant a good deal to some of them. So I decided to make my observer a young man.

6. For a discussion of the emergence of this self-consciousness and of the loss of "innocence" attendant on it, see Faderman, 297–331.

7. For a fuller exploration and discussion of the issues involved in such a decision, see Lambert, 676ff.

8. See Lambert for a detailed analysis of the stages by which Ántonia is "reduced to an uttterly conventional and asexual character."

WORKS CITED

Bennett, Mildred. The World of Willa Cather. Lincoln: Nebraska Univ. Press, 1961.

Brown, E. K., and Leon Edel. Willa Cather: A Critical Biography. 1953. Rpt. New York: Avon, 1980.

Cather, Willa. My Ántonia. 1918. Rev. 1926. Rpt. Boston: Houghton, 1980.

Faderman, Lillian. Surpassing the Love of Men: Romantic Friendship and Love between Women from the Renaissance to the Present. New York: Morrow, 1981.

Fields, Annie, ed. The Letters of Sarah Orne Jewett. Boston: Houghton, 1911.

Gelfant, Blanche. "The Forgotten Reaping Hook: Sex in *My Ántonia.*" *American Literature* 43 (1971): 60–82.

Lambert, Deborah. "The Defeat of a Hero: Autonomy and Sexuality in *My Ántonia.*" *American Literature* 53 (1982): 676–90.

O'Brien, Sharon. *Willa Cather: The Emerging Voice.* New York: Oxford Univ. Press, 1987.

Rule, Jane. *Lesbian Images.* Garden City, N.Y.: Doubleday, 1975.

Russ, Joanna. "To Write 'Like A Woman': Transformations of Identity in the Work of Willa Cather." *Journal of Homosexuality* 12 (1986): 77–87. Reprinted in *Aspects of Lesbianism.* Ed. Monika Kehoe. New York: Hawthorne, 1986.

Stuckey, William J. "*My Ántonia*: A Rose for Miss Cather." *Studies in the Novel* 4 (1972): 473–83.

Woodress, James. *Willa Cather: Her Life and Art.* Lincoln: Nebraska Univ. Press 1970.

ELEVEN

Sapphistory: The Woolf and the Well

Jane Marcus

The purpose of this essay is twofold: to return to Virginia Woolf's book *A Room of One's Own* (1929) the circumstances of its material production, its historicity, and to suggest a reading based on its relation to the trial of Radclyffe Hall's novel *The Well of Loneliness* (1928) for obscenity. In this reading we can identify the heroine of the essay, Judith Shakespeare, as Radclyffe Hall herself, and the narrator, the unnamed Mary (Hamilton) of the old Scots "Ballad of the Four Maries," as speaking in the voice of Mary (Llewelyn), Stephen Gordon's lover in *The Well of Loneliness*. (Woolf's narrative Mary is generic, but it is interesting to note if one doubts the generic power of "Mary" that Lovat Dickson, in his biography of Radclyffe Hall, calls Stephen's lover Mary *Hamilton* instead of Mary Llewelyn three times and calls her Mary Henderson once.)[1] The essay as fictive "Mary (Hamilton)'s" gallows' song sings sisterhood in homoerotic tones, slyly seducing the woman reader and taunting patriarchal law just this side of obscenity. The metaleptic echo of the absent name of Mary (Hamilton) is, in Jefferson Humphries's words[2] a "haunted trope," a ghostly allusion to an absence, and it mirrors the primal absence in the text of women's books on the shelves of the British Museum.

The unverbalized allusion to the narrator of the ballad and the lost beloved of Hall's novel cannot reverberate as an echo without the reader's recognition of the source of the echo. Since the success of *A Room* depends on the reader's collaboration in the conspiracy of its making, the critic's role here is to embody the historical context in which the disembodied voice of Echo can be reconstituted, to collect some of the scattered parts of the woman artist's body. The classical Echo is buried in pieces all over the earth, pieces that shriek and speak when stepped on, endlessly repeating the tag ends of statements as questions. Woolf's Judith is buried at the elephant and Castle in one piece, or rather two pieces, since she is pregnant, and "she never wrote a word." Her resurrected self is Mary Hamilton, the narrator, who sings her ballad before she is publicly hanged for sexual transgression. Mary (Hamilton) echoes Judith Shakespeare and both voices echo Radclyffe Hall. Woolf's narrative voice is sexually and politically exciting for the woman reader because it simultaneously rings with fear of male reprisal for sexual and verbal transgression, it mourns our martyrs, and it also resurrects them. A Room of One's Own is a chamber of echoes, an echo chamber, in which Echo, the woman artist, who transgressed both sexually and verbally in the myth, may cease to seduce the self-loving narcissistic male with his own words, and may speak in her own words, having "put on the body which she has so often laid down," as Woolf says of Judith Shakespeare (118).

The second point I want to explore is the way A Room of One's Own lectures women students on the necessity of the female mentor, with the name of Jane Harrison (she had died that April), triumphantly initialed as "the great J.H.," used as another haunted trope, the shabby "phantom" of "terrible reality," which is set against the melodramatic villainy of Oscar Browning, whose name evokes the even more terrible reality of academic homosexual misogyny. The origin of the metaleptic troping of his name is far more complex and personal. Woolf could not fault the Cambridge homosexuals of her own circle, Strachey and Forster or Lowes Dickinson, for their misogyny, but she could attack all they stood for in the name of Oscar Browning.[3]

In a brilliant essay, "Literary Allusion as Feminist Criticism in A Room of One's Own," Alice Fox traces and analyzes Woolf's turning of allusion into a strategy for feminist criticism. She rightly argues that the contemporary educated audience understood and responded to its fundamental feminist attack on patriarchal hegemony over culture, especially in the allusions to Milton, the Manx cat, and the Scots ballad. What I want to suggest here is that allusion or echo cannot function now without the reader's recognition of these allusions and the reader's response. Otherwise, Woolf's horror that she had lost her audience, the "No echo" confided to her diary just before her death, will be true. The critic must help the ghostly echo put on not only a body, but the body she wore in 1928 and 1929. Echo's voice needs both a literary and historical context.

> Talks to Girls
> But my book isn't a book — it
> only talks to girls.
> (Letters 4:102 [to Ethel Sands])

A *Room of One's Own,* two lectures in six chapters, given at Newnham and Girton in October 1928, is, first of all, a feminist subversion of the form of the academic *lecture.* Unschooled herself, Woolf despised lectures, seldom heard one and seldom gave one, except to audiences of women and working men. Several Stephens had lectured here before her. But no romantic old-girl nostalgia for Cambridge Octobers endowed her visit with a sense of carrying on a great tradition, though her grandfather had been a radical in making "Modern History" a field and her father's lectures on eighteenth-century great men were radical with religious doubt and Victorian angst. Her first cousin, Katherine Stephen, Principal of Newnham, had recently died, but I suspect the kinship Woolf felt was to her mystical aunt Caroline Emelia Stephen's informal lectures to young Quaker outsiders—plain, unpretentious, and sincere in their presentation.

In her memoirs, Kathleen Raine[4] describes Woolf's "talks to girls" at Girton. Her vivid recollection is of the presence of Vita Sackville-West with Virginia Woolf descending "like goddesses" with the "divine manna" of their beauty and fame: "In the fairy land of the Girton reception room, then, members of the Literary Society were gathered for coffee, after Hall; young Eton-cropped hair gleaming, Chinese shawls spread like the plumage of butterflies." The walls were embroidered with birds and flowers in wool on ivory satin, and oriental embroidery was draped over the grand piano. So the setting was as seductive as the speech. Despite Woolf's emphasis on the poverty of the women's colleges, the atmosphere was luxuriously feminine and relaxed. The presence of Vita Sackville-West was not only real but symbolic. *Orlando* had just appeared—a lesbian love letter, including photographs of Vita Sackville-West—and it was *not* on trial for obscenity. When Woolf asked the students to check whether Sir Chartres Biron or Sir Archibald Bodkin was not eavesdropping, that they were all women in the room, the obscenity trial for *The Well of Loneliness* was still in progress.[5] The names of the patriarchs, while deliciously fictional in quality, were in fact real. Lesbianism itself was on trial as well as literary free speech, and it was well known that Vita had devoted much energy to organizing support for Radclyffe Hall. The audience would have known of Sir Chartres Biron's role as presiding magistrate in the case, and his refusal to consider "literary merit" as an issue and that Bodkin was director of public prosecutions. In responding to Woolf's command to see that the offending magistrate was not hiding in a cupboard, the audience accepts the plot of the talk, that literary women gathered in a room to discuss women and writing are, at least symbolically, lesbians, and the Law is the enemy. The conspiracy she sets up with her audience is of women in league together against authority.[6] When she told the sad tale of Shakespeare's sister, her audience knew that Radclyffe Hall was descended from Shakespeare's daughter and that the supporters of Hall had tried to use Shakespeare's sonnets as evidence in the trial.[7] Like all great propagandists, Virginia Woolf exploited in her speech the death of a martyr in her cause. That Judith Shakespeare was a fiction did not prevent the audience from seeing her death as a sign of the suppression of lesbianism in the obscenity trial. Judith Shakespeare is certainly the universal figure of the oppressed woman artist, but she was also, in the context of the times, "Radclyffe Hall." The informal "talks to girls" was an antilecture in form, but it also served as discourse of feminist conspiracy— both, one thinks, to connect the nonfeminist lesbians (like Vita Sackville-West and the Radclyffe Hall circle) with women's political cause, and to connect all women with the plight of lesbians. Much of A Room was meant simply to convert her beloved Vita to feminism, its seductive tone an extension of her love letters. By adopting Vita's lesbian cause (see her letter to The Nation, 8 September 1928) in a public lecture, she was seducing Vita into accepting a larger feminism. Appearing with Vita at Girton in October before the final trial (November 9) was a public statement in a way of her own "sapphism." She often felt that she would be "hinted at for a Sapphist" for writing this book, but her appearance with Vita at Girton was more than a hint.

Readers of A Room are part of a conspiracy, that word Woolf used to define "us against them" with her sister in the nursery, with Margaret Llewelyn-Davies and the Cooperative Working Women's Guild. We are all breathing together in the relaxed antiacademic rhythm of her prose. Soon she has us breathing hard (when we realize the exclusion of men from this text and begin to fear their interruption or reprisal)—and then she has us breathing heavily as the erotic nature of her verbal enterprise becomes clear. The Virginia Woolf who gives "talks to girls" harbors, and in this case practices, a powerful and barely disguised desire to seduce. In fact, I would argue that for the woman reader this text is irresistible. I would agree with Sylvia Townsend Warner reading Mrs. Dalloway: "I felt like Joseph resisting Potiphar's wife" (7).

What, then, will we call it when the woman writer seduces the woman reader? I have suggested Sapphistry as a suitable term for this rhetorical seduction. It requires compete mastery of the structure of classical rhetoric to subvert powerlessness, acute consciousness of female otherness and difference to even wish to make maleness other and different. An earnest feminist appeal to political solidarity would not be half so effective as shameless flirtation, Woolf seems to feel. Not only narration but even punctuation is enlisted in her seductive plot: "Chloe liked Olivia. They shared a . . ." Dot dot dot is a female code for lesbian love. The draft of this lecture reveals that before writing "a laboratory," Woolf declared that she "thought of the obscenity trial for a novel." She didn't think much of *The Well of Loneliness* as a work of fiction or truth to female experience. Perhaps her asides and sexual jokes are meant to show Radclyffe Hall a trick or two, how to suggest that women do sometimes like women and avoid both the censor and lugubrious self-pity at the same time.

I turned the page and read . . . I am sorry to break off so abruptly. Are there no men present? Do you promise me that behind that red curtain over there the figure of Sir Chartres Biron is not concealed? We are all women, you assure me? (A *Room* 85)

The question marks and ellipses, to which we supply silent assent and fill in the blanks, seal the pact of our conspiracy. The rest of this flirtatious passage ("Do not start. Do not blush.") asserts as the norm that "women like women."

Woolf's analysis of the style of Mary Carmichael's new novel is also couched in sexual terms. Her style seems to lack a sense of an ending: "To read this writing was like being at sea in an open boat"; "She was 'unhandling' herself as they say in the old plays." Reading *Life's Adventure*, "I feel as one feels on a switchback railway when the car, instead of sinking, as one has been led to expect, swerves up again. Mary is tampering with the expected sequence. First, she broke the sentence; now she has broken the sequence" (85). It is perhaps not necessary to gloss the open boat as the vulva or the rising and falling without a single climax to female orgasm, to see an example of Woolf's usual references to language in sexual terms. As for "unhandling herself," it certainly can be read sexually. But "Unhand me, Sir," is also the cry of the damsel in danger of male violence, from which she rescues herself. The "expected sequence" is the structure of the novel on the model of male sexual experience. When she breaks it, "Up one went, down one sank." "I tried a sentence or two on my tongue" is also extremely suggestive. If Cixous wanted an example of "writing with the body" it is to be found here. If Radclyffe Hall wanted an example of lesbian writing, "the shortest of shorthand, in words that are hardly syllabled yet," it is here. If Mary Carmichael is to "catch those unrecorded gestures, those unsaid or half-said words" of the language of women, "she will need to hold her breath . . ." (88). We are, of course, as breathless as Mary Carmichael at Woolf's daring half-said suggestion that fiction is structured on the model of one's own sexual experience. But she leaves us in no doubt about this in her discussion of nonandrogynous super-male texts, novels of "unmitigated masculinity":

Do what she will, a woman cannot find in them that fountain of perpetual life which the critics assure her is there. It is not only that they celebrate male virtues, enforce male values and describe the world of men; it is that the emotion with which these books are permeated is to a woman incomprehensible. *It is coming, it is gathering, it is about to burst on one's head,* one begins saying long before the end. That picture will fall on old Jolyon's head; he will die of the shock; the old clerk will speak over him two or three obituary words; and all the swans on the Thames will simultaneously burst out singing. But one will rush away before that happens and hide in the gooseberry bushes, for the emotion which is so deep, so subtle, so symbolical to a man moves a woman to wonder. (106)

This passage is not merely amusing. It seems to me that it took great courage to say this on a public platform in 1928. Woolf's next assertion, that the novel of "unmitigated masculinity" leads directly to "the Fascist poem," foreshadows the analysis of the origin of fascism in the patriarchal family in *Three Guineas.* She calls it "a horrid little abortion." Since to Woolf writing is always a sexual act, abortion as the product of male writing is a significant epithet. Then Woolf moves on to her well-known celebration of the androgynous mind of the artist. What I want to point out here is that Woolf's feeling for sexual difference privileges the female and describes the male literary product as a two-headed monster "in a glass jar in a museum in some country town" (107).

Let us look again at the opening pages of *A Room of One's Own.* Woolf identifies herself as a writer of fiction, a "liar"; she invents Oxbridge and Fernham, rejects "I" as unreal, and claims anonymity through the three Marys rather than identity as the descendant of Jane Austen and George Eliot.[8] (Here she outmaneuvers those who would call her a bourgeois feminist literary critic who merely wants to replace the canon of great men with a canon of great women.)

In *A Room of One's Own* the narrator, divested of "Virginia Woolf," then tells us how she sat on a riverbank and looked at the reflections of a "burning tree" and a weeping willow, cast out her line (the image of the woman writer as fisherwoman which she works out later in "Professions for Women"), and caught a thought, too small a fish to keep. "I will not trouble you with that thought now, though if you look carefully you may find it for yourselves in the course of what I am going to say" (5).

By now we are hooked, like her thought, the small fish. We women readers have been tangled in the net of a narrative seduction by the woman writer. A *Room* is not simply a declaration of difference from male writing, but a questioning of the difference within difference. She asks not only how is women's writing different from men's, but who speaks for working-class women? How is the lesbian writer to say "Chloe likes Olivia?" The idea of the androgynous mind of the artist comes directly after the leaf falls, the ambiguous taxi floats the couple downstream, and Woolf expresses her discomfort with notions of sexual opposition and unity. In trying to deal with the maternal imperative, the definition of the feminine as the opposite of the masculine, the imaginary "cooperation of the sexes," Woolf hits on a temporary solution in the idea of androgyny: "Ought not education to bring out and fortify the differences rather than the similarities? For we have too much likeness as it is" (92). Androgyny means erasure of difference. How can she hold both views at once? Androgyny, it becomes clear, is a good idea for overly masculine writers to try, though the opposite does not hold true. That is, the arguments are not logical. She is biased in favor of women. When she says "the book has somehow to be adapted to the body" (81), she means the female body.

How to write in a notebook is the subject of chapter two. The scene has shifted to London's British Museum, a public library which does not reject her as the university library did. The narrator's tone is light and amusing but a "little fish" is thrown out for the students to catch. Explicit instructions are given in how to do research, how to use the card catalogue, and how to collect notes. Her audience is being instructed in how to take her place on the platform and told what questions to pursue as feminist historians. (The difference between lecturer and lectured is erased.) She is no longer standing but sitting—we are all readers and note-takers. Procne is reading Philomel's text; we are reading with her—the original meaning of the word *lecture* is restored. Both admonition and domination have disappeared. She demystifies scholarship but warns women to wear "claws of steel and a beak of brass" to protect us while we work. Later she says, "The history of men's opposition to women's emancipation is more interesting perhaps than the story of that emancipation itself. An amusing book might be made of it if some young student at Girton or Newnham would collect examples and deduce a theory—but she would need thick gloves on her hands, and bars to protect her of solid gold" (57). She is under no illusion about the dangers inherent in feminist history or feminist literary criticism. Before a select audience of women students at Newnham and Girton, she reads aloud the contents of this notebook and the list (28) is a rhetorical device used to great effect. I have often read *A Room of One's Own* as the first modern text in feminist history and literary criticism, concentrating on its instructions and demonstrations of "thinking back through our mothers," finding and evaluating women's works and lives. But I had ignored her simultaneous practice of criticism of male texts, her insistence that her student followers look up the letter M in the British Museum, as well as the letter W, to find out why "women do not write books about men," why women are "so much more interesting to men than men are to women?" (27). The seduction of the woman reader by the writer of *A Room of One's Own* had two purposes: to inculcate sexual solidarity by establishing difference and claiming that difference as superior, and to recruit and enlist a new generation of women in the cause of feminist scholarship. The artist, the historian, and the critic have all been assigned their tasks in the conspiratorial "cell" of our "room." Secrecy has not only been sexually suggestive but politically primary. When we leave these lectures we have particularly pledged ourselves to "write like women." We have been seduced into sisterhood.

The complex naming in *A Room of One's Own* also invites readers to unveil the Sapphic figures half glimpsed as Mary Hamilton and J. H. Virginia Woolf's use of the ballad of the "Four Maries" for her narration of *A Room* has complex roots: her reading of D. Hay Fleming's *Mary Queen of Scots* (1897) during a difficult adolescent period, as Louise de Salvo's research illustrates; the publication of *Orlando;* and the obscenity trial. The ballad of the Queen's Maries was *in fact* based on the story of a Scots lady-in-waiting to Queen Catherine of Russia. *That* Mary Hamilton had a child by Tsar Peter and was hanged. But Woolf would have known the ballad from its attribution in Sir Walter Scott's *Minstrelsy* as a legend of Mary Queen of Scots. Scott took this from John Knox's attack on the queen and her four Maries in his *Monstrous Regiment of Women*. Mary Beaton and

Mary Seton were in reality the queen's handmaidens. Mary Carmichael and Mary Hamilton were not the actual names of the other two, who were Mary Fleming and Mary Livingstone.

There was, however, another historical Mary Hamilton, whose story may have surfaced during the meetings regarding the defense for the Radclyffe Hall trial, which both Virginia and Leonard attended. In 1746, Henry Fielding, novelist and judge, published a pamphlet called *The Female Husband: or, the Surprising History of Mrs. Mary Alias Mr. George Hamilton.* . . . Fielding found her guilty of marriages to three women and ordered her whipped publicly in four market towns in Somerset (Faderman 68). The result of all of these allusions and echoes behind the names of her narrators is a muddle and confusion regarding women that exactly mirrors Woolf's experience in the British Museum as a historian bent on "truth." There is no truth about women. What one finds are comradeship in chastity of the queen's Maries and the equation of pregnancy with death, as in the life of her own Judith Shakespeare. The cross-dressing of Mary and her maids, including their ability to ride and hunt, was also important, and this, as well as Shakespeare's heroines, contributed to *Orlando*.

A Room of One's Own has another echo of *The Well of Loneliness*, which Angela Ingram points out. The Fernham passage where Jane Harrison appears like a phantom ends an excited description, in denial of the "fact" that it was fall, of the spring garden, dim and intense "as if the scarf which the dusk had flung over the garden were torn asunder by star or sword— the flash of some terrible reality leaping, as its way is, out of the heart of the spring. For youth—."[9] This echoes chapter 38 of *The Well* and its love scene in the dim, sweet garden "and something in the quality of Mary's youth, something terrible and ruthless as an unsheathed sword, would leap out at such moments and stand between them." The star or sword that tears the veil to reveal the leaping reality could be read in many ways. Here it is a reference to the lesbian novel. For not only did Chloe like Olivia, Jane Harrison liked Hope Mirrlees, and they appear to have shared more than their research on the mythology of Russian bears. Surely some of the Cambridge audience would have thought of Harrison in this connection as well as for her great and pioneering role as a scholar.

Although Jane Harrison is given her full name later in the text, here in this emotional passage she is not only ghostly in body but her name is reduced to initials. The use of initials in this text is as complex as the narrative Marys and the ellipses. The absences indicated by anonymity and unsaid words reflect woman's absence from history, but they are also sexually suggestive of women's love of women. We note that "Professor von X" suggests professional misogyny; the von suggests the aristocracy and also plays on England's ambivalent attitude toward Germany between the wars. Mr. A, the novelist, and Mr. B, the critic, lose some of their power over us by their reduction to initials. The absence of their whole names, unlike women's absences, tends to equalize them with women. Robbed of their fame, they intimidate us less as A or B or "old Professor Z." It may be a coincidence that the men are designated by letters at the beginning and the end of the alphabet, but it does make them somehow terminal, and unreal, suggesting a solid chunk of reality in between. By naming them in such a truncated way, she is also verbally castrating them in a sense, even as Mary Carmichael is fully named in the text as the imaginary novelist. The Marys, with their suggestion of maidenhood and anonymous disguise, are Woolf's literary ladies-in-waiting. She is having a fling as the slightly Sapphist author of *Orlando,* queen of the literary world at least for a day, and a "figure" to the students. She is also capitalizing on the obscenity trial for a lesbian novel in a book about women's writing, forever linking the two subjects in her pages.

The rhetorical strategies of *A Room of One's Own* construct an erotic relationship among the woman writer, her audience present in the text, and the woman reader. In the holograph draft notes for *A Room of One's Own* after "Chloe liked Olivia. They shared a . . ." Woolf wrote:

The words covered the bottom of the page; the pages had stuck. While fumbling to open them there flashed into my mind the inevitable policeman . . . the order to attend the Court, the dreary waiting; the Magistrate coming in with a little bow . . . for the Prosecution, for the Defense—the verdict; this book is obscene + flames sing, perhaps on Tower Hill, as they compound (?) that mass of paper. Here the paper came apart. Heaven be praised! It was only a laboratory. Chloe-Olivia. They were engaged in mincing liver, apparently a cure for pernicious anemia. (Monks House Papers, B.6)

Woolf feels fearful and complicitous with the author of *The Well of Loneliness.* The paper of her own pages is singed by the flames that burn the banned book.

The brilliance of *A Room of One's Own* lies in its invention of a female language to subvert the languages of the patriarchy. Like her novels, it is about reading and it trains us to read as women. Its tropes figure new reading and writing strategies, enlisting punctuation in the service of feminism with the use of ellipses for encoding female desire, the use of initials and dashes to make absent figures more present and transforming *interruption,* the condition of the woman writer's oppression, as in the citations to Jane Austen's experience, into a deliberate strategy as a sign of woman's writing. The narrator of *A Room* continually interrupts herself. In following the interrupted text, the reader reproduces the female experience of being interrupted and joins Woolf in making interrupted discourse a positive female form. The tyranny of the interrupter is forgotten as the woman writer interrupts herself. I began by insisting on the contextualization of *A Room of One's Own* as historically the last series of women's suffrage pamphlets. I will end by suggesting that the literary strategy of interruption was intended to transform a feminist political strategy which truly voiced women's rebellion at enforced silence into a literary trope which captures the radicalism of the movement in a classic tribute.

In her deliberate marriage of *A Room of One's Own* to *The Well of Loneliness,* Woolf's narrative strategy of intertextuality with a banned and "obscene" lesbian novel is a political effort to keep lesbian texts in print, if only by allusion. She wins her "room" only to share it.[10]

The critical task which Woolf leaves us is the incorporation of the lost and banned books of the other into the canon of the read. *The Well* is at the center of Evadne Price's *Not So Quiet . . . ,* published under the pseudonym of Helen Zenna Smith in 1930 and now reprinted by the Feminist Press. It seems to me to be a deliberate attempt to counter the romantic story of lesbian ambulance drivers in World War I with a lesbian-bashing scene calculated to reconnect the collusion between motherhood and war. The story is continued in Rosemary Manning's powerful novel *The Chinese Garden* (1962), set in an English girls' school in 1928, where veterans of women's war work expel the readers of *The Well of Loneliness* from a school where masculine values prevail. The teachers are lesbians who ban lesbianism and its books. To continue the project of *A Room* is to read these texts together, to see that their intertextuality constitutes a countertradition of double difference within difference in the historical construction of gender identity. What a difference this tale makes in the reading of modern British fiction.

NOTES

The editors of this volume have condensed the argument and removed the digressions from my study of the narrative strategies in A Room of One's Own. The argument locates lesbianism in the reader. See "Sapphistry: Narration as Lesbian Seduction" in my Virginia Woolf and the Languages of Patriarchy.

1. See Dickson, 132 and 71. An analysis of the tone of this book would yield interesting results. Dickson creates sadomasochistic love scenes without supporting evidence to titillate an audience, one assumes, of male readers. He insinuates that lesbianism was somehow responsible for England's naval problems in World War I, when searching for a reason for Admiral Troubridge's failure to pursue the German fleet. Had his sex life been in order, the admiral, we are asked to believe, would have followed orders. Dickson says that he cannot believe Lady Troubridge's story that her aversion to her husband coincided with his syphilis. See also Rebecca West's review of Dickson's book (London Telegraph, 27 July 1975). See also Letters 3: 487 (27 April 1928) where Woolf wrote to Vita Sackville-West "I rang you up just now, to find you were gone nutting in the woods with Mary Campbell, or Mary Carmichael or Mary Seton, but not me. . . ."

2. Humphries's reading does not see Echo outside of her relation to Narcissus. For a feminist reading of the myth, see Greenberg. Greenberg uses the myth to explain a non-Oedipal female textuality where the relationship of the reader to the texts is seen in the same terms. "If the text can come to be seen as a locus of processes, as speaking itself, then it can cease being represented by and occupying the political position of dead women. It will no longer be open to critical or creative dominance. . . . Instead, domination or mastery of the text must disappear as a political necessity of criticism" (302).

3. The relation of women to male homosexuals and of homosexuals to women deserves further discussion. Jeffrey Weeks in Coming Out and in his fine essay in The Making of the Modern Homosexual actually does discuss the other important issue, that of class, as well as the social construction of homosexual in Britain. The field is a young one, of course, and it is to be expected that homosexuals of the late nineteenth and early twentieth centuries should appear heroic to their historians. But what concerns me here is that for women like Virginia Woolf, the homosexual men of Cambridge and Bloomsbury appeared to be not the suffering victims of heterosexual social prejudice, but the intellectual aristocracy itself, an elite with virtual hegemony over British culture. E. M. Forster, Lytton Strachey, Goldsworthy Lowes Dickinson, and their friends were misogynist in their lives as well as their writing. Virginia Woolf, already exacerbated by her own sense of sexual difference was, I think, confused and disturbed by the woman-hating of her male homosexual friends, and this is the origin of that difficult passage in A Room of One's Own on Oscar Browning, which appears to be uncharacteristically intolerant in a writer who produced so

many sympathetic portraits of homosexuals in her fiction. See my *Virginia Woolf and the Languages of Patriarchy* for more on Oscar Browning.

4. Kathleen Raine's memoirs (from *The Land Unknown*) are reprinted in *Virginia Woolf Miscellany* 10 (Spring and Summer 1978). I am indebted to Catherine Smith for pointing this out. Woolf's lecture at Newnham was perceived quite differently according to the memoirs published in *A Newnham Anthology*, ed. Ann Phillips. E. E. Duncan-Jones, the first woman to write for *Granta*, recalled that I. A. Richards told her that the master of Madgalene vowed to vote for the most "masculine" poem submitted anonymously for the Chancellor's Prize. Since women were not allowed to wear academic dress because they weren't members of the university, she was going to appear in the Senate House in a flounced summer dress until her tutor talked her out of it. She claims that the notorious dinner was ruined because Virginia Woolf was late *and* she had unexpectedly brought her husband. She found Woolf "formidable" and only remembered from her talk high praise of Stella Gibson's poem, "The Hippogriff." When *A Room* appeared, she found the exposé of the poverty of the women's colleges "disquieting." U. K. M. Stevenson recalled the joy of having a room of her own, where she served biscuits and coffee to Virginia Woolf and the students after her talk. Her room was where

> Virginia Woolf stood and sat, and looked and spoke . . . fixing me with that wonderful gaze, at once luminous and penetrating, what she actually said was, "I'd no idea the young ladies of Newnham were so beautifully dressed." The prig in me was chagrined, even if my vanity sat up and purred; but over the years what has persisted has been the quality of her look, which seemed to say so much more than the words that came with it. The look held a hint of a smile, a hint of compassion, but it was above all an absolutely ruthless look; my pretty frock was no proof against it. (Phillips, 173)

My thanks to Martha Vicinus for pointing out these passages.

5. See Woolf, *Diaries* 3: 206, also 193 for her letter to *The Nation* about the trial. Woolf thought *The Well of Loneliness* was a "meritorious dull book" but joined vigorously in the protest at its suppression. Possibly she felt guilty that she had escaped the censors with her own comic treatment of sexuality in *Orlando*. Note that Victoria Glendinning in *Vita* (London: Weidenfeld and Nicolson, 1983) minimizes Sackville-West's role in the defense of Radclyffe Hall.

6. Her diary (3:200) describes Girton's "starved but valiant young women," and she regrets that all "the splendour, all the luxury of life" is lavished on the male students, not the women. "I felt elderly & mature. And nobody respected me. They were very eager, egotistical, or rather not much impressed by age & repute" (201). She worried that her strong desire "to write a history, say of Newnham or the women's movement" in the sparkling vein of *Orlando* might have been "stimulated by applause" (203). But Desmond Macarthy annoyed her:

> And the egotism of men surprises & shocks me even now. Is there a woman of my acquaintance who could sit in my arm chair from 3 to

6:30 without the semblance of a suspicion that I may be busy, or tired, or bored; and so sitting could talk, grumbling & grudging, of her difficulties, worries; then eat chocolates, then read a book, & go at last, apparently self-complacent & wrapped in a kind of blubber of misty self satisfaction? Not the girls at Newnham or Girton. They are far too spry; far too disciplined. None of that self confidence is their lot. (204) She recalls how relieved her student hostesses were when she and Vita paid for their dinner "and they showed us the chocolate coloured corridors of Girton, like convent cells."

7. Virginia Woolf attended the trial on November 9 and described Sir Chartres Biron as a "debonair and distinguished magistrate," "like a Harley St. specialist investigating a case. All black & white, tie pin, clean shaven, was coloured & carved, in that light, like ivory" (*Diaries* 3; 206–7). She was impressed by the law as "a very remarkable fence between us and barbarity. . . . What is obscenity? What is literature?" and relieved that she did not have to testify. She met Lady Troubridge, whom she had known as a child, and "John" (Radclyffe Hall) whom she described as "lemon yellow, tough, stringy, exacerbated." It is testimony to her principles that she was there and ready to testify on behalf of a novel and a novelist whom she disliked personally but defended politically. She Angela Ingram's "Unutterable Putrefaction and Foul Stuff: Two Obscene Novels of the 1920s," *Women's International Forum* 9 (1986): 341–54.

8. Alice Fox has argued that Woolf omits the fourth Mary of the ballad, Mary Hamilton, because, unlike other victims, she was betrayed by a woman. Nelly Furman, in a provocative essay (*"A Room of One's Own:* Reading Absence," in *Women's Language and Style,* ed. Douglas Butturff and Edmund L. Epstein. Studies in Contemporary Language No. 1, Department of English, University of Akron) points out that "the disappearance of the subject," her death, is the theme of the Scottish ballad that forms Woolf's collective voice. Mary Hamilton, who is the actual speaker of "Once there were four Marys," in the song, is indeed absent from Woolf's text. She died on the gallows for killing an unwanted child, like Judith Shakespeare who commits suicide when she is pregnant. *A Room* does point out that few great women artists had children. Perhaps Woolf is not only claiming anonymity by being Mary Whatshername, but also speaks *for* the absent Mary Hamilton as she speaks *for* Judith Shakespeare.

9. See Ingram. In 1912 Virginia Woolf wrote to Lytton Strachey anticipating the Cambridge performance of Walter Headlam's Greek play "afterwards *in the dusk, in the college garden,* with Jane Harrison to make proclamation, we have the tragedy from start to finish" (*Letters* 1; 498). Woolf supposedly contributed to Walter Headlam's translation of the *Agamemnon.* It would be interesting to compare her translation (in the Berg Collection, unpublished) with his.

10. By incorporating allusions to *The Well of Loneliness* in *A Room of One's Own,* Virginia Woolf "lifts the ban" on the lesbian novel. She resurrects *The Well* from its cultural state-imposed "death" under the ban of obscenity. She brings Radclyffe Hall, her novel and the trial into literature forever in a narrative

strategy calculated to emphasize that the privacy of the woman writer's room is in fact collective and not private at all, since the company she keeps there includes the ghosts of all the women writers before her and the presence of Radclyffe Hall and others like her who have been censored by canonical patriarchy. Woolf gives Hall's novel classical status as the work of "Shakespeare's sister," and routs the enemies of free speech by reducing Sir Archibald Bodkin and Sir Chartres Biron to comic idiots. The fantastic and comic play of her text as in the drama of "Chloe liked Olivia . . ." locates lesbianism securely in the lap of the reader (not in the text) and so thumbs its nose at the judges in the obscenity trial who cannot arrest us all for reading as lesbians. Politically, Judith Shakespeare and Stephen Gordon are linked by their inability to escape from the ideological and biological imperative of the reproduction of mothering.

WORKS CITED

Dickson, Lovat. *Radclyffe Hall at the Well of Loneliness: A Sapphic Chronicle.* New York: Scribners, 1975.

Faderman, Lillian. *Scotch Verdict: Miss Pirie and Miss Woods v. Dame Cumming Gordon.* New York: Quill, 1983.

Fox, Alice. "Literary Allusion as Feminist Criticism in *A Room of One's Own.*" *Philological Quarterly* (Spring 1984): 145–61.

Greenberg, Caren. "Reading Reading: Echo's Abduction of Language." In *Women and Language in Literature and Society.* Ed. Sally McConnell-Ginet, Ruth Borker, and Nelly Furman. New York: Praeger, 1980. 300–309.

Hall, Radclyffe. *The Well of Loneliness.* 1928. Rpt. New York: Comici Friede, 1930.

Humphries, Jefferson. "Haunted Words or Deconstruction Echoed." *diacritics* (Summer 1983): 29–38.

Ingram, Angela. "Unutterable Putrefaction and Foul Stuff: Two Obscene Novels of the 1920s." Paper delivered at South Central Modern Language Association, Tulsa, Okla., 1985.

Manning, Rosemary. *The Chinese Garden.* 1962. Rpt. London: Brilliance, 1984.

Marcus, Jane. *Virginia Woolf and the Languages of Patriarchy.* Bloomington: Indiana Univ. Press, 1987.

Monks House Papers. The Virginia Woolf Manuscripts from the Monks House Papers at the University of Sussex. Brighton, England: Harvester Press Microform Publications, 1985.

Phillips, Ann, ed. *A Newnham Anthology.* Cambridge: Cambridge Univ. Press, 1979.

The Radclyffe Hall Obscenity Trial Papers. Harry Ransom Humanities Research Center, University of Texas, Austin.

Smith, Helen Zenna. *Not So Quiet . . .* New York: Feminist, 1989.

Warner, Sylvia Townsend. *Letters.* Ed. William Maxwell. New York: Viking, 1982.

Woolf, Virginia. *The Diaries of Virginia Woolf.* Ed. Anne Olivier Bell, 5 vols. New York: Harcourt, 1977–84.

———. *The Letters of Virginia Woolf.* Ed. Nigel Nicholson and Joanne Trautman. 6 vols. New York: Harcourt, 1975–80.

———. *A Room of One's Own.* New York: Harcourt, 1929.

PART III

Lesbian Themes, Sources

TWELVE

Expatriate Sapphic Modernism: Entering Literary History

Shari Benstock

Only a decade ago, the exploration of *Sapphic modernism* would not have been possible. The titles of two 1979 publications by Blanche Wiesen Cook link the reasons behind that impossibility: "The Historical Denial of Lesbianism" and " 'Women Alone Stir My Imagination': Lesbianism and the Cultural Tradition." The denial of all forms of lesbian experience, including artistic and aesthetic experiences, and the suppression of lesbianism by and within history have defined it as an excluded Other within cultural tradition. Virginia Woolf, for instance, has only rather recently gained admission to the modernist canon, where her status rests primarily on experiments in "stream of consciousness" narrative method. She has not yet been accorded full status with T. S. Eliot, James Joyce, and Ezra Pound as one of the "giants" of modernism. Were the critics who confer canonization to take seriously Cook's claim that Woolf's imagination was fueled by Sapphic erotic power, they would be forced to redefine modernism in ways that acknowledge its Sapphic elements. If this erotic power were theorized as Sapphic modernism, as Cook claims is possible for Woolf (1979), as Susan Lanser does for Djuna Barnes (1979), as Susan Friedman and Rachel Blau DuPlessis do for H. D. (1981), and as Catharine Stimpson has done for Gertrude Stein (1977), it could profoundly change not only our notions about modernist art, but also redefine the erotic in relation to the creative sources for all art. Cook claimed in 1979 that "we have just begun to name our own world and to consider the full implications of women's friendships and the crucial role played by female networks of love and support, the sources of strength that enabled independent, creative, and active women to function" ("Cultural Tradition" 720). Within modernist studies our efforts to "name our own world" have met with (mostly silent) resistance. While many scholars have accepted feminist remappings of modernism in

London, Paris, New York, and Berlin, few believe that our work offers serious challenges to the theoretical and critical definitions of modernism. That is, we may have proven that there were Sapphists who wrote, but our claims for Sapphic modernism are open to question.

Modernism is itself a disputed terrain. Within this past decade the modernist cultural construct created by literary historians and critics has begun to crack under pressure from poststructuralists, semioticians, social historians, and theorists of mass culture. There is tremendous debate these days regarding definitions of modernism, but as Bonnie Scott acknowledges in her introduction to *The Gender of Modernism,* this activity in modernist studies is still primarily devoted to canonical male authors.[1] That is, this work starts from a knowledge of who the great modernists are (or were), even if it is not possible to say what modernism is (or was). Scholarly discussions of these issues further compound critical confusions: in the past decade the differences among modernism, postmodernism, and the avant-garde have been argued from a variety of theoretical viewpoints, but we still understand these terms—and the artistic movements they presumably describe—only very imprecisely. Perhaps most troublesome to scholars of English-language literature is the notion of *Modernity,* an umbrella term associated with French theories of art that denotes the range of twentieth-century "postrealist" cultural-artistic movements.

Most disturbing to me, however, is the absence of feminist work that comes to definitional terms with modernism as an aesthetic-cultural-historical concept. Feminist studies have had enormous impact on the field of modernist scholarship, rewriting history and restoring women's lives and texts, but they have avoided any direct confrontation with the conceptual categories of modernism.[2] In this chapter I suggest why we can no longer "map" modernism without mapping its conceptual definitions and founding assumptions, especially the political and artistic divisions evident in conservative, Anglophilic *high modernism* and the internationally-based and politically fragmented "avant-garde" movements of the early twentieth century. The relationships of these groups within modernity or to postmodernism are beyond the scope of this essay, but they certainly need greater study, especially by feminist critics. To avoid these questions, however, is to risk being "edited out" of the current modernist debate, much as the work of Sapphic modernists has been excluded. We have posed the question "Was there a modernism for women?" without asking "What was modernism?"[3] The attempt to define Sapphic modernism cannot elude these earlier questions, especially as it seeks to discover the relations among gender, sexual orientation, and creativity. A better question might be: how many (female) modernisms were there?

SERIOUS AND PLAYFUL

Yes its [sic] done—Orlando—begun on 8th October, as a joke; & now rather too long for my liking. It may fall between stools, be too long for a joke, & too frivolous for a serious book. (Virginia Woolf, *Diaries* 3:177)

Admitting the overwhelming difficulties in postulating Sapphic modernism—that we lack the necessary textual information, that theories of creativity remain speculative at best, that we are saddled with inadequate definitions of modernism and restrictive notions of lesbianism—let us begin. In general, we can distinguish between those women of the London and Paris communities whose writings followed traditional models of form and style, but whose subject matter was Sapphism (Radclyffe Hall's *The Well of Loneliness* is a well-known example, as is Colette's *The Pure and the Impure*), and those writers who filtered the lesbian content of their writing through the screen of presumably heterosexual subject matter or behind experimental literary styles (Virginia Woolf, Gertrude Stein, H. D.). Sapphic modernism, however, wore many necessary and elaborate disguises, making it almost impossible for the literary historian to categorize and group its various occurrences.[4] What happens, for instance, if we divide these works between the "traditional" and the "experimental," and—following Woolf's comments about *Orlando*—between the "serious" and the "playful"?

Immediately we realize how difficult and risky this venture is. Modernism presumably constituted a break with traditional forms—a serious break—and high modernism, like the High Church Anglicanism of its conservative party leader, T. S. Eliot, took itself very seriously. On the other side of this great divide, modernist experimentation admitted no "play" whatsoever. The business of "making it new" (the slogan of the other camp leader, Ezra Pound) was no joking matter: the future of culture and civilization rested on it. Indeed, the term *play* suggests to a contemporary ear another kind of serious business, the free play of the signifier within the bounded field of signification postulated by deconstruction and Lacanian psychoanalytic theory. This division of the textual body appears to reinforce destructive binary oppositions and hierarchical power structures: "playful" = "not-to-be-taken-seriously."

Moreover, this division overlooks the ways modernism constructed itself on a political agenda of exclusion—the exclusion of the Other. There are two pulsations that direct modernism: one is the urge toward polarities and oppositions (the proclamation of an adversary culture); the second is the effort to separate art from history (the proclamation of artistic autonomy).[5] In fact, these pulsations are the same, and they lead to high modernism, which justifies continuity, and exclusivity, in literary traditions. A different kind of modernism, what I call avant-garde modernism (the excluded Other), announces itself as a rupture, a break with the past, and marks a cultural-historical shift. Texts that belong to avant-garde modernism are sometimes written by "high modernists" (Joyce's *Finnegans Wake*, Pound's *Pisan Cantos*, perhaps Eliot's *Four Quartets*), but often avant-garde works are entirely excluded by high modernism. A large number of highly experimental works are produced by woman-identified writers: Djuna Barnes, H. D., Gertrude Stein, and Virginia Woolf.

Where, for instance, does one place Djuna Barnes's work in such a scheme? *Nightwood,* according to T. S. Eliot a work of "a creative order," employs traditional methods of plotting and characterization, but shadows its serious study of cultural and social repression behind archaic language. *Nightwood*'s richly anachronistic language is its modernist "signature." *Ladies Almanack,* described as a "slight satiric wigging" by its author (who signs herself "A Lady of Fashion") belongs to no recognizable literary genre and employs richly arcane and anachronistic language (Foreword, n.p.). Of the two works, the *Almanack* is stylistically the more experimental ("outrageous" by high modernist standards) and is no less socially and sexually complex for its satire. Indeed, the satire cuts both ways: the *Almanack* addresses a small and select audience of lesbians well known to Barnes (members of Natalie Clifford Barney's salon), but the attitudes supporting its satire belong to the modernist mainstream, which in general hated Sapphism and in particular resented the wealth and leisure of this group. If *Nightwood* carefully conceals the psychosexual premises on which it establishes its social-cultural critique, *Ladies Almanack* reveals Barnes's enormous ambivalence about the sexual and social privilege it satirizes. By describing this work as a "slight satiric wigging," however, its anonymous author protected herself against reprisals both from her male modernist colleagues and from Barney's group. She also insured that the *Almanack* would not be taken seriously.

Fear of contamination is the founding premise of modernism, and as

Andreas Huyssen remarks, the movement operates under the sign of this anxiety (vii). It is ironic, of course, that modernism was unable to recognize itself in *Nightwood*, which exposes the "depravity" under the bedrock of culture. It was only able to recognize the "Otherness" of *Nightwood* and not to see its own relation to that Otherness. Despite Eliot's laudatory introduction to the text, *Nightwood* has for years been a cult item, never legitimated by canonized modernism: indeed, Eliot's introduction suggests the ways high modernism was unable to read Barnes's text, blinded to the truth of its representation. From first sentence to last Eliot announces his own reading deficiencies: "What I would leave the reader prepared to find is the great achievement of a *style*, the *beauty* of phrasing, the *brilliance* of wit and characterisation, and a *quality of horror* and doom very nearly related to that of Elizabethen tragedy" (xvi, emphasis added). Eliot could not determine its generic boundaries, saying that it would "appeal primarily to readers of poetry" (xi) but also claiming that it was not "poetic prose" (xii). If its genre was in question so was its gender, to which Eliot—struggling against his own latent homosexuality and concomitant homophobia—was blinded. *Ladies Almanack* raises these same questions in the extreme, even as it mocks the premises on which they rest: to what degree was Djuna Barnes's art sexually ambivalent, shuttling between homophobia and lesbian desire, between cultural conservatism and artistic experiment?

If we think of the distinctions between high and avant-garde modernisms less in terms of their formal properties, aesthetic purity, or artistic programs, and distinguish them instead in terms of address (the place from which they speak to the audiences they hoped to engage), we might better be able to suggest the reasons why some lesbian writers of the period embraced Sapphic modernism and others fled from it. We could also remap the ground on which modernism staged its claims. I would argue that *Nightwood* and *Ladies Almanack* address quite separate audiences and that their creative powers come from different places within Barnes. This is a rather obvious comment: *Nightwood* invokes the underside of high modernism while *Ladies Almanack* is addressed to the women who are themselves the subjects of its satire—the *Almanack* holds up a cracked looking glass in place of Lady Fashion's mirror.[6] What is not as obvious is the position from which each of these texts speaks: *Nightwood* examines the cultural unconscious from a belief in conscious artistic control (one of the reasons this text has been so widely misread, even by feminists). Barnes positioned herself as a "modernist," believing in the powers of the conscious mind and the ability of the modernist writer to control and direct the text. *Ladies Almanack*, however, speaks not only to a different audience but from a different place—it speaks from the unconscious as it *ruptures* the cultural text.[7] The *Almanack* speaks from the other side of the psychosexual fault line: it crosses the "double-cross" of the Sapphic boundary. In so doing, it relinquishes the power of cultural control over the text, letting the text "speak itself" as the writer retracts the psychic fissures.

I use the term *fault line* here and elsewhere to call attention to revised understandings of the ways our minds work. In the early years of modernism, following Freud's discoveries of the unconscious and Jung's work on the "collective unconscious," differences between the conscious and unconscious were often described in spatial terms: the conscious mind was conceived as existing at a higher plane than the unconscious, which was located at the dark "bottom" of our psyches. Virginia Woolf often speaks of fishing up an idea from the depths; Matthew O'Connor describes himself as that which crawls out from under a rock when it is moved. The conscious mind is defined as light and reason, the unconscious mind as the dark and irrational. These are the terms of *Nightwood*'s moral dialectic. But we know from Jacques Lacan's work that the spatial divisions of upper and lower psyches and the division of spheres into rational/irrational, light/dark are incorrect—or, rather, entirely metaphorical. According to Lacan the conscious and unconscious minds cannot be separated from each other; they are not distinct spheres but interlocking structures. Each is essential to the existence of the other: without the unconscious, there could be no conscious; the unconscious is the culturally excluded Other necessary to the existence of culture. This description, indeed, retraces a major theme of *Nightwood*—the relation of culture to cultural repression.

The unconscious, which Lacan claims is "structured like a language," cannot speak directly. Yet its workings pattern our individual usages of the symbolic system of language. Moreover, the unconscious takes up a sexual position, which initiates our entrance into the cultural-symbolic and determines our place in it (Mitchell and Rose, 28–57). My use of the term *fault line* is an effort to suggest this structural relation, which is marked in a pattern of cracks and fissures, evidence of the cultural imprint that the unconscious constantly unsettles and undermines. Sexuality is itself structured along this fault line, and language reveals the psychosexual positioning by either tracing its contours or attempting (however "unconsciously") to erase its patterns. In highly conscious forms of writing, such as modernism claimed to be, linguistic structures trace and erase the psychosexual contours in a single gesture. Djuna Barnes's works are excellent examples of this double inscription, which reveal the fissured patterns of her sexual ambivalence. In *Nightwood,* the cultural-social "Other" is characterized by sexual, political, cultural, and racial "deviancy," for which the text offers many examples. The psychosexual Other of the text, however, is found in its writing—its use of tropes and images, which are themselves the disguises of the unconscious. In giving expression to the cultural and personal violence that are the effects of repression, *Nightwood* reinscribes its most oppressive elements—the repressed returns with a vengeance.

Ladies Almanack presumably speaks delight, pleasure, laughter—what in poststructuralist terms is called *jouissance*—and yet this text displays a disturbing otherness, the otherness of the cultural norm that recognizes its Other only in fear or mockery. The *Almanack*'s distinguishing feature may be the effort to mask its fear of the image of its (unconscious) sexuality in the looking glass through wit and word play. Again, the Other is revealed in writing practices that appear to belong to *écriture féminine*, a writing that stays as close to the unconscious as possible and that produces jokes, puns, slippages of grammar, and rhetorical and lexical extravagances. It risks falling *inside* oppositions, where the difference between laughter and tears, anger and love can no longer be differentiated. This writing constantly (but not consistently) retraces sexual desire as linguistic excess.[8] Whereas *Nightwood* shines a cold light on the fear of alternative sexualities and the force of their repression, *Ladies Almanack* skates along the sexual-cultural lines that divide the acceptable from the outrageous. The risk of this writing should not be underestimated, nor should its energy, which turns on the terms of (sexual) address, be overlooked: there is no address *other than* the sexual in the *Almanack*. The Sapphic spirit that Evangeline Musset (Natalie Clifford Barney) courts and whose collective creative energies she encourages regulate the seasons of this *Almanack* and direct its "speaking in tongues."

IMAGINATION AND IDENTITY

We travel far in thought, in imagination or in the realm of memory. (H. D., *Tribute to Freud* 35)

But what of Virginia Woolf's concerns, noted earlier, that *Orlando*—a "biography" of her lover, Vita Sackville-West—was "a joke"? What is the difference between a "joke" and a "serious book"? Or between Djuna Barnes's "satiric" almanack and Woolf's "joke" biography? Do these jokes that mix up genders and genres have something to do with bisexuality? Djuna Barnes, in later life, denied a woman-loving center to her psyche (Field 201). Virginia Woolf lived her adult life as a middle-class married woman, but her sexual and creative responses were to women, who "stirred" her imagination. For H. D., however, the difference between sexual genders and literary genres was no joke. She was determined to understand the unsettledness of her own sexual identity; further, she explored with Freud the relation of what he called her "perfect bisexuality" to her writing (Guest 209). H. D. feared that the visions of writing she saw projected on a wall in Corfu were the workings of an artist's mind "got out of hand, gone too far, a 'dangerous symptom' " (*Tribute to Freud* 51). Like Woolf, H. D. feared expression of the unconscious.

If we trace the workings of sexual identity through these women's writings, we find ourselves retracing psychosexual fissures. The place of address shifts from text to text, as we have already seen in Barnes's work. In H. D., the place of address is located in separate genres (in general, her poetry speaks from the position of heterosexuality and her prose from the position of lesbianism). For Woolf, the Sapphic disrupts address and shifts the terms of narrative development in texts that appear to speak from the cultural position of heterosexuality. The works that speak from the Sapphic (for example, *Orlando, A Room of One's Own, Three Guineas, Between the Acts*) revise both genre and gender. These are works rarely included in Woolf's "modernist" canon, which is limited to *To the Lighthouse* and *Mrs. Dalloway; The Waves* constitutes her officially sanctioned "post-modernist" contribution. It is true that Woolf's writing has been rather consistently misread by male critics, but this is particularly true of the works that "speak from the Sapphic." Commenting on *A Room of One's Own,* Jane Marcus explains that this happens because "the male reader is forced to deny the superiority of his gender if he is to read . . . sympathetically" (*Languages* 159). In this text, Woolf's "Sapphistry" shifts the place of enunciation, the forms of address, the subjects of that address, *and* resituates the reader as a (Sapphic) woman. Marcus also argues that Woolf demonstrates in *A Room* a poetics of interruption, instances of a break with the cultural past, achieved here by reinscribing the cultural tyranny of interruption into a strategy of women's writing. I would add that Woolf's

"Sapphic" texts are themselves interruptions in her oeuvre, moments where sexual difference leads to a poetics of difference.

We see in Woolf's Sapphic practices a radical re-formation of language. Signaling such changes are very particular uses of grammatical forms and conventions of punctuation that alter the syntax and rhythm of these texts. For Jane Marcus, these features belong to a "female language" whose "tropes figure new reading and writing strategies, enlisting punctuation in the service of feminism with the use of ellipses for encoding female desire, the use of initials and dashes to make absent figures more present and transforming interruption . . . into a deliberate strategy as a sign of woman's writing" (*Languages* 187). These discoveries are crucial to an understanding of Woolf's writing methods and to women's contribution to modernism. They also hold the potential for moving feminist theory beyond its concerns with representation-of-woman-as-figure to the analysis of the structural terms of figuration itself. Marcus shadows forth a poetics of figuration whose terms are nonrepresentational and which mark the failure of representation.

Woolf's radical revisions of syntax and punctuation point to a truth within linguistic structures: representation is always premised on the loss of that which cannot be represented. In general, feminist criticism has overlooked this truth, having necessarily fixed its attention on images of women in film, literature, and art—images that support phallocentric notions of the "feminine" and deny women strength, energy, courage, and possibilities beyond the heterosexual script. Virginia Woolf, however, directs our eyes elsewhere, to places in her texts where representation inscribes its failure. The ellipsis is one figure of unrepresentability within Woolf's writing, as Jane Marcus and, more recently, Rachel Bowlby have observed. Both *A Room of One's Own* and *Three Guineas* are broken by ellipses, which serve as rhetorical figures and grammatical functions—they leave "something to be understood." In grammar, the figure of the ellipsis refers to the omission of one or more words in a sentence whose presence is required to complete the grammatical construction or fully express the sense. The rhetorical sense of ellipsis comes from ellipse, a "noun of action," whereas in geometrical figures the shape is constituted by a "falling short." An elliptical is therefore made up of curved planes, ovals, or circles, which are created by deviations from the straight line and which curve back. In both the grammatical and rhetorical senses of the term, the ellipse figures an absence, a fault, a defect: it marks the impossibility of figurability and the failure of representation. As such, it serves to figure woman-in-culture, where she denotes absence (of the phallic signifier), silence, and nonpresence. Woolf's texts, which elliptically interlock with each other, turn these figures and tropes inside out (the turning is always signaled by ellipses) so that "deviation" constitutes a new form of structure. I believe that this form of grammatical-rhetorical "deviation" figures not merely the experimental or avant-garde, but the Sapphic.

The ellipsis is an example of a structural term that is unread and unheard in the text: we are trained as readers to "skip over" it, and as writers (often) to take ellipses, dashes, and other marks of punctuation for granted. Demonstrating such instances in Woolf's text, Marcus shows *A Room* to be an echo chamber, one of whose "unverbalized allusions" is to Radclyffe Hall's *The Well of Loneliness,* a text that silently modulates Woolf's writing. Hall's "Sapphic Chronicle" has always been praised for the courage of its political convictions, but never (to my knowledge) for attributes inherent to Woolf's modernist writing—its literary style, psychological subtlety, artistic innovation, and tropic complexity. Indeed, on these scores, *The Well* has always been something of an embarrassment. Is it ludicrous to suppose that *The Well* served Woolf as wellspring for arguably the most brilliant examples of her creativity—*A Room* (1929) and *Orlando* (1928, published exactly one month before the obscenity trial of *The Well of Loneliness* began)? Marcus thinks not, and I agree with her. For it was precisely the style and tone of *Orlando*—a joke not to be taken too seriously —that allowed Woolf to escape the public censure brought against Radclyffe Hall. Writing in her diary on Saturday, 10 November 1928, the day following the Bow Street trial, Woolf commented: "What is obscenity? What is literature? What is the difference between the subject & the treatment?" (*Diaries* 3:207). These are the questions that have haunted feminist critics, haunted us perhaps too literally so that the fixtures supporting these "differences"—the strings and pulleys of the textual operation—are obscured by the terms of their representation. Woolf's poetics of interruption calls attention to the textual scaffolding that supports representability itself, not by showing it forth and opening it to speculation, but rather by revealing its *effects.*[9]

Before turning to Gertrude Stein's dynamic theories of the relation between representation and narration, we must underscore Marcus's conclusion that *A Room of One's Own* is an example of "narration as lesbian seduction" 163). Sapphic modernist fiction may be defined in such terms, and Woolf's text is arguably the best example in English. But it is not the only example, nor is H. D., for instance, any less attentive to the structural supports of female figuration or the stylistic, rhythmic, and thematic terms of these writing forms. Whereas Woolf explored the dimensions of fiction, essay, diary, and letter (all of which develop by narrative gestures), H. D.'s work was more radically divided between poetry (in which she reinvented both lyric and epic forms) and fiction. Although her work seems also to divide along lines of sexual orientation, her fiction does not escape the imprint of cultural heterosexuality, nor does the poetry remain unmarked by Sapphistry. Images of women attempting to read the script on walls erected by Western culture are to be found in numerous texts by H. D.— indeed, these scenes might almost be described as her "signature pieces."[10] H. D.'s work with Freud was an effort to read the writing, to unveil the structural supports of the cultural unconscious. Parenthetically, it is interesting to note that H. D.'s creative process seemed to be more in tune with Jung's notions of the collective unconscious, whereas she found with Freud ways of translating the "suppressed desire for 'forbidden signs and wonders' " into her own woman-script (*Tribute* 51). H. D.'s female figures are caught in contradiction—Helen, "hated of all Greece" (*Helen in Egypt* 2), but also the object of male desire; Hermione caught between the terms of heterosexuality and Sapphic desire; H. D. herself negotiating the terms of dream and reality.[11]

H. D.'s writing exposes the awful dichotomies and hierarchies of Western culture as they capture and violate women. Her writing is a kind of interminable analysis, to borrow a Freudian phrase, of history and culture and her own relation to them. This analysis is haunted by its own lesbian shadow, as Hermione Gart is haunted by Fayne Rabb. H. D. and Virginia Woolf examine in their writing moments of simultaneous forgetting and remembering. What is "forgotten" (because culture suppresses it) and "remembered" (because it is a source of artistic creativity) is the Sapphic. H. D. describes the ways the Sapphic is veiled by culture in an effort to divest it of its powers, which threaten the definitional categories on which culture rests (male/female; heterosexual/homosexual; power/weakness, etc.). The Sapphic is a structure of the unconscious; it is not a language, but it structures language; it is mysterious and shadowy, not directly accessible, not immediately available to view. It exists in another realm, like the Minoan-Mycenaean civilization behind Greece (to which Freud made reference), and when it finds a medium through which to speak, it radically restructures the rules of the cultural game. It can rewrite narrative as lesbian seduction. It can create a revolution in poetic language, refiguring the cultural images of women. It can redefine entire genres and renegotiate the boundaries between grammar and rhetoric, aesthetics and ideology. In artistic practices, it resituates the relation of conscious to unconscious and resists modernist claims to full aesthetic control over the text.

RHETORIC AND ROSES

Poetry and prose. I came to the conclusion that poetry was a calling an intensive calling upon the name of anything and that prose was not the using the name of anything as a thing in itself but the creating of sentences that were self-existing and following one after the other made of anything a continuous thing which is paragraphing and so a narrative that is a narrative of anything. That is what a narrative is of course one thing following any other thing. (Stein, *Narration* 25–26)

If there is such a thing as Sapphic modernism, then its philosopher-theorist is Gertrude Stein, whose writings have remained outside the gates of classic modernism. These writings are both special cases of the "Sapphic" and of the "modernist" *because* they are assaults upon Western ways of knowing and categorizing. Marianne DeKoven has commented that "there is no principle of 'the same' running through [Stein's] writing, no spinal column along which her works could be arranged from head to bottom" (15).[12] But Stein's writing interrogates the relation of sameness to itself and to a principle of difference within the field of representation. Stein took identity as her philosophic subject, rejecting out of hand identity as it has been constructed in the Western, European tradition and reconstructing (an)other id-entity (as Shirley Neuman has suggested in an examination of the compositional process of *Ida A Novel*).[13] The question of identity was personal to Stein—a theoretician of the domestic—because her own identity was thrown into crisis by her lesbianism, and as Henry Sayre points out, her work questions "what it means for the female artist to adopt what in effect has been set out in Western painting as the masculine position" (31). While one might argue that Stein's poetic-philosophical pursuits were spurred by purely intellectual concerns, I contend that these endeavors were responses to Sapphic impulses that she first concealed and later celebrated. Analysis of genres, names, pronominal categories, and verbal constructions provide a (Sapphic) plot to the Stein oeuvre. Her efforts were, as DeKoven has commented, a "lifelong commitment to freeing language from the hierarchical grammars of patriarchy" (9). Stein knew, in advance of everything I have said and all that modernism and postmodernism has written, that tropes of representation are structured by the unrepresentable. She was perhaps the most literal-minded of twentieth-century writers because she took nothing for granted, not even the literal. Here I would caution against too literally "decoding" the lesbian structures supporting Stein's writing, which risk reducing them to the formulaic and conventional.

Recalling Stein's interest in individual words, in the assemblage of their parts and etymological relations, she took seriously the prefix "re" in words I have used in delineating specificities of Sapphic modernism: *remembrance, representation, recognition,* and (implied in my discussion of writing) *reiteration.* As Charles Caramello has pointed out, Stein eschewed the traditional (Western) stance of theory—the *spectatorial,* the seeing-from-a-distance—in order "to express concretely not only the meaning of the thing being observed but also the meaning of the manner of observation and the meaning of the mode of its presentation" (4). Her effort was to determine how predetermined conventions (grammar, for instance) place phenomena within a culturally determined structure. Thus she rejected the "remembered," which participates in the received ideas of convention; she rejected description in favor of a kind of composition in which "observation and its statement would *develop* simultaneously" (Caramello 5), and she was profoundly suspicious of a belief in material referentiality. Caramello has claimed, using Rosalind Krauss's work in support of his argument, that Stein understood literally the "re" of *representation:* her work is a re-presentation that stages a dematerialization of the object of representation. We know from deconstructive theories that representation calls forth absence (of the object) and opens the way to repetition (of the word) within an echo chamber of simulacra and phantasms. For Stein this realization opens the way to her later work on the structure of representation, where she reveals the power structures of representation. This breakthrough, as Henry Sayre and others argue, could only have been made in the wake of her own crisis of identity as woman, specifically as Sapphic woman.[14]

Poetry calls the name of identity into an abyssal structure that can only repeat (echo) the name it calls. In *Lectures in America* (1935), Stein writes:

When I said
A rose is a rose is a rose.

And then later made that into a ring I made poetry and what
did I do I caressed completely caressed and addressed a noun. (231)

She makes a ring of the rose and in so doing makes "poetry," which caresses
and addresses a *noun,* a name. The copula "is" does not operate either in its
usual philosophic sense (it does not represent sameness or equivalency but
rather difference and absence) nor in its grammatical sense (the linkage of
subject with object) nor in the structure of heterosexuality (coupling in
order to reproduce). Sayre hears in "A rose" a pun, "Eros." Eros calls to
itself, addresses itself, caresses itself, echoes itself. In another context I
have called this the "apostrophe-effect," in which the obsessive calling of
the name is an address to genre (and therefore to gender) across the space
of the grammatical mark of apostrophe (') in which the poetic genre of
apostrophe situates itself.[15] When Stein speaks theoretically, rather than
poetically, she fixes the difference between poetry and prose in relation to
the name (the sign of identity): "poetry was a calling an intensive calling
upon the name of anything and . . . prose was not using the name of
anything as a thing in itself but the creating of sentences that were self-
existing and following one after the other" (25–26). When "A rose is a rose
is a rose" is formed into a ring, its successional apparatus—that which
constitutes narrative—is replaced by invocation. The "rose" no longer
follows itself but echoes itself in the "O." More precisely, Stein writes: "If
poetry is the calling upon a name until that name comes to be anything if
one goes on calling on that name more and more calling upon that name as
poetry does then poetry does make of that calling upon a name a narrative
it is a narrative of calling upon that name" (26). Stein's "narrative of calling upon that name" is the narrative of calling upon the name of (Sapphic)
love.

My insistent calling upon the name of "Sapphic modernism" has resulted
in a "narrative of calling upon that name," an echoing of its effects as
"Sapphic modernisms." Our desire is to learn something about the specificities of these woman-centered modernisms and to discover their creative
sources in the wellsprings of Sapphic desire, which calls its name across
the space of difference and sameness. We can feel the resistance of Sapphic
modernisms to the canonical modernism that reinforces cultural norms
while appearing to stage a revolution against those forms. We are suspicious
of postmodernism's embrace of Sapphic literary celebrations or angered at
modernist definitions that exclude lesbian writers who dared to speak the

name of Sapphic love rather than cloak the Sapphic textual body in a style
à la mode. But Gertrude Stein's thoroughgoing interrogation of the cultural
power of symbolic structures (language, image) reveals the consistency of
the patriarchy's will to power. The Otherness against which that power
structure shores up its reserves is not defined either as "same as" (itself) or
"different from" (patriarchy). It is cross-hatched by a network of relations,
conscious and unconscious, whose designs shape creative expression. In
privileging conscious artistic control, modernism refused to admit its (unconscious) Other and consciously refused admittance to others.

Only the most fully attentive readings of Sapphic modernist texts could
illustrate the interworkings of this structural network. I am not suggesting
that such readings rediscover the structuralist dynamics of twenty years ago
(for example, Barthes's S/Z). Rather, such analyses reveal the ways in
which structural categories (grammar, rhetoric, genre, punctuation, etc.)
cannot maintain the definitional boundaries they establish. Even apparently
conventional texts that employ traditional literary forms (for example, *The
Well of Loneliness*) reveal the impossibility of structuralist poetic claims, but
"avant-garde" texts—such as those by Barnes, H. D., Stein, and Woolf,
different as these writers are from each other—position themselves *structurally* in the interstices, gaps, and overlaps inherent in literary orders.
Working both within and outside these structural forms, they expose the
fallacious terms of literary conventions. Not surprisingly, these writings are
difficult to place according to genre. Because they insist upon writing
beyond-the-boundaries of our inherited critical traditions, readers have
difficulty in knowing what to say, where to begin an analysis. Collectively,
these texts are the "dangerous symptoms" of a system that cannot tolerate
difference.

NOTES

1. Scott's list of recent work devoted primarily to male modernists includes (among
   others) Bradbury, Dasenbrock, Levenson, and Schwartz to which I would add
   Longenbach and Menand.
2. I include myself among feminists who have avoided open confrontation with
   modernist definitions (see "Précisions terminologiques" in *Femmes de la rive
   gauche*, 443–44). Alice Jardine, a theorist who has expanded our notions of the
   relation between French theory and American critical practice on questions of
   "modernity," also fails in *Gynesis* to distinguish the place of "modernism" within

the larger sweep of modernity, although she discusses postmodernism (65–67), taking its "modernist" base for granted. "Modernism," as it is used by critics and educators who have established, and continue to valorize, the canon of twentieth-century literature, is not the same as Jardine's "modernity." Modernism is undoubtedly part of the field of modernity, but its shape and distinctive characteristics remain an internal exclusion in Jardine's analysis. She avoids the most difficult avenues of this terrain by remaining silent on the crucial question of terminology, while several of her theoretical subjects (Derrida, Kristeva, Sollers) are right now enmeshed in its disputes. From theoretical perspectives, *Gynesis* displaces feminist modernists. In similar ways, Sandra Gilbert and Susan Gubar's work on modernism, especially the first two volumes of *No Man's Land,* is silent on the conceptual definition of modernism (*the* constructive term of their discourse). They discuss "not just literary history but social history" (1:xi), but they do not place modernism in the literary-social history they construct; indeed, they provide no historiography for modernism. Astradur Eysteinsson's *The Other Modernity: The Concept of Modernism and the Aesthetics of Interruption* (Ithaca: Cornell Univ. Press, 1990) addresses these complex questions in ways productive of feminist modernist critical theories.

3. It has been difficult to theorize female modernism because we do not yet have available—edited and in print—all the literary works and supporting materials that allow us to pose such metatextual questions. *The Gender of Modernism,* edited by Bonnie Scott, is an anthology of unpublished materials by some twenty-eight modernists, the collective research work of twenty scholars, which extends the range of modernist writing. Its Sapphic modernists include Djuna Barnes, Willa Cather, H. D., Charlotte Mew, Sylvia Townsend Warner, and Virginia Woolf. The diverse nature of these women's works suggests that Sapphic modernism is not founded on notions of self-sameness (including the "sameness" of sexual orientation). Rather, Sapphic modernism constitutes itself through moments of rupture in the social and cultural fabric.

4. I discuss the sexual and social politics of lesbian writers of the early twentieth century in "Paris Lesbianism and the Politics of Reaction, 1900–1940." Although there was a complicity of right-wing ideologies and avant-garde cultural practices in this period, women who took lesbianism as literary subject matter (Radclyffe Hall, Natalie Clifford Barney, Liane de Pougy, Renée Vivien, Vita Sackville-West) employed highly traditional—even old-fashioned—forms of expression. The subject matter may have been shocking, but its expression (like its politics) was highly conservative. The artistic risk takers (Djuna Barnes, Gertrude Stein, Virginia Woolf) disguised the lesbian content of their writing within experimental forms. Did the "Sapphic" support and nurture the experimental in the writing of Barnes, Stein, and Woolf? There is a greater measure of inconsistency in the sexual and artistic politics of this second group of women in comparison to the first. A distinguishing feature may be the wealth and upper-class privilege that defines the first group (members of Barney's salon) in contrast to the mixed social, religious, and economic backgrounds of the second

group (defined here by their artistic productions not by personal relationships).

5. Andreas Huyssen examines how literary history has generally disregarded these pulsations (which are aspects of the same thrust toward aesthetic purity and formalist hegemony). Thus "modernism" and the "avant-garde" are either interchangeably used terms or the avant-garde is excluded altogether from modernism, so that Gertrude Stein's writings remain uncategorizable. Huyssen admits that "the boundaries between modernism and avantgardism remained fluid" (viii), but I reinforce the division of the two here in order to illustrate how modernist literary innovation was premised on repression—specifically, an unwillingness to acknowledge the workings of the unconscious.

6. See Karla Jay's comments on the economic and social factors that structure Barnes's satire. The implications of social class and economic status within the Paris artistic community have for too long been overlooked by critics of modernism. Jay's analysis of the distance between the millionaire heiress, "Dame" Natalie Clifford Barney, and the economic and sexual isolation of Djuna Barnes, the "Lady of Fashion" who dared not sign her own name to the *Almanack,* opens the way to much-needed study of the relation within modernism of art sexuality, and economics. Lady Fashion's mirror, in which the *Almanack* reflects members of Barney's group, is not far from Stephen Dedalus's "cracked lookingglass of a servant" (*Ulysses* 1:146), his definition of Irish art. The mirror reflects, among other things, differences in economic and social privilege.

7. *Nightwood* and, to an even greater degree, *Ladies Almanack* employ outmoded and archaic modes of language that on the surface seem to undercut any self-conscious *modernist* positioning. Yet modernism reappropriated earlier forms of writing, especially medieval and Renaissance vocabulary and turns of phrase, as texts by T. S. Eliot, James Joyce, Ezra Pound, Edith Sitwell, and Virginia Woolf attest.

8. Lacan's work teaches that language does not substitute for sexuality but "makes up" for it. Language is supplementary, always trying to make good on the inevitable failure of its own meanings, whose vanishing point *is* sexuality (see Mitchell and Rose 44–52). Hélène Cixous instructs us in how, precisely, writing does this, describing it in such texts as "The Laugh of the Medusa" and practicing it in her own texts (see *Entre l'écriture*), where she claims to stay as close to her unconscious as possible. *Ecriture féminine* is her term for writing practices that follow the "feminine" against the grain of its cultural inscription in passivity and weakness. Overlooked by most commentaries on *écriture féminine* are: (1) it can be written by either women or men (it is not dependent on biological sex); (2) as it rewrites cultural repression it necessarily reinscribes that repression and all that has been lost to it. For women, this practice necessarily involves a redisovery of the lesbian in us—the woman-centeredness of living and loving structures declared by social culture to be "taboo." For men, this practice involves a rediscovery of the feminine "other" that society must repress in order to construct its code of masculinity. But the ambivalence

and unease of this writing on the edges can never be erased; indeed, it is crucial to *écriture féminine*.

The writing is always risky. James Joyce, for instance, called his daughter, Lucia—who suffered from schizophrenia and was hospitalized for the entirety of her adult life—the "shadow of my mind." *Finnegans Wake* was written, in part, in an effort to understand what he called her "genius," which twinned itself to his own creativity. This shadow genius was, of course, constructed by Joyce's own *disregard* for Lucia's psychic and physical needs, which explains perhaps its haunting qualities. Lucia is not the only example of suppressed female creativity on which male genius constituted itself: one thinks of Zelda Fitzgerald, Vivien Eliot, Camille Claudel. A "dangerous symptom" (in its clinical sense) is the instance of female insanity and instability necessary to the production of modernism. Heirs to modernism continue to cover up these symptoms: Stephen Joyce, for instance, forced the censorship of portions of Brenda Maddox's biography, *Nora,* which dealt with Lucia Joyce's schizophrenia and the particularly artistic symptoms of her disease, and destroyed Samuel Beckett's correspondence with Lucia and her correspondence to Stephen Joyce (see my "Portrait of the Artist's Wife"). Quentin Bell's repeated denials of Virginia Woolf's woman-centered sexuality (or her socialist politics) are well known, and his version of her life, unfortunately, continues to hold pride of place among her biographies.

9. Any effort to examine the structure of representation raises the issue of Western notions of cognition, which privilege the coincidence of "I" and "eye." Indeed, our critical vocabulary rests on the belief that "to see is to know." The word *theory* (drawn from Latin *theoria* and Greek Θεωρία) means what is available for "looking at, viewing, contemplation, speculation." What forms of representation hide is, of course, everything that is not available to the visual, what is not a "sight" or a "spectacle." In Western culture, woman *is* a spectacle for man's viewing (sexual pleasure), and sexual difference is reduced to *visible* difference—woman's "lack," or the absence of a penis. The textual elements I describe are, for the most part, invisible to our usual reading practices.

10. See Peggy Kamuf's reading of Woolf's *A Room of One's Own,* "Penelope at Work," in her *Signature Pieces,* 145–73.

11. Cassandra Laity's chapter in this book, "Decadence and Sapphic Modernism," provides a different reading from mine in *Women of the Left Bank* on the relation of lesbianism and heterosexuality in H. D.'s *HERmione.* Providing important documentation of H. D.'s interest in Swinburne's writing, Laity does not see in the metonymic allusion to his poetry ("sister my sister") the impossibility of women's sisterhood under patriarchy, a division that is marked by Fayne Rabb's treachery with George Lowndes. There is great risk in figuring the Sapphic through the demonic (as Gilbert and Gubar have done) and in overlooking the misogyny and homophobia of Victorian-Romantics such as Swinburne. H. D. herself, however, seems not to have recognized these disturbing elements in his work.

12. Marianne DeKoven's "Gertrude Stein and the Modernist Canon" confronts the

question of Stein's simultaneous placement inside and outside the modernist canon: "because Stein is central to so many divergent twentieth-century cultural phenomena, she inevitably becomes marginal or eccentric to any *unified, coherent tradition*" (16, emphasis added). Alan R. Knight's essay, "Masterpieces, Manifestoes and the Business of Living: Gertrude Stein Lecturing," (In *Gertrude Stein and the Making of Literature*. Ed. Shirley Neuman and Ira B. Nadel [Boston: Northeastern Univ. Press, 1988], 150–67) provides very helpful distinctions between the modernism of continuity and tradition (high modernism) and avant-garde modernism, which constitutes a rupture in the cultural-historical fabric. These distinctions are important to any study that confronts questions of literary definitions. Evidence of the differences between editorials and essays that weave a coherent literary tradition and manifestos that constitute a break with traditions is to be found in the little magazines that published modernist writers. These periodicals grounded modernism in the social and cultural history of its development, illustrating modernist unease with both its immediate past history and its contemporary moment. They provide documentation that has for the most part been overlooked by students of modernism and which holds important implications for definitions of modernism in its social-historical contexts. Bernard Benstock and I examine these materials in *Modernism Made Manifest*.

13. See " 'Would a viper have stung her,' " 168–93. *Ida* is one of Stein's most philosophic texts, interrogating identity (especially female identity) through various kinds of visual and verbal wordplay.

14. This crisis of identity took place during and following her affair with May Bookstaver and resulted in her move to Paris in 1903. The experience of this first love affair was crucial to Stein's writing, especially to *The Making of Americans*, parts of which she drafted during the relationship with Bookstaver.

15. See my *Textualizing the Feminine*, chapter 2, which examines apostrophe in terms of its position of address. The grammatical effects of apostrophe seem to bind the subject to that which the subject (already) possesses, and it also opens this assumption to question. As a rhetorical figure, the apostrophe deflects its message: it is a strategy of indirect address (see Quintilian) or an effort to call up that which is not there. In calling the name of that which is not present (the absence figured in the "O" that usually initiates apostrophe, as in "O Wild West Wind"), apostrophe eschews description. (This last is crucial for understanding Stein's writings, which also avoid description.) The genre of apostrophe calls out to voice, but that voice is represented through an *image* of voice in the text: "O." Apostrophe problematizes systems, bodies (including the human body), origins, delivery points, and points of departure. It undoes the structure of hierarchies and resists closure, this last a way of resisting the narrative drive from origin to closing. That is, apostrophe calls the question of genre to account—to present itself and account for itself. As a grammatical marker, apostrophe marks that which cannot be fully accounted for.

WORKS CITED

Barnes, Djuna. *Ladies Almanack*. New York: Harper, 1972.

———. *Nightwood*. New York: New Directions, 1937.

Benstock, Shari. *Femmes de la rive gauche: Paris, 1900–1940*. Trans. Jacqueline Carnaud et al. Paris: Femmes, 1987.

———. "Paris Lesbianism and the Politics of Reaction, 1900–1940." In *Hidden from History: Reclaiming the Gay and Lesbian Past*. Ed. Martin Bauml Duberman, Martha Vicinus, and George Chauncey, Jr. New York: NAL, 1989, 332–46.

———. "Portrait of the Artist's Wife." *Times Literary Supplement*, 30 Sept. 1988, 1065.

———. *Textualizing the Feminine: Essays on the Limits of Genre*. Norman: Univ. of Oklahoma Press, 1990.

———. *Women of the Left Bank: Paris 1900–1940*. Austin: Univ. of Texas Press, 1986.

Benstock, Shari, and Bernard Benstock. *Modernism Made Manifest: The Impact of Literary Periodicals, 1890–1940*. Austin: Univ. of Texas Press, forthcoming.

Bowlby, Rachel. *Virginia Woolf: Feminist Destinations*. Oxford: Blackwell, 1988.

Bradbury, Malcolm. *The Social Context of Modern English Literature*. New York: Schoken, 1971.

Caramello, Charles. "Gertrude Stein as Exemplary Theorist." In *Gertrude Stein and the Making of Literature*. Ed. Shirley Neuman and Ira B. Nadel. Boston: Northeastern Univ. Press, 1988, 1–7.

Cixous, Hélène. *Entre l'écriture*. Paris: Femmes, 1986.

———. "The Laugh of the Medusa." Trans. Keith Cohen and Paula Cohen. In *The Signs Reader: Women, Gender, and Scholarship*. Ed. Elizabeth Abel and Emily K. Abel. Chicago: Univ. of Chicago Press, 1983, 279–97.

Cook, Blanche Wiesen. "The Historical Denial of Lesbianism." *Radical History Review* 20 (1979): 60–65.

———. " 'Women Alone Stir My Imagination': Lesbianism and the Cultural Tradition." *Signs* 4 (1979): 718–39.

Dasenbrock, Reid Way. *The Literary Vorticism of Ezra Pound and Wyndham Lewis: Towards the Condition of Painting*. Baltimore: The Johns Hopkins Univ. Press, 1985.

DeKoven, Marianne. "Gertrude Stein and the Modernist Canon." *Gertrude Stein and the Making of Literature*. Ed. Shirley Neuman and Ira B. Nadel. Boston: Northeastern Univ. Press, 1988, 8–20.

Field, Andrew. *Djuna: The Life and Times of Djuna Barnes*. New York: Putnam, 1983.

Friedman, Susan Stanford, and Rachel Blau DuPlessis. " 'I Had Two Loves Separate': The Sexualities of H. D.'s *Her*." *Montemora* 8 (1981): 7–30.

Gilbert, Sandra M., and Susan Gubar. *No Man's Land: The Place of the Woman Writer in the Twentieth Century*. 2 vols. New Haven: Yale Univ. Press, 1988–89.

Guest, Barbara. *Herself Defined: The Poet H. D. and Her World*. New York: Doubleday, 1984.

H. D. *Helen in Egypt.* New York: New Directions, 1961.
———. *Tribute to Freud.* New York: New Directions, 1956.
Huyssen, Andreas. *After the Great Divide: Modernism, Mass Culture, Postmodernism.* Bloomington: Indiana Univ. Press, 1986.
Jardine, Alice. *Gynesis: Configurations of Woman and Modernity.* Ithaca: Cornell Univ. Press, 1985.
Joyce, James. *Ulysses.* New York: Vintage, 1986.
Kamuf, Peggy. *Signature Pieces.* Ithaca: Cornell Univ. Press, 1988.
Krauss, Rosalind. "In the Name of Picasso." *October* 16 (Spring 1981): 14–21.
Lanser, Susan Sniader. "Speaking in Tongues: *Ladies Almanack* and the Language of Celebration." *Frontiers* 4 (1979): 39–46.
Levenson, Michael H. *A Genealogy of Modernism: A Study of English Literary Doctrine, 1908–1922.* London: Cambridge Univ. Press, 1984.
Longenbach, James. *Modernism Poetics of History: Pound, Eliot, and the Sense of the Past.* Princeton: Princeton Univ. Press, 1987.
Marcus, Jane. *Virginia Woolf and the Languages of Patriarchy.* Bloomington: Indiana Univ. Press, 1987.
Menand, Louis. *Discovering Modernism: T. S. Eliot and His Context.* New York: Oxford Univ. Press, 1988.
Mitchell, Juliet, and Jacqueline Rose, eds. *Feminine Sexuality: Jacques Lacan and the école freudienne.* New York: Norton, 1985.
Neuman, Shirley. " 'Would a viper have stung her if she had only one name?': *Doctor Faustus Lights the Lights.*" In *Gertrude Stein and the Making of Literature.* Ed. Shirley Neuman and Ira B. Nadel. Boston: Northeastern Univ. Press, 1988, 168–93.
Sayre, Henry M. "The Artist's Model: American Art and the Question of Looking like Gertrude Stein." *Gertrude Stein and the Making of Literature.* Ed. Shirley Neuman and Ira B. Nadel. Boston: Northeastern Univ. Press, 1988, 21–41.
Schwartz, Sanford. *The Matrix of Modernism: Pound, Eliot, and Early Twentieth-Century Thought.* Princeton: Princeton Univ. Press, 1985.
Scott, Bonnie Kime, ed. *The Gender of Modernism.* Bloomington: Indiana Univ. Press, 1990.
Stein, Gertrude. *Lectures in America.* New York: Random, 1935.
———. *Narration.* 1935. Rpt. New York: Greenwood, 1969.
Stimpson, Catharine R. "The Mind, the Body, and Gertrude Stein." *Critical Inquiry* 3 (1977): 491–506.
Woolf, Virginia. *The Diaries of Virginia Woolf.* Ed. Anne Olivier Bell. 5 vols. New York: Harcourt, 1977–84.

THIRTEEN

The Outsider among the Expatriates: Djuna Barnes's Satire on the Ladies of the *Almanack*

Karla Jay

When Djuna Barnes died on 19 June 1982, we lost not only a noteworthy writer but also the last witness to that fabulous era of American expatriates in Paris in the early 1900s. With her demise, the curtain fell on that great stage; far from having opened the show, however, Barnes made the last entrance when she disembarked in France in the early 1920s. Natalie Clifford Barney and Gertrude Stein had arrived and set up their salons more than a decade earlier, and the avalanche of American and British expatriate writers and artists, including Radclyffe Hall, Una Troubridge, Mina Loy, Sylvia Beach, Janet Flanner, Alice B. Toklas, and Romaine Brooks, had solidly landed. The party was firmly under way.

It was not merely the timing of her arrival that distinguished Barnes from most of her sister expatriates. Unlike most of the other women, Barnes had to work for a living and had little enough to get by on comfortably, since she lacked the fortune of Natalie Barney[1] or Peggy Guggenheim or even the relative security of Gertrude Stein or Romaine Brooks. If others wrote or painted, it was because they *chose* to: Barnes *had* to. Whereas her peers could overlook the drearier economic aspects of writing, Barnes could not. Barney could take her literary output lightly and quip that her "only books/Were women's looks" (Wickes 15), and Stein could play the brilliant hostess while awaiting her discovery by American audiences. Barnes had to earn her living as a journalist and illustrator, at which she had more than a modicum of success. Her work was published in most of New York's important newspapers. Therefore, when Barnes began in Paris to venture into long, hermetic, and uncommercial fiction, she was risking a starvation that none of the others would ever have to contemplate. As a consequence, she ultimately wound up at the economic mercy of the other women, not just of Peggy Guggenheim, as Andrew Field reports in his biography, but also of Natalie Clifford Barney, who frequently sent Barnes checks for one hundred dollars and paid bills for repairs in Barnes's apartments. Once, she even sent her own housekeeper, Berthe Cleyrergue (who owed her position in Barney's household to Barnes's introduction), to tend Barnes when the latter was ill at the Hôtel d'Angleterre (France Culture).[2] Sometime in the late 1920s another unnamed "rich American woman" provided Barnes with a monthly stipend of fifty dollars (Josephson 83).

Rather than inspiring gratitude, occasional handouts of fifty or one hundred dollars from the generous who have millions tend to create bitterness, resentment, and anguish in the recipient, negative reactions usually not perceived by the donor. Barnes's letters to Natalie Barney are filled with complaints about finances and problems with her living quarters; they were likely veiled requests for additional funds. The wealthy clique of expatriates in Paris would probably not have understood the emotional toll of poverty on Barnes, who was perpetually placed in the role of the beggar at the feast, the celebrant in the borrowed gown, the one to partake of others' hospitality without being able to return it in kind. With Barnes's elegant looks and stylishness, it was probably easy for them to overlook her impoverishment. But it was not easy for Barnes to live with it, and much of her bitterness emerged when she depicted her wealthy friends in Ladies Almanack.

In addition to aiding Barnes financially in an extremely modest way, Natalie Barney included her friend in her literary circle. Barney's Academy of Women attempted to create a milieu in which elite women artists would nurture one another, provide supportive criticism for each other's work, and publish one another when necessary (Jay 33). Still, this salon was not for everyone; Barney deeply detested the masses and envisioned herself as writing for and surrounding herself with the chosen few. She attempted to reify this dream, first by going to Lesbos in 1904 with Renée Vivien (Pauline Mary Tarn) and later in 1927 by establishing the Academy of Women as an addition to her already prestigious Paris salon. Certainly, Barney considered Djuna Barnes one of the select few qualified to breathe her rarified air. But did Barnes feel comfortable breathing it? The biting satire, verging on viciousness, which is found in Ladies Almanack, strongly suggests she did not; instead, she bit the very hands that brought Ladies Almanack into existence.

As part of the cultural mission of her salon, Barney subsidized the anonymous publication of *Ladies Almanack* in 1928. Though Barnes's name did not appear on the book for several decades, it was commonly known that she was the "Lady of Fashion" who had penned the wicked satire of Barney and her circle. Barney, in her role as "patroness" of the arts, never admitted directly to Barnes that she saw any ill intent in Barnes's portrayal of her as the seductive Evangeline Musset; in fact, in 1935, Barney wrote Barnes a letter in which she called the work "a never failing delight" and thanked Barnes for the "many new admirers" the work had attracted to her (1). Friendly letters were exchanged between the two until Barney's death in 1972. However, in a rough draft of an essay on Barnes, Natalie Barney wrote, "Djuna Barnes *[sic]* pistol has too easy a trigger with no safety catch" ("Impression" 4). In other words, Barnes wrote too quickly without perceiving the consequences, but Barney obviously noticed the bullets. It would be consonant with Barney's character to choose to overlook publicly (in the published version of the essay in *Aventures de l'esprit*) and privately (in her letters to Barnes) the poison in the barbs. If she confessed Barnes had wounded her, she would violate the codes of knightly chivalry that she tried to emulate.

While Barney and some of the others, such as Solita Solano who also reacted positively (in public at least) to the *Almanack,* preferred to ignore the more venomous side of Barnes's humor, it is nevertheless there, commencing with the title. Although Barney admired knights and virgins, she never labeled herself a "lady," preferring to be called a "woman"; in her epigrams, she said that a lady was no more than an "expurgated woman" (*Pensées* 97). Yet Barney was very much a lady—a lady of leisure and a lady who ran a salon in the tradition of the best noblewomen in France, such as Mlle. de Scudéry or Mme. de Staël. It was only at the beginning of the twentieth century with the advent of rich Americans such as Gertrude Stein, Mina Loy, and Natalie Barney that salon hostesses reflected such bourgeois origins. In the *Almanack,* Barney is called Dame Evangeline Musset, the term *dame* underscoring her generational claims, if not to a title, at least to wealth. Without a doubt, Barney was much more of a grande dame than the "Lady of Fashion" who penned the work. If Barnes were a "dame," she was so only in the coarse American usage of the word.

The book begins with the unflattering account of Barney/Musset and her father, Albert (called "Father" in the *Almanack*), who is perturbed because his daughter Evangeline has not turned out quite to his liking.

He had Words with her enough, saying: "Daughter, daughter, I perceive in you most fatherly Sentiments. What am I to do?" And she answered from High enough, "Thou, good Governor, wast expecting a Son when you lay atop of your Choosing, why then be so mortal wounded when you perceive that you have your Wish? Am I not doing after your very Desire, and is it not the more commendable, seeing that I do it without the Tools for the Trade, and yet nothing complain?" (8)

The belief that lesbianism was caused by parents who strongly desired a son during or after the child's conception would have been disputed by Barney, who believed herself to be "naturally unnatural" (*Traits* 166). She thought herself very much a woman, not a "pseudo-man," as she is portrayed here in the beginning of the *Almanack*, especially when Barnes proclaims Musset's sexual anatomy to be lacking only an inch (15). Such a description of Barney was insulting on several levels. To begin with, Barney not only considered herself to be completely feminine, but she also pursued beauty in its myriad feminine forms, as Liane de Pougy later described: "We loved long hair, pretty breasts, pouts, simpers, charm, grace, not boyishness. 'Why try to resemble our enemies?' Nathalie-Flossie [Barney] used to murmur in her little nasal voice" (253).

Moreover, the idea that a lesbian was a woman whose anatomy was similar but not equal to that of a man's was a negative stereotype that had long been present in the laws of Great Britain and other countries. It was erroneously believed that lesbians engaged in sex by penetrating other women with unnaturally elongated clitorises. This widely believed but biologically unproven premise had been brought into the public eye a century earlier (1811) in the notorious slander case in Edinburgh, Scotland, brought by schoolmistresses Marianne Woods and Jane Pirie against Dame Cumming Gordon, whose niece had accused the two of engaging in lesbian practices in the boarding school they ran. The teachers were vindicated by the court in part because the judges believed that no such deformed women existed in Scotland! (Faderman 153–55). While feminist critics, such as Susan Sniader Lanser, defend *Ladies Almanack* partly as a celebration of oral sexuality (39–45), they fail to explain this demeaning definition of lesbianism created by patriarchal, misogynistic law courts which could not conceive of sexuality without a phallus or a substitute for one. The deformation of Musset's/Barney's anatomy undercuts the prowess attributed to her tongue, which superficially at least outweighs all other forms of sexual techniques referred to in the *Almanack*.

Barnes may have gone so far as to mock Barney's renowned sexual prowess. For instance, it is claimed that when she was thirty, Musset "made a Harlot a good woman by making her Mistress" (17). This deed, of course, is a direct reference to Barney's love affair in 1898–99 with Liane de Pougy, who was the most famous courtesan of her day, and whom Barney did succeed in seducing. However, the rest of the story contradicts the facts as Barney and her circle would have known them. Barney, who was only twenty-two or so when her affair with de Pougy transpired, failed to "reform" her: that transformation was accomplished by a man, Prince Georges Ghika, whom Liane de Pougy married. Barney desperately tried but did not succeed in persuading de Pougy to abandon her life in the demimonde. In other words, what is on the surface related as one of Barney's greatest triumphs was, in fact, one of her greatest failures. Barney was unable to accomplish what a "real" man did. Barnes is not so much rewriting history as holding up failure in the guise of success, a tactic which might be intended to irritate Barney but go unnoticed by the unwary reader.

Nor is Barney portrayed as the kindest of lovers. In one episode, Musset leaves Doll Furious (Dolly Wilde, with whom Barney was lovers during the 1920s) in the middle of their lovemaking in order to pursue another woman, Bounding Bess (Esther Murphy),[3] despite the protests of Doll Furious (31–32). "Fickle" would be a euphemism for the way in which Musset leaves her, despite her rationale of converting another woman to the "cause." Dolly Wilde, the niece of Oscar Wilde, was known to be as witty as he. In fact, she once remarked, "I am more Oscar-like than he was like himself" (quoted in Wickes 183). It is not her wit, however, which is exhibited in the *Almanack;* rather, she is portrayed as a "slave" to Musset's sexual prowess, begging her to stay and continue their lovemaking. Not only does she ignore the presence of Nip and Tuck (Janet Flanner and Solita Solano, respectively), but in addition she clearly has no qualms about making love on the carpet in front of her acquaintances.

Barney/Musset pursues not only Bounding Bess, but several other women, as well. Nevertheless, her primary relationship during this era was with American artist Romaine Brooks, with whom Barney was involved for over half a century. Although Brooks is not sexually satirized as is Dolly Wilde, Barnes also manages to attack Brooks on the points she felt most sensitive about. In the *Almanack,* Brooks, thinly disguised as Cynic Sal, is reduced to the role of a servant: "She dressed like a Coachman of the period of Pecksniff, but she drives an empty Hack" (36), a clear reference to Brooks's mode of dressing in somber women's suits with black top hats. Brooks was insecure about her social standing within Barney's circle and with herself in general since Brooks's mother had treated her much like a servant (and by some accounts gave her away to be raised by one) until her sickly brother, St. Mar, whom her mother greatly preferred, finally died. As a result, Brooks suffered emotional and economic scars from her childhood, which Barnes does not refrain from digging up (or into). The empty hack might refer to a loveless life, and Barnes's remark that Brooks "still cracks as sharp a Whip" (26) is a comment upon Brooks's reputedly dour and antisocial personality, which caused her often to remain alone in her own apartment or studio rather than attending Barney's salon. Brooks is further described as "the Woman . . . who is of so vain and jealous a Nature that do what you will you cannot please her" (36), a comment that alludes to Brooks's well-known jealousy over Barney's love affairs with other women, especially Dolly Wilde, whom Brooks finally drove from Barney's bed after nearly a decade of struggle. Thus, Brooks was a "servant" in another regard —that is, she was a slave to her love for Barney and to her own jealous nature.

Barnes does not linger long on each of Barney's lovers; instead, she rushes Barney quickly toward eternity and her elevation to lesboerotic sainthood. Dame Musset dies in the book at the age of ninety-nine, which ironically is just a bit older than Barney's actual death in 1972 at the age of ninety-five.

When Musset dies, her followers carry her body here and there and finally cremate it:

And when they came to the ash that was left of her, all had burned but the Tongue, and this flamed, and would not suffer Ash, and it played about upon the handful that had been she indeed. And seeing this, there was a great Commotion, and the sound of Skirts swirled in haste, and the Patter of much running in feet, but Señorita Fly-About [Mimi Franchetti] came down upon that Urn first, and beatitude played and flickered upon her Face, and from under her Skirts a slow Smoke issued, though no thing burned, and the Mourners barked about her covetously. (84)

Finally, after all the mourners have taken their turn over the tongue, they place Musset's ashes "on the Altar in the Temple of Love" (84).

Barney/Musset appears to have been elevated to sainthood, but on closer analysis, she has been reduced to a sexual acrobat in life and beyond. Barney's tongue gives pleasure in life, and is hotter than the flames of cremation, but only the sexual talents of her tongue transcend mortality.

She is not portrayed in the book as the charismatic salon hostess, witty speaker, and creative writer that she was. In her postmortem state, she mechanically gives pleasure to others because her eyes and brain have not risen from the flames along with her tongue. The fact that Musset is interred in a Temple of *Love* is ironic, for what can the nature of such an indiscriminate love be? The fact that Musset's posthumous prowess delights as well as amazes her devoted followers reduces them to Musset's level, for their adoration of the mobile relic seems to them more than an adequate replacement for the deceased woman or at least metonymy for what she was. Barney could hardly be thrilled to see all her intellectual accomplishments forgotten—for despite her pose of anti-intellectualism she was a prolific writer—while her sexual athleticism alone is immortal.

Furthermore, this reductionist vision of Barney as a conscienceless nymphomaniac negates much of what she most valued in life: friendship. Barney prided herself on being a fine friend as well as an outstanding lover, and the fact that almost all of Barney's lovers remained close friends with her when the sexual aspect of their relationship ceased seems to prove that she attained her goal. Barney detested Don Juanism and emphasized the "Platonic" element of her relationships (in both the modern and original meaning of the concept). The shift from the Temple of Friendship to the Temple of Love may seem slight, but it drastically alters the scale of values Barney upheld throughout her writing where the former held the higher place. In the final analysis, Barnes does not elevate Barney; rather, she flattens her into a one-dimensional, slightly pornographic caricature. Even if Musset does attain sainthood in the *Almanack*, what does her immortal state consist of? The lives of the saints often begin with accounts of sinning that lead to a visitation, transformation, or rebirth, any of which creates a higher, purer self. Musset in the end is reduced to ashes, and what has risen is the relic of her most carnal self, a testament to unrestrained, undirected, uncontrolled, and indiscriminate cunnilingus.

Barney and her lovers are not the only ones to be sniped by Barnes's bullets; the others become targets as well, most notably Radclyffe Hall and Una Troubridge, presented as Tilly Tweed-In-Blood and Lady Buck-and-Balk, respectively. According to Barnes, Troubridge "sported a Monocle and believed in Spirits" (18). Hall "sported a Stetson and believed in Marriage" (18). Unlike some of the more obscure references in this roman à clef, there can be no doubt about the identity of these two women, for Troubridge did indeed favor a monocle, and Hall, a stetson. Both Troubridge and Hall were greatly devoted to Catholicism and believed that they would be reunited in heaven, despite the teachings of the Church on the subject of homosexuality.[4] When the two have tea with Musset, the pair insists that English law should legalize their union: "For the equal gold Bands . . . shall make of one a Wife, and the other a Bride" (19).

After the publication of *The Well of Loneliness*, Radclyffe Hall was tried on charges of obscenity in both England and the United States because of the novel's lesbian subject matter (although Stephen Gordon is portrayed as so self-sacrificing and helpless in her sexual preferences that one can hardly blame her for her "deformity" as it is presented). It is illogical for Hall and Troubridge to expect the privilege of marriage, considering the legal consequences of merely writing about the topic. In view of their satirized dress, especially that of the masculine Radclyffe Hall, who liked to be called "John" and who cropped her hair like a man, their demand for the legalization of their union both within the *Almanack* and against the mores of their time can only serve to make the readers guffaw at Hall and Troubridge, not sympathize with them. The couple certainly forms a vivid contrast to Barney's infidelities, but they do not emerge in a sympathetic light, and the pity Hall hoped to evoke from the public in her novel is totally lacking in Barnes's cruel satire of her. Even Musset, upon hearing their pleas for marriage, proclaims that one might do equally well to take the law into one's own hands: "But then there are Duels to take the place of the Law," she facetiously proclaims (20).

Satire and caricature by definition exaggerate and flatten the people they depict, but other bawdy characters (one thinks of Chaucer's Wife of Bath) manage to retain their humanity while Barnes's characters do not. Some might argue that the work is an almanac, not a tale or a novel, but it does not belong to the first genre, either. Despite organizing the book by months, Barnes's work does not fit the traditional description of an almanac, which usually contains such items as weather forecasts, tide tables, and lists of facts. Nor is it for a specific profession, such as farmers. Neither can the *Almanack* be classified as a novel, for the only plot is a rather sketchy biography of Musset.

Perhaps by placing the work beyond recognizable genres, Barnes also hoped to escape the limitations of expectations of such forms, but the structure of the *Almanack* itself does not explain the heartlessness of the joke. Part of the explanation, of course, lies in Barnes's monetary situation discussed earlier. She resented being poor, and the willingness of the others to support her work financially may have ironically increased her anger at them. *The Antiphon* strongly suggests that Barnes had been bought or sold at least once in her youth, and she might have perceived well-meaning gestures of literary admiration and financial backing as having hidden strings or ill intent.

A further irony is that Barnes's satire was so extreme that most of the women in the *Almanack* failed or refused to identify themselves though, purportedly, the work was an "in-joke," written for and, in part, privately subsidized by the other women in the work. Even Natalie Barney, who provided most of the characters' identities in marginalia of her own copy of the *Almanack*, was unable to name all the figures in the book, though they were all supposedly either her lovers or intimate members of her circle. For example, Barney could not identify the three women who were the sources for Maizie and the two Doxies.[5] Similarly, Janet Flanner, who admitted in *Paris Was Yesterday* that she was depicted in the *Almanack*, was not sure whether she was Nip or Tuck (xviii). Barney, however, was sure that Flanner was Nip, a journalist who "could not let a Morsel go, though she knew well that it could be printed nowhere and in no Country" (34). We can only assume that members of the café circle among whom the book was circulated were even further afield in their speculations about the identities of the wild ladies of Barnes's Sapphic calendar.

Humor, it is traditionally suggested, is based on, among other things, recognition. But if the members of Barney's coterie did not recognize themselves or one another, even in a caricaturized form, one wonders what they were laughing at. The bawdy humor was most likely the source of laughter and praise. The *Almanack*'s ribald Joycean humor and puns have sold copies of the book to admiring readers who most likely are unable to identify *any* of the characters in the book.

If one were to attribute kindness to Barnes (a trait that never seems conjoined with her name), one might suggest that in her satire she hermetically protected the identities of her friends. However, through the veneer, those somewhat acquainted with the period and group can easily recognize Barney, Brooks, Wilde, Hall, and Troubridge. It is not, however, the witty Barney or Wilde, the artistic Brooks, or the brave Hall and Troubridge who are depicted; instead, Barnes presents a reductionist vision of them which flattens them to a one-dimensional level, usually sexual, in which their lifetime achievements are diminished or omitted. It is questionable whether Saint Musset's followers are liberated lesbians or sexual slaves.

Several critics, including Susan Lanser (39–45) and Gayle Rubin,[6] have described the book as a joyous celebration of lesbianism, but they have somehow overlooked this reductionist element, and most importantly, Barnes's sexual alienation from the other members of the circle. For one thing, Barnes seems to identify most closely with the character of Patience Scalpel, whom Barney identified as Mina Loy. Loy, who was a poet and salon hostess in Paris at the time, provides a distinct counterpoint to the lesbians. In contrast to Barney's lusty sexuality, Loy is described as being frigid and is represented by the month of January (10).

Yet it is too simplistic to label Loy as a "foil" to Barney/Musset as does Louis Kannenstine (54). Loy's position in the group is unique. Though she had dabbled in Sapphic love, she is a heterosexually identified woman, and as such she is forever an outsider of some sort, no matter how deeply she shares the literary preoccupations of the others. She "could not understand Women and their Ways" (11), and her liberalism and sympathy for the group have obvious limits. She rejects the life-style of Barney and her circle for her own daughters, whom, she insists, "shall go a'marrying" (13).

Therefore, Loy was in some fashion simultaneously within and outside the group, intellectually in one camp and sexually in the other. Her position strongly reflects that of Barnes herself. While their economic situations were not analogous, Loy was Barnes's closest friend within the circle, the one with whom she identified. Like Loy, she refused to label herself a lesbian. Despite Barnes's decade-long affair with artist Thelma Wood, she insisted, "I'm not a lesbian. I just loved Thelma" (quoted in Field 101). Since her relationship with Wood appears to have been longer than any other relationship in her life and since she also had affairs with other lesbians, including Natalie Barney (Field 123), there is quite obviously a strong element of self-denial here, not that Barnes or Loy would be the first woman to be a lesbian yet thoroughly and totally deny it. The negation comes across clearest when we note who is *not* in the *Almanack*. Barnes manages to mention, if only in passing, almost all the members of Barney's intimate circle during this era, *except* herself and Thelma Wood. Their absence from the sensual circle seems more telling than their presence, even if briefly noted, would have been.[7]

Although the narrative voice occasionally uses "I" and "we," the effect of omitting herself from the cast of characters is to create a chasm between "I" and "they." The text has been traditionally interpreted as being about the Barnes/Barney circle, but the curious lack of the encompassing "we" and Barnes's absence undercut this possibility and suggest another intention. Barnes's role here is as outsider, an observer of a "sexual and social institution" to which she does not claim membership. Her choice of signature may provide the clue here. She is the "Lady of Fashion": As previously noted, the "ladies" represent Barney and other elite, upper-class lesbians of her coterie. The "Lady of Fashion" is thus either the one who participates solely because it is the rage at the time (the "fashion") or perhaps the one who dresses for a role she plays rather than being a real lesbian (as in a lesbian "after a fashion" or someone masquerading as a lesbian but who is not truly one).

From her own perspective, Barnes must have found herself in a historically and otherwise unique situation. Usually, lesbians were persecuted by the Church or the state, sometimes both. In traditional social circumstances, a woman like Barnes, who was trying to make her way in the world, would go out of her way to avoid the scandal associated with such women. For a variety of reasons, lesbians moved to the forefront of the literary and artistic movements in Paris in the 1920s. To make her way among the literary denizens, Barnes had to ingratiate herself with a group she might be expected to shun under other circumstances. She was torn, therefore, between two sets of mores, and I believe she managed to accommodate both by joining the group on the one hand and mocking and denouncing them on the other.

Even had Barnes wanted to join wholeheartedly in the Sapphic circle, she was not a "real" lady like the others who were economically independent women, free to choose not only where they lived but how they lived, sexually and otherwise. On the contrary, Barnes was not financially free to be a lesbian and could not afford to live like the salon set. She was at the mercy of a phallocentric literary establishment in the States, from which she earned her living as a journalist and illustrator. She knew too well that the fortunes of publishing are more fickle than Barney's trust or Brooks' inheritance. She did not sign the *Almanack* because of a fear of scandal— certainly the book is no more obscene than Joyce's *Ulysses* or Gide's *Corydon;* rather, she did not sign it because she could not afford to be publicly identified as a lesbian or to identify herself as one. Should the world discover the identity of the "Lady of Fashion," the negative relationship to the world portrayed within the *Almanack* would protect her reputation. After all, there were limits, even to bohemianism.

Thus, Barnes underscores her economic and sexual isolation from the rest of the circle by removing herself from the family album. Had Barnes been willing or able to accept her lesbianism, the *Almanack* might not have existed or might have been different. The same could probably be said for *Nightwood* and some of her other works. And were some critics not so eager to salvage whatever positive lesbian material that can be gleaned from this era to counterbalance the pits of solitude and despair into which other authors disparagingly tossed us, then they might see that *Ladies Almanack* is not quite the light-hearted prolesbian romp we would like to embrace wholeheartedly. What is contained within the book is problematic at best because of its reductionist vision of lesbianism, and what is missing is perhaps even more so because of all the questions we must ask about Barnes's absence. Barnes left us no final answer as to whether her barbs were meant to vex or please and whether the trigger went off accidentally or on purpose. But unlike Dame Musset, whose tongue survived even death, Barnes left us only silence for the last half of her life and an only partially solvable enigma of an intriguing roman à clef, which in its funhouse mirror reflects not only Barney's Paris coterie but fragments of the expatriate Barnes herself who stood on the doorstep, half in and half out of the club.

NOTES

Grateful acknowledgment is made to the National Endowment for the Humanities for a Travel to Collections Grant, which enabled research in Paris for the essay to be undertaken. I would also like to thank the Scholarly Research Committee and the Summer Research Grant Program of Pace University for their support. Finally, I would like to thank Jean Chalon for permitting me to see Natalie Barney's copy of *Ladies Almanack*.

1. Natalie Clifford Barney's fortune is usually estimated at between two and one half and four million dollars, the equivalent of which today would be about a billion dollars (Jay 2).
2. Later on, particularly after Barnes's return to the United States, a number of other people provided financial aid, emotional care, and donated time and energy to sustain Barnes.
3. Esther Murphy had several husbands, including John Strachy and Chester Arthur, before becoming a lesbian.
4. See Joanne Glasgow's essay in this collection for a more detailed discussion of their religious beliefs.
5. The two Doxies are described as, "One (Low-Heel) protesting that women were

weak and silly Creatures, but all too dear, the other (High-Head) that they were strong, gallant, twice as hardy as any Man, and several times his equal in Brain, but none so precious" (50).

6. Gayle Rubin has presented a slide show on Natalie Barney's life in Toronto in 1984 and in other places as well, which defines the *Almanack* as a celebration of lesbian sexuality.

7. Although the work was partially subsidized by Barney and the book was sold by subscription to members of her circle, it is difficult to imagine that Barney would have asked Barnes to leave herself out of the book, since it was common during the era to portray oneself along with one's coterie, as in several group portraits of the Cenacle.

WORKS CITED

Barnes, Djuna. *Ladies Almanack*. 1928. Rpt. New York: Harper, 1972.

Barney, Natalie Clifford. "An Impression of Djuna Barnes and Her Book by the Amazon of Remy de Gourmont." MS, NCB 85, 789.10. Bibliothèque Jacques Doucet, Paris, France.

———. Letter to Djuna Barnes, 17 Nov. 1935. Natalie Clifford Barney Collection. Bibliothèque Jacques Doucet, Paris, France.

———. *Pensées d'une amazone*. Paris: Emile-Paul, 1920.

———. *Traits et portraits*. Paris: Mercure de France, 1963. New York: Arno, 1975.

Cleyrergue, Berthe, and Michèle Causse. Interview with Françoise Werner. *France Culture*. Radio France, Paris, 2 Nov. 1983.

Faderman, Lillian. *Scotch Verdict: Miss Pirie and Miss Woods v. Dame Cumming Gordon*. New York: Morrow, 1983.

Field, Andrew. *Djuna: The Life and Times of Djuna Barnes*. New York: Putnam, 1983.

Flanner, Janet [Genet]. *Paris Was Yesterday, 1925–1939*. New York: Penguin, 1981.

Jay, Karla. *The Amazon and the Page: Natalie Clifford Barney and Renée Vivien*. Bloomington: Indiana Univ. Press, 1988.

Josephson, Matthew. *Life among the Surrealists: A Memoir*. New York: Holt, 1942.

Kannenstine, Louis F. *The Art of Djuna Barnes: Duality and Damnation*. New York: New York Univ. Press, 1971.

Lanser, Susan Sniader. "Speaking in Tongues: *Ladies Almanack* and the Language of Celebration." *Frontiers* 3 (1979): 39–45.

Pougy, Liane de. *My Blue Notebooks*. New York: Harper, 1979.

Wickes, George. *The Amazon of Letters: The Life and Loves of Natalie Barney*. New York: Putnam, 1976.

FOURTEEN

H. D. and A. C. Swinburne: Decadence and Sapphic Modernism

Cassandra Laity

In the summer of 1952, just weeks before H. D. began composing the epic poem, *Helen in Egypt*, Bryher sent her A. C. Swinburne's posthumously published novel *Lesbia Brandon*. Startled from a peacefully lethargic summer by this "thunder bolt," H. D. wrote excitedly to Norman Holmes Pearson that Swinburne's "exotic and erotic" fictional account of his sexual history had sent her into an "electric coma." "The book is really the turn of the tide," she wrote, "I have waited for the 'romantics' to come really back . . . so now, I can just get caught up in the tide, no more swimming against the breakers."[1] At first glance, H. D.'s rediscovery of the Romantics resembles that of her male modernist contemporaries, who despite the anti-Romantic bias of modernism, acknowledged their debt to the Romantic past late in their careers.[2] H. D.'s "Romanticism," however, hardly resembles the "Romanticism" that Harold Bloom, Frank Kermode, and other critics of Romantic revisionism have demonstrated in modernists such as Eliot, Pound, Yeats, and Wallace Stevens.[3] Male modernists consistently maintained a safe distance from Swinburne, whose "effeminate" and "unwholesome" poetics they repeatedly invoked to exemplify the lapse of Romanticism into decadence and decay. Indeed, as Frank Kermode's *Romantic Image* affirms, modernist continuities with the Romantic past passed over the Decadents' explorations of "forbidden" sexualities, androgyny, and role-reversal in favor of the less disruptive "Romantic image" of the muse which sustained the I-thou relation between male subject and female object.[4] Had any of the major modernists recognized a "forefather" in A. C. Swinburne, he would not have claimed *Lesbia Brandon* as a precursor text: Swinburne's narrative of indeterminate gender roles and unconventional sexualities represented the Victorian-Romantic at his most "effeminate" and "perverse." H. D.'s "electric coma" is therefore understandable: she mistakenly believes that

217

the publication of *Lesbia Brandon* signals a shift in male literary history ("the turn of the tide") away from the poetics of male desire toward its disruption in the fluid sexualities of Decadent-Romanticism.

H. D. was not alone, however, among women modernists in her identification with Swinburne and the Decadent poets. Katherine Mansfield's early letters and journal entries reveal an almost obsessive identification with the sexual ambiguities of Oscar Wilde and a devotion to the Decadents which one critic describes as persistently "deeper than fashionability." Violet Hunt, a self-professed New Woman who lived openly with the still-married Ford Madox Ford, declared that Swinburne's odes to "free love," "Ilicet" and "Felise," "constitute almost my bible—one that needs no clumsy revision." Other women writers appear to have constructed a patch-work "female" tradition which traced a line from Sappho through the Victorian Hellenists and particularly Swinburne. Willa Cather praised Swinburne as "thoroughly Greek" and linked him as a successor to Sappho —"he has even imitated the Sapphic measures perfectly." Sharon O'Brien cites Cather's early reading in the French and British Decadents as instrumental in shaping her "consciousness of 'unnatural' sexuality." Similarly, Renée Vivien, like many twentieth-century women writers, found an empowering female "mask" or "fantasy precursor" in the more remote Sappho, but the sensuous imagery of Vivien's erotic "Mytilene" and particularly her portraits of the lesbian *femme fatale* derived from her extensive reading in Swinburne. As Susan Gubar observes in her important "Sapphistries," Vivien regarded Decadence as "fundamentally a lesbian literary tradition."[5]

The Decadence of the 1890s provided, I suggest, a "female" tradition for modernist women poets in particular who, unlike twentieth-century women novelists, did not claim to "think back through" their mothers, the strong women poets of the past. Unable or unwilling to recognize a tradition of women poets in the nineteenth century, H. D. and others "used" the Decadents to fashion a feminist poetic of female desire.[6] While Yeats, Eliot, and Pound found Swinburne's experimental articulations of desire "perverse," several women modernists, including H. D. and Renée Vivien, discovered in Swinburne's more fluid explorations of sexuality and gender roles a radical alternative to the modernist poetics of male desire which, as Shari Benstock and others have noted, silenced and effaced the twentieth-century woman writer.[7]

This chapter inquires into the discrepancy between the "myth of manhood" that emerged from the male modernists' anti-Romantic program for early modernism and the Romantic "myth of womanhood" exemplified by H. D.'s *HER*. H. D's fictional history of her sexual and aesthetic beginnings in which poems from Swinburne articulate the young woman poet's discovery both of her bisexuality and of her poetic vocation contrasts radically with similar myths of poetic "origins" generated by Eliot, Yeats, and other modernists. In Eliot's and Yeats's personal "scripts" of their poetic development, the achievement of a "virile" modernism depends on separation rather than connection with the "effeminate" influence of Romanticism. Contrary to Harold Bloom's Oedipal model of father-son combat, male modernists appear to have perceived their Romantic precursors as insidiously possessive "foremothers" whose influence threatened to feminize both their psyches and their art, stripping them of masculine autonomy and creative power. I suggest that the male modernists' assessment of a certain strain of Decadent-Romanticism as "women's writing," was, in part, correct. Eliot, Yeats, Pound, and others recognized that the disruptive sexuality and textuality of the Decadent Romantics in particular posed a threat to the early modernist program for poetry. By contrast, H. D.'s Romantic myth of origins as expressed in *HER* reestablished connections with those aspects of Romanticism the male modernists had dismissed as "effeminate" and "perverse." This discussion therefore attempts to suggest how differing responses to the Romantic past distinguish at least one strain of female modernism from the prevailing male modernism.

However, feminist transformations of Decadent-Romanticism required an extremely careful maneuvering through the straits of the feminist revisionary process. Feminist revisions of the self-described "religion of vice" risked inscribing the very censure and self-abasement women modernists sought to escape. As feminist critics have pointed out, Decadent influence could be dangerous—both to the feminist text and the female psyche. Catharine R. Stimpson describes the lesbian romanticism of several modern novels as "at . . . worst, an inadvertent parody of *fin de siècle* decadence." Lillian Faderman goes so far as to attribute Renée Vivien's lurid death by starvation to her identification with Swinburne's Lesbia Brandon, among other Decadent sadomasochistic images of the "doomed lesbian."[8] Instead of barring us from a consideration of Decadent influence, such unfortunate examples should help uncover the conflicts and contradictions of the feminist revisionary process. At worst, Decadent influence clearly marked the ways in which the feminist revisionist text falls prey to its submerged male discourse. At best, however, the "use" of the Decadent precursor might provide an arena for the sexual/textual debate between the sobering confines of "perversity" and the heady freedom of disruption which must accompany the practice of feminist revisionism. I hope to demonstrate that in H. D.'s successful maneuverings of the process, she devises textual strategies which carefully distinguish her feminist transformations of Decadent influence from the darker side of the Decadent poetic.

MODERNIST ANTIROMANTICISM: SWINBURNE AND "WOMEN'S WRITING"

It is taken for granted that theories of modernism emerged in reaction against Romanticism and particularly the Decadent Romanticism of the nineties; however, even a cursory glance at the misogynist rhetoric which attended the early twentieth-century rejection of the "effeminate" Romantics for a "virile" modernism suggests that theorizers of modernism such as T. E. Hulme, Eliot, Pound, and Yeats socially constructed the Romantic past as a pernicious form of "women's writing." In keeping, perhaps, more with Nancy Chodorow's speculations about the formation of male gender identity than with Freud's, male modernist "anxiety" of Romantic influence translated as sexual anxiety toward an apparently overpossessive and domineering "foremother" who threatened to "womanize" the modernist enterprise.[9] Widely publicized theories of early modernism developed by T. E. Hulme, Pound, Eliot, and others, repeatedly evoked the specter of Romanticism as a domineering *femme fatale* and recounted her ruinous effect on the last generation of poets.[10] This suppression of women's writing inscribed in the early modernist poetic,[11] I suggest, compelled women writers to seek out and evolve other "modernisms." However, before considering H. D.'s revisions of Swinburne, it would be useful to examine the conception of "women's writing" that evolved from the Imagist program for early modernism, focusing on the male modernists' pronouncements against Romanticism, the "case histories" of their own battle with Romantic influence, and finally, on the theories of language and the "image" that defined early modernism.

One recognizes the familiar dismissals of women's writing in the charges leveled by the male modernists against Romanticism: sentimentalism, effeminacy, escapism, lack of discipline, emotionalism, self-indulgence, confessionalism, and so forth. Further, a gender-biased, binary construct of Romanticism and modernism informed much of the rhetoric of anti-Romanticism in the early twentieth century. T. E. Hulme's "Romanticism and

Classicism," an important essay on the tenets of the early modernist Imagist doctrine, divided literary history into strict gender categories: the "Romanticism" of Swinburne, Byron, and Shelley was defined as "feminine," "damp," and "vague"; Classicism, which formed the model for Imagism, "dry," "hard," "virile," and "exact."[12] Explicit or implicit rejections of "women's writing" for the "masculine" virtues of intellect, "unity," objectivity, and concreteness lay behind Pound's professed "contempt" for the "softness of the 'nineties.'" Eliot's arguments against Romantic "dissociation" of intellect and emotion, and Yeats's scorn for the "womanish introspection" of the "tragic generation."[13] Finally, modernists frequently linked Romanticism with women writers in dismissals of both. T. E. Hulme blamed the present decayed state of Romanticism for giving license to the self-indulgent sentimentality, confessionalism, and flowery imagery of women writers:

The carcass is dead and all the flies are upon it. Imitative poetry springs up like weeds, and women whimper and whine of you and I alas, and roses, roses, roses, all the way. It [Romanticism] becomes the expression of sentimentality rather than of virile thought. (*Speculations* 69)

Similarly, Richard Aldington's review of a novel by Violet Hunt in the *Egoist* maintained that women writers were "incapable" of the "indirect method of writing," and could only imitate the confessional mode he equates with Rousseauistic Romanticism, thus relegating them to the "great second class" of writers (17).

A similar gender-biased dualism characterized Yeats's and Eliot's personal histories of their poetic development from a childish and effeminate Romanticism to a mature and virile modernism. These "scripts" had a profound and far-reaching impact in the influential models of literary history and aesthetics created by both poets which socially constructed the Romantic dissociation of sensibility as "female," and "unity" as "male."

Yeats's self-conscious myth of the "phases" of his own personal and poetic development best demonstrates the pervasiveness of the gender-biased binary construct in modernist schemes of literary history. Yeats's critics have reconstructed the path that Yeats himself traced from his early "effeminate" Aestheticism to the "movement downwards upon life"[14] he associated with the modernist poetic. Yeats's narrative of this shift, which he initiated in *Memoirs* and continued in the later *Autobiographies*, prose essays, and letters, begins with an account of the early Yeats as an "effeminate" Romantic. Dominated and consumed by his obsession for a masterful woman both in life (Maud Gonne) and art, the Aesthete poet wrote poems of "longing and complaint" to the nineteenth century *femme fatale* that ruled his imagination. Yeats described his early poetry as "effeminate" and escapist—"a flight into fairyland and a summons to that flight" (*Letters* 90)— and overshadowed by a "sentimental sadness" and "womanish introspection" (*Letters* 434). Yeats's depiction of his early Romantic imagination incorporated the common modernist conception of Romanticism as a dangerous, erotic, and potentially unmanning female power which leads the poet more and more deeply into his own solipsistic fantasies and away from the "virile" forces of aggressive sexual energy, "will" and "intellect." T. E. Hulme warned against the seduction of Romanticism which he compared to "a drug": "accustomed to this strange light, you can never live without it" (*Speculations* 127). Similarly, Yeats cautioned George Russell against a nineties' Aestheticism he described as "that region of brooding emotions . . . which kill the spirit and the will, ecstasy and joy equally [and whose dwellers] speak with sweet, insinuating, feminine voices" (*Letters* 435). Under the spell of Romanticism's siren song, the early Yeats felt powerless and "alone amid the obscure impressions of the senses"; he produced a fragmented and "sterile" art "full of decorative landscape and of stillife" (*Essays* 271). Yeats described his radical shift in sensibility at the turn of the century from an effeminate Romanticism to a virile modernism as a summons to "hammer [his] thoughts into unity." At the climax of Yeats's personal history, he cast off his former, Romantic persona for a more vigorous modernism and wilfully executed a "movement downwards upon life," recreating himself as "the man of action."

Yeats projected a similar movement from an effeminate Romanticism to a virile modernism in one of his many schemes of literary history and its corresponding phases of imagination. In *Autobiography*, Yeats described the late Romantic "tragic generation" as having lapsed symbolically into the sensuous trap of the deadly *femme fatale* and her island paradise: "in those islands . . . certain forms of sensuous loveliness were separated from all the general purposes of life. . . . I think that the movement of our thought has more and more so separated certain images and regions of the mind and that these images grow in beauty as they grow in sterility" (209). Yeats thus envisioned the literary imagination as a progression of male desire which had been temporarily stalled in the "feminine" thrall of Romanticism.

Eliot also reconstructed his early Romanticism as a period of "daemonic possession" associated with the early, susceptible period of adolescence:

I took the usual adolescent course with Bryon, Shelley, Keats, Rossetti and Swinburne. . . . At this period, the poem, or the poetry of a single poet, invades the
youthful consciousness and assumes complete possession for a time. We do not
really see it as something with an existence outside ourselves; much as in our
youthful experiences of love, we do not so much see the person as infer the existence
of some outside object which sets in motion these new and delightful feelings in
which we are absorbed. . . . it is . . . a kind of daemonic possession by one poet.[15]

Eliot's depiction of his early Romanticism as an "invasion" and "daemonic
possession" shares the modernist conception of Romantic influence as robbing the poet of both sexual and imaginative autonomy. Under the influence
of Romanticism, the young Eliot, like Yeats, finds himself absorbed by self-
indulgent, erotic fantasy (resembling the experience of first love) in which
the "other" exists as an extension of his own ego. Eliot identifies Romanticism with "the first period of childhood," as a passive and implicitly "feminine" phase of uncontrolled passions and self-indulgence. In Eliot's account
of his early Romanticism, he makes it clear that a persistent Romanticism
indicates arrested development, and that the assumption of an autonomous
poetic identity requires the passage from an adolescent Romanticism to a
responsible modernism/manhood: "it [the Romantic period of adolescence]
is, no doubt, a period of keen enjoyment; but we must not confuse the
intensity of the poetic experience in adolescence with the intense experience of poetry." Neither Yeats's nor Eliot's narratives of their struggles to
overthrow Romantic influence recall the Bloomian Oedipal combat between
father and son; rather both male modernists appear to be resisting the pre-
Oedipal attachment to an eroticized "foremother" whose hold over the
young man must be broken.

Eliot's and Pound's famous indictments of Swinburne's evasive signification in their formulations of the Imagist doctrine establish a further
connection between the Romantics' "perverse" or "unmanly" sexuality and
"unhealthy" textuality. While Eliot maintained that Swinburne's poetry is
neither "morbid" nor "erotic," Eliot's sexual repugnance toward the Decadent-Romantic's "perversities" is discernible in the rhetoric of his attack on
Swinburne's language which still concludes that Swinburne is sick:

[Swinburne's] morbidity is not of human feeling but of language. Language in a
healthy state presents the object, is so close to the object that the two are identified.
   They are identified in . . . Swinburne solely because the object has ceased to
exist, because the meaning is merely the hallucination of meaning. . . . It is in fact
the word that gives him the thrill not the object. When you take to pieces any verse

of Swinburne, you find always that the object was not there—only the word. (*Essays* 284, 285)

Swinburne's refusal to evoke a concrete "meaning," to make the one-to-one correspondence between "word" and "thing" which characterized the early modernist poetics of "the Image" is implicitly attributed to his disturbed sexuality. Language in a "healthy" state, Eliot implies, aims straight for the object of its desire; Swinburne is distracted by a pornographic fetishization of "words"—"the word gives him the thrill not the object." Pound's similar criticism of Swinburne's use of language suggests a misplaced sexuality/textuality. Pound asserts that in Swinburne, "the word-selecting, word-castigating faculty was nearly absent. Unusual and gorgeous words attracted him." Pound warns against such a surrender to the "unusual" and "gorgeous" siren song of Romanticism; "this is of all sorts of writing the most dangerous to an author, and the unconscious collapse into this sort of writing has wrecked more poets in our time than perhaps all other faults put together.[16] Both Pound and Eliot would seem to agree that an appetite for the "unusual" breeds psychological and textual corruption.

Eliot's and Pound's criticisms of Swinburne's deliberate evasions of an easily conceptualized meaning suggest that their antipathy to the "effeminate" subject matter and style of the Romantics extends to the subtler, disruptive characteristics which contemporary feminist theory has identified with "women's writing." If women's writing, according to Hélène Cixous, attempts to open up the text and disrupt conventional dualisms through the practice of "différance," or deferred meaning, then Eliot's and Pound's critique of Swinburne may be read as a dictum against such "women's writing" in favor of an androcentric theory of "presence."[17] Taken as a whole, however, the male modernists' anti-Romanticism issued an unconscious warning to men and women writers alike: to stray from the modernist program for poetry was to risk a shallow or "childish" art, a "dissociation of sensibility," or worse, sexual and moral deviance.

DECADENCE AND MODERNIST WOMEN'S WRITING: H. D.'S *HER*[18]

While many modernist women writers shared in their male contemporaries' anti-Romanticism, others did not. Women modernists who participated in their male contemporaries' anxiety of Romantic influence risked internalizing its implicit suppression of women's writing. Further, the male modernists' specter of a castrating and demonic female "Romanticism" too closely resembled the male image of the woman writer as the "unnatural," predatory "madwoman."[19] Paradoxically, the enforced exile of Romanticism may have created a "wild zone" of creative power for some women writers who sought alternatives to the modernist poetics of male desire.

From the early days of Imagism, H. D. distinguished herself from the anti-Romanticism she had heard expressed so often by her close friends in the modernist enterprise, Pound, Aldington, and Lawrence. As early as 1916 in her review of Yeats's *Responsibilities*, H. D. called for a poetic alliance between modernist realism and Romantic visionary intensity that would heal the ravages of war. Looking back nostalgically at the Victorian-Romantics, she wrote, "the nineties were ill-starred, but they had, at least, a star." In the unpublished review, H. D. proposed her own agenda of "responsibilities" for modern poetry, urging a revised Romanticism that would "spiritually join our forces" with the poetry of the nineties to "reinvoke some golden city, sterner than dream cities and wrought more firm."[20] Later, in the forties, H. D. openly acknowledged her "sense of continuity" with the Victorian-Romantics. Commenting on her recent novel set in the Pre-Raphaelite period *(White Rose and Red)*, H. D. indicated a familial rather than adversarial relation to her Romantic past:

The [Pre-Raphaelite] artists of the *Rose* . . . seem near, familiar, *familiars* almost . . . perhaps because of my early devotion to their legend. I know more about them or sometimes seem to know more about the Rossetti-Morris circle than I do of my own contemporaries. . . . It is the sense of continuity that inspires me.[21]

H. D.'s persistent need for connection rather than rupture with the Romantic past departed significantly from her contemporaries' vehement rejection of the "effeminate" late Romantics.

Although H. D. did not write essays detailing the "dos' " and "don'ts' " of Imagist poetry, her formulations for the future of poetry are contained in her private, unpublished "notes" on writing, in her memoirs, and in the unpublished prose fiction of the twenties.[22] These works, and particularly *HER*—a fictional representation of H. D.'s early poetic development— trace a woman modernist writer's response to the Romantic past, creating an alternative "case history" to the personal "scripts" shared by such male modernists as Yeats and Eliot. Indeed H. D.'s fictionalized autobiographies of her own poetic development reverse the order of Yeats's and Eliot's personal histories which moved from the early suffocating attachment to a "female" Romanticism toward severance from the past and the assumption of an autonomous, "male" modernism. By contrast, H. D.'s young women poets attempt to work backward toward recovery of a former Romantic "self" which experienced a primary and frequently homoerotic bond with a "sister" muse, and to extricate themselves from the strict sex-gender codes that polarize the sexes and efface the woman poet in the London literary circle. In narratives such as HER and "Paint It Today" the adolescent Romantic "self," under the influence of Swinburne in particular, discovers poetic and prophetic power through a homoerotic bond with a "twin-self sister" who is boyishly androgynous.[23] Unlike the "scripts" of her male contemporaries, H. D.'s fictionalized histories of her involvement in the Imagist circle, "Asphodel" and "Paint It Today," describe the break with Romanticism and the subsequent transition to a modernist poetic as a painful indoctrination into the predatory, patriarchal sexual politics H. D. associated by turns with World War I, the "modern aesthetic cult of brutality,"[24] and her own confining role as muse to Lawrence, Aldington, and Pound. In "Asphodel" the sequel to HER, and "Paint It Today," the poetry of Swinburne is frequently evoked to signify the "real" poetic tradition that has been lost or crushed by the brutish sensibility of war and the modern age. In "Asphodel," Hermione pronounces herself and her female beloved the inheritors of the authentic poetic tradition of the Victorian-Romantics, "We are legitimate children. We are children of the Rossettis, of Burne-Jones, of Swinburne. We were in the thoughts of Wilde. . . ." Later in "Asphodel," Hermione laments the wartime devastation of the "true" poetic tradition she associates with Pater's "Mona Lisa" and Swinburne's "Itylus": ". . . prose and poetry and the Mona Lisa and her eyelids are a little weary and sister my sister, O fleet sweet swallow were all smudged out as pompei and its marbles had been buried beneath obscene filth of lava, embers, smouldering ash and hideous smoke and poisonous gas."[25] H. D. began composing fiction in 1917, hoping to regain what she called her "artist personality" by writing through the emotional "tangle" that obscured her poetic powers following the related crises of World War I, the breakup of her marriage, and her disenchantment with the London literary circle.[26]

HER

HER fictionalizes the events that occurred following H. D.'s withdrawal from Bryn Mawr in her sophomore year, focusing on her simultaneous relationships with Frances Gregg and Ezra Pound, to whom she was briefly engaged. Recently expelled from college, and painfully aware of her failure to "conform to [her family's] expectations," Hermione initially rebels against familial constraints in her engagement to the unconventional young rebel-poet George Lowndes, only to find herself further circumscribed as the "decorative" object of his patronizing affections and clumsy sexual over-tures. However, Fayne Rabb (based on Frances Gregg), the sister-love she meets through a mutual friend, provides the way out of the morass: both the marginal nature of Hermione's newly discovered "forbidden" sexual identity, and the intense, self-identifying nature of her love, enable Her-mione to escape her position as object into "another country" where her powers might fully emerge.[27] Swinburne's formidable presence in the nar-rative, however, —inscribed by Hermione's almost obsessive litany of quo-tations from his poetry and references to the Decadent-Romantic himself— has yet to be fully explored.

Susan Friedman and Rachel DuPlessis first discussed *HER* in the con-text of 1920s' lesbian novels such as Radclyffe Hall's *Well of Loneliness*.[28] Recent feminist scholarship has attributed the rise of lesbian novels in the 1920s such as Radclyffe Hall's *The Well of Loneliness* to the debates about female sexuality provoked by sex reformers such as Havelock Ellis. H. D. and Bryher knew Havelock Ellis and read with interest his theories about lesbian sexuality. However, one can not overlook the widespread influence of Swinburne on modern poets and specifically on H. D., Pound, and Frances Gregg, who apparently read Swinburne to themselves and each other during the years described in *HER* as obsessively as the text indicates. Further, Ellis's theory that the lesbian woman is the victim of a "congenital inversion," which traps a "man" in a woman's body, does not describe the celebratory "sister-love" or the fluid androgyny of both Fayne and Her-mione.[29] Although the sexologists certainly prompted much of the public and literary debates about female sexuality in the 1920s, once sparked, modernist women writers such as H. D. turned back to the literary tradi-tion which first introduced them to the subject of variant sexualities and which, unlike the psychoanalytic literature, was authored by poets who admitted to their own "deviance." H. D.'s early reading in Swinburne, and particularly the *Poems and Ballads,* is a more likely source for *HER*'s celebration of multiple forms of "deviant" desires and gender role-reversals. Swinburne's celebrated explorations of narcissism, androgyny, "free love," lesbianism, homoeroticism, and other "forbidden" subjects, do not take one moral stance, but represent a range of attitudes and debates about "deviant" and "illicit" sexualities.[30] In reply to the moral outrage that immediately followed the publication of *Poems and Ballads*, Swinburne described his individual "studies of passion or sensation" as "dramatic, many faced, multifarious (*Replies* 18, 3)." Indeed, the volume offers several conflicting "studies" of "deviant" sexual behavior or gender-identification. For example, two poems which H. D. quotes in "Asphodel," "Hermaphroditus," and "Fragoletta," present contrasting views of the dual sexualities of the androgyne.[31] In the former, the hermaphrodite is portrayed as a sterile, deprived creature whose dual gender-identities cancel each other out:

Love stands upon thy left hand and thy right
Yet by no sunset and by no moonrise
Shall make thee man and ease a woman's sighs,
Or make thee woman for a man's delight . . .

But "Hermaphroditus" is immediately succeeded by an ode to androgyny, "Fragoletta," in which the beautiful boy-girl is a "double-rose of love's," rendered more desirable by his (he is male) "double" sexualities. H. D. used the above quotations in "Paint It Today" to project her own ambiguity toward her bisexuality. Swinburne may have been the first to articulate for H. D. the debate about her "two loves separate" which resonated throughout her career. One can not ignore the strong presence of the Decadent-Romantics in the literary discourse on "deviant" sexuality that began in the 1920s.

I suggest therefore that Swinburne's erotic *Poems and Ballads* serve not only to affirm and encode Hermione's lesbian identity, but to articulate a spectrum of desires and gender-disruptions which helped shape H. D.'s early awareness of "deviant" sexuality and which were not available to her in the high modernist discourse of the 1920s. The novel might therefore represent one modernist woman poet's attempt to dislocate herself from the prevailing poetic of male desire and to forge a "female" poetic from the Decadent-Romantic past.[32] Through Swinburne's multiple explorations of "forbidden" desire, Hermione steps outside the narrow linguistic and sexual conventions imposed upon her by the young male poet, George Lowndes, based, significantly, on Ezra Pound. From the opening pages of the novel in which Hermione describes her predicament, she feels herself "clutch toward something that had no name yet" (8); significantly, Hermione's impulse toward freedom remains nameless until the insistent beat of Swinburne's "words" attunes her to those movements of desire, language, and prophecy which form the radical, homoerotic discourse of the novel—a discourse which persists even after Fayne Rabb herself briefly abandons the "sister love" for George Lowndes. Swinburne's explorations of androgyny, homoeroticism, narcissism, and maternal-eroticism shape the successive erotic personae Hermione projects on Fayne Rabb who is at once the boy-child, "Itylus," the "sister swallow," and the narcissistic "sister" of Swinburne's "Before the Mirror." Through her Decadent heritage, therefore, Hermione disrupts the poetic of male desire and becomes the speaking subject of her emerging poetic powers. The complex weave of Swinburne's poems that winds through the narrative recreates a countermyth of womanhood, drawing on those Romantic linguistic practices, forms of desire, and theories of imagination that H. D.'s modernist contemporaries had pronounced "effeminate" and "unwholesome." H. D.'s and Hermione's "use" of Swinburne to disrupt conventional gender roles and sexuality is worth examining in more detail.

Quotations from five of Swinburne's works recur throughout HER, including "Faustine," "Itylus," "Before the Mirror," and "The Triumph of Time" from Poems and Ballads and lines from the opening of Swinburne's play, Atalanta in Calydon: "When the hounds of spring . . ." The most frequently quoted lines derive from "Itylus" and "Before the Mirror," both central to the emerging complex of gender-disruptions and forms of desire which Hermione experiences in her love for Fayne. "Itylus" (CW 187–89), and particularly the line, "sister, my sister, O fleet, sweet swallow," dominates the narrative of HER, inscribing the homoerotic and sympathetic love between Hermione and Fayne, as well as the prophetic, and poetic dimensions which emerge from the "sister-love." H. D. appears to have avoided Swinburne's overtly lesbian poems, such as the sadomasochistic "Anactoria" (which succeeds "Itylus" in the volume) in favor of the more sympathetic bond expressed in "Itylus." H. D.'s "use" of the poem derives in part from Swinburne's "feminist" revision of the Procne/Philomel legend which places the emphasis on the bond between the sisters—Philomel had slain her own son, Itylus, in order to revenge her husband's rape and mutilation of her sister, Procne. While Philomel's romantic call to the "sister swallow" evokes homoeroticism, H. D.'s more overtly lesbian interpretation of the poem led her to misquote Swinburne's line, "the heart's division divideth us" as "the world's division divideth us" (124 and throughout) suggesting the heterosexism that denies lesbian love. Indeed, Swinburne's "Itylus" must stand as H. D.'s chief Romantic precursor poem: the lines resonate throughout her career, from *HER* to the later *Helen in Egypt,* always signifying the search for the kindred "spirit-love" that was to distinguish H. D.'s philosophy of love.[33] The refrain from "Itylus" hovers spectrally behind the narrative of *HER* from Hermione's first apprehension of the sexual and spiritual awakening inaugurated by Fayne. Sitting at the breakfast table where she receives Fayne's invitation to *Pygmalion,* Hermione perceives "something like a dynamo vibrating with electricity from some far distance." These prophetic stirrings are decoded in part by Hermione's simultaneous call to the sister-spirit she vaguely apprehends in her compulsive incantation of Swinburne's "Itylus," — *"sister my sister, O singing swallow, the way is long to the sun and south"* (123, 124, H. D.'s emphasis). Thereafter, Hermione's chanting of "Itylus" forms a prelude to the lovers' erotic and prophetic sessions in her workroom where "prophetess faced prophetess" (146). The lines of the poem haunt the physical as well as spiritual union of the lovers in Hermione's workroom; lying across the body of the sleeping Fayne, Hermione imagines their hearts beating to the rhythm of the poem: *"O sister my sister O fleet sweet swallow* ran rhythm of her head and *hast thou the heart to be glad thereof yet* beat rhythm of a heart that beat and beat . . ." (180, H. D.'s emphasis).

The homoeroticism implied by the opening lines of "Itylus" forms part of a spectrum of desires and gender-disruptions articulated by Swinburne's poems, including narcissism, androgyny, and maternal-eroticism, which in turn lead Hermione to the complexities of signification and to her poetic vocation. Swinburne's overtly narcissistic "Before the Mirror" (CW 260–62) forms yet another strand in the matrix of "forbidden" desires which inscribe Hermione's love for Fayne. Swinburne's poem is dedicated to Whistler, and inspired by his painting, *The Little White Girl,* of a young girl in white leaning languidly against a mantle whose mirror reflects her dreamy expression. Swinburne used Whistler's painting to create a romantic and erotic portrait of female narcissism; the poem alludes both to the sentimental love for a "sister" image and to masturbation: "Nought else exalts or grieves/ the rose at heart, that heaves/ with love of her own leaves and lips that pair." H. D. quotes most frequently from the lines which suggest a spiritual fusion between the girl and her ghostly "sister" image: "Art thou the ghost, my sister,/ White sister there,/ Am I the ghost, who knows?" These lines recur frequently in conjunction with the opening lines of "Itylus" and contribute to the evolving myth of womanhood constructed by Swinburne's poems, whereby Hermione taps her spiritual, erotic, and poetic powers through intimate self-identification with a "twin-self sister."

The homoeroticism and narcissism of "Itylus," "O sister," and "Before the Mirror" are joined by Fayne's shifting identity in "Itylus" as female "sister" and slain boy-child, "Itylus," further complicating the sexual/textual configurations inscribed by Swinburne. Significantly, Hermione forgets Fayne's name following their initial meeting, and fails to recognize the import of Fayne's appearance in her life until she has "named" her "Itylus." By "naming" Fayne with Swinburne's "Itylus," Hermione articulates a spectrum of "forbidden" desires associated with the Decadent Romantic which remain "nameless" in the dominant discourse and simultaneously discovers the infinite possibilities of language. As the slain boy-child, Fayne is not only the lost "sister" but the lost "child" in the shifting erotic-familial bonds which characterize Hermione's relation to Fayne. Further, Fayne's cross-gender identities as twin-sister and boy, "Itylus," join the several masks of androgyny which Hermione projects on her beloved, who is successively, the beautiful boy Pygmalion, the huntress Artemis, a "boy hunter," and the boy Itylus. While H. D. does not refer in *HER* to Swinburne's actual poetic explorations of androgyny, "Hermaphroditus," and "Fragoletta" (as mentioned above), she quoted Swinburne's reference to the boygirl Fragoletta as a "double rose of love's" in "Paint It" to evoke the "double" and more fluid sexualities of the androgyne and the bisexual. Hermione's articulation of her own and Fayne's "double" sexual identities in the "naming" of Fayne as the boy Itylus releases her from her object-position in the discourse of male desire and gives Hermione access to the multiple, polysemous, power of "words." Hermione's discovery of her bisexuality, a "name" for Fayne, occurs, appropriately, while she endures the "obliterating" kisses of George Lowndes. Musing on his earlier quotation from Swinburne's *Atalanta,* she reflects, "The kisses of George smudged out her clear geometric thought but his words had given her something . . . *the brown bright nightingale amorous . . . is half assuaged for . . . for . . .* her name is *Itylus* (H. D.'s emphasis)." In the same meditation, Hermione lights upon her "heritage": "Words may be my heritage. . . ." and "mythopoeic mind (mine) will disprove science . . . she could not say how or when she saw this; she knew it related back to an odd girl" (73, 76). Hermione's simultaneous discovery of the "mythopoeic mind," the multiple meanings of "words," and the plurality of her "forbidden" desires demonstrates the sexual/textual configuration Eliot and Pound deplored in Swinburne's "unwholesome," evasive signification which failed to make the rigid one-to-one correspondence between "word" and "thing." One might also accuse the text of *HER* itself—a lesbian novel written in deliberately disjunctive and associative prose—of such Swinburnian "effeminacy."

"FAUSTINE": THE DARK SIDE OF DECADENT REVISIONISM

However, H. D.'s construction of a "female" tradition in her countermyth of Romantic origins poses problems for the individual female talent not encountered by her male contemporaries. While male poets constructed an opposition between an "unhealthy" and inferior Romantic poetics and an autonomous, vigorous modernism, both assumed a place in the tradition. By contrast, Hermione experiences an aggravated form of "anxiety of authorship," as she wavers between a feminine identity that would entirely silence her, or a marginal "Decadent" poetic identity which threatens, in the second half of the novel, to self-destruct. Hermione's use of Swinburne does not ensure that she will continue to write poems. Indeed, in assuming the Romantic "forbidden" and "effeminate" poetic, she risks the ostracism and censure of her male contemporaries, and equally, if not more destructive, her own internalization of the "Decadent" discourse that would efface her powers. H. D. consciously introduces Hermione's self-doubt through evoking the double-edged sword of feminist revisions of Decadence. While Hermione is initially successful in finding a way out of the "silencing system" imposed by George Lowndes through her transformation of Swinburne, she is finally defeated and driven to madness by the relentless resurfacing of the "Decadence" inscribed in the Romantic poetic. Two Swinburnes begin to form toward the end of the novel; the empowering Swinburne of "Itylus" gives place to the "Decadent" creator of the demonic *femme fatale* "Faustine," as Hermione begins to doubt the integrity of the visionary and erotic powers she has discovered in Fayne. Both Hermione's and Fayne's reentrance into the heterosexist discourse of the novel is signaled by their shifting attitude toward Swinburne who once articulated the nonhierarchical "sister-love," and now speaks the erotic perversities of a religion of vice. Swinburne and George Lowndes thus appear temporarily in collusion; both agreed that Fayne and Hermione should be "burned as witches."

The lines from "Faustine" (*CW* 238–43) relate the erotically cruel encounter between Fayne and Hermione (162–64), transforming Fayne from sister-child to lesbian vampire, "Faustine." The poem's description of the sadistic empress's face on the Roman coin — "curled lips long since half kissed away. . . . long ere they coined in Roman gold, your face, Faustine" —continually interrupt the narration which reinforces its suggestively sadistic strain of sensuality. Fayne's "empress mouth made its down-twist, made its up-twist that scarred the line of the face." Fayne puts "into her low voice the sort of scorn that went with *curled lips long since half kissed away* (H. D.'s emphasis)." The self-conscious "decadence" of the scene that encodes the kiss between Fayne and Hermione enacts a ritualized celebration of "vice," complete with the gothic props of swirling "wine-colored" curtains and the obsessive incantation of "Faustine."

I feel the fringe of some fantastic wine-colored parting curtains. Curtains part as I look into the eyes of Fayne Rabb . . . curtains parted, curtains filled the air with heavy swooping purple. Lips long since half kissed away. Curled lips long since half kissed away. . . . Long ere they coined in Roman gold your face—your face—your face—your face—your face—Faustine. (165)

Immediately following the kiss, Hermione looks up into Fayne's face which is "too white" and feels as if they "had fallen into a deep well and were looking up." While the scene effectively conveys the powerful eroticism which is lacking in Hermione's clumsy encounters with George Lowndes, the image of the well conjures up yet another form of confinement, perhaps more dangerous. H. D. deliberately evokes the dark side of Swinburne to demonstrate the rupture of the "sister-love" that climaxes in Fayne's betrayal of Hermione with George Lowndes. Shortly after the kiss, Fayne asks Hermione pointedly, "[I]sn't Swinburne Decadent?" To Hermione's confused question, " In what sense exactly decadent, Fayne?" Fayne cryptically pronounces their relationship "indecent" and "immoral": Oh innocence holy and untouched and most immoral. Innocence like thine is totally indecent" (165). Fayne's new assessment of their intimacy and her subsequent repetition of George Lowndes's words, "he said you and I ought to be burnt for witchcraft," signals her betrayal with George Lowndes (165). Shortly afterwards, Hermione's assimilation into the heterosexist discourse is complete when she concludes, "she knew that they should be burnt for witchcraft . . . she knew that George was right" (165). Significantly, Lowndes also turns the very words from Swinburne that affirmed her sister-love into a mocking pronouncement against what he perceives as a perverse, but titillating (to him) narcissism—"art thou a ghost my sister? Narcissi, are you a water lily?" (208). H. D. continues to manipulate the Janus face of Swinburne to convey Hermione's struggle to place her newfound desires and prophetic power either as "perverse," isolating, and therefore annihilating, or as liberating and empowering. Abandoned by both Fayne and George, Hermione descends into mental and physical illness. In the climactic mad scene of the novel, Hermione's disassociated thoughts consider whether she should go on "arguing" or conform to the consensus that would pronounce her and Fayne "Decadent." While she repeatedly calls to Fayne through Swinburne's "Before the Mirror"—"my sister there"—Hermione just as abruptly switches back into the discourse of her family, fiancé, and the betraying Fayne, warning herself, "remember always that Swinburne being decadent there's no use arguing . . ." (H. D.'s ellipsis).

However, the novel remains distinct from those lesbian novels of the twenties such as Radclyffe Hall's *The Well of Loneliness* or Renée Vivien's earlier sadomasochistic Swinburnian poems of homoerotic thralldom to a cruel "maîtresse."[34] Unlike Vivien and Hall, H. D. self-consciously maintains an equal tension or dialectic between the affirming myth and its potential negation which is never deliberately resolved. In retaining the dialectic, Hermione both explores the impossibility of creating an entirely empowering myth within the male discourse and preserves the trace of Hermione's exuberant escape into prophetic and erotic power with Fayne Rabb. While the novel closes enigmatically with the maid's report that Fayne Rabb is in Hermione's "workroom," Fayne's alleged return to the scene of their intimacy momentarily conjures the "ghost, my sister there" Hermione, fashioned from Swinburne.

H. D. was not always so successful at preserving the delicate balance of Decadent revisionism. Returning once more to her Romantic origins during the forties, H. D.'s research notes for her Pre-Raphaelite novel, *White Rose and Red,* indicate that she began to identify too closely with Swinburne the "perverse" and ostracized Decadent. Acutely sensitive about the critical misunderstanding of her own work (frequently labeled "Romantic" and escapist). H. D.'s research notes underscored in red the public "vendetta to suppress" Swinburne's *Poems and Ballads.* Anxious about her writing "delays," H. D. quoted disconcertingly from Swinburne's self-pitying "The Leper" (CW 250–55):

Yea, though God always hated me—
It may be all my love went wrong—
A scribe's work writ awry and blurred,
Scrawled after the blind evensong—
Spoilt music with no perfect word . . .[35]

H. D. seemed, momentarily, to have internalized the male modernists' perception of Swinburne's sexual and linguistic depravity. However, unlike Renée Vivien, H. D. did not allow the "dark" side of Decadence to rule her imagination for long. Her excitement over Swinburne's *Lesbia Brandon* five years later indicated that she still found strength in the Decadent's fearless defiance of conventional gender-roles and sexuality. This time she was bolstered by her discovery that Swinburne "had some of the same sort of ideas and delays."[36] Just weeks later, H. D. began the quest-romance of her own sexual history, *Helen in Egypt;* she had, perhaps, once more tapped the prophetic and poetic power of her Romantic "origins."

NOTES

A Visiting Fellowship to the Beinecke Library, Yale University (Summer 1987) enabled me to research and write parts of this chapter.

A version of this chapter first appeared in *Feminist Studies,* 15, no. 3 (Fall 1989): 461–84, under the title, "H. D. and A. C. Swinburne: Decadence and Modernist Women's Writing."

1. Letter to Norman Holmes Pearson, 8 August 1952, Beinecke Library, Yale University.
2. Both Harold Bloom in *The Anxiety of Influence* (New York: Oxford Univ. Press, 1973) and George Bornstein in *Transformations of Romanticism in Yeats, Eliot and Stevens* (Chicago: Univ. of Chicago Press, 1976) trace a tripartite structure in the pattern of influence from early imitation to rejection and finally reconciliation with the literary "forefather."
3. For studies of Romantic and Victorian influence in the male modernist tradition see: Harold Bloom's *Yeats* (Chicago: Univ. of Chicago Press, 1970); Frank Kermode's *Romantic Image* (New York: Vintage, 1964); George Bornstein's *Transformations of Romanticism;* Robert Langbaum's *The Poetry of Experience: The Dramatic Monologue in Modern Literary Tradition* (New York: Norton, 1963); and Carol T. Christ's *Victorian and Modern Poetics* (Chicago: Univ. of Chicago Press, 1984).
4. Frank Kermode's *Romantic Image* defines the paradigmatic modern image as the Romantic figure of the female muse. See also Margaret Homans's essay, " 'Syl-

lables of Velvet': Dickinson, Rossetti, and the Rhetoric of Sexuality," in *Feminist Studies* 11, no. 3 (Fall 1985); 569–93. Homans asserts that the " 'I' of romantic lyric is constitutively masculine" and that "the romantic lyric depends on the plot of masculine heterosexual desire. . . . The poem crosses the space between the questing self and the feminine object of his desire . . ." (570). Her essay demonstrates how Rossetti and Dickinson disrupt the heterosexual plot of romantic lyric.

5. Kaplan, " 'A Gigantic Mother,' " 166. Violet Hunt's "My Oscar," reproduced by Robert Secor in "Aesthetes and Pre-Raphaelites: Oscar Wilde and the Sweetest Violet in England," *Tulsa Studies in Language and Literature* 21, no. 3 (Fall 1979): 401. Hunt's "My Oscar" is a reminiscence of her relationship with Oscar Wilde. Willa Cather, *Courier*, 30 November 1895, reproduced in *The World and the Parish*, ed. William M. Curtin (Lincoln, Neb.: Nebraska Univ. Press, 1970), 277. O'Brien, " 'The Thing Not Named,' " 588. Gubar, "Sapphistries," 49. Gubar describes Sappho as a "fantasy precursor" whose remoteness allows the modern woman writer to "write 'for' or 'as' Sappho and thereby invent a classical inheritance of her own." However, modernist writers such as H. D. and Vivien also looked to Swinburne for a more recent and accessible range of poetic conventions which would concretize the "fantasy precursor" they perceived in Sappho.

6. See Alicia Ostriker's discussion of modernist women writers' unwillingness to claim the influence of their contemporaries, "What Do Women (Poets) Want?: H. D. and Marianne Moore as Poetic Ancestresses," *Contemporary Literature* 27, no. 4 (Winter 1986).

7. Shari Benstock's *Women of the Left Bank* (Austin: Univ. of Texas Press, 1986), Marianne DeKoven's *A Different Language: Gertrude Stein's Experimental Language* (Madison: Univ. of Wisconsin Press, 1983), and Taffy Martin's *Marianne Moore: Subversive Modernist* (Austin: Univ. of Texas Press, 1986) and others, inquire into how modernist women writers disrupt the patriarchal constructs of the high modernist aesthetic.

8. Stimpson, "Zero Degree Deviancy," 253. Faderman, *Surpassing the Love of Men*, 268. Feminist critics often deny Swinburne's influence because his lesbian images are perceived as pornographic male fantasies shaped by the "male gaze." Similarly, Sydney Kaplan describes Oscar Wilde as a "curious" model for Katherine Mansfield, stressing that "even in his supposed androgyny" the Decadent Aesthete is a "male" figure (Kaplan 166, 167).

9. See Nancy Chodorow's *The Reproduction of Mothering: Psychoanalysis and the Sociology of Gender* (Berkeley: Univ. of California Press, 1978). Masculinist and feminist critics alike have accepted Freud's Oedipal construct as the configuration behind the psychology of "influence" in the male literary tradition. However, it would seem that Chodorow's model for the social construction of male identity which insists on separation from the mother better suits the pattern of modernist "anxiety" toward an eroticized "foremother."

10. See Gilbert and Gubar's second volume of *No Man's Land, Sexchanges* (New Haven: Yale Univ. Press, 1989), particularly chapter 1, "Heart of Darkness:

The Agon of the Femme Fatale," for further discussion of the *femme fatale* in male modernist writing.

11. Sandra M. Gilbert and Susan Gubar attribute the misogynist attitude of high modernism toward the female "scribblers" to male anxiety about the proliferation and success of "women's fiction" during the first decades of the twentieth century in "Tradition and Female Talent," in *The Poetics of Gender,* ed. Nancy K. Miller (New York: Columbia Univ. Press, 1986).

12. Hulme, "Romanticism and Classicism," in *Speculations,* ed. Read. (Hereafter cited in the text as *Speculations.*)

13. Pound, "Lionel Johnson," 362. Eliot's argument concerning the Romantics' separation of "emotion" from "intellect" pervades his critical work, but is most clearly put forth in his essay "The Metaphysical Poets," in *Selected Essays,* 241–50. Yeats actually accused his own work during the nineties of a "womanish introspection." See *The Letters of W. B. Yeats,* ed. Allen Wade (New York: Macmillan, 1955), 434. (Hereafter cited in the text and notes as *Letters.*)

14. First expressed in a 1906 letter to Florence Farr (*Letters* 469).

15. Eliot, "On the Development of Taste," 33–34. Bornstein discusses this passage on Eliot's description of his early Romanticism in *Transformations of Romanticism* (96, 97) as evidence that Eliot feared and suppressed the powerful sexuality of the Romantics.

16. Pound, "Swinburne Versus his Biographers," 294, 295. Interestingly, when Pound wishes to defend Swinburne he insists upon Swinburne's "masculinity," appealing to Swinburne "the strong swimmer" and the "intemperate drinker."

17. Hélène Cixous presents her project for "feminine writing" in "The Laugh of the Medusa," in *New French Feminisms,* ed. Elaine Marks and Isabelle de Courtivron (New York: Schocken, 1981) and in "Castration or Decapitation?" *Signs* 1 (Summer 1981); 41–55. See also Leslie Brisman's "Swinburne's Semiotics," *Georgia Review* 30 (1977): 578–97. Brisman maintains that Eliot and Pound are correct about Swinburne's evasive signification and that Swinburne deliberately avoids concrete "meaning" in order to reveal the complexities of signification itself.

18. H. D. originally entitled the book *HER,* but her publishers renamed the work *HERmione* to avoid overlap with another novel of the same name. Here I use H. D.'s original title.

19. A reference to Gubar and Gilbert's discussion of the male image of the woman writer as "unnatural," castrating, and/or mad in *The Madwoman in the Attic.*

20. Unpublished review of Yeats's *Responsibilities* which was reprinted in *Agenda* 25, nos. 3–4 (Autumn/Winter 1987–88); 51–53. For more on H. D.'s use of eroticized landscapes to realize this agenda in her poetry, see my essay "H. D.'s Romantic Landscapes: The Sexual Politics of the Garden," *Sagetrieb,* H. D. Issue, 6, no. 2 (Fall 1987): 57–75.

21. See "H. D. by Delia Alton," 194, 195.

22. Critics have attributed H. D.'s silence to her indifference to the narrow Imagist doctrine which her own art surpassed; however, H. D.'s letters to Amy Lowell in 1916 (Beinecke Library, Yale University) during the preparation of the Imag-

ist anthology reveal that she was actively engaged in the compilation of the anthology and well aware of the tenets of Imagism.

23. Nancy Chodorow's model for the social construction of gender identity provides a plausible psychoanalytic theory for the differing relation of H. D. and her male contemporaries to their Romantic "foremother." While Yeats's and Eliot's program for a "virile" modernism depended on separation from the Romantic "foremother," H. D.'s young poet-heroines achieve creative autonomy through connection to the "female" tradition.

24. Letter to Amy Lowell, 19 July 1919, Beinecke Library, Yale University. H. D. complained to Amy Lowell about the "cynicism" (September 1918) and undue stress upon "originality and cleverness" of the "modern cult of brutality" she perceived in writers such as Joyce and Eliot.

25. "Asphodel," pt. 1, p. 96, pt. 2, p. 20, Beinecke Library, Yale University.

26. Letter to John Cournos, 9 July 1917, Beinecke Library, Yale University.

27. Susan Friedman and Rachel DuPlessis identify HER as essentially a lesbian text whose heroine discovers poetic, prophetic, and erotic power through union with a "twin self sister" in " 'I Had Two Loves Separate.' " While I disagree with Shari Benstock's perception of the lesbian relationship in HER (Women of the Left Bank, 335–49) as "split" by its internalization of various patriarchal prerogatives and therefore destructive, Benstock's emphasis on Hermione's quest to "make herself the subject of her language" has been helpful to this discussion.

28. In " 'I had Two Loves Separate,' " Friedman and DuPlessis touch on Swinburne's poems as a means of encoding the lesbianism of the novel. Shari Benstock (Women of the Left Bank) does not attempt to describe his role in the semiotics of Hermione's quest for subjectivity.

29. Ellis, "Sexual Inversion," 1: 22. See also Esther Newton's "The Mythic Mannish Lesbian: Radclyffe Hall and the New Woman," Signs 9, no. 4 (Summer 1984), 557–75. Newton discusses the relationship between the sexologists' theories of "congential inversion" and the character of Stephen in The Well.

30. Rachel DuPlessis argues convincingly that H. D. repeatedly used shifting familial-erotic bonds in her work to escape "romantic thralldom" to male power in "Romantic Thralldom in H. D.," Contemporary Literature 20, no. 2 (Summer 1979): 179–203. I suggest here that H. D. found an early model for her feminist experiments with alternative sexualities in Swinburne.

31. Swinburne, The Complete Works, 1: 213, 215. (Hereafter cited in text as CW.) H. D. quotes from these passages in "Paint It Today," chap. 6, pp. 11, 12.

32. Benstock also perceives HERmione as a critique of high modernism, and particularly of the Imagist enterprise (Women of the Left Bank, 335–49).

33. The line "O sister, O shadow" is quoted in reference to Clytaemnestra in Helen in Egypt (New York: New Directions, 1974) bk. 7, pt. 6, p. 103. Interestingly, Eliot also quotes from "Itylus" at the end of the Wasteland—"O swallow swallow." Far from signifying the "sister-bond," Eliot's reference points toward the rape and mutiliation of Procne as one more evocation of loveless sexuality in the wasteland of modern culture. One might speculate that Eliot's implicit

condemnation of Swinburne's sexuality enters into his choice of "Itylus" as well.

34. I use Hall's *Well of Loneliness* as an example of a lesbian novel which internalizes heterosexist attitudes toward "inversion." However, Gillian Whitlock argues convincingly that *The Well* has not received a fair critical reading, and that Hall is struggling to create a specifically lesbian language and imagery. See " 'Everything is out of Place': Radclyffe Hall and the Lesbian Literary Tradition," *Feminist Studies* 13, no. 3 (Fall 1987): 555–82. Several of Vivien's poems are written to a domineering "mistress"; but Vivien's "After Swinburne" directly acknowledges the influence of the Decadent-Romantic.

35. "Notes on Pre-Raphaelites," 25, 27, Beinecke Library, Yale University.

36. Letter to Norman Holmes Pearson, 8 August 1952, Beinecke Library, Yale University.

WORKS CITED

Aldington, Richard. "Violet Hunt." *The Egoist.* 1 January 1917, 17, 18.

Eliot, T. S. "On the Development of Taste in Poetry." In *The Use of Poetry and the Use of Criticism.* London: Faber, 1964, 32–36.

———. "Swinburne as Poet." In *Selected Essays.* New York: Harcourt, 1932, 281–85.

Ellis, Havelock. "Sexual Inversion." In *Studies in the Psychology of Sex.* Vol. 1, pt. 4. New York: Random, 1942, 1–384.

Faderman, Lillian. *Surpassing the Love of Men.* New York: Morrow, 1981.

Friedman, Susan, and Rachel Blau DuPlessis. " 'I Had Two Loves Separate': The Sexualities of H. D.'s *HER.*" *Montemora* 8 (1981): 7–30.

Gilbert, Sandra M., and Susan Gubar. *The Madwoman in the Attic: The Woman Writer and the Nineteenth-Century Literary Imagination.* New Haven: Yale Univ. Press, 1979.

Gubar, Susan. "Sapphistries." *Signs* 10, no. 1 (Autumn 1984): 43–62.

H. D. "Asphodel." Beinecke Library, Yale University.

———. "H. D. by Delia Alton." *The Iowa Review* 16, no. 2 (Fall 1986): 194–95.

———. *HERmione.* New York: New Directions, 1981.

———. Letter to John Cournos, 9 July 1917. Beinecke Library, Yale University.

———. Letter to Amy Lowell, 19 July 1919. Beinecke Library, Yale University.

———. Letter to Norman Holmes Pearson, 8 August 1952. Beinecke Library, Yale University.

———. "Notes on Pre-Raphaelites." Beinecke Library, Yale University.

———. "Paint It Today." Beinecke Library, Yale University.

———. "Responsibilities." *Agenda* 25, nos. 3–4 (1987–88): 51–53.

Hulme, T. E. *Further Speculations.* Ed. Sam Hynes. Minneapolis: Univ. of Minnesota Press, 1955.

———. "Romanticism and Classicism." In *Speculations.* Ed. Herbert Read. New York: Harcourt, 1924, 113–40.

Kaplan, Sydney Janet. " 'A Gigantic Mother': Katherine Mansfield's London." In *Women Writers and the City: Essays in Feminist Literary Criticsm*. Ed. Susan Merrill Squier. Knoxville: Univ. of Tennessee Press, 1984, 161–75.

O'Brien, Sharon. " 'The Thing Not Named': Willa Cather as a Lesbian Writer." *Signs* 9, no. 4 (1984): 576–99.

Pound, Ezra. "Lionel Johnson." In *Literary Essays*. Ed. T. S. Eliot. New York: New Directions, 1968, 361–70.

———. "Swinburne versus his Biographers." In *Literary Essays*. Ed. T. S. Eliot. New York: New Directions, 1968, 290–94.

Stimpson, Catharine R. "Zero Degree Deviancy: The Lesbian Novel in English." In *Writing and Sexual Difference*. Ed. Elizabeth Abel. Chicago: Univ. of Chicago Press, 1982: 243–59.

Swinburne, A. C. *The Complete Works*. Volume 1. Ed. Sir Edmond Gosse and Thomas Hames Wise. London: Heinemann, 1925.

———. *Swinburne Replies*. Ed. Clyde Kenneth Hyder. Syracuse, N. Y.: Syracuse Univ. Press, 1966.

Yeats, W. B. *The Autobiography*. New York: Collier, 1963.

———. *Essays and Introductions*. New York: Macmillan, 1961.

FIFTEEN

What's a Nice Lesbian Like You Doing in the Church of Torquemada? Radclyffe Hall and Other Catholic Converts

Joanne Glasgow

Catholicism has had a long and tangled connection with homosexuality. In present-day America, the Catholic church is seen as one of the archenemies of homosexuality, even while some may argue that it is one of the largest employers of homosexuals in the country. Catholic forces joined with ultraorthodox Jewish forces in a last-ditch effort to stop the gay rights legislation passed in New York City in 1986. The authorities in Rome silenced the efforts of the Jesuit John J. McNeill to minister to lesbian/gay male Catholics in America. Dignity, a community of lesbian/gay male Catholics, holds monthly protests outside St. Patrick's Cathedral in New York City, in the hopes of beginning a dialogue of reconciliation with the church. Lesbian Catholics in huge numbers have flocked to the nondenominational gay Metropolitan Community Church, to Wicce, to private religious gatherings, and alternative religions. Many have repudiated religion altogether in their despair at finding a secure "home" in the Roman Catholic church. Countless lesbian and gay male Catholics have stayed in the church, troubled, struggling, making personal, often very private "contracts" to preserve their faith. These struggles and protests are well known. Yet all the official voices of Roman Catholicism remain obdurate: They speak against homosexuality as if there were and always has been ("world without end") a prohibition, natural and ordained by God, against the abominations of the flesh represented by homoeroticism.

How startling, then, to find in the early years of this century significant numbers of lesbians deliberately choosing Roman Catholicism as their professed faith. That there have always been lesbian Catholics we know quite well. But it has been easy to assume that they were women brought up as Catholics, not women who in their maturity and in full knowledge of their lesbianism *chose* to become Catholics.

Yet in 1901 Violet Shiletto, lifelong friend of expatriate poet Renée Vivien, converted to Catholicism. In 1909, on her deathbed, Renée Vivien (born Pauline Mary Tarn) made that same profession. In 1907 Una Troubridge, for twenty-eight years the lover and companion of "John" Radclyffe Hall, became a Catholic. Five years later, but before she knew Una, so did Radclyffe Hall. During the years of World War I the painter Tony Atwood joined this "communion of saints," as did writer Christopher St. John, feminist, novelist, and editor of Ellen Terry's memoirs. And there were others, many of them (Auerbach 406–7).

Why? What did Catholicism mean to these writers and artists? Did they see the church differently from so many of their latter-day sisters? Was it a different church from the one I knew growing up? Or was it rather that they were different from those of us who have struggled to find reconciliation with church teaching today? In short, was the difference in the church or in the women?

I would argue from the evidence of church documents, catechisms, conduct manuals, and the writings of the women themselves, although these are generally circumspect, that their lesbian sexuality was seen as innocent by the church. Indeed, lesbianism did not exist as a Catholic reality.[1]

It is thus an epistemology of lesbianism that I propose to explore in this essay, a study of the construction of the meaning (or more accurately the nonmeaning) of lesbianism which was to influence early twentieth-century lesbian Catholic converts. While the essay does not, therefore, offer any close textual analysis, it does, like Bonnie Zimmerman's essay in this volume and like Lillian Faderman's important historical/linguistic studies *Surpassing the Love of Men* and *Scotch Verdict,* examine some linguistic epistemological interstices important to an understanding of the context in which some lesbian writers of the early twentieth century positioned themselves.

In simplest terms, the Catholic church of the early twentieth century had effectively erased lesbianism through the agency of language. Specifically, in Catholic popular teaching sexual acts by definition required ejaculation by a penis. Other sexual behaviors were certainly discouraged as what was usually termed "occasions of sin," which were, of course, to be avoided. If phallic agency is the reality denoted by the word *sex*, then acts performed by lesbians were not sex. Masturbation, in this understanding, is therefore a sin only for men. Indeed, Catholic popular teaching as late as the 1950s confirms this view. When I was in school, the nuns never mentioned masturbation to us girls, although my brother was taught that it was evil. The nuns certainly never suggested, probably did not consider possible, that my own adolescent experiments alone and with other girls might be sinful. They weren't. Sex was completely phallocentric.

Such personal anecdotal evidence, however, provides little more than the hunch or guess from which one might proceed. It by no means accounts for what are clearly major differences between Catholic teaching then and now, nor does it explain the self-understanding of such introspective, articulate, and highly self-aware adult women as "Ladye" Mabel Veronica Batten, Renée Vivien, Una Troubridge, and Radclyffe Hall. They were not simply living out the unselfconscious nineteenth-century "romantic friendship" that Faderman proposes as linguistic/epistemological reality in *Surpassing the Love of Men,* and that Zimmerman illustrates so well in her discussion of George Eliot. They were, after all, twentieth-century women for whom the linguistic/symbolic reality of lesbianism had been permanently altered by the work of Havelock Ellis and Krafft-Ebing, Freud, and other psychologists and sexologists. The priests may not have known what these women were doing, but the women themselves certainly did.

To understand what lesbianism meant to them *as Catholics,* therefore, we have to examine not only what they said—and did—about it, but also the sources that informed their thinking. We need to know just what catechetical manuals or methods were used in the early 1900s when these English and expatriate French lesbians converted. In the cases of Violet Shiletto and Renée Vivien in turn-of-the-century France, the question may be unanswerable, since both converted on their deathbeds. We can surmise, however, from the much later conversion of Alice B. Toklas (1957) that at least for Shiletto, another English-speaking convert, the catechism, if any had been used at all, would have been the English "penny catechism" (Toklas 355). This catechism was based on Bishop Richard Challoner's eighteenth-century *An Abridgment of Christian Doctrine,* itself derived from the 1566 Roman Catechism of the Council of Trent (*New Catholic Encyclopedia* 212, 214). In typical fashion, this catechism treats sexuality as a moral subject and, like most Catholic teaching in other documents, proscribes it outside of marriage. By implication, of course, this would mean that lesbianism, because it can occur *only* outside of marriage, is proscribed. Yet, lesbianism itself is never mentioned. When homosexuality is discussed (and it is discussed only obliquely), it is generally treated as a moral subject for males only.[2]

We know a bit more, though not much, about Una Troubridge's conversion, which was effected in Florence in 1907, when she was twenty. According to her biographer Richard Ormrod, Troubridge (or Margot Taylor, as she was then) had probed in that rather typical adolescent fashion for deeper religious meaning and truths than her Anglican faith seemed to offer. She flirted with Buddhism and other Eastern religions (Ormrod 37). In 1907 her extended visit to her Florentine cousins, the Tealdis, finally precipitated her decision to become a Catholic. Surrounded as she was by unquestioning and long-established Catholic families, for whom religion was a part of the daily fabric of life, with its rituals, devotions, celebrations, and food, as well as the "true path" to salvation, Troubridge felt herself an outsider, even perhaps outside the divine plan of salvation. Catholicism offered what was for her a more profoundly experienced religious satisfaction than Anglican Christianity. It also offered comfort, belonging, and eternal salvation, as well. At that time, there seems to have been no conflict about sexual morality, as Troubridge was not to adopt a lesbian identification until much later, when in 1915 she met and fell in love with Radclyffe Hall, usually called "John." Even then, however, she appears to have suffered no crisis of conscience over sexual morality and the teachings of her adopted faith. Indeed, if we are to trust one of her last pronouncements, made the year before her death in 1963, she never did experience any struggle on this account. Asked by a friend how she and John had reconciled their "inversion" with their Catholicism, what they did about confession, Troubridge replied very simply, "There was nothing to confess" (Baker 357).

One might be tempted to attribute this absence of conflict to the assuagements of habit and time, to speculate that by the end of their life together they were not sexually active, or to assume that Troubridge's Catholicism had been integrated into her identity firmly enough not to be dislodged by later developments. Certainly we know that there are a good many lesbians who have grown up Catholic and have been able to reconcile their sexuality with religious practice. But in almost all such instances, the reconciliation is achieved only after considerable intellectual and/or emotional struggle.[3] The startling realization in Troubridge's case is that there was no recorded struggle at all. And this is remarkable precisely because Troubridge kept extensive and very intimate diaries in which she recorded almost everything that weighed on her mind or her conscience. If there had been any struggle, as there was over the church's condemnation of psychic mediation—and her beloved Ouija boards—it would have been recorded.

In the case of Mabel Veronica Batten, Hall's lover from 1907 to 1915, we have even less evidence. "Ladye," as she was called, had always been a Catholic. She was a married woman, as well. What she thought of her relationship with John as it might have affected religious teaching, we simply do not know. Ladye is known to us only through Hall's and Troubridge's accounts. But it seems safe to conclude that she, too, saw no conflict. Hall's conversion was aided and encouraged by Ladye, and together they visited churches, shrines, even the Pope. They were both enthusiastic, devout, and wholehearted about religious observances. Their behavior betrays neither doubt nor struggle.

The figure about whom we know the most is, of course, Radclyffe Hall. Raised in the Church of England, but most influenced in religion by her American grandmother Sarah Diehl, Hall, like Una Troubridge with whom she was to live for twenty-eight years, found most of her deepest religious yearnings unfulfilled. Her early religious training had stressed a God of judgment, which she later identified as the Protestant God, strenuous, stern, and rigorous. But in Ladye's Catholicism she witnessed a more relaxed and easy-going attitude, what Michael Baker characterizes as a southern European or Italian attitude, one in which religion and God were part of the sunny Mediterranean way of life (43). In January 1912, Hall and Ladye went to see Max Reinhardt's *The Miracle,* a play featuring a fallen nun who is redeemed by a statue of the Madonna. Hall records that the play moved her deeply (Baker 43), and she decided to become a Catholic.

Her religious instruction was provided by Father Sebastian Bowden, one of the most fashionable of the Brompton Oratorians to whom many of the wealthy or talented or famous turned for spiritual guidance and instruction (Ellmann 93–94). Within a month Bowden had received Radclyffe Hall into the church.

One cannot but wonder what he thought of his unusual convert. He certainly knew she was living with Ladye. Her remarkable appearance—in tailored suits, stetson and all—was already generating familiar gossip in London. She was neither self-effacing nor closeted. But appearances, no matter how semiotically revealing, are not declarations. Besides, Bowden was by that time nearly eighty years old. He was approached as a priest by a sincerely religious woman looking for guidance. Both John and Ladye were pious, wealthy, and well placed. As an Anglican, John would have been familiar with most of the doctrines and moral standards of Christianity. What remained for her to know and accept were those few areas of difference between the two forms of Christianity. It seems reasonable to conclude that Bowden saw no difficulties in his priestly task. He raised no objection. And nothing in his instructions to her threw up any insurmountable barriers to conversion. In fact, the process was rapid, smooth, uncomplicated.

What, though, of John herself? Although *The Well of Loneliness* was still sixteen years from being written, Hall's own awareness of her sexuality was firmly in place. She was thirty-two years old. She could not be accused of innocence or naïveté or even simple ignorance, as one might say of Una Troubridge. Yet never in all the years to follow did Hall once express a conflict between her religion and her sexual behavior. Her faith was deep and fervent and permanent. She went to Mass almost daily. She kept relics, including one she believed to be of the True Cross. She spent many hours conversing with priests, and in her early years with Troubridge was so rigorously devout and bigoted that Una swore John was likely to become another Torquemada herself (Troubridge 48).

After Ladye's death, John and Una offered Masses for her, included her in their prayers, and lit votive candles in her memory. These small pieties, combined with their enthusiasm for the larger, more public religion of magnificent ritual, and their appreciation of the richness of visual and sensory expression—that is, the art, literature, and music of Catholicism —answered a lifelong need for spiritual wholeness and connectedness. If Hall had seen her sexual identity, which was central to her self-definition, as problematic, one could never discover that conflict in her religious practices.

Indeed, Hall is as explicit as Troubridge was to be many years later. After the vicious newspaper attacks on *The Well* and on Hall as a perverter of Christian decency, she was, according to Una, in such

deep spiritual pain that throughout the remaining years of her life she could scarcely bear to speak of it, even to me. Once she did say: "To think that I should have been used as a means of disrespect to Him . . ." (Troubridge 104)

In support of her defense at the obscenity trial, Hall made clear her conviction that she had in no way subverted traditional moral or religious or social teaching.

I claim emphatically that the true invert is born and not made. I have behind me in this claim the weight of most of the finest psychological opinion [Havelock Ellis]. . . . Only when this fact is fully grasped can we hope for the exercise of that charitable help and compassion that will assist inverts to give of their best and thus contribute to the good of the whole. When I wrote The Well of Loneliness [sic] I had in mind the good of the whole quite as much as the good of congenital inverts. (Baker 238)

This "good of the whole" is for Hall a traditional concept, a vision of people, classes, interests, all hierarchically ordered and fitting together, the harmony coming from the infusion of God's goodness throughout. She did not claim a special place for inverts, much less an exalted one. She even willingly designated that place to be lower than the usual low rung women occupied in the hierarchy, a conclusion which has often pained lesbians in our own time. At the end of that same deposition quoted above, she argued that "[f]or the sake of the future generation inverts should never be encouraged to marry" (Baker 238).

More emphatically, in an interview with Evelyn Irons in the Daily Mail, Hall stated, "To be a good wife and mother is the finest work a woman can do" (Baker 248). To plead for understanding for inverts, even to insist that they are made by God as they are and so are not to be condemned, is not for Hall a radical or subversive stance. It was rather a profoundly Catholic stance. She so believed that her views upheld the established order and added to the great harmony that God's love promised to all that she could still be vulnerable to deep shock at the attacks on her. Her lesbianism was not anti-Catholic or anti-Christian. It was simply a part of her God-given nature, hence outside morality altogether. So what conflict could there be?

Clearly, then, when we examine what these individual women thought about the reconcilability of lesbianism and Catholicism, we see that for them resolution was simple. The reality represented linguistically as inversion (or lesbianism) may have been problematic in secular terms, as the trial of The Well illustrates, but it was not problematic in religious terms.

Nor did their religious advisors find it problematic in teaching and catechetical terms, where the general instructions were simple. Of the three main categories (creed, code, and cult), the teachings on code provided guidelines for moral action. Usually these guidelines followed the "Ten Commandments" of the Old Testament as revised and reinterpreted by Christianity and by centuries of Catholic tradition, and the "Six Commandments" of the Church itself. Sexuality was regulated by Commandments six and nine of the first group, commandments against adultery, also interpreted after Paul and early church fathers to include fornication. If one neither fornicated nor committed adultery, one did not violate the code.

It is precisely at this point, it seems to me, that one begins to make sense of the apparent contradiction between lesbianism and Catholicism and to see why it presented no obstacles to any of the women who embraced both. When one begins to look at church teaching about sexuality as it was generally interpreted, two major factors emerge—first, the erasure of women as instrumental agents of sexuality, an erasure which is itself a result of deep misogyny in the church; second, the instrumentality of language itself in determining the reality of individual acts.

The erasure of women as agents of sexuality, and hence the erasure of lesbianism, has a long history in Catholic teaching. It was accomplished by an almost total silence on the subject, a silence which itself provides an illustration of the process through which early twentieth-century Catholics were able to accommodate positions which late in the century lesbians have found almost impossible to reconcile.

According to John Boswell, in what remains the best, most thorough, and most scholarly history of Roman Catholicism and homosexuality, *Christianity, Social Tolerance, and Homosexuality,* widespread discrimination against homosexuals and the theological inquiries and official proclamations and papal bulls that supported that discrimination did not really begin until the fourteenth century, despite sporadic attempts on the part of some notable church fathers, teachers, and saints in earlier times. Moreover, according to Boswell, even in the centuries leading up to this fourteenth-century prohibition, the church was notably silent on lesbians. While some brief mention was made of women who engaged in unnatural practices and while a few of the reformers of each age included women in their general condemnations, almost universally the reformers dealt with men and with male homosexuality. In *The Church and the Homosexual,* a plea for inclusion of gays in the ministry of the Catholic church, John J. McNeill repeats this assertion that lesbians are absent from almost all patristic and medieval documents on homosexuality.[4] When women I would describe as lesbian are mentioned in the documents, they are discussed not as transgressors of sexual moral absolutes, but rather as sinners against Christian orthodoxy. They are, in effect, erased.

Historians of church attitudes toward lesbianism, then, find themselves with scant material from which to construct an official doctrine. Lesbianism has been almost totally erased. The rest is silence. And that silence, I would argue, is based on an almost complete misogyny in which male sexuality is privileged and invested with agency, while female sexuality exists only as a function of male activity.

This misogyny is so pervasive, ancient as well as modern, and so thoroughgoing as to defy comprehensive demonstration. Almost every major text from Genesis to John Paul II provides examples. Both Boswell and McNeill in their analyses of the church and homosexuality demonstrate conclusively that the church was little interested in lesbianism, since only male activity really mattered. In text after text, women are presented as the "Daughters of Eve," necessary for reproduction, but like Eve sexually dangerous, if not evil. Sexuality itself is seen as problematic for men since it distracts them from God. The roots of this attitude stretch back to Abraham and the early Hebrews. And for medieval scholastics like Aquinas this misogyny is buttressed by similar views about women's inferiority drawn from Aristotle and the Greeks. Women's sexuality is never seen as something separate from male desire. Church teachings exemplify Adrienne Rich's "compulsory heterosexuality," or at least compulsory *female* heterosexuality.[5]

It is not that women aren't sexual. They are. But their sexuality exists only insofar as it elicits sexual responses from men. It is precisely because it does so that women are so dangerous to men.[6] If women's sexuality were self-referential, then it would have to be redefined within the general doctrines and practices of sexual morality. Such a redefinition has not been attempted until recently, and it is not yet complete, since the basic misogyny still operates.

Misogyny, thus, accounts in significant ways for the official neglect of lesbianism. Homosexuality, however much it may have been tolerated prior to the fourteenth century, as Boswell asserts, became problematic to reformers only insofar as it concerned men. The main charge against gay men was that they debased the Adamic and Christ-like nobility of the male body by becoming "like females." The reverse was not possible. Women could not become "like men." Sexuality, therefore, couldn't properly exist between them; hence, what the witch doctors Kramer and Sprenger characterized as "women's filthy lusts" (47) existed only as pollutants to male godliness. This invisibility or erasure of lesbianism is, I believe, central to an understanding of Catholic attitudes.

One must acknowledge, however, that such erasure was not exclusively a Catholic attitude. Lillian Faderman has explored the same phenomenon extensively in *Surpassing the Love of Men*. And Boswell amply illustrates its development among ancient Hebrews and Romans. The key to this widespread dismissal of lesbian existence is more properly the function of language as the embodiment of reality. When we read through the historical texts and the catechisms, even when we read the most popular religious manuals of the time, we cannot escape the conclusion that sex is always by definition, almost *a priori,* heterosexual in nature and requires penetration by the penis.

Most of the popular manuals of the late nineteenth and early twentieth centuries were, of course, not so explicit as that. One of the most widely known was Father George Deshon's *Guide for Catholic Young Women,* interestingly subtitled *Especially for Those Who Earn Their Own Living.* It was first published in 1871 in New York, and had been reprinted thirty times by 1892. It was also translated into German and became one of the most popular manuals in Germany. It is therefore instructive to read Deshon's advice to young women, particularly about "purity." He devotes seven chapters (63–69) to this subject without once delineating what is or is not "pure." He refers to chastity, to modesty, to custody of the eyes and dress and thoughts, and he assumes that his general language will be understood. He implies that we all *know* what impurity is. Later in discussions of what intimacies to form (chapter 72), he makes it clear that his vision of chastity is completely heterosexual. Girls often introduce the poison of impurity among themselves by talking of "beaux and getting married" (239). Every specific example he gives, and there aren't many in this vaguest of works, is heterosexual.

The same is true about manuals for young Catholic men of the time, as is evident from Father F. X. Lasance's *The Young Man's Guide* (1909). The chapters on purity are again completely heterosexual, with sins against chastity stemming from unwise "company keeping" with members of the opposite sex (336–37). This is to be expected, given the general moral teaching of these manuals. But in his introduction, Lasance makes an even more interesting point, one thoroughly congruent with my reading of Catholic erasure of lesbianism. "There is more than a grain of truth," he writes, "in the adage, 'Take care of the boys, and the girls will take care of themselves' " (v).

If sex is by definition what happens between men or between men and women, if for women its reality is determined by intercourse, then Vivien and Shiletto, Hall and Troubridge, Christopher St. John and all other lesbians were indeed innocent. And from all the evidence, it seems clear that their sexuality was seen as innocent by the church. Lesbian sexuality did not exist as a Catholic reality.

It is only a small step from this realization to the more radical conclusion that they would have seen Catholicism as one of the most hospitable forms of Western religion for them. As Nina Auerbach so perceptively recognized in her discussion of Christopher St. John, whose novel *Hungerheart* details her spiritual journey and conversion to Catholicism in ways that are almost emblematic of the lesbian convert of the period:

Catholicism gave Christopher a God who would affirm spirit's ascendancy, but the hunger for that ascendancy was not hers alone; it gave faith to a generation of feminists. Like male disguise, the triumphant spirit insured the integrity and boundaries of the body: anger, sexual love, the appetite for victory and power, all purged themselves out of physical life. (406–7)

St. John is one example of this liberation from conventional sexuality that Catholicism offered lesbians. But perhaps the most striking illustration is Renée Vivien. What Vivien wanted passionately, almost desperately, was a return to her "chaste love for Violet [Shiletto]," a love which "seemed to embody a passion untouched by impurity" (Rubin xxi). Violet had died alone in the South of France in 1901, unaided by her dearest friend (Vivien) and consoled only by the priest called to her bedside. It is clear from Vivien's autobiographical novel *A Woman Appeared to Me* that Vivien's grief at her friend's death was inextricably bound up with guilt at having been at the time in the arms of her new lover, Natalie Clifford Barney (Jay 13). Restless and searching, never satisfied, Vivien wrote, loved, repented, fled, returned, and finally found peace and a recovery of innocence and, to her mind, virginity and thus a special purity in her own deathbed conversion to the Catholicism that had consoled her dead friend Violet.

Most of us would ask how one can ever recover virginity. But Vivien sought to do just that. And it is clear from *A Woman Appeared to Me* that she believed lesbian love, even in all its physicality, was not sex. Sex was base and required men and penises. Her lost innocence was about desire and not about actions. In Catholicism she could recover that innocence and virginity. Whatever one thinks of the mental constructs that Vivien seemed to find so consoling, one must admit that Catholic teaching would not have found them incomprehensible.

Finally, in the case of Radclyffe Hall, we come to see that the erasure of lesbian existence and the phallocentric ontology of sex that Catholicism presents actually provided, as Auerbach suggests although in a different context, the necessary space and lack of intrusion or control that allowed Hall to find her place in a radically alien universe. She did not have to fight a church or a God to be a lesbian. She could concentrate on finding a way to serve that church and love that God, to find her place both in time and in eternity—finally to *belong*.

There are, thus, some rather wonderful ironies in lesbian Catholicism. Despite its policy of "open admission" to heaven for women, which was no mean principle, as an institution the Catholic church never ministered well to adult women, except as asexual beings—nuns, widows, virgin martyrs. The ultimate irony, therefore, is that in its phallocentric blindness it made asexual beings of lesbians and created for some of them a refuge from the virulent homophobia and misogyny of the secular world.

From this "secure" place, Hall could write novels such as *The Well of Loneliness* and *The Master of the House,* and St. John could produce *Hungerheart.* These novels continue to puzzle or distress many lesbian as well as nonlesbian readers, but they are, I think, less disturbing when we understand the realities constructed by the language the authors used and the realities they were thus inscribing in a language many of us cannot accept today. Lesbian readers will probably, as I do, continue to battle the patriarchal structures and language that these authors adopted so wholeheartedly when they adopted the Church of Torquemada, but, by understanding their conversion to Catholicism, we can also, I believe, read them with more accuracy, discrimination, and ultimately with more real understanding.

NOTES

I am indebted to Karla Jay, David Kievitt, and Jane Marcus for their insights and encouragement as I explored the ideas presented in this essay.

1. Terminology is slippery and treacherous when we attempt to speak about same-sex relationships between women as they were/are viewed by the Catholic

church. I use the contemporary term "lesbianism" throughout this text, despite the fact that it is anachronistic and would not have surfaced in church writings of the time, nor even in the writings of the twentieth-century authors under discussion. Still, it is useful in that it conveys more clearly than earlier language the sexual as well as emotional relationships that are referred to in this essay. What is most interesting, of course, is that the church had no term at all that conveyed what the present-day term lesbianism means. Language constructs reality/constructs language, in the familiar loop.

2. The only specific catechetical reference to lesbianism that I was able to find occurred in an eighteenth-century guide for missionaries to South America. One must speculate, therefore, on the racist Eurocentrism of this document. Since South Americans had to be instructed about the evil of this practice, but not Europeans, presumably Europeans were immune from the sinful dangers so mentioned. It reminds one of Lillian Faderman's analysis of Scottish reactions to charges of lesbianism; that is, that perhaps one could believe women in India might be guilty, but not Scottish women! (See Faderman's *Scotch Verdict*.)

3. For an understanding of the complexity of this phenomenon, see Curb and Manahan's *Lesbian Nuns*.

4. Boswell and McNeill are both very careful to cite the rare occasions when lesbians are specifically mentioned in these works. Even more specific information can be found in Arthur Evans's *Witchcraft and the Gay Counterculture* (159–64). I would also direct readers' attention to the erasure of lesbianism in recorded documents of the infamous witch trails of the fourteenth through seventeenth centuries. No comprehensive study of lesbianism and the witch burnings has yet appeared, to my knowledge. Mary Daly in *Gyn/Ecology* and Andrea Dworkin in *Woman Hating* both provide provocative beginnings for such a study. It must be noted, of course, that "marginal" women, many of whom were lesbians, were the primary targets of these witch hunts. Again there is an erasure of sexuality through language that stresses witches' "disagreeable" or unwomanly qualities.

5. See Rich's "Compulsory Heterosexuality."

6. Perhaps the most misogynistic text ever sanctioned by the Catholic church was Kramer and Sprenger's *Malleus Maleficarum*, used widely throughout Europe to fuel what Daly calls the "witchcraze." The entire text is remarkable for its virulent woman hating.

WORKS CITED

Auerbach, Nina. *Ellen Terry: Player in Her Time*. New York: Norton, 1987.
Baker, Michael. *Our Three Selves: The Life of Radclyffe Hall*. New York: Morrow, 1985.
Boswell, John. *Christianity, Social Tolerance, and Homosexuality: Gay People in Western Europe from the Beginning of the Christian Era to the Fourteenth Century*. Chicago: Univ. of Chicago Press, 1980.

Brown, Judith. *Immodest Acts: The Life of a Lesbian Nun in Renaissance Italy*. New York: Oxford Univ. Press, 1986.

Curb, Rosemary, and Nancy Manahan. *Lesbian Nuns: Breaking Silence*. Tallahassee, Fla.: Naiad, 1985.

Daly, Mary. *Gyn/Ecology: The Metaethics of Radical Feminism*. Boston: Beacon, 1978.

Deshon, Rev. George. *Guide for Catholic Young Women: Especially for Those Who Earn Their Own Living*. New York: Catholic Book Exchange, 1892.

Dworkin, Andrea. *Woman Hating*. New York: Dutton, 1974.

Ellmann, Richard. *Oscar Wilde*. New York: Knopf, 1988.

Evans, Arthur. *Witchcraft and the Gay Counterculture*. Boston: Fag Rag Books, 1978.

Faderman, Lillian. *Scotch Verdict: Miss Pirie and Miss Woods v. Dame Cumming Gordon*. New York: Morrow, 1983.

————. *Surpassing the Love of Men: Romantic Friendship and Love between Women from the Renaissance to the Present*. New York: Morrow, 1981.

Jay, Karla. *The Amazon and the Page: Natalie Clifford Barney and Renée Vivien*. Bloomington: Indiana Univ. Press, 1988.

Kramer, Heinrich, and James Sprenger. *The Malleus Maleficarum*. Trans. Rev. Montague Summers. 1928. Rpt. New York: Dover, 1971.

Lasance, Rev. F. X. *The Young Man's Guide*. New York: Benziger, 1909.

McNeill, John J. *The Church and the Homosexual*. 3d ed. Boston: Beacon Press, 1988.

The New Catholic Encyclopedia. Vol. 3. New York: McGraw, 1967.

Ormrod, Richard. *Una Troubridge: The Friend of Radclyffe Hall*. London: Cape, 1984.

Rich, Adrienne. "Compulsory Heterosexuality and Lesbian Existence." In *Powers of Desire: The Politics of Sexuality*. Ed. Ann Snitow, Christine Stansell, and Sharon Thompson. New York: Monthly Review Press, 1983, 177–205.

Rubin, Gayle. "Introduction." In *A Woman Appeared to Me*. By Renée Vivien. Tallahassee, Fla.: Naiad, 1976, iii–xli.

St. John, Christopher. *Hungerheart: The Story of a Soul*. London: Methuen, 1915.

Summers, Montague. *The History of Witchcraft and Demonology*. London: Kegan Paul, 1926.

Toklas, Alice B. *Staying on Alone: The Letters of Alice B. Toklas*. New York: Liveright, 1973.

Troubridge, Una. *The Life and Death of Radclyffe Hall*. London: Hammond, 1961.

SIXTEEN

Making the World Safe for the Missionary Position: Images of the Lesbian in Post–World War II America

Kate Adams

Browse book publishing's trade journals for the year 1952 and discover how mainstream culture imagined the future roles of postwar middle-class women. Contemplate, for example, what it would mean for women in the decades after the war that, beginning in 1952, the works of Freud could be bought in any drugstore, edited for the layperson and produced in cheap, mass-market paperback editions. Or that the publication of new home economics titles rose by 20 percent, the greatest percentage gain of any category of books that year. Among them was Robert Loeb's *She Cooks to Conquer*, advertised as "especially designed for bachelor girls" wanting to "prepare such man-trapping dishes as Pomme Aphrodite." After the man was trapped, children were sure to follow—and so along with the boom in the home economics category came a flood of children's books, the category which saw the second-largest increase in publishing that year.[1] Freud, cookbooks, thin volumes for children full of colorful pictures—all of these shaped the industry's year, but nothing could compare to the success of the single, biggest-selling title of 1952: the brand-new Revised Standard Version of the Bible.

The new Bible received enormous attention. Its publisher opened an account with a Madison Avenue advertising agency and bought $500,000 worth of flyers, posters, window displays, and commercial spots on radio and television. The U.S. Post Office issued a stamp, commemorating the printing of the Gutenberg Bible five centuries earlier as well as the new Bible's September publication. In Korea, army chaplains held special celebratory services, and at home, *Colliers* and *Life* featured them in their illustrated articles introducing Americans to the new translation, while

Saturday Review printed columns of verses from the old King James and the new RSV for easy comparison. In eight short weeks, Americans bought one million copies of the new Bible, its entire first printing, and bookstores garnered a backlog of 600,000 orders. It was the publishing event of the year, and almost everyone was happy—except perhaps the harried booksellers who had to tell disappointed Christmas shoppers there would be no more Bibles until after the New Year, and one notable Baptist minister who gained the newswires' attention when, one Sunday night in November, "furious over the substitution of 'young woman' for 'virgin' in Isaiah 7:14," he burned the offending page in front of his North Carolina church.[2]

One wonders how that Baptist minister, or all those Bible buyers, might have responded to another, much less celebrated event in publishing that same year: four months before the RSV Bible, a novel called *The Price of Salt* appeared, in which two women living in New York meet, fall in love, travel the country together, and successfully persevere in a homophobic environment without ending up unhappy, insane, or dead. The book received a brief, lukewarm review in the *New York Times Book Review,* and then, silence: its publisher, Coward-McCann, launched no advertising campaigns featuring it; no library loudly banned it; no minister burned its pages on the steps of his church. Yet the novel appeared in a decade notable for its increasingly conservative attitude toward lesbianism in particular and women's sexual and social identity in general. In the early 1950s, a reactionary medical community damned Alfred Kinsey's sex research and his relatively progressive findings regarding the nature of women's sexual response and homoerotic experience. In the same years, the psychoanalytic establishment institutionalized a "sickness theory" model of homosexual behavior which would affect the medical and cultural treatment, as well as the self-perception, of the lesbian for years to come. And mirroring the homophobia of the federal government, the military establishment replaced its unusually lenient wartime policy toward lesbianism with a series of "sex hygiene" lectures that encouraged women to think of the lesbian as a neurotic, immoral threat to "normal" womanhood. The mood of the country would certainly have better supported the burning of lesbian novels than the burning of Bibles: 1952 was not a good year for authors to write sympathetically of lesbians or communists, nor for libraries to subscribe to Russian newspapers, nor for booksellers to display paperback novels with sexy covers where minors might get hold of them. Perhaps this national taste for censorship and censure prompted the author of *The Price of Salt,*

Patricia Highsmith—whose first book, *Strangers on a Train,* had been the basis for a popular Hitchcock thriller—to publish her second novel under a pseudonym, "Claire Morgan." In any case, her novel escaped public "burning." It did not receive much positive or negative mainstream attention in 1952 and it has not gathered much since, even though generations of women have read it, have written the author thanking her for writing it, and various paperback houses and feminist presses have kept it in print more or less continuously for over thirty years.[3]

Given the treatment that Radclyffe Hall's pioneering novel *The Well of Loneliness* received in the British and U.S. obscenity trials following its 1928 publication, one might reasonably expect that *The Price of Salt* would have been soundly denounced for its sympathetic treatment of lesbianism, especially during a postwar decade of conservative cultural retrenchment. Instead, mainstream culture ignored Morgan's text and its positive image of the lesbian, preferring to acknowledge images it could endorse, images that emphasized the lesbian's maladjustment and immorality. In 1952 this hegemonic image of the lesbian received widespread notoriety through the efforts of the U.S. House of Representatives' Committee on Current Pornographic Materials. The Committee's primary intent was to expose the paperback, comic book, and magazine publishing industries as a potential threat to the moral fiber of American youth. An attack on lesbianism became the coincidental by-product of the Committee's work when one paperback novel received enormous attention during the hearings—Tereska Torrès's autobiographical wartime novel, *Women's Barracks* (1950), which portrayed lesbianism in conventionally pathological as well as sensational terms.

Together, *Women's Barracks* and *The Price of Salt* present two contrasting images of the lesbian in postwar U.S. culture. The pathological images of the lesbian in *Women's Barracks* do the dominant culture's work by representing lesbian sexuality and the independent woman as threats to bourgeois culture and to its ideals of "normal" womanhood. The other novel, *The Price of Salt,* creates a positive image of the lesbian and thus delivers an extraordinarily subversive message, but it does so in a highly conventional, genteel narrative structure; consequently, it never received the attention that a highly sensational—and highly conservative—text such as *Women's Barracks* received. Reading the novels together suggests that a homophobic culture chooses either to represent the lesbian as pathological or to render the lesbian invisible; in such a context, we then learn to recognize the lesbian only when she comes clothed in the cultural assumptions which make her the Other and which mask or distort her fundamental humanity.

Arkansas Democrat E. C. Gathings and the Congressional antipornography committee he chaired found in Torrès's *Women's Barracks* a novel they could "love to hate." The Committee's majority report, published in December 1952, damned the book as a prime example of "the so-called pocket-size books, which originally started out as cheap reprints of standard works" but "have largely degenerated into media for the dissemination of artful appeals to sensuality, immorality, filth, perversion, and degeneracy" (U.S. Cong. 3). The Gathings Committee cited sixty paperback novels in its report, "selected on the basis of obscenity, violence, lust, use of narcotics, blasphemy, vulgarity, pornography, juvenile delinquency, sadism, masochism, perversion, homosexuality, lesbianism, murder, rape, and nymphomania, or other objectionable features" (12). Among the novels cited were John Steinbeck's *The Wayward Bus* and titles by James Farrell, Mickey Spillane, and Erskine Caldwell, but *Women's Barracks* received a great deal of attention during the hearings for a number of reasons—perhaps not the least of which was that, because the novel depicted recognizably lesbian characters, the committee found it ipso facto guilty of so many other of the "objectionable features" on its list as well.[4]

The Committee cited the immorality of "girlie" magazines and comic books as well as paperbacks in its majority report, but during the five days of hearings in early December 1952, the Committee focused its attack primarily on paperback books. Paperbacks, because of their widespread availability and their increasingly risqué cover art featuring "lurid and daring illustrations of voluptuous young women" (3), were an especially dangerous influence on the morality of American youth, or so the Committee claimed; but beyond that, paperbacks made an easy target. Ever since Robert de Graff's Pocket Books began the "paperback revolution" in 1939, paperback houses had been the poor cousins of the establishment publishing industry. In spite of the paperback publishers' claims that their books enlarged the ranks of the reading public and made literature and ideas affordable to the masses, and in spite of their monumental effort to provide reading material and entertainment for the armed services during World War II, paperback publishing was only grudgingly tolerated by the industry at large, and then primarily because paperback reprinting was too lucrative a field to ignore.[5] The success of paperback publishing made it easier for all publishers to define a "good" book as one that sold millions, an ethically dubious definition that the Gathings Committee exploited.

Even among paperback publishers themselves, there was a pecking order, and the house that published *Women's Barracks* was at the bottom. Fawcett Gold Medal was the first major house to publish paperback *originals* as well as reprints. Their original paperbacks bypassed the hardcover houses, the book reviewers, and the hardcover reprinters and book clubs, taking a direct route from manuscript to drugstore counter and thereby avoiding many of the regular costs of conventional publishing as well as some of its "quality control" mechanisms. Fawcett Gold Medal originals were cut entirely adrift from the editorial decorum of hardcover publishing, leading Bernard DeVoto to suggest that "what Gold Medal proved is we didn't know how lousy novels could be" (Bonn 50). DeVoto was half-right: paperback original publishing expanded the market for potboilers, but it also allowed controversial or marginal texts to come into print. Few hardcover houses would have touched the lesbian romances of Ann Bannon, Paula Christian, Valerie Taylor, and others in the 1950s, yet Fawcett Gold Medal published all these authors in paperback from 1957 to 1962, thereby helping to create what has been called the "golden age" of lesbian pulp fiction, a phenomenon which in turn helped establish that lesbian culture existed outside the boundaries of Greenwich Village, and which would influence the spread of the gay liberation movement in the sixties and seventies.

The mere existence of these later lesbian texts suggests that the controversy stirred up by *Women's Barracks* did not have the effect on popular culture that the Gathings Committee intended, and the novel's later sales confirm this. As one of Fawcett's first million-selling "manuscript-to-drugstore" originals, *Women's Barracks* had a hand in making the golden-age lesbian romances possible, even though Torrès's novel is not itself a lesbian romance. Still, its publication acted as a wedge, a way into print for other texts which would in the future treat lesbianism more positively and radically than *Women's Barracks* itself did. For in spite of the notoriety that surrounded it in 1952, Torrès's novel does not challenge the conventional wisdom about lesbians which the Gathings Committee would support. Her depiction of the lives of women soldiers during wartime is nothing more than a racy potboiler hiding an extremely conservative cultural message. A

Frenchwoman's text translated into English by her American novelist husband,[6] *Women's Barracks* reaffirms what postwar U.S. culture was telling itself about lesbianism and about women's place in society.

The novel describes the lives of French women soldiers in an army barracks in war-torn London, a milieu that Torrès's own five-year stint in the Women's Army Corps of the Free French forces made familiar. The narrative focuses almost exclusively on the sexual revelations of four or five young women soldiers who, if the novel's word is taken literally, did nothing during their army years except have affairs with men, have affairs with women, talk to each other about the affairs they were having, and try to get over the affairs they had already had. In some places the narrative reads like an adolescent's fantasy sex manual with characters walking through it, an impression that the narrator's first-person limited—or first person voyeur—point of view does nothing to diminish.

The voyeurism begins early, in the first scene of the novel: the main characters are introduced as they stand naked in a recruitment office awaiting physical examinations. The narrator appraises the bodies of the nude women around her in a kind of smorgasbord style: hips, legs, breasts, hair, facial features are compared and critiqued, and in this way readers and characters become "acquainted with the bodies of our future comrades before we even knew their names" (9).[7] The objectification continues in another early scene, in which the recruits are caught tailoring their regulation khaki underwear into more form-fitting briefs; as punishment, they are made to stand inspection the next morning. One by one, each woman raises her skirt, revealing thighs "rimmed in khaki" to the officer performing the inspection who, the narrator tells us later, is a lesbian.

For some readers, scenes like these went a long way toward confirming the popular wisdom that life in a women's army corps promoted erotic contact between women. In the case of the U.S. Women's Army Corps, popular wisdom may have been fairly accurate. Historian John D'Emilio, in his research into the creation of homosexual communities in the United States, suggests that both popular images of the lesbian and official wartime army policies gave the military "an especially prominent role in fostering a lesbian identity and creating friendship networks among gay women":

In an era that frequently associated homosexuality with the reversal of gender roles, the Women's Army Corps became the almost quintessential lesbian institution. . . . Ironically, military policy contributed to a situation that it took pains to deny. . . . Anxious to counter its reputation of moral laxity, the military sought to avoid unwanted pregnancies by keeping its female personnel segregated, often having women's only nights at canteens or providing separate space for women to socialize. A training manual for officers praised the desire for intense "comradeship" in service as "one of the finest relationships" possible for women. (D'Emilio 27)

The "training manual" D'Emilio mentions here consists of a set of "Sex Hygiene" lectures prepared for WAC officers in 1943. The lecture on lesbianism is extraordinarily tolerant in tone and language, cautioning officers to "expect more consciousness of sex and more difficulties concerning it" during times of war, counseling them not to engage in witchhunts against lesbians, and suggesting that lesbians "are exactly as you and I, except that they participate in sexual gratification with members of their own sex" (Bérubé and D'Emilio 761).

However, military tolerance of lesbianism did not survive the end of the war; with the McCarthy era came a new set of sex hygiene lectures, these published by the navy in 1952. Mirroring the increased homophobia of the federal government at large, the new navy lectures presented legal, medical, and religious warnings which declared that a charge of lesbianism meant the ruination of women's professional, personal, and social lives. The lectures encouraged the navy woman to avoid the "practising homosexual" who might lure her first into friendship and then into the one "foolish mistake" which could ruin her "delicate reputation" and her chances for marriage and motherhood (Bérubé and D'Emilio 759). This sea change in military policy reflects larger cultural forces signaling the end of what limited tolerance lesbians and other women on the margins of social norms could expect during the war. As postwar America's need for women soldiers and female factory workers decreased, so did women's social, sexual, and financial freedoms, both inside and outside the military.

The Gathings Committee attack on *Women's Barracks* reflects this postwar reaction to wartime license, in spite of the fact that the novel's depiction of lesbian lives has more in common with the 1952 mainstream than it does with an earlier, wartime era of relative tolerance. Although not as hysterical as the navy's lectures, Torrès's novel is equally homophobic, building its portrayal of lesbians on implicit and traditional stereotypes. Her narrator, who "had known so little of these matters when [she] came to the barracks," becomes through her observations of four other soldiers a vicariously trained clinician, able "to distinguish between the various grades" of homoeroticism between women (68) and to comment on the sexual and emotional adjustment of her barracks-mates.

The narrator describes Ann, the major lesbian character in the novel, as young, friendly, "a strapping large girl with a boyish haircut" and "a heavy, almost masculine voice" (11) who looked immediately natural in her uniform. The only new recruit "who seemed to know how to knot her tie properly," Ann seems "like a big brother" (12) to the other recruits in spite of her youth. Large and innocent, Ann is a perfect foil for another lesbian soldier in the novel, the barracks warrant officer. An older, more experienced "career Army" lesbian, Petit is "a smallish woman who had the look of a little old man . . . looking over the girls with a friendly eye" (16). Taken together, the two women comprise a single caricature of the masculine life cycle, from boyish youth through wise "old fellow" (16). A "special current" passes between Ann and Petit, the narrator feels: they share an instinctual knowledge that "they could count on each other in the eternal battle between themselves and other women" (17).

Following the line of nineteenth-century scientists, Torrès's narrator understands Ann and Petit and Ann's lover, Lee, to be "real" lesbians— authentic, manly lesbians—what Krafft-Ebing would have called "congenital inverts." As in the Krafft-Ebing model, Torrès's real lesbian is born, not made, reprimanded in childhood for "not conducting herself like a good little girl who plays with her dolls" and doomed in adulthood to an "exhausting love which dies of its own sterility between brief flashes of passion" (69). "No one could ever change" the condition of real lesbians, and the narrator observes that this makes them irrevocably unhappy, living "separately from the rest of the world, cloistered among themselves . . . going to lesbian night clubs together" (106). They are "women outside human society, profoundly solitary," cut off from the family, from children, and all men except pederasts, "the only men with whom they had anything to do" (119, 106).

On the whole, Torrès's "third sex" lesbians are stridently masculine, unnaturally "inverted," and peculiarly out of date for the 1950s. Ann and Petit do not resemble the Freudian neurotic model of the lesbian, more current at the time, whose troubled passage through the feminine Oedipal crisis is the source of her arrested and aberrant sexuality. Nevertheless, while Torrès leaves Ann and Petit to their nineteenth-century fates, she does pull one latent lesbian character into the modern age of psychiatry. Ursula, a young girl who is afraid of men, begins the novel with a crush on Claude, a "dangerous" nymphomaniac who "went to bed with colonels and generals, and with all the women of London" (122). Jilted by Claude and afraid that "she would remain doomed to solitude all her life, like Ann, like Petit" (90), Ursula embarks on a series of episodes which result, finally, in her satisfactorily making love with a man, an event which breaks her immature attachment to Claude and leaves her feeling "suddenly grown," imbued with "a sort of pride in no longer being a little girl" (98). Ursula marries her mild-mannered soldier soon after they make love, but not before Claude explains to her the lesbian fate she has just escaped. Claude's "technical explanation" of the causes of lesbianism is the closest Torrès ever comes to articulating the psychoanalytic model of lesbianism whose currency grew in the decade after the war. Claude explains that "some women could experience only an exterior climax. They were frigid within, and could never be satisfied by men" (106). Taken together, Ursula's experience and Claude's comments on the relative merits of vaginal and clitoral orgasm sketch in outline the Freudian psychoanalytic model of lesbianism: a girl's normal sexual development is arrested at an autoerotic, pre-Oedipal stage, resulting in prolonged attachment to her first love object, the mother; thus arrested, the girl will become a "man-hating" or "man-fearing" lesbian unless she can successfully translate her Oedipal penis envy into erotic attachment to her father and subsequently to an appropriate male (who can provide her with a penis substitute in the form of a child).[8]

Whether the individual members of the Gathings Committee leaned toward the Krafft-Ebing "third sex" or the Sigmund Freud "arrested development" model of lesbianism, they could breath a collective sigh of relief over Torrès's homophobic depiction of lesbian lives and her handling of Ursula's story. In spite of the war and barracks life, Ursula gets a chance at normal, married, adult womanhood; and like a good order-restoring comedy, the novel ends with a total of three marriages before a bomb destroys the barracks and the women's "period of military life" which had "brought nothing but a series of disillusions" comes to an end (95).

If *Women's Barracks* had not been so "smutty"; had there been no naked women scenes and fewer sentences of the "Mickey pressed herself to him while he kissed her arched lips" variety; had the book managed the clever trick of negatively portraying lesbianism without ever actually *mentioning* it —perhaps then the Gathings Committee could have admitted the debt of gratitude they owed the novel's sexual politics. In spite of its impropriety in the eyes of many in 1952, *Women's Barracks* does promote mainstream cultural ideals by confirming popular images of World War II moral laxity (and from a conveniently safe Gallic distance) and by conflating negative images of lesbianism with women's occupation of traditionally male spheres. The novel reinforces the dominant cultural belief that independent women, whose lives do not center on the family and marriage, are or will be generally unhappy and unfulfilled. Minus the naughty bits, the novel's message is conservative and palliative; or, in the words of Ursula on her first night with her future husband, the novel confirms that in the postwar years, everything would be "normal, so wonderfully and utterly normal, coming out of these mad years" (141).

What constituted "normal" sexuality for women was of great interest to the public and the medical and psychiatric establishments in the 1950s, thanks in great part to Kinsey's study of female sexual behavior and the controversy following its 1953 publication.[9] What made Kinsey's study so controversial was the extent to which it engendered *popular* as well as professional discussion of sexuality in general and homosexuality in particular. The postwar era saw both sexuality and its professional interpreters come out of the closet into popular discourse.

The "mishmash" of Krafft-Ebing pathology and Freudian psychoanalysis in Tereska Torrès's treatment of lesbianism probably accurately reflects the general confusion in popular attitudes toward homosexuality in the United States at mid-century. Long considered either a sin or a crime, homosexuality was now most often discussed as a curable disease by doctors and psychiatrists whose medical models of homosexuality confronted well-established religious and legal definitions. John D'Emilio has noted that up until the 1940s, medical and psychiatric investigations of homosexuality were primarily limited to the pages of professional journals, while the general public's perception of the homosexual—usually male—was shaped by sensational news stories about the sex criminal or religious morality tales about the sex sinner. But during World War II, the armed services began large-scale psychiatric screening of military inductees, a program which "catapulated the psychiatric profession into the lives of millions" for the first time, and paved the way for the incursion into popular culture of a psychoanalytically produced image of the homosexual (D'Emilio 17). "Psychiatry emerged from the war with its status enhanced," D'Emilio writes, and homosexuality emerged from the pages of professional journals to be more openly discussed in popular magazines and books (17–18). The war did a lot for psychiatry and in turn, psychiatry made its reputation in part on its ability to interpret sexual behavior—"normal" and otherwise—to a large public.

As young Ursula in *Women's Barracks* teetered on the brink of establishing a sexual identity, the narrator reports that she "told herself the things that Catholics tell their priests during confession, and that Americans tell their psychoanalysts" (91). Had a woman like Ursula or Ann approached a psychiatrist to discuss her lesbianism in the 1950s, she would most probably have been encouraged to think of her sexuality as profoundly abnormal but curable. For in spite of Kinsey's conclusions that homosexuality among women was more common and clitoral orgasm more dominant than had been previously believed, the prevailing psychiatric approach to the lesbian in postwar America was to treat her as a sort of normal woman in disguise, thwarted in her pursuit of fulfillment and happiness by an unfortunate wrong turn on her road out of childhood. And the lesbian who entered analysis could expect her doctor to insist that her abnormal sexuality could be cured if only she was willing to be normal.

Dolores Klaich, in analyzing the evolution of psychiatry's "sickness theory" of homosexuality, stresses that "the 'curing' of homosexuals is a peculiarly American preoccupation" (88). In the same decade that Britain's Wolfendon Committee was effecting more tolerance for the homosexual in that country, U.S. legislators were calling federally employed homosexuals "security risks" and medical professionals were attempting cures with treatments ranging from psychoanalysis and aversion therapy to electroshock and lobotomy.[10] Although there were some researchers, Evelyn Hooker and Harry Benjamin for example, who approached homosexuality as a nonpathological behavior, the "sickness theory" still held as the dominant view, partly because the professionals who employed it—Irving Bieber, Lawrence J. Hatterer, and Edmund Bergler among others—were the ones most often published in the popular media.[11] Even when a writer's main subject was not homosexuality, the sickness theory was often and easily incorporated into more general treatments of sexuality, marriage, or related subjects. For example, Dr. Edmund Bergler's popular book *Kinsey's Myth of Female Sexuality* (1954) begins as an attack on most of Kinsey's 1953 conclusions and ends as a promotion of the Freudian-based "sickness theory" laced with a kind of McCarthy-esque "conspiracy theory" in which Kinsey becomes a dupe of the homosexuals: Bergler argues that "homosexuals have taken Kinsey for a ride" and Kinsey has provided them "with an 'irrefutable,' 'statistical' and 'scientific' argument enabling them to maintain and spread their perversion without conscious guilt" (141, 155). Bergler's paranoid suggestion that homosexuals who resisted cure were consciously proselytizing for their sexuality is fairly common in the popular discussion of homo-sexuality of the day; it is reminiscent as well of the righteousness and paranoia with which the Gathings Committee pursued the immorality they perceived in paperback publishing.

For the most part, popular studies of homosexuality published in the 1950s dealt exclusively with male homosexuality; the notable exception is Dr. Frank Caprio's *Female Homosexuality*, published in 1954. The book's influence has been considered profound since at the time of its publication it was, according to Dolores Klaich, "The only mass-marketed book written by a psychiatrist devoted solely to lesbianism," and it remained in print until 1972, a year before the American Psychiatric Association voted to delete homosexuality from its list of mental illnesses (98). Caprio, like other sexologists of his time, perceived lesbianism as a disease with the potential of undermining the nation: he wrote *Female Homosexuality* to alert the nation to "the prevalence of female homosexuality" and its threat to "the stability of our social structure."[12]

Whenever lesbianism appears in Caprio's numerous works on sexuality, he reveals a narrow, punitive, vision of the lesbian as the antithesis of the passive, maternal, domestic "normal" woman. In his 1955 book, *Variations in Sexual Behavior*, Caprio diagnosed lesbians as "emotionally unstable and neurotic" sufferers of a "sexual immaturity" caused by the lesbian's inabil-ity to accept that "women consciously prefer to fulfill their maternal role and to be loved by a man." Caprio believed that as "modern women" became "rapidly defeminized as a result of their overt desire for emancipation," they ran the risk of a "psychic masculinization" which could lead them "to a homosexual way of living or thinking" and all sorts of pathological behav-iors. Living like a lesbian, Caprio maintained, would result in "sadistic and psychopathic trends," "kleptomaniac tendencies," "antipathy toward the male sex," a "will to dominate" and extreme jealousies leading to passionate crimes. Thinking like a lesbian, another name for latent homosexuality, could produce "frigidity," "a preference for masturbation" and other sexual acts, "namely fellatio, cunnilingus, coitus per anum, and various positions such as the wife who prefers to lie on top and assumes the active role" (162–66).

As a sickness theorist, Caprio offers psychoanalysis as a cure for sexually maladjusted women who "voluntarily renounce the desire for masculinity, reverting to their original role of women" (161). He recites histories of successful treatments from his own practice, histories that seem to have been selected with an audience's taste for the sensational in mind. In the chapter on lesbianism in *Variations in Sexual Behavior*, Caprio includes case histories involving a triangular seduction between a married woman, her sister-in-law, and her husband; a narcissistic lesbian's mother-fixation, alcoholism, and incestuous relationship with her brother; and finally, the story of an unhappily married woman which Caprio entitled "A Case of Latent Homosexuality in a Wife Who Admitted a Compulsive Urge to Bite Her Husband's Penis" (172–74).[13]

It was not only the readers of popular sexology who could expect this sort of titillating material; increasingly, the readers of respectably published and reviewed middle-brow fiction could also revel in stories which were not only sexy, but "kinkily" so. In popular fiction of the 1950s, lesbian experience was almost exclusively represented by the terms which the psychiatric profession's sickness theorists had codified in their admonitions and case histories. Psychiatric co-optation of lesbian experience was followed by fictional representations of lesbian lives which rivaled even the most sensational of Caprio's case histories.

Take, for example, the novel *The Hearth and the Strangeness;* Macmillan published it in 1956, and it garnered review attention from over a dozen major periodicals. Published under the ambiguously androgynous pseudonym "N. Martin Kramer," the novel was written by Beatrice Wright, a professor of psychology and division president of the American Psychiatric Association. The "hearth" in Kramer's title refers to that of Sumner Grange, eccentric inventor and failed husband/father, and his wife, Lisette, religious fanatic and sexual prude. The "strangeness" refers, for the most part, to their children, for as the novel's Freudian family romance unfolds, the novelist implies that an unorthodox home life led the two youngest Grange children to their unhappy homosexual ends.

Actually, only one of the two youngest children is unhappy: Gareth Grange becomes more preoccupied and tortured by his fear of his own homosexual tendencies as the novel progresses. Neither his marriage to a seductive Southern belle, nor his impressive success in the masculine world of military service can allay his fears. His adoring sister, Aliciane, makes a more positive "adjustment" to her own homosexuality. She moves away from him, finishes law school, and settles into domestic tranquility with her lover Jeradine while her brother Gareth is in Korea. Aliciane's homosexuality is made "unhappy" only in the novel's final scene, when Gareth returns from overseas and, in a homophobic panic, stalks his sister to her bedroom where, as Aliciane's hysterical (and nude) lover looks helplessly on, he stabs her to death.

All of the novel's sordid drama and Freudian hint-dropping resulting in a madman's panic, a grisly murder, and a nude lesbian's shrieking response to her blood-spattered bed—all this would be laughable, like a bad horror movie, if it weren't so common in the fiction of the day. Lesbians, when they appeared in novels—and they seemed to appear more and more often, a bit of spicy relish in a hearty heterosexual page-turner—most often appeared as doomed characters, fated to end up by novel's end heterosexual, unhappy, and/or dead.

Leonard Bishop, for example, embellished his third novel, *Creep into Thy Narrow Bed* with a minor but sensational lesbian subplot. While Bishop's lusty hero, Adam, is fighting for his soul in the sordid world of an underground New York abortion ring, his lesbian sister, "Petey," is attempting to throw off her unnatural affections in an even more sordid world: Petey works as an attendant in an insane asylum. Only in this asylum, the live-in attendants are locked up at night just like the inmates, under the orders of the gruff, masculine, and homosexual head nurse. While Nurse Kovack makes eyes at Petey's roommate, the newly hired Myrna, Petey herself alternately burns with desire for Myrna and attempts to seduce her homosexual co-worker Sheldon in the hope that sleeping with a man, any man, will allow her to embrace "the legend of mystery" that "embraces other women" (91). All of this nighttime activity is, of course, accompanied by the hysterical screams of the asylum's inmates.

Insane, murderous siblings and incongruously sordid surroundings often accompany the lesbian presence in postwar mainstream fiction, and the lesbian character when she does appear is almost always "explained" psychoanalytically, with reference to her horrible parents, her traumatic youth, or abominable heterosexual experience. The cold-hearted career woman Lesley Winter in James Ronald's *The Angry Woman* is the victim of all three. Originally published serially in *McCall's* before Lippincott published it in hardcover in 1947, James Ronald's "mystery/romance" is memorable because its narrator, a novelist, "poses" as a psychiatrist in order to discover the story behind Lesley Winter's pathological "itch to prove she's the equal of a man" (11). In the novel's prologue, the narrator, a novelist, convinces a vulnerable young woman named Janet to talk about her close but troubled relationship with Lesley Winter, a woman whose evil the novelist hints at by noting that "she affects rather severe suits of sharkskin and saxony, so admirably cut that I have considered asking the name of her tailor" (10). Sensing that there "might be a novel in" Janet's story about Winter, the novelist persuades Janet to come up to his room for some therapeutic talk. Janet relents, and they retire to his room where he lays her out on a couch, puts a glass of water at her elbow, and then, so that nothing can "disturb the flow of her thoughts," moves his chair out of her range of vision. Thus arranged in classic analyst/analysand position, the novelist milks his flesh-and-blood muse, disappearing from the narrative until her story has been told. Finally, in the epilogue, the novelist brings the emotionally spent Janet a martini and then hurries her out his door, so anxious is he to begin the work which will turn the "case history" she has provided him with into the novel he owes his publisher. Even though his manipulations have made him feel "like a brute," the freeloading novelist—or psychiatrist, or vampire—begins telling "his" story to the readers of McCall's.

Figuratively or literally, then, in fiction and in "science," psychoanalysis became the lesbian's chaperone whenever she came out into the mainstream of popular culture. Like a kind of postwar Cinderella, the lesbian's presence in society was strictly circumscribed by an explicatory "godfather's" presence, who rendered her identifiable as a lesbian according to culturally sanctioned preconceptions. The proof of this is, first, in the works of writers like Caprio and Torrès; but obversely, in a text like Claire Morgan's *The Price of Salt,* the obvious absence of culturally produced preconceptions proves the rule as well. What Morgan's text and its reception proves is that without the trappings of her psychoanalytically produced and approved identity, the lesbian is rendered invisible to mainstream culture. Unless she enters dressed in the culture's preconceptions, unless she is arrayed, so to speak, in the glass slippers and gown which the culture recognizes as her appropriate attire, she cannot attend the cultural ball.

At the kind of ball to which their interpreters were likely to go, the lesbians in Claire Morgan's *The Price of Salt* would have been as anonymous as maids: they are not "mannish" women seeking out "masculine" pursuits; they are not irreparably scarred by childhood or adult sexual traumas; they exhibit none of the characteristics which make the culturally produced lesbian so recognizable. Therese Belivet, a nineteen-year-old artist making her way in New York, falls hopelessly in "love at first sight" with Carol Aird, an upper-middle-class mother of an eight-year-old daughter, newly separated from her husband. Therese pursues Carol with the stricken, innocent, and obvious fervor of first love, and Carol, the more experienced of the two women, makes no declaration of her own feelings until Therese has been prodded into more mature consideration of the real nature of her own. Their long and romantic courtship gives way finally to the women's wholehearted acknowledgment and physical consummation of their affection, an affection which is rendered with a modesty even the Gathings Committee could approve and which seems thoroughly appropriate for this thoroughly old-fashioned love story. When late in the novel Carol's ex-husband reveals that he has had the two women followed, that he knows the true nature of their relationship, and that he will use his knowledge in court to keep Carol away from her daughter if she continues to see Therese, the love story triumphs over blackmail in true romantic form: forced to choose between her child and her lover, Carol chooses Therese over motherhood—and Claire Morgan makes lesbian literary history by ending her story without one suicide, murder, or insane asylum ever insinuating its wormy head into her romance.

Morgan's Therese and Carol do not resemble lesbians cast in the dominant culture's mold primarily because Morgan seems not to assume that the prerequisite to writing a lesbian love story is to first address the cultural stereotypes which her story's particulars will deny. There is little defensive posturing in the novel, and less deep probing into its characters' developmental traumas. The only forum that the novel presents for the articulation of the negative stereotypes of the lesbian appears well after the relationship between Carol and Therese has, in its unfolding, refuted such an articulation's validity. Richard, Therese's sometimes-boyfriend, writes her a letter in which he warns her of the error of her ways and simultaneously "clears" himself of the self-imposed charge of ever having been in love with a lesbian:

I know I had stopped loving you then, and now the uppermost emotion I feel toward you is one that was present from the first—disgust. It is your hanging onto this woman to the exclusion of everyone else, this relationship which I am sure has become sordid and pathological by now, that disgusts me. I know that it will not last, as I said from the first. It is only regrettable that you will be disgusted later yourself, in proportion to how much of your life you waste now with it. It is rootless and infantile, like living on lotus blossoms or some sickening candy instead of the bread and meat of life. . . . The slightest memory or contact with you depresses me, makes me not want to touch you or anything concerned with you. (238–39)

In Richard's letter the lesbian image that the professional explicators have made gets its airing; but because by this point in the novel Richard's own tendencies toward self-deception and immaturity have been thoroughly revealed, because his own wounded pride figures so prominently in the letter, Richard's presentation of the "lesbian as immature invert" message here does not have much force, wrapped as it is in his own palpable insecurity. In spite of Richard's righteous assertion of his authority to analyze Therese's sexuality, his letter is a fairly ineffectual tool for conveying the censure of mainstream culture, an effect which Morgan surely calculated when she made Richard her standard-bearer in the cause of normalcy.

In the same calculated way, Morgan makes Therese and Carol ineffectual vehicles for the standard assumption made about lesbians. Carol, who has had a relationship with a woman previous to her relationship with Therese, does not fit the standard image of the "practiced homosexual" out to seduce innocent heterosexuals promoted by the military's 1952 "sex hygiene" lectures. On the contrary, Morgan makes her naive innocent the aggressor at the start of the relationship while Carol plays a more hesitant and passive role. Therese, for her part, fails to exhibit the psychic twitches so prevalent in the helping professions' image of the lesbian and in the work of novelists like Torrès, Wright, and Ronald. If Therese is a typical "image" of anything, it is of the adolescent female *or* male, fascinated and amazed by the power of her recently discovered emotions and the depth of her own capacity for passionate response.

Morgan makes her lesbians so relentlessly "atypical" in light of the popular stereotype that they remind us of nothing more than typical lovers in a traditional romance—which is exactly what they are. If Morgan's lovers had been any less eccentric, any more predictable, they would have been named Carol and Thomas, or Carl and Therese. In fact, C. J. Rolo, in his brief review of the book for the *New York Times,* complained of exactly this "blandness" in Morgan's treatment of her theme:

Obviously, in dealing with a theme of this sort, the novelist must handle his explosive material with care. It should be said at once that Miss Morgan writes throughout with sincerity and good taste. But the dramatic possibilities of her theme are never forcefully developed. (23)

A more thoughtful critic might have deduced that Morgan's failure to surround her lesbian characters with the "explosive" trappings of other popular fictions dealing with lesbians is precisely the "failure" which makes her text so successfully radical: when the lesbian enters culture without an escort of popular image and assumption, as she does in Morgan's text, nobody recognizes her as a lesbian.

Rolo goes on to mention, with mild astonishment, that "Therese apparently cannot conceive of there being anything questionable about this new relationship" with Carol. It is as if without Therese's exhibiting the kind of "sincere anguish" which Dr. Caprio looks for in latent lesbians, C. J. Rolo cannot recognize Therese as a woman or as lesbian: that is, it's not normal for Therese to assume that she's normal. Drawing attention to this without resorting to sensationalism or defensive retort is Morgan's strategy for "crashing" the postwar cultural ball.

Near the end of the novel, as Carol recounts her meeting with her ex-husband's lawyers in a letter to Therese, she regrets her failure at that meeting to make "the most important point I did not mention and was not thought of by anyone":

—that the rapport between two men or two women can be absolute and perfect, as it can never be between man and woman, and perhaps some people want just this, as others want that more shifting and uncertain thing that happens between men and women . . . [but] to live against one's grain, that is degeneration by definition. (246)

This point, which might have been as incomprehensible to the lawyers in the novel as it was to psychoanalysts like Caprio, is precisely the point which Morgan's text and its representation of the lesbian is intent on making. Unlike *Women's Barracks* or the other novels which "handle explosive material" with tremendous sensationalism while delivering conservative, culturally sanctioned messages, Morgan's *The Price of Salt* is able to deliver a profoundly radical message by couching that message in the most conventional of terms. Morgan's calculated underplaying of "the dramatic possibilities of her theme" makes her text, in the end, more subversive than any of the paperback novels on Congressman Gathings's hit list.

NOTES

1. *Publishers Weekly*, 29 November 1952:2161; *Publishers Weekly* 24 January 1952:260; *Publishers Weekly*, 6 September 1952, 30 August 1952:801–3, 860.
2. *Publishers Weekly*, 16 August 1952:694–95; *Colliers*, 4 October 1952:15–17; *Life*, 20 October 1952:91–92; *Saturday Review*, 20 December 1952:1971.
3. After it had been rejected by one house, Coward-McCann published the first edition of *The Price of Salt* in 1952. Bantam bought paperback reprint rights in 1953 and kept the book in print until approximately 1964. In 1969, Macfadden reprinted it in paperback; in 1975, Arno issued a hardcover reprint. The novel's

most recent publisher is Naiad Press, Tallahassee, Florida (1984). All page references in the text refer to the Naiad Press edition, which also includes an afterword by Claire Morgan written in 1983. For publishing history, see Barbara Grier's bibliography *The Lesbian in Literature*, 3rd ed. (Naiad, 1981) and *Lesbiana: Book Reviews from THE LADDER* (Naiad, 1976) 162.

4. Even before the Gathings Committee hearings or the publication of its report, *Women's Barracks* had been the subject of a *Newsweek* article (20 August 1951:92–93) focusing on the book's impressive sales, its subject matter, and its cover art (which depicted a seated, uniformed woman looking on as two of her barracks-mates, clad only in bras and girdles, continue dressing). In the Gathings Committee majority report, *Women's Barracks* is prominent among the books denounced for the same reasons that *Newsweek* had found it newsworthy, but also because the managing editor of the book's publisher (Ralph Daigh of Fawcett Gold Medal) was a witness at the hearings, and because the book had been declared obscene by a Canadian judge, from whose opinion the Committee quotes in its report. See U.S. Cong, 16, 36–40. See also Kenneth C. Davis, *Two-Bit Culture: The Paperbacking of America* (Boston: Houghton, 1984), 216–47.

5. For a thorough treatment of the effects of paperbacking on the publishing industry, see Kenneth C. Davis. See also Freeman Lewis, "Paperbound Books in America," *Publishers Weekly*, 15 November 1952:2012–18 and 22 November 1952:2081–85; *Newsweek*, 20 August 1951:91–92.

6. In 1948, Tereska Torrès married U.S. novelist and war correspondent Meyer Levin, a friend of her father, whom she had known since the age of four. Apparently Levin translated *Women's Barracks* from Torrès's original manuscript, in French, although Levin did not originally take credit for his translation. Kenneth Davis writes that *Women's Barracks* was ostensibly written by Tereska Torrès, but [Fawcett Gold Medal managing editor] Ralph Daigh later revealed it had been translated by Meyer Levin, not yet known as a best-selling writer (155). Torrès's biography in *Contemporary Authors* lists Levin as translator, "from the original manuscript," of five of her nine novels.

There was as well some controversy over whether *Women's Barracks* should be called a "novel" or an "autobiography." Ralph Daigh claimed it was a "true story" adapted from Torrès's diary (U.S. Cong. 37–38). Judge A. G. McDougall of Ottawa, Canada called it "fiction" (U.S. Cong. 40). Torrès's 1970 autobiography asserts that although many of her novels, including *Women's Barracks*, were autobiographically inspired, they are works of fiction nevertheless.

7. Fawcett Gold Medal sold its rights to *Women's Barracks* in 1968 to Dell Publishing, New York. All page references in the text are to the Dell edition, first printing, 1968. As of that edition, three million copies of *Women's Barracks* had been printed.

8. Sigmund Freud, "The Psychogenesis of a Case of Homosexuality in a Woman" (1920), *Standard Edition of the Complete Psychological Works of Sigmund Freud*, ed. James Strachey 18:147–72; "Female Sexuality" (1931), *Standard Edition* 21:223–43.

9. Kinsey's study was not the first of its kind undertaken by an American: in 1918, social scientist Katharine Bement Davis conducted a survey of 2,200 single and married women which challenged traditional assumptions about women's sexual experience. Nor was Kinsey's study the first to suggest that homoeroticism among women was much more common than generally assumed: Davis's study, too, showed that between 30 and 50 percent of American women reported having "intense emotional relationships with other women" that were accompanied by sexual intimacy 15 to 25 percent of the time. See Rosalind Rosenberg, *Beyond Separate Spheres: Intellectual Roots of Modern Feminism* (New Haven: Yale University Press, 1982), 197–200.

10. Klaich, *Woman + Woman*, 188–118; Jonathan Katz, *Gay American History* (New York: Crowell, 1976), 170–93; D'Emilio, *Sexual Politics*, 16–18.

11. Klaich, 95; 99, 102–5; D'Emilio, 144, 215.

12. As quoted in Klaich, 89, 99. All other page references to Caprio's work in the text refer to his *Variations in Sexual Behavior*.

13. Dolores Klaich asserts that some of Caprio's case histories are plagiarisms, citing one example whose origin is Krafft-Ebing's *Psychopathia Sexualis*. She calls into question Caprio's research methods in other areas as well. See Klaich, 99–102.

WORKS CITED

Bergler, Edmund, M.D., and William S. Kroger, M.D. *Kinsey's Myth of Female Sexuality*. New York: Grune & Stratton, 1954.

Bérubé, Allan, and John D'Emilio. "The Military and Lesbians During the McCarthy Years." *Signs* 9 (1984): 759–75.

Bishop, Leonard. *Creep into Thy Narrow Bed*. New York: Dial, 1954.

Bonn, Thomas L. *Undercover: An Illustrated History of Mass–Marketed Paperbacks*. New York: Penguin, 1982.

Caprio, Frank S., M.D. *Variations in Sexual Behavior*. New York: Citadel, 1955.

D'Emilio, John. *Sexual Politics, Sexual Communities: The Making of a Homosexual Minority in the United States, 1940–1970*. Chicago: Univ. of Chicago Press, 1983.

Klaich, Dolores. *Woman + Woman: Attitudes toward Lesbianism*. New York: Morrow, 1974.

Morgan, Claire [Patricia Highsmith]. *The Price of Salt*. Tallahassee, Fla.: Naiad, 1984.

Rolo, Charles J. Review of *The Price of Salt* by Claire Morgan. *New York Times Book Review* 18 May 1952:23.

Ronald, James. *The Angry Woman*. Philadelphia: Lippincott, 1947.

Torrès, Tereska. *Women's Barracks*. New York: Dell, 1968.

United States Cong. House. *Report of the Select Committee on Current Pornographic Materials*. 82nd Cong., 2nd sess. House Report 2510. Washington, D.C.: Government Printing Office, 1952.

SEVENTEEN

The "Queen B" Figure in Black Literature

SDiane A. Bogus

The Black Lesbian writer must create our home, unadulterated, unsanitized, specific and not isolated from the generations that have nurtured us.
—Gomez, "A Cultural Legacy"

The "Queen B" is a euphemism for Queen Bulldagger or Bulldyker. Judy Grahn traces the linquistic and historical etymology of the word, citing the female warrior of A.D. 61, Boudica (pronounced boo-uh-dike-ay), a leader/queen of the Celtic, Iceni tribe, who led an uprising against Roman imperialism to be captured ultimately and flogged, her daughters raped, but not before (with a confederation of Celtic tribes 120,000 strong) she burned to the ground what are now London and Colchester. Grahn asserts: "I believe there are modern attempts to soften her character and hide her ferocious history" (137)—just as her name was driven undergound by the attempts of the Roman governor, Seutonius, to find her grave and defile it. To speak her name at that time in history, in the wrong company, could mean death. So the name *Boudica* carries with it a legacy of danger and secretiveness, but also a hidden history that speaks of valor, pride, and strength. Such is the dichotomy of gay people today, at once proud and apprehensive in an unaccepting culture. Grahn also speculates that the name *Boudica* "could have been a title as well, meaning: bullslayer-priestess" (139). As high priestess of her people, perhaps the queen performed the ceremonial killing of the bull (who was also the god) on the sacred altar, embankment, or dyke. Thus, the modern bullfight or the bull dogging of rodeos recalls, secularly, the ancient rituals of slaying/subduing bulls.

This association is linked to black culture in that the man who introduced "bulldogging" as a rodeo event was a black cowboy, Bill Pickett

(1860–1932), known especially for his participation in rodeo events from Poncha City, Oklahoma to Mexico. It was in South America that he found fame in the 1923 movie, *The Bulldogger*. It is likely that Pickett's participation in the sport and in film brought the word *bulldogger* into black culture and, in time, *"bulldogger"* mutated into *bulldagger*.

The term *bulldagger* comes, too, from cattle farms such as the one Pickett worked on. Ranch hands from time to time witnessed one bull mounting another to make stabbing motions familiar to bull and cow. Perhaps the mutation from "dogger" to "dagger" reflects this observation and explains the lexical change. Whatever the case, the black woman who assumes the male sexual prerogative is called a bulldagger by the genteel as well as by the ignorant of the community. The name, though linked to a ritual past, has been understood to be generally pejorative. Here, I will attempt to resuscitate it and reinterpret the character to whom it refers. In the 1940s and 1950s these terms were used by black and white lesbians themselves to make distinctions of class, race, and proclivity toward cross-dressing among themselves (Pinson 8).

Gomez's quote, which begins this essay, belongs to the "black lesbian-feminist aesthetic" (Bogus, "Notes" 13), and it could not have been uttered before 1974, the year that the first contemporary and undeniably homosexual black woman appeared in a work of American fiction by a black woman (Roberts, "Black Lesbians before 1970" 103–9). Before the introduction of Renay Johnson, in Ann Allen Shockley's *Loving Her,* no critical dialogue regarding black women as lesbians in American fiction existed, nor did literary or biographical research about this image (Cornwell 18–19; Roberts, "Black Lesbians before 1970" 103–9). Shockley's "black lesbian," a term in need of definition, broke through the barriers obscuring this image of black woman. In the past, taboo had silenced others (Walker, "Breaking Chains" 285), and in 1974 Shockley's "daring" portraiture excited such reactionary critical response in the fields of Afro-American and women's studies that it may not be an overestimation to credit Shockley with literally *provoking* the critical dialogue about the black lesbian character by her 1979 essay "The Black Lesbian in American Literature."

In one sense, she may even have inspired the studies which followed the publication of her book, notably J. R. Roberts's *Black Lesbians* and biographical work by Gloria T. Hull on Alice Dunbar Nelson (Hull, *Give Us This Day*) and on Angelina Weld Grimke (Hull, " 'Under the Days' "), both resurrected "lesbian" writers once tabooed. Hull asks, "What did it mean to be a Black lesbian/poet in America at the beginning of the twentieth century?" (*Give Us* 77). And the answer is nearly the same for all black lesbian writers in the mid-to-late twentieth century: "First, it meant that you wrote (or half wrote) in isolation—a lot which you did not show and knew you could not publish. It meant that when you did write to be printed, you did so in shackles chained between the real experience you wanted to say and the conventions that would not give you voice" (*Give Us* 77).

Shockley understood this. Her early work, particularly two first novels, *A World of Lonely Strangers* (1960) and *Not to Be Alone* (1950), were rejected by many publishers. She came to understand the resistance to her subject matter, but even more limiting was the fact that no woman writer could tackle the lesbian theme without being called gay (Shockley, Letter to the author, 28 August 1983), a phenomenon that plagues her career as a novelist even now.

Still, for all of Shockley's explorations, and perseverance, critics often consider her portraiture of the "black lesbian" as lacking viability and authenticity (Gomez 118). Some do not even recognize the import of that "first" published black lesbian portrait drawn by a black woman.

Gloria Wade-Gayles, for example, believes, "As a distinct group in Black women's literary history, they [Black lesbians] were not written in between 1946 and 1976" (18). Though they were not portrayed as a "group," individual black lesbians did appear in the literature of others. Moreover, the contemporary "black lesbian" appeared in 1974, two years before the date assigned by Wade-Gayles. The figure also appears in two 1967 novels, Ed Bullins's *Clara's Old Man* and Ishmael Reed's, *The Free-lance Pallbearers*, though neither portrait is one of a Queen B. The former includes a portrait of Big Girl, a health care worker who dominates the life of her lover, and the latter, of Fannie Mae, a caricature of a gossipy, superstitious, shopping-crazed bisexual. The latter characterization is satirical and difficult to evaluate as a serious portraiture. Nevertheless, the belief that only black lesbian feminists can speak the truth about their lives denies the contribution of the nonlesbian Shockley who seemingly lacks the political credentials of a black lesbian writer.

Yet Shockley is instrumental in introducing the figure of the black lesbian as Queen B—Bulldagger. Although the prototype of this figure already existed in Afro-American history and although not all of Shockley's black lesbians are Queen B's, still a focus on Shockley's characters who approach the type will enable me to suggest a fundamental and new critical perspective by which Shockley's black lesbian can be interpreted.

It is inconceivable to me that any novel about the lives of black women fails to include the black culture from which black people spring, yet Gomez, when contrasting the black lesbian portraiture in Ann Allen Shockley's *Say Jesus and Come to Me* with Alice Walker's *The Color Purple*, applauded Walker for her "diligent attention to the details and essences of Black life" while denouncing Shockley for "trivializing" the lives of black lesbians because of her "inability to place Black lesbians in a believable cultural context in an artful way" (118). Gomez especially liked the way *The Color Purple* "bursts at the seams with details of the folk history of juke joints, the nascent art of the Blues, [and] extended families" (118). These remarks, while evoking the timeless argument about the role of the black writer and the purpose of his or her art, also assume that there is no likeness in "details" between these two novels. According to Gomez, the "folk history" of black people and the "art of the Blues," can be credited to Walker but not to Shockley.

However, my own study of both works reveals the very specific black woman character who "speaks of the generations that have nurtured" her image. She is an incarnation of folk history, a carrier of the "nascent art of the Blues" and a product of black culture, if not of extended families: the female blues singer who bonds with other women. She is also an artist with an "Afro-American sensibility," a "triumphant spirituality," who exhibits "an exuberant emotional expression" when she sings or performs. She clearly knows "the value of human freedom," for her woman-loving choices compel her to "confront life's adversities and grapple with them" (Benjamin 12). She does not always remain calm or possess grace and dignity when grappling with life's adversities, but the trials of her life infuse her music and her life with purpose. She also draws strength from her lover because when she is fulfilled by her music, she can allow and indulge an unaffected, unselfconscious sensuality. She is, in short, the Queen B.

Using this definition, the Queen B appears in Shockley's work as Renay Johnson in *Loving Her*, Holly Craft in the short story, "Holly Craft Isn't Gay" (69–77) in *The Black and White of It*, and Travis Lee of *Say Jesus and Come to Me*. She is also Shug Avery in *The Color Purple* (Walker) and Congo Rose in *Home to Harlem* (McKay), Sybil of *Strange Brother* (Niles) and Josephine Jordan of *Young Man with a Horn* (Baker). Upon reexamining these texts closely, and by allowing for the representation of the figure in American novels by nonblack women (even when the figure may appear stereotyped or minor), one can argue for the general existence of the archetype that I am calling the Queen B.

The Queen B aspires to be and generally succeeds as a singer whose music contributes to and influences the world in which she lives (or with which she identifies). Her vocation makes her a kind of "Queen of Soul," like Aretha Franklin, or a "Queen (also Empress) of the Blues" like Bessie Smith. Like these real-life figures, the Queen B has talent and style. She has, whether her behavior reflects it or not, a conferred regality that has been assigned to black women by writers and poets since Tyye and Hatshepsut of Egypt, and Hathor and Nzinghu of Africa. This royalty is reflected in Travis Lee of *Say Jesus,* who is the "Pristine Goddess of Song," and in Walker's Shug Avery, "The Queen Honey Bee," in *The Color Purple.* These epithets add no emotional or spiritual dimension to the character of the Queen B, but they do give her color and class among those of a kind: the black woman blues singer of the 1920s and 1930s.

As Dolores Barracano Schmidt theorizes in "The Great American Bitch":

When a character appears and reappears virtually unchanged in the work of a number of different authors over a period of time, we may theorize (a) that the character is derivative, the writers having used a common model, (b) that the character is a product of social conditioning. . . , or (c) the character is a symbolic fulfillment of the writer's needs. (900)

Schmidt's theory, particularly the first two parts, is applicable to the appearance of the Queen B type in the fictions of American writers since the 1920s.

The common model for one variety of the Queen B can be said to have derived from social conditioning. Compare and contrast Langston Hughes's description of Gladys Bentley (1894–1960) of Harlem cabaret fame to Blair Niles's fictional representation of Sybil in *Strange Brother:*

Some of the small clubs had people like [Miss] Gladys Bentley [who] sat and played a big piano all night long. . . . Miss Bentley was an amazing exhibition of musical energy—a large, dark, masculine lady, whose feet pounded the floor while her fingers pounded the keyboard—a perfect piece of African sculpture animated by her own rhythm. . . . The old magic of the woman and the place and the night and the rhythm being one is gone. (*The Big Sea* 225–26)

The strange figure whose hands passed with such incredible speed up and down the piano . . . [had] what rhythm! [She kept] her feet . . . beating on the floor as if it were a drum.

Where on earth could she have come from? She looked like the heart of Africa . . . the heart of darkness! (Niles 70)

The "social conditioning" that made for the character of Sybil was the exalted notion of "the primitive" during the Harlem Renaissance. In *Novels of the Harlem Renaissance,* Amritjit Singh discusses the development of the worship of the primitive as having come into vogue with Carl Van Vechten's *Nigger Heaven* (1926) which popularized a facet of black culture. Singh calls it a "bandwagon effect" that writers such as Claude McKay, Eric Walrond, and Langston Hughes "got in on" (25). The idea was to "exalt the exotic, the sensual, and the primitive" (25). Generally, this was done by showing what creatures of joy black people were. Though W. E. B. DuBois and Benjamin Brawley, among other writers and critics, felt the emphasis on the bawdy depiction of the Negro was detrimental to the black's political future (Singh 25), some images took hold; among them were the "large, masculine lady" of nightlife, song, energy, and African spirit. This image was modeled after Gladys Bentley, alias "Bobbie Minton," who was "known to be queer, to cross-dress," often "sporting a girlfriend" on her arm in "daily marches down Seventh Avenue dressed in men's clothes" (Roberts, *Annotated Bibliography* 70). (Bentley is reputed to have married a woman in Atlantic City in the 1930s.) Sybil has the same traits, even a "wife" (57). Her cross-dressing and overt woman-loving behavior serve as one common model for the Queen B.

Another common model, less masculine but no less woman-loving or talented, is represented by black singer Bessie Smith. She "transformed our collective shame at being rape victims, treated like dogs or, worse, the meat dogs eat by emphasizing the value of our allure. In doing so, she humanized sexuality for Black women" (Michele Russell, quoted in Spillers 8). The Bessie Smith model generally is not at war with men. Often she leads an active lesbian lifestyle while married and raising a family (Pinson 8). By contrast, however, today's lesbian cannot be seen as "politically correct" if she sleeps with men (Cohen 48).

Thus, it is important to note that during the 1920s and throughout the 1930s "most urban Blacks—whether they indulged or not, accepted homosexuality as a fact of life" (Albertson 125). This attitude did not mean there were no blacks who felt same-sex coupling to be wrong. Jake, the lead character in *Home to Harlem,* is repulsed by "faggoty men" and "bulldyking women" (McKay 68), yet he attends their cabarets regularly. Just as it was believed that marriage legitimized sexual relations between males and females, moving it from "dirty" fornication to sanctified conjugal relations, there was an element of black society that thought women sexually intimate with one another were both sinful and man-hating as exemplified by the title of Bessie Smith's 1930s' blues tune, "It's Dirty But It's Good." And while Bessie Smith was not politically active, she was socially cognizant (Albertson 149). From the stage, she "chided, embraced, inquired into the nature of (Black) womanhood through the eloquence of form that she both made use of and brought into being" (Spillers 87). So transcendent and essential were her translations of the nuances of black culture that James Baldwin attributes his being "reconciled to being a nigger" through the "tone and cadence" of Bessie Smith's recordings while he was exiled in Paris (quoted in Charters, *The Poetry of the Blues* 5).

Even when she is not an international star, however, the Queen B model can emerge, as did Gladys Bentley, as "a bigger than life lesbian star" (Shockley, "Black Lesbian Biography" 8). Ideally, the world, either accepting of, ignorant of, or repulsed by her sexual behavior, ought to "tramp to the doors" (Bentley 9) to see her perform.

Often the Queen B can transcend the conflicts of her sexuality, the effects of oppression, racial or gender-related, and the distractions of ordinary life; when she does, she gains the potential to become as historic a figure as was Bentley or Smith, the latter of whom is said to have achieved "heroic stature" because "her music far exceeds the facts of her life" (Oliver 71).

So how do the fictional Queen B's compare to their once-living counterparts, the models on whom they are based? Congo Rose, Sybil, Josephine Jordan, and Shug Avery constitute a fictional coterie of first-generation Queen B's who, in fact, sing the blues between the 1920s and the 1930s. Those of Shockley's canon—Renay Johnson, Holly Craft, and Travis Lee —comprise the second generation who sing or play popular music such as rhythm and blues or jazz, between 1960 and the present.

What traits are common to the first generation of Queen B's and those of Shockley's second? Which not? Where do we find, in both generations, "an Afro-American sensibility," "an exuberant emotional expression," and "a deep and abiding sense of the value of human freedom," as Benjamin suggests (12) is true of the black singer in these traditions? What conclusions can we draw about the Shockley portraiture?

In examining the portraiture, I found two obvious features of the Queen B that are physical in nature. Generally, the earlier Queen B's are stouter and darker than Shockley's, perhaps reflecting the physical characteristics of their real-life counterparts. In contrast, Shockley's Queen B's are slimmer and lighter-skinned. I suspect that in the thirties when Shockley was growing up, she, like most Negroes of the time, received messages from white culture that called for assimilation. Thus many Negroes straightened their hair, used skin lighteners, and strove to imitate the behavior of the dominant culture. This need to assimilate prompted many black people to appreciate that which was European and to downplay their African heritage, as the singer does in Shockley's "Song of Hope." A certain antagonism toward and shame about being "too dark" sprang up. Perhaps the pain of being black in white America gave rise to this discriminatory chant that I recall from my own childhood: "If you're white, you're right; if you're yellow or brown, stick around, but if you're black get back."

Ultimately, however, the color of the Queen B's skin is unimportant to her self-definition as woman and singer. It is significant, as Playthell G. Benjamin has said, that she is black because blackness is the source of her "African-American sensibility," her "exuberant emotional expression," her "triumphant spirituality" (12).

Thus the characterization of Sybil and Josephine as dark-skinned blues singing women is anything but a "joke" (Walker "Embracing" 67). Having achieved stardom, they demonstrate an Afro-American sensibility and an "exuberant emotional expression," triumphantly, spiritually. This ability to confront life without any undue racial selfconsciousness allows Sybil, the star of the Lobster Pot, to appear "extraordinary," to put "herself over by sheer genius" (Niles 42). Sybil can sing and dance "as though to live was so gorgeous an experience that one must dance and sing thanksgiving." (42) And Josephine, a well-known recording star, cannot go into a public place without "somebody yelling Jo, and then somebody else . . . until the room [is] full of it" (Baker 174). Wherever and whenever, Josephine sings in "the fine wild way she had." They are treated seriously because within each are the agonies of spirit that give depth to their singing.

Part of the Queen B's importance, thus, is her role as a musical artist, which in turn makes her a central figure in the community at large. It is important to remember that the themes of blues idiom are love, disappointment, and anger. In her music, the blues singer finds release from the emotions that trouble. The impulse to sing, Benjamin has summarized, is an attempt to squeeze from brutal experience a near-tragic, near-comic lyricism (18). To achieve this lyric dimension takes a depth of insight, a compassionate response, and an artistry that can reverberate in others, that can become, as it were, "universal." This ability belonged to Bessie Smith, to Mamie Smith, to Gladys Bentley, to the legion of blues singers whose direct concern with the trials of being black or alone or financially insolvent were real. This ability to translate experience, says Hortense Spillers, has created one of the "truest" images of the black woman, America's black female vocalist (86). Thus, later Queen B's may not sing the blues as did their prototype, but they bring to their art a knowledge of the tradition, the honesty of it. They share a living legacy of blues transformations. "When I sing," says Travis Lee, "I try to impart my true and undiluted feelings." (*Say Jesus* 66). Renay Johnson, on the other hand, loves and hates the blues. When Terry Bluvard requests a tune by Debussy, and Renay plays it on the piano, Renay feels she overcomes the stereotype that "a nigger knows nothing but blues and jazz" (19). Yet, at another point, after she and Terry become romantically involved, she is asked to play for a friend of Terry's on whom Renay decides not to "waste the blues" because:

The blues are for deep inside where they all start and sometimes never end. You don't just listen to the blues. *You feel it* twisting around inside like a serpentine knife, hurting and sometimes healing. (34, emphasis added)

Of all the Queen B's, Renay alone doesn't sing, but since childhood she has had "a dedication to and a love for music" (11). She is the only one who has allowed motherhood to keep her from developing her career. The Queen B is generally determined and persistent; therefore, she is able to overcome personal challenges as she engages her art. She allows no distraction, major or minor, to sabotage her determination to sing or perform. For example, Mister's jealousy does not keep Shug from singing "Miss Celie's Song" to Celie before an intimate crowd. Shockley's characters also overcome abusive men on the road to becoming the singers or musicians they have determined to be.

In broad application, then, if the singer is successful at taking the theme and genre of her song and affecting an audience in such a way that the audience identifies with the emotional experience of it, then the Queen B can be said to approximate the prototype of the blues tradition from which she springs. Bessie Smith's performance can serve as a model for the first- and second-generation Queen B's. As Carl Van Vechten noted about a Bessie Smith performance:

This was no actress; or imitator of women's woes; there was no pretense. It was the real thing: a woman cutting her heart open with a knife until it was exposed for us all to see so that we suffered as she suffered. (Quoted in Albertson 140)

If the mark of a Queen B is her ability to sing so as to move her audience to empathy, then the following descriptions of Sybil's and Josephine's blues styling align them with the model provided by Smith:

Sybil mopped her forehead . . . and began at first in slow, carefully enunciated, chanting syllables:
As I passed St. James infirmary
I saw my sweetheart there
Aw-aw-h Aw-aw-h
It seemed to June that a corpse actually lay in the room . . . they were all wailing around it. . . . And suddenly an incredibly sweet, prolonged trembling cry from Sybil. (Niles 59–60)

Josephine has been recognized at a local club and asked to sing impromptu. She takes the mike:

She sang . . . quietly and you could hear every word as if she were close to you, talking to you. . . . But they hadn't taught her to do what she was doing with the song. . . . [It stood] for all the trust and betrayals of all time. It was the true, tragic thing, from her mouth, and to hear it was to know it. (Baker, 175–76)

The Queen B of these two fictions is shown in her element—performing before people. Her effect on the audience is clear and immediate. One could say she translates, even if troubled, both the "exuberant emotional expression" and "African-American sensibility" that Benjamin attributes to the music of black Americans (12). However, Congo Rose is given only brief moments in the spotlight. Her performances are not closely examined for the effect she has on the audience. In Rose's case, she sings "a wonderful drag blues that was the favorite of all the low-down dance halls." Couples dance. One man gives her money. "The excitement" is said "to have mounted" (19–20). But Rose is treated like a whore. She stops singing to sit with Jake and a friend because "that was part of her business. She got more tips that way, and the extra personal bargains that gave her the means to maintain her style of living" (61). She is treated unsympathetically by McKay who makes her seduction of Jake the act of a sex-hungry "animal" whose "tireless activity" made Jake "her big, good slave." Despite her negative treatment by men, Rose's intimate friends include men as well as women. Nevertheless, she sings the ironic lyrics: "There's two things in Harlem I don't understan'/It is a bull dyking woman and a faggoty man." If Rose is really "free in her ways," it is curious that her woman-friend never surfaces as a romantic figure. Thus, Rose appears to be whorish and self-hating when she encourages Jake to beat her and take her money (63). Her portraiture is so contradictory as to deny all else except her devotion to her art. After making love with Jake and telling him that she loves him "Moh'n anything," she realizes—two hours later—that she has been "honey-dreaming some" (65) and from the romantic interlude following Jake's beating she jumps up, smoothing her frock, to head out for the Congo.

This theme of female abuse shared between the Queen B's of both generations is not particularly reflected in the lives of their prototypes, although Bessie Smith was known to instigate fights (Albertson 148). Holly Craft, unlike Congo Rose who perversely craves manhandling, was "a woman whose body had been used" (Shockley, *Black and White* 74), and as a result she "crooned to the soft hidden faces of the women who could understand what she was singing about—them—mired in their sorrows, happiness, secrets, loves" (74).

Travis Lee is a more typical figure than Congo Rose. Rose wanted her men to live "in the usual sweet way to be brutal and take her money from her" (61). Travis, on the other hand, is, unluckily, "a magnet that drew the same type of man over and over again—the husky, macho stud with no qualms about living off his woman and slapping her around" (41).

Suffering a nasty beating from Rudolph Valentino Jones, after she accuses him of infidelity, Travis, a singer whose roots are in the black church, salves her wounds while listening to a religious broadcast. Understood to be the "pristine Goddess of Song," principally of rhythm and blues, Travis undergoes a spontaneous religious conversion that leads her back to church music and to the arms of Myrtle Black, despite the fact that Travis "doesn't like dykes" (72). Eventually Travis, feeling "used and used and used," joins Myrtle's Universal Church for All People where she sings:

Travis's music came out sweet and plaintive, an undiluted melancholy sound, analogous to a lonely, pliant voice floating from a cabin window beneath a waning, pink southern sky. As she sang, a cauldron of emotions engulfed the church. There were those who eased tears and others who listened in joy and sorrow. . . .

When she finished, pleasure and appreciation was indicated in the ancestral African custom of feet patting the floor. . . . (147)

One can see, then, that between the once-living models and the original "common model" for the Queen B, there are traits common to both, some easily traceable and applicable, others not. In this eclectic contrast between the Queen B's and their prototypes, one can sense in "the whole envelope of circumstances" that their commonalities are strikingly similar. The appeal and depth of these images make for "an exuberant emotional expression" in the face of abuse, personal crises, and other distractions. The link between them all is the "Afro-American sensibility" which bears the legacy of slaves who sang spirituals to free themselves spiritually and physically (Benjamin 14).

The abiding sense of "the value of human freedom" that Benjamin highlights is partly articulated by the Queen B's woman-loving choices—except for Congo Rose for whom a particular friend is never seen. The relationships of the Queen B nevertheless do not distract her from her art. In most instances, for the first- and the second-generation Queen B's, their relationships nurture them as artists. For example, Amy North follows Josephine Jordan about to support her career; Sybil's "wife" comes to the club; Celie nurses Shug back to health so that she can perform again; Adrienne welcomes Holly into her life whenever she desires to come; Terry encourages Renay to return to her music studies. The best example of the difference her female lover made in the life of a Queen B is Travis Lee. Once a virulent heterosexist, Travis comes to discover, much to her surprise, that "you never know where your heart is going to lead you" (170). But beyond this discovery, even knowing that she had much to lose if her lesbianism was discovered ("those in the entertainment world whose homosexuality was whispered about" suffered much "rancor"), Travis "felt like shouting [her love for Myrtle] from the housetops" (170).

Although her love for Myrtle is wonderful, the "confrontation" between the black female singer and a hostile world is present as well. The second-generation Queen B in Shockley's Say Jesus, Loving Her, and her "Holly Craft Is Not Gay" all must struggle with their lesbianism in an unaccepting world. By contrast, the earlier Queen B is unselfconscious though not without her trials. She does not often try to hide her sexual and emotional commitment to a woman, nor does it seem an affront to her immediate circle of friends and acquaintances. The first-generation Queen B, as blues singer, confronts the dismal and delightful specters of life so evenhandedly, she seems inexplicably balanced. Her bisexuality, her multiple relations, her liaisons, her lesbianism, and questionable heterosexuality—whatever we call her romantic involvements—are free of strain because she is freed by the liberty of singing and by the subjects of her song. Her life, the audience she sings for, are transformed by "the directness of expression in the sexual attitudes of the blues" (Charters 82). It is small wonder that one 1920s' blues tune attests: "Women loving each other. . . . They ain't playing it secret no more. These women playing a wide open hand" (Charters 82).

Ann Allen Shockley's Queen B is also freed by the possibility of transformation that music offers. Holly becomes famous and has a following because she sings the secrets, sorrows, and happiness of women, but she, Renay, and Travis all have to confront a shift in social mores regarding homosexuals, which had not been very pronounced in the 1920s. So although they find a freedom of expression in singing or playing their respective genres of music, they are constantly in internal conflict about what it means to love a woman and what others will think if they find out. Renay comes to understand too clearly one aspect of the dilemma of a black woman-loving woman when she tries to decide if she should share her newfound lesbianism with Fran, her best friend:

Black women were the most vehement about women loving each other. This kind of love was worse to them than the acts of adultery or incest, for it was homophile. It was worse than being afflicted with an incurable disease. Black women could be sympathetic about illegitimacy, raising the children of others, having affairs with married men—but not toward lesbianism. . . . (31)

None of Shockley's Queen B's fare too well when they confront the society of the 1970s and 1980s. Jerome Lee, angry because he can no longer control or dominate Renay, becomes stereotypically selfrighteous about the effect of Renay's new life on his daughter: "The shitting-ass nerve of you, bringing my daughter up around bulldikers" (128). Renay ends up hospitalized from the beating by Jerome Lee. In *Say Jesus and Come to Me* Rudolph, jealous and ego-crushed by Travis's having spurned him, plans to destroy the career of Myrtle (and thus hurt Travis, too) because Myrtle "was a bulldagger with a church full of faggots, dykes, squares and Jesus freaks . . . pretending to be praising the Lord" (191). Eventually, he spreads this insidious truth to those who would support Myrtle's march and she is forced to admit her homosexuality publicly.

Shockley's Queen B's struggle for every freedom, every kiss with the women they love, and though clearly showing a preference for women, they have unwelcome dealings with men, sometimes living with them while carrying on relations with women, sometimes leaving them for women. Unlike the first-generation Queen B's, Shockley's protagonists are not un-selfconscious though they are brave, confronting life's adversities with varying degrees of grace and integrity.

These similarities and differences between the first- and second-genera-tion Queen B in relationship to their handling of their romantic involve-ments distinguishes them from each other without dividing the portraiture in these fictions. One thing is certain: none of these Queen B's is "isolated from the generations that have nurtured them," as Gomez seemed to feel was the case with Shockley's black lesbian.

The fact is, the black lesbian is a recent incarnation of lesbian-feminist politics, and the term is used as a handy label by those who must call the woman-loving black woman *something* to give her presence and identify her, even at the risk of separating her from the culture of which she is so integrally a part.

The black lesbian Queen B has a common source which is unadulter-ated, unsanitized, and as specific as any figure can be. She is weak or wanton, like Shug or Congo Rose. She is vulnerable and foolish, as are Renay and Holly. She is centered and career-oriented, as are Josephine and Sybil. She is at one point unselfconscious about loving women, and at another, repressed as well as oppressed by society. Still, and above all, she is an artist in a great and long tradition of American music infused with the rhythms and memories of an African/slave past. Even in fiction, she helps to establish the proposition that the musical contribution of black America is an original contribution to the artistic heritage of the world, representing a unique sensibility in Western culture (Benjamin 33). It is as unique a sensibility as the Queen B is a unique figure. She stands out boldly in American fiction from the 1920s to the present, but she is especially re-born, if not duplicated, in the work of Ann Allen Shockley whose interest in the blues/jazz/popular singer as a character made this beginning link pos-sible.

WORKS CITED

Albertson, Chris. *Bessie*. New York: Stein & Day, 1972.
Baker, Dorothy. *Young Man with a Horn*. Boston: Houghton, 1938.

Benjamin, Playthell G. "The Afro-American Musician: Messengers of a Unique Sensibility in Western Culture." *The Black Nation* (Summer/Fall 1986): 11–33.

Bentley, Gladys. "I Am a Woman Again." *Ebony* (August 1952): 92+.

Bogus, SDiane. "Notes on the Black Lesbian Aesthetic in Literature." *Mama Bear's News and Notes* (August/September 1986): 3+.

———. "The Reality of the Black Lesbian." *GPU News* (October 1978): 17, 19–20.

Bullins, Ed. *Clara's Old Man. Five Plays by Ed Bullins*. New York: Bobbs, 1968.

Charters, Samuel. *The Poetry of the Blues*. New York: Oak Publications, 1963.

Cohen, Jennifer Dawn. "The Phenomenon of Previously Self-Identified Lesbians Who Are Presently Relating Sexually to Men." Master's Thesis. San Francisco State University, 1983.

Cornwell, Anita. *Black Lesbian in White America*. Tallahassee, Fla.: Naiad, 1983.

Gomez, Jewell. "A Cultural Legacy Denied and Discovered: Black Lesbians in Fiction by Women." In *Home Girls: A Black Feminist Anthology*. Ed. Barbara Smith. New York: Kitchen Table/Women of Color, 1983, 110–23.

Grahn, Judy. *Another Mother Tongue*. Boston: Beacon, 1984.

Hughes, Langston. *The Big Sea*. New York: Hill and Wang, 1940.

Hull, Gloria T., ed. *Give Us This Day: The Diary of Alice Dunbar Nelson*. New York: Norton, 1984.

———. "Rewriting Afro-American Literature: A Case for Black Women Writers." *Radical Teacher* (December 1977): 10–14.

———. " 'Under the Days': The Buried Life and the Poetry of Angelina Weld Grimke." *Conditions Five* (Autumn 1979): 133–42.

McKay, Claude. *Home to Harlem*. New York: Harper, 1928.

Niles, Blair. *Strange Brother*. New York: Liveright, 1931.

Oliver, Pat. *Bessie Smith*. New York: A. S. Barnes, 1961.

Pinson, Luvenia. "The Black Lesbian: Times Past—Times Present." *Woman News* (May 1980): 8.

Reed, Ishmael. *The Free-lance Pallbearers*. Chatham, N.J.: Chatham Bookseller, 1967.

Roberts, J. R. *Black Lesbians: An Annotated Bibliography*. Tallahassee, Fla.: Naiad, 1981.

———. "Black Lesbians before 1970: A Bibliographical Essay." In *Lesbian Studies: Present and Future*. Ed. Margaret Cruikshank. Old Westbury, N.Y.: Feminist, 1979. 103–9.

Schmidt, Dolores Barracano. "The Great American Bitch." *College English* 32 (1971): 900–905.

Shockley, Ann Allen. *The Black and the White of It*. Tallahassee, Fla.: Naiad, 1980.

———. "Black Lesbian Biography 'Lifting the Veil.' " *Other Black Woman* 1 (1982): 1–13.

———. "The Black Lesbian in American Literature: A Critical Overview." *Conditions Five* (Autumn 1979): 133–42.

————. "The Black Lesbian: Invisible Woman in American Literature." SAMLA Convention. Atlanta, 1 November 1979.

————. Letter to the author. 28 August 1983.

————. *Loving Her.* 1974. Rpt. Tallahassee, Fla.: Naiad, 1987.

————. *Say Jesus and Come to Me.* 1982. Rpt. Tallahassee: Naiad, 1987.

————. "Song of Hope." *Fisk Herald,* October 1946, 26–29.

Singh, Amritjit. *The Novels of the Harlem Renaissance.* University Park, Pa.: Penn State Univ. Press, 1976.

Spillers, Hortense. "The Politics of Intimacy: A Discussion." In *Sturdy Black Bridges: A Vision of Black Women in Literature.* Ed. Roseann P. Bell, et al. Garden City, N.Y.: Anchor, 1979.

Wade-Gayles, Gloria. *No Crystal Stair.* New York: Pilgrim, 1984.

Walker, Alice. "Breaking Chains and Encouraging Life." *In Search of Our Mothers' Gardens.* New York: Harcourt, 1983.

————. *The Color Purple.* New York: Harcourt, 1982.

————. "Embracing the Dark and the Light." *Essence* (July 1982): 67+.

EIGHTEEN

A Revolutionary Signifier:
The Lesbian Body

Namascar Shaktini

If one speaks the unspeakable—breaks the taboo on lesbianism—can one continue to speak in the language which we all know, but which assumes the phallocentric subject imposing the taboo? If not, is it possible to write while repositioning subjectivity? Monique Wittig, in a remarkable text, *The Lesbian Body,* has struggled with this problem by rupturing with the phallocentric subject, and, as I hope to show, has produced a lesbian signifier —what Elaine Marks has called a "revolutioanry signifier" (Marks 360). *The Lesbian Body* is a systematic movement to affirm lesbian intersubjectivity, in spite of the negating or decentering effect of phallogocentrism, the organizing principle of the symbolic order which centers meaning in relation to the phallic body as point of reference. Lacan has called the phallus the "primary signifier" (Lacan 287). Through a major reorganization of meaning within Monique Wittig's text, the lesbian body has displaced the phallus as the central point of reference.

The sex-gender system in the symbolic order organizes the structures of phallic oppression. This system turns biological females into wives (objects of exchange by men) and, in order to continue to do this, maintains the myth that women are only sexual objects, not subjects. Obviously, as sexual subjects and nonwives, lesbians cannot exist for the sex-gender system; we are, by our very existence, a double contradiction of this system. In the rare cases where a lesbian has been recognized, she has been perceived by the phallic subject as manlike, monstrous, "the demonic corrupter" (Marks 361).

This chapter focuses on Monique Wittig's deconstruction of some central phallic image-concepts of women and lesbians as part of the process whereby she constructs a revolutionary signifier. First, at the materialist level, the concept of the exchange of women (affirmed by Lévi-Strauss) is metamorphosed. Second, at the ideological level, the black continent metaphor for female sexuality (affirmed by Freud) is distanced as the lesbian signifier moves metaphorically away from it. Third, the lesbian-monster figure is ironically assumed and deconstructed as only one of a multiplicity of signifieds of the intersubjective pronouns, "I," "you," and "we."

Let us first examine Wittig's deconstruction and rewriting of the wife-exchange concept of Lévi-Strauss. His view of women as wives to be exchanged like words and money by a male-identified subject is too well known (after forty years) to need another discussion here. Gayle Rubin's article "The Traffic in Women" has shown that, for his theory, "the incest taboo and the exchange of women are the content of the original social contract" (Rubin 192). Let me simply refer to Wittig's one-sentence comment establishing her political position toward this concept: "Since, as Lévi-Strauss said, we talk, let us say that we break off the heterosexual contract" (Wittig, "Straight Mind" 110). Written from a lesbian point of view, that is, a view from outside the system of wife exchange, Wittig's essay theoretically critiques "the language of the exchange of women where human beings are literally the signs which are used to communicate" (Wittig, "Straight Mind" 104).

In *The Lesbian Body*, Lévi-Strauss's anthropological wife-exchange concept becomes a component of the writer's material which is figured in a distanced, displaced manner. In Wittig's metamorphosis, the objects of exchange are no longer women; the objects exchanged are now attributes of color, and the women have now become the subjects of exchange. Thus, in the following two quotations, we see Wittig's metamorphosis of the exchange system; the color attributes are first assigned (by the author) to the figures of the women and then they are reassigneed, at the level of narration, by the women themselves. The first series of name/attribute pairs is presented thus:

I watch you holding the hand of Artemis with leather laced over her bare breasts, then that of Aphrodite, the black goddess with the flat belly. There is also the triple Persephone, there is sun-headed Ishtar, there is albina eldest of the Danaïds, there is Epone the great horsewoman, there is Leucippa whose mare runs in the meadow below white and shining, there is dark Isis, there is red Hecate, there are Pomona and Flora holding each other by the hand, there is Andromeda of the fleet foot, there is blonde Cybele, there is Io with the white cow, there are Niobe and Latone intertwined, there is Sappho of the violet breasts, there is Gurinno the swift runner, there is Ceres with the corn in her hair, there is white Leucothea, there is moon-headed Rhamnusis.[1] (My translation)

Then the new order of meaning (new set of relationships between women and their attributes) is signaled by Aphrodite: "At a sign from blessed Aphrodite all around you exchange their colours. Leucothea becomes the black one, Demeter the white, Isis the fair one, Io the red, Artemis the green, Sappho the golden, Persephone the violet" (70).[2] We see that lavender, which in every other instance in the book is actually or potentially identified with Sappho, now becomes the attribute of Persephone. Wittig's image shows us that attributes are relative, not absolute—meaning can and does change.

Wittig metamorphoses the structuralist theoretical concept of women into a poetic image. To do this, she goes for her materials to a progressive poetic tradition, that of Rimbaud's "Alchemy of the Word," and his famous sonnet "Vowels," where an element internal to language, vowels, becomes the signified rather than the signifier of some reality which would be exterior to language. But in Wittig's alchemical process, different from Rimbaud's, it is the attributes of figures, not the attributes of phonetics, that change their status from siginifiers to signifieds. Rimbaud provides Wittig with deconstructive material which she uses in a political way—to deconstruct the concept of the exchange of women. This shift breaks the relation of identity that representationalism demands. If poem 43 were representational (if it referred to a reality exterior to language), we would call this change a poetic flaw, a violation of the verisimilitude of representationalism. Sappho "signifies" lavender and lavender "signifies" Sappho in *The Lesbian Body*. But in poem 43 this relation of identity is deconstructed. Similarly, though Sappho is represented and invoked elsewhere by the speaker-writer as a muse, in poem 43 she is identified as just one of the figures in the library books: "/I know them all by their names from having studied them in the library books" (*Lesbian Body* 69).[3]

Meaning is therefore constructed in this poem in a nonrepresentational way. Phallic meaning is deconstructed. By turning the theoretical concept of wife-exchange into a poetic image, Wittig creates a remarkable image-concept. In poem 43, women are not objects, but subjects of the exchange. By exchanging their own attributes, they redefine themselves. Wittig envisions here a communication-exchange network in terms not of universal heterosexuality, but of lesbianism. In a politico-poetic act, she breaks the "heterosexual contract" (Wittig, "Straight Mind" 110).

To maintain the wife-exchange system, a supporting ideology must also be maintained. Women's sex and reproduction can best be kept in male hands if it is believed that only men are subjects of desire—that women are passive sex objects. Not surprisingly, when Freud constructed his theory of sexuality from the point of view of the phallus he found that the sexual life of women is unknowable—a "dark continent."[4] We can see a recurrent movement away from the "dark continent" in *The Lesbian Body*.

Unlike Cixous, who claims in "The Laugh of the Medusa" that *"the Dark Continent is neither dark nor unexplorable,"* and that she has been there often, Wittig presents the black continent as a metaphor for what she wants to escape (Cixous 255). In *The Lesbian Body* the three occurrences of the phrase "the black continent" are weighed against the three occurrences of the phrase "the lesbian body." But the placement of "the lesbian body"— as title, and as first and last phrase of the list—establishes the central importance of this phrase, while the placement of "the black continent"— always at the very end of prose poems—connotes a phrase at the end of its usage.

According to the *Petit Larousse*, one of the surnames of Aphrodite is Cyprine, etymologically related to the island of Cyprus where Aphrodite/ Cyprine was honored. In a politico-poetic act, a lexical metamorphosis, Wittig has reintroduced the word *cyprine* with a new usage. Just as the phallic subject, on the bodily level, produces semen, and on the symbolic level, seminaries and seminars and seminal words,[5] the lesbian as sexual subject produces *cyprine* (*Lesbian Body* 139). In the list (in the French original), *cyprine* is the first of the attributes listed after the phrase "the lesbian body." (In the list, David Le Vay unfortunately translates Wittig's poetic neologism as "juice.") The beloved is addressed as "m/y glory of cyprine" (50).[6] Poem 11 hyperbolically describes the cyprine or cyprin[7] in which the lovers are swimming as a rising tide, gushing forth through the window into the sky, where it has the color and consistency of clouds: "the rising wave emerges in the sky, farewell black continent of misery and suffering farewell ancient cities we are embarking for the brilliant and radiant islands for the green Cytheras for the black and gilded Lesbian Islands" (my translation).[8] Wittig thus evokes and pluralizes Cythera, an island of the Aegean sea, where there was a magnificent temple to Aphrodite. She also evokes and lesbianizes a scene of heterosexuality, "L'Embarquement pour Cythère," the well-known painting for which Watteau was named to the French Academy in 1717. No one would think of this poem as representational, in the sense that it would describe a consistent reality "exterior" to language. The voyage takes place on many levels, but there is no level which would be represented or "mirrored" as in the case of Stendhalian "reality."[9]

Cyprin is bodily like semen, and here Wittig has coined a term which is very political, because it names as a fact of reality what had not before been named (and therefore known) by the phallic subject. Freud had not been able to recognize (for example in *Portrait of Dora*) female-female sexuality, independent of the penis. He consistently considered the "libido," whether in male or female, to be masculine. It is generally consistent with his theory that female sexuality, except to the extent that it exists from the point of view of the phallic subject, cannot be known. The black continent, or unknowable female sexuality, denies, in effect, the female as a subject of desire. In another sense, the black continent metaphor is a metaphor for the blindness of the phallic "primary signifier." The metaphor poses the basic epistemological problem of phallogocentrism.

Through the magic of metaphor, cyprin as a word-concept undergoes a metamorphosis in *The Lesbian Body*, swelling until it can no longer be contained. Cyprin gushes out, produced as part of the female orgasm, much as semen is produced during the orgasm of the phallic subject. In this hyperbolic metamorphosis, the cyprin, first produced as empirical proof of female sexual pleasure, turns into a rising tide which, cloudlike, rises to the sky, refuting, by its very existence in the world of words, the phallocentric notion that female sexuality cannot be known. This poem about cyprin "means" only in relation to the lesbian body, the primary signifier of Wittig's text. Here, "the black continent" for Wittig is the phallogocentric gehenna we are trying to leave, the place to push off from as we embark for the lesbian islands. The movement against the phallic metaphor gives momentum toward the metaphorical "place" of lesbian metaphor.

Wittig uses description and evocation of islands for the construction of lesbian presence in the poems of *The Lesbian Body*. On the level of description, lesbian love is "located" on, around, or above islands. Islands are thus the recurring "setting" (to the extent that there is any) for the prose poems. In contrast to the three references to the black continent, there are twenty-nine references to islands. The island images evoke Sappho's island, Lesbos, as well as the island of Aphorodite, Cythera.

In the second poem in which the black continent is mentioned, poem 34, we are still in the black continent, but we know we are on its edge since we are "on the edge of the sea." This is one of the poems where the speaker invokes the divine Sappho who, as the prototypical lesbian, evokes the presence of lesbianism. Here, as in nine of the poems, Sappho is specifically named. She is recurrently invoked, glorified, or prayed to as a muse. It was Plato who ostensibly started the intertextual tradition of Sappho as the tenth muse, and this image-concept appeared as early as the seventeenth century in a French dictionary.[10] In poem 34 Wittig uses this image-concept of Sappho. But Wittig elsewhere deconstructs the concept of Sappho as muse, for example in poem 43, where Sappho appears as one of the figures in the "library books."[11] In poem 34 Sappho performs the divine function of marking the lovers with a violet mark.[12] The lavender colors—violet, mauve, purple, lavender, and lilac—appear seventy-two times in the text, adding, as signifiers of lesbianism, to the sense of lesbian presence.

/I wait for the arrival of the comets with their smoky flashes, they are here thanks be to Sappho, the stones of her star are fallen, those which marked you above your cheek at the level of the temple with a violet seal exactly like m/y own, glory to Sappho for as long as we shall live in this black continent.[13] (My translation)

Here is the suggestion that we will not always live in this black continent.

We encounter the black continent metaphor for the third and last time in poem 52. In this poem the lovers undergo a bodily metamorphosis: they become covered with hair, hair that has the properties of wings in that they are able to "catch the wind," "seek a current," and "fly away." In this case, as in the first, the relation to the black continent is to say farewell and steer for the island of the living: "I float m/y arms on your arms, the wind mingles our hairs, it combs them, it brushes them, it gives them luster, farewell black continent you steer for the island of the living" (my translation).[14] In these three poems, we see a recurrent metaphorical movement or implied desire for movement away from the black continent, upward and onward.

Wittig thus transcends the nineteenth-century European colonialist metaphor—not only at the level of Freud's signified meaning—"unknowable" female sexuality, but also at the level of the signifier—"black." Where Freud used "black" to mean the absence of light (since his perspective of dominance caused an epistemological "blackout" in regards to the oppressed), Wittig assimilates this usage into a multiplicity of usages. In her phrases "black glistening" (*Lesbian Body* 111), or "black and shining" (18 and 22), for example, black is used in combination with (not polarized in opposition to) light.

Black appears also as one of the colors, like the lavender colors. Black and lavender are the only colors used as epithets for the beloved by Wittig:

"m/y so black one" (163), "m/y . . . lilac purple one" (50), "m/y most mauve one" (116). They are the colors which appear most frequently in her text— black occurring seventy-nine times, as compared with the 72 occurrences of the lavender colors.

Instead of being just a negative term, black is in a position of power in Wittig's text. For example, in poem 43, where the white goddess of fertility disappears, the exchange of colors is caused by a sign from Aphrodite, "the black goddess with the flat belly," and "Leucothea becomes the black one." In another example, poem 97, it is the "black star" which empowers the beloved, here addressed as "unknown": "May the black star crown you finally, giving you to sit at m/y side at the apogee of the figuration of lesbian love m/y most unknown."

The movement away from the black continent is, on another level, a romantic escape to another country. (The influence of Baudelaire's "L'In-vitation au voyage," quoted almost in its entirety in Wittig's *L'Opoponax* [*The Opoponax*], should not be overlooked.) The movement of the eyes reading from left to right, from the first to the last of the text, moves the reader from gehenna (the initial "setting," if we may speak as though there were such a thing) to one of the lesbian islands. This metonymic movement culminates in the last prose poem (110) on the last page.

We start out in Wittig's text from gehenna where we say our "fare-wells."[15] We are leaving. Why do we start out in hell? Perhaps because Charles Baudelaire also interchangeably used the term "damned women." That is, the image-concept of lesbian which he introduced is inextricably intertwined with his construction of a metaphor of lesbians as damned women, both in his book, *Les Fleurs du mal* (*Flowers of Evil*), and during the defense of his book at the trial of 1857. Baudelaire brought the word "lesbienne" into common usage in France, but he was not the first to use it. According to Marie-Jo Bonnet, the first to publish the word in French was Emile Deschanel in *Revue des deux mondes*, 15 June 1847, p. 343 (Bonnet 34). Although Baudelaire puts an apology of lesbianism into the mouth of one of the characters, he follows the example of Diderot's *La Religieuse* in linking the lesbian image to that of monster-victim. If Wittig's text is to begin with the beginning of the word "lesbian" in French (the beginning of knowledge of lesbianism), she (and we) must deal with the monster-victim concept that accompanies it.

In the gehenna of the first poem, the beloved "you" signifies a monster that no one can stand seeing: "You know that not one will be able to stand seeing you with eyes turned up lids cut off your yellow smoking intestines spread in the hollow of your hands your tongue spat from your mouth long green strings of your bile flowing over your breasts, not one will be able to bear your low frenetic insistent laughter" (my translation).[16] In Baudelaire's poem entitled "Femmes damnées" ("Damned Women"), the two lesbians are depicted as a monster and a victim. Handily for Wittig's purposes, there is also a poem by Baudelaire problematizing the monster-victim relation, "L'Héautontimorouménos," which she uses to deconstruct the linkage of "lesbian" to "monster-victim." This poem is in effect rewritten by Wittig in poem 2 of *The Lesbian Body,* which seems, like poem 1, set in hell, until we get to the last line. There, we have a movement away from hell. But this same movement is a movement toward lesbianism: "At this point/I invoke your help m/y incomparable Sappho, give m/e by thousands the fingers that ease the wounds, give m/e the lips the tongue the saliva which draw one into the slow sweet poisoned country from which one cannot return" (my translation).[17] There are oscillating movements from hell to lesbianism and back again throughout the poems which are without any apparent linear arrangement (they are reversible) until we reach the final poem.

In the last poem, we have arrived in a lesbian setting. Here, we see a reconstruction after all the processes of fragmentation and recombination. We are no longer nowhere.[18] We are on the principal center of an island in the midst of an assembly and carnival. The beloved body has been reassembled and may be contrasted with the initial fragmented signified of the beloved "you": The speaker-writer now cannot take her eyes off the beloved. But the beloved is not looking at the subject, she is looking at her surroundings. It is through the eyes of this beloved lesbian that we see those surroundings: "Your eyes are turned in the direction of the sea which prolongs the principal center of the island, it is visible as a pastel blue between the snowy-flowering cherry trees specified in the architecture of their branches and their inflorescences. A sudden gust of wind shakes them, causing them to a shed a great quantity of petals, their slow fall continues between the now stationary trees" (My translation).[19]

Thus it is in terms of the lesbian relation that the world is finally "visible" and representable. We have arrived at the destination of our voyage. We are able to see the world from the lesbian point of view; we are able to "mean" and "represent" in terms of a lesbian symbolic order. Because of Wittig's many deconstructive techniques, her representation is different from Balzac's or Stendhal's realism.[20] In this last poem, the represented "reality" is specified as simply what "is visible." It is a view, that's all. In this view, there is a movement of the eyes from the center to include what is marginal.

The point of arrival can be contrasted with Odysseus's homecoming at the end of his voyage. (The lesbian subject, in poem 8, is "not part of this voyage" (*Lesbian Body* 23). Unlike the male hero who arrives at his private house *(domus)* with his household of dependents (domestics and housewife and heir), the questing lesbian arrives at a carnival in a public place. The male hero and his wife, Penelope, each with a proper name, have been replaced here by anonymous people—one in the watching crowd, the other, part of a group of itinerant entertainers identified only by a number.

Wittig's ending is open. There is an openness of the circle, of the real structure to potentiality: "The circle breaks, the troupers of group number seven lend their balls to those who wish to juggle" (my translation).[21] If we see an allegorical meaning here, it is structural. Like the circular structures (complete poetic paragraphs) of Wittig, the circle here opens; new jugglers[22] (new poets) can take over the balls (words) since they desire to juggle (write) them. Wittig's text opens onto circulation in a new (lesbian) network of exchange and communication of potential texts to be written with reference to the lesbian body. Indeed, Wittig's own oeuvre will participate in this intertextuality: In the book that follows *The Lesbian Body*, Wittig cites the first line of this prose poem (Wittig and Zeig 32). In other examples, her French neologism, *cyprine*, has reappeared in the text of another lesbian writer, Nicole Brossard, whose translator, Susanne de Lotbinière-Harwood, has proposed the English translation, "cyprin." A computerized concordance of *The Lesbian Body* has been produced by Sally Douglas, permutating in alphabetical order every word in Wittig's text (Shaktini, Appendices C–E). And of course, the present discussion is in an obvious intertextual relationship to *The Lesbian Body*. A lesbian intertext has in fact begun. And the lesbian quest (the quest for the female subject) continues, as we see in the last line of the text: "/I look for you m/y radiant one, across the assembly" (my translation).[23]

Wittig's specific movements against the black continent and toward the lesbian islands are also part of a general movement away from the phallocentric organization of meaning. By deconstructing Lévi-Strauss's concept of the exchange of women, and creating a *Verfremdungseffekt*, an estrangement effect, from Freud's black continent metaphor, Monique Wittig in effect refutes the two major theories which deny the existence of women as subjects of desire. At the same time, *The Lesbian Body* affirms, through its very existence in literary discourse, the concept of a female subject of desire. And by representing the monster image as only one of a multiplicity of lesbian identities, Wittig refutes the reductionism of the phallic representation of lesbians. To affirm what has never before been written, Wittig must take apart meaning as it has been constructed from the point of view of the phallic body and put it together again from the point of view of the lesbian body. Monique Wittig has created a remarkable text. Her restructuring of meaning establishes the lesbian body in its place as a new primary signifier not only in this text but, through intertextual relations, in the symbolic order.

NOTES

This is a revised version of a paper delivered 10 May 1988 at the Second International Conference on Writing and Language: The Politics and Poetics of Feminist Critical Practice and Theory at the Inter-university Centre of Post-Graduate Studies, Dubrovnik, Yugoslavia. The author gratefully acknowledges a grant from the Center for the Study of Women in Society, University of Oregon, which supported research for this article.

1. J/e te regard tenir la main d'Artémis lacée de cuir sur ses seins nus puis celle d'Aphrodite, la noire déesse au ventre plat. Il y a aussi Perséphone la triple, il y a Ishtar à la tête soleille, [note that here Wittig has coined a feminine adjectival form of the masculine French word, *soleil,* in a usage that evokes "le Roi-Soleil"] il y a Albina l'aînée des Danaïdes, il y a Epone la très cavalière, il y a Leucippe dont la jument court dans le pré en contrebas blanche et brillante, il y a Isis la noire, il y a Hécate la rouge, il y a Pomone et Flore se tenant par la main, il y a Andomède au pied Léger, il y a Cybèle la blonde, il y a Io à la blanche vache, il y a Niobé et Latone enlacées, il y a Sappho aux seins violets, il y a Gurinno la rapide coureuse, il y a Céres du blé dans ses cheveux, il y a Leucothéa la blanche, il y a Rhamnusie à la tête lune" (43, 13–24).
2. "A un geste d'Aphrodite la bienheureuse, toutes autour de toi elles échangent leurs couleurs. Leucothéa devient la noire, Déméter, la blanche, Isis la blonde, Io la rouge, Artémis la verte, Sappho la dorée, Perséphone la violette" (43, 39–43).
3. "J/e les connais toutes par leurs avoir étudiées dans les livres de la bibliothèque" (43, 2–4).
4. Sigmund Freud used the "dark continent" metaphor as follows: "Another characteristic of early infantile sexuality is that the female sexual organ proper as yet plays no part in it: the child has not yet discovered it. Stress falls entirely on the male organ, all the child's interest is directed towards the question of

whether it is present or not. We know less about the sexual life of little girls than of boys. But we need not feel ashamed of this distinction; after all, the sexual life of adult women is a "dark continent' [in English in the original] for psychology. But we have learnt that girls feel deeply their lack of a sexual organ that is equal in value to the male one; they regard themselves on that account as inferior, and this 'envy for the penis' is the origin of a whole number of characteristic feminine reactions." "The Question of Lay Analysis," 212.

5. It doesn't matter that the popular connection of semen to these more abstract words is by way of what Barthes has referred to as a "false etymology."

6. "m/a gloire de cyprine" (29,1).

7. As the translator, Susanne de Lotbinière-Harwood has proposed in her translation of Nicole Brossard's *Sous la langue: Under Tongue.*

8. le flot montant débouche dans le ciel adieu continent noir de misère et de peine adieu villes anciennes nous nous embarquons pour les îles brillantes et radieuses pour les vertes Cythères pour les Lesbos noires et dorées" (11, 30–34).

9. There is none such as that which situates Flaubert's Emma Bovary, or Stendhal's Mathilde de la Môle. We recall Stendhal's famous definition of the realistic novel: "Un roman: c'est un miroir qu'on promène le long d'un chemin." *Le Rouge et le noir* (Paris: Garnier 1964), 100; see also 361.

10. See Louis Moreri, *Grand dictionnaire historique* . . . (1681): "Sapho, qu'on surnomma la dixième muse," (cited in Bonnet, *Un Choix sans équivoque*, 238, n. 17).

11. The other example is in poem 77 where the "i," as self-disclosing writer, addresses Sappho as a figure she can "interpret."

12. Barthes refers to the creation of "markedness" as a divine act. The divine subject is implicitly the point of origin of the distinction "marked" and "unmarked." It is the absolute point from which meaning is constructed.

13. "J/'attends que viennent les comètes dans des éclairs fuligineux, elles sont là grâces en soient rendues à Sappho, elles sont tombées les pierres de son étoile, celles qui ont marqué le haut de ta joue à hauteur de la tempe d'un sceau violet tout comme la m/ienne, gloire à Sappho pour aussi longtemps que nous vivrons dans ce continent noir" (34, 17–23).

14. "j/e flotte m/es bras sur tes bras, le vent démêle nos chevelures, il les peigne, il les brosse, il les lustre, adieu continent noir tu mets le cap pour l'île des vivantes" (52, 27–30).

15. Wittig, *Le Corps lesbien.* The text begins as follows: "Dans cette géhenne dorée adorée noire fais tes adieux . . ." (1, 1–2). For cross-reference of poem and various edition page numbers, see endnote below.

16. "Tu le sais, pas une ne pourra y tenir à te voir les yeux révulsés les paupières découpées tes intestins jaunes fumant étalés dans le creux de tes mains ta langue crachée hors de ta bouche les longs filets verts de ta bile coulant sur tes seins, pas une ne pourra soutenir l'ouïe de ton rire bas frénétique insistant" (1, 11–17).

17. "A ce point-là j/e t'appelle à m/on aide Sappho m/on incomparable, donne m/oi les doigts par milliers qui adoucissent les plaies, donne m/oi les lèvres la langue

la salive qui attire dans le lent le doux l'empoisonné pays d'où l'on ne peut pas revenir" (2, 20–24).

18. Martha Noel Evans sees the text as a voyage: *"The Lesbian Body . . .* is, in a sense, nowhere because it is itself a movement. From the opening sentence it describes itself as a voyage—a voyage that involves a radical break precisely with the place where we are" (187–88). But she fails to comment on the point of arrival.

19. "Tes yeux se portent dans la direction de la mer qui prolonge la place principale de l'île, elle est visible d'un bleu pastel entre les cerisiers en fleur ennuagées précis cependant dans l'architecture de leurs branches et de leurs inflorescences. Un coup de vent subit les secoue faisant tomber une grande quantité de pétales, leur chute lente continue entre les arbres à présent immobiles" (110, 17–24).

20. Margaret Homans, intent on attacking the "paradox of separatism," and homophobically ignoring *The Lesbian Body* (which had been available in English translation for eight years when her *Signs* article was published) misunderstands Wittig's revolutionary signifier: "To the extent that we can read her book, we recognize the dependence of both writer and reader on the system of representation that her characters are represented [in *Les Guérillères*] as demolishing" (190).

21. "Le cercle se rompt, les bateleuses du groupe numéro sept prêtent leurs balles à celles qui désirent jongler" (110, 26–28).

22. The first women poets in France probably grew out of the "jongleuse" tradition. See Bogin's *The Women Troubadours*. Wittig's text thus comes full circle, evoking at the ending the beginnings of nonphallic writing in France.

23. "J/e te cherche m/a rayonnante, à travers l'assemblée" (110, 35–36).

WORKS CITED

Baudelaiire, Charles. *Les Fleurs du mal*. Paris: Livre de Poche, 1972.

Bogin, Meg. *The Women Troubadours*. New York: Norton, 1976.

Bonnet, Marie-Jo. *Un choix san équivoque*. Paris: Denoël, 1981.

Brossard, Nicole. *Sous la langue: Under Tongue*. Trans. Susanne de Lotbinière-Harwood. Montreal: L'Essentielle, 1987.

Cixous, Hélène. "Laugh of the Medusa." In *New French Feminisms*. Ed. Elaine Marks and Isabelle de Courtivron. New York: Schocken, 1981, 245–64.

Diderot, Denis. *La Religieuse*. Paris: Garnier, 1968.

Diner, Helen. *Mothers and Amazons*. Garden City, N.Y.: Anchor-Doubleday, 1973.

Evans, Martha Noel. *Masks of Tradition: Women and the Politics of Writing in Twentieth-Century France*. Ithaca: Cornell Univ. Press, 1987.

Freud, Sigmund. "The Question of Lay Analysis." In *Standard Edition of the Complete Psychological Works of Sigmund Freud*. trans. James Strachey. Vol. 20. London: Hogarth, 1953–74.

Homans, Margaret. " 'Her Very Own Howl': The Ambiguities of Representation in Recent Women's Fiction." *Signs* 9, no. 2 (1983): 186–205.

Lacan, Jacques. "Signification of the Phallus." In *Ecrits: A Selection*. Trans. Alan Sheridan. New York: Norton, 1977.

Marks, Elaine. "Lesbian Intertextuality." In *Homosexualities and French Literature: Cultural Contexts/Critical Texts*. Ed. George Stambolian and Elaine Marks. Ithaca, N.Y.: Cornell Univ. Press, 1979, 353–77.

Rimbaud, Arthur. *Rimbaud: Complete Works, Selected Letters*. Trans. Wallace Fowlie. Chicago: Univ. of Chicago Press, 1966.

Rubin, Gayle. "The Traffic in Women: Notes on the 'Political Economy' of Sex." In *Toward an Anthropology of Women*. Ed. Rayna R. Reiter. New York: Monthly Review Press, 1975, 157–210.

Shaktini, Namascar. "The Problem of Gender and Subjectivity Posed by the New Subject Pronoun j/e in the Writing of Monique Wittig." Ph.D. Dissertation. University of California at Santa Cruz, 1981. Ann Arbor: UMI, 1983. 8218623.

Wittig, Monique. *Le Corps lesbien*. Paris: Editions de Minuit, 1973.

———. *The Lesbian Body*. Trans. David Le Vay. 1975. Rpt. Boston: Beacon, 1986.

———. "The Straight Mind." *Feminist Issues* (1980): 102–10.

Wittig, Monique, and Sande Zeig. *Lesbian Peoples: Material for a Dictionary*. New York: Avon, 1978.

NINETEEN

Nicole Brossard: A Differential Equation of Lesbian Love

Alice Parker

An image is a stop the mind makes between uncertainties
—Djuna Barnes, *Nightwood*

The word is of a tenuous chemical substance which performs the most violent alterations.
—Roland Barthes, A *Lover's Discourse*

Nicole Brossard has spent the last decade and a half engaged in a multifaceted project to evacuate the space occupied by Woman, a male fantasy that hangs over our heads "like a threat of extinction," and whose images are scattered through the artifacts of Western culture. The first volume of her lesbian triptych, *These Our Mothers or the Disintegrating Chapter,* begins with a declaration of hostility: "It's combat. The book. Fiction begins suspended mobile between words and the body's likeness to this our devouring and devoured mother" (*These Our Mothers* 8). The writer struggles between a language that excludes female and particularly lesbian subjectivity, produced by a discourse that reduces woman to biological functions and oppressive roles, and a vision she tries to generate through her writing. "Fiction" has a double aspect for Brossard; it is alien (patriarchal) scenarios ("fantasies [that] made her lose her sense of reality" [13]), and a "fictive theory" the author is elaborating. Reconstruction begins with the alphabet, with words, with the body, with desire.

This leads us to the second movement in Brossard's texts, the creation of a space for the woman/lesbian subject of writing to articulate her desire, to refigure/revalue her self-apprehension. A revised subjectivity inclines us toward the "essentielle," inflected in the feminine. Combining "essence" or ontological status and the female pronoun "elle" (she), *essentielle* becomes a sign in Brossard's texts for an ideal or "aerial" woman, a figure to orient her desire and focus her vision. Michèle Causse calls this last project a "psychic parthenogenesis," in which we would give birth to ourselves, and which she sees as preliminary to an "ontogenesis," that would grant woman genuine access to "human" being (147). In a discussion with Adrienne Rich in 1981, Brossard noted:

We have the imaginary of our bodies, of our sex, and especially of our skins, which synthesize time and space. The imaginary travels through our skin, on all its surfaces. The skin of a woman which slides on to the skin of another woman provokes a sliding of meaning creating the possibility of a new version of reality and of fiction, which I would call a tridimensional vision. (Quoted by Godard, 153)

Thus, says Michèle Causse, "each sentence is a utopia, which in working through my body becomes my real" (148).

As an avant-garde writer associated with movements for Québécois nationalism and radical feminism (Rosenfeld 232), Brossard has continued to revise "reality" through textual in(ter)ventions in every genre, including those for which we do not yet have the name. She thus joins other Québécois writers who characterize their writing practices as "modernity," many of whom worked together on the journal *La Barre du jour,* which she co-founded in 1965 and which became *La Nouvelle barre du jour* in 1977. Although the theoretical insights of poststructuralism and the experiments of the "language" poets seem remote from the agendas of radical lesbian/feminism, for Brossard the ferocious power of patriarchal ideologies can be dismantled only from within discourse. To reconceptualize gender, power, and sexuality requires fundamental changes in the language or symbolic system.

Although only in her mid-forties, Nicole Brossard has produced well over twenty volumes. Using the tools developed by postmodern textuality, which she adapted to her own purposes in *A Book,* (1970), *Sold-Out* (1973) and *French Kiss* (1974), she turned her attention after the mid-seventies to the inscription of a specifically lesbian desire. She experiments with the lexicon, with syntax, grammar, and graphesis in order to emphasize writing and book production, as well as to problematize the inherited terms for our experience, our reality, our self-perception and our bodies. She has left no word unturned, no image or concept unchallenged in her ongoing project to create a just future for the woman or more precisely the lesbian subject of writing. Her poetry, prose, and fiction-theory that defy generic definition project a new space of the imaginary and of the symbolic. Brossard makes no excuses for the difficulty of her texts: all revolutions require intense discipline, intelligence, and vision. But unsuspected treasures await readers who are not intimidated by the praxis of experimental texts.

There are sentences that have the power to reorient your life: "If it were not lesbian, this text would make no sense." This phrase, from *These Our Mothers,* "insolently deposited on the tomb of the [lesbian] secret (also called the 'inadmissable')," Michèle Causse writes, is what first signaled to her that an exciting new writing was in process (147). A male reader characterizes Brossard's project as an "ecology of the mind" (Nepveu 142–43). In fact, it is an ecology of the *lesbian* mind, a continuing exploration of the (hitherto) unthinkable/unedited. Brossard's notion is that in inherited discourses lesbian desire is unrecorded, occulted: "each time the strategy of the books must be unmasked and we leave foundering there in the course of the reading, our biological skins" (*Lovhers* 28).

Brossard's political *engagement* with writing (Forsyth 157–72) is summed up in her preface to *The Aerial Letter* (1988):

I believe there's only one explanation for all of these texts: my desire and my will to understand patriarchal reality and how it works, not for its own sake, but for its tragic consequences in the lives of women, in the life of the spirit. Ten years of anger, revolt, certitude and conviction are in *The Aerial Letter,* ten years of fighting against that screen which stands in the way of women's energy, identity and creativity. (35)

I underscore the political intention (tensions) of the Brossardian oeuvre precisely because it is complex and experimental. Traditional critical praxis has reflected a (sometimes unexamined) desire to sever literature from politics so these domains will not infect each other. But is politics not the most amazing fiction? And do we really think that literature, even avant-garde, texts, is exclusively self-referential? Explanations on Brossard's part like "the source of my writing is writing" ("Entretien" 186) or "I write on the side of pleasure and desire," as she stated in a 1988 interview, can easily be misread. However, if language mediates or even constructs our perception of and experience of "reality," as has been established in the last two decades at least, it is surely "political" to intervene through language, to operate on the image and the word in order to reconstitute the imaginary and subjectivity.

Marcelle Marini says of Marguerite Duras that she writes "under the pressure of politics, not on it but in its horizon" (recalling a figure of Georges Bataille [Marini 39]). Similarly, we could say of Brossard that she writes "in the horizon of the political," recognizing that the term *lesbian*, like an (ex)tension bridge, occupies the span between the private and the political. The terms Brossard uses to locate her writing are "picture theory," "fiction-theory," and "desiring writing." Throwing into question narrativity, logocentrism, and the paternity of the text, she blurs generic boundaries and problematizes binary oppositions of which the prototype is of course gender marking. Even the most radical among us have trouble extricating ourselves from the heteropatriarchal ideology that constructs the female body and female sexuality. How can the writer evacuate concepts of gender that have been reinforced through millennia of male fantasy and domination in order to create a space for the infinite play of sexual difference? Brossard deploys the term *lesbian* to collect the visionary potential of hitherto unexplored female desire. What better way is there to disrupt the discourses that found and maintain the social order(s) than to intervene "on the side of desire," as a lesbian-feminist writer?

Stealing terms from technology, science, and mathematics, Brossard regrounds her vision by de-signing texts (literally inventing new signs) for a symbolic order within which words will respond to revised codes. Figures like the hologram and the laser drawn from the new optics, references to differential equations and a fourth dimension, focus unsuspected energy on dormant centers of our minds. As Louise Dupré observes in her preface to *These Our Mothers*, "[Brossard] submits writing to the abstraction of a mutating, desexualized, aerian woman, a fictive body, present/absent, in the last resort unrepresentable, in the geometry of the spiral, favoring new perceptions" (11). Nicole Brossard is preparing the ground so that "when we dead awaken" from the nightmare of phallogocentrism, a luminous continent in the form of a floating island of our desire will be prepared to receive us.[1]

DOUBLE IMPRESSION

Roland Barthes writes in *A Lover's Discourse:* "The more I experience the specialty of my desire, the less I can give it a name. What is characteristic of desire, proper to desire, can produce only an impropriety of the utterance" (20). Recognizing the cautions we have learned from recent theorists, this then is the challenge: to write a "differential equation" for lesbian love. The "indescribable sensation" we derive from reading, Brossard notes, can "keep us up until dawn," when "our mind is extravagant, wandering in unspoken zones and we have no choice but to explore them" ("Certains mots," LA 152–53).[2] Not the least of the pleasures in store for those who are willing to take the "trouble" to decipher Brossard's texts is an erotics of reading and of writing. The desiring text becomes a desire for the text: "we cannot believe the truth that erupts in us like a memory of shadow and of passion." Reading (Brossard) like theory allows us to "become what we desire": "a subtle and complex woman" awaits us. "Words are a way of devouring the desire that devours us" (LA 153). With "our wet fingers we turn the pages, going from terror to ecstasy"; we become "the precision of desire in the unrecountable space of the brain." These sensations can only be expressed by underlining: "with each reading the intimacy of eternity is an intrigue we invent" (LA 154).

Brossard's latest "novel," *Le Désert mauve* (*The Mauve Desert*), is the first prose work in which she willingly moves from "modernity" to postmodernism," although English readers would place all of her works including the lesbian triptych, *These Our Mothers, Le Sens apparent* (*Surfaces of Meaning*), and *Lovhers,* in that category. From her earliest books of poetry (1965) through her works of fiction-theory in "prose," Brossard has sought consistently new horizons:

> to open onto mental
> space, with words of lightning, sequence
> of unreason, episode of recommencements
> and of breasts unrecorded web: the mouths
> science of the real, skin/intinerary
> going away to slip gently
> into the continent of women.
>
> (*Lovhers,* 82)

A primary focus of Brossard's work is an investigation of the "ritual" of the written word. What interests her are the "hidden spaces" behind words, the "enigmas, messages, proofs which confirm our intuitions and our beliefs" ("Access" 8), the echoes of "magical, ancient, dormant formulas" (9).

There are three movements I identify in the work of Nicole Brossard: a practice of reading, a practice of writing, and a practice of love, movements I separate only arbitrarily and which reinforce each other. For the woman subject, as opposed to the object-Woman projected by phallocentric discourse, access to writing is of critical importance, because, as Lacan noted, woman does not speak (herself) in the symbolic system we call language: woman is "excluded from the nature of things which is the nature of words, . . . they do not know what they say, which is the whole difference between them and me" (*Encore* 68). Lacan states that Woman has no access to the universal, and can only be written with the "the" barred (68). "I" has for centuries been co-opted by Man, Brossard declares, which "occupies in all its splendor, all its mediocrity, with all its fears and ecstasies, the semantic and imaginary field" ("Access" 9). Western thought requires that we reread and overwrite the phallic subject:

To render visible the woman whose sense and presence we intuit in us as a motive of identity, is a writing task which necessitates shifts in meanings as yet unedited in the imaginary realm of language. ("Access" 10)

A complication of the task of inscribing woman in language is "Man's WOMAN . . . living in us like a perverse habit" ("Access" 11). Like Monique Wittig, Brossard looks critically at the figures of "mothers, wives and whores [that] maintain service," which are "frozen in tautological dailiness" ("Access" 11). A significant breach in this system, the "fente" that Brossard eroticizes in her own texts, is produced by terms that elude phallic control, notably *amazon* and *lesbian*. Whether or not they were "invented" by Man, they record an excess: they are at once "utopic and damned, figures forbidden access, like desirable writing" ("Access" 11). Barred from language, the woman subject has a difficult location in discourse: obliged to deny her perceptions, her feelings, she "can only stammer, lie and contradict [herself]," she "can only perceive herself as a (masculine) other" ("Access" 13). Brossard uses the "fabulous" (as in fable) lesbian subject to trespass the forbidden space of (male-centered) letters and to move into desirable writing / the writing of desire. Thus she engages in a process that Elizabeth Meese calls "crossing the double cross" by doubling as the subject of her desire, the desiring woman in/of/for her.

A point of intersection for the political and the textual, Brossard's "aerial woman" is a space in which the writer and her creation can "move together" (Discussion with author, Paris 1988). This double who takes the form of one's desire is essential, real, and virtual; it is a model that permits the writer access to the universal and to her self. If Lacanian psychoanalysis is a description (which is of course not value-free) rather than a *prescription*

of the status of woman, then we can see how from the male perspective—
Lacan with his "Ding," the "Freudian Thing," the phallus that *fixes* his
attention—woman can only be the mystic or maternal Other. In Lacan's
"The Love Letter" the (m)other is accorded the privilege of *prime mobile*
(*Encore* 74–75), since she provides the space for man to speak, the "dit-
mension" (88). Thus Lacan does not fare any better than Freud with female
subjectivity. The woman subject inhabits language as an echo or reflection
of the male "not-all" (74). Unless she is satisfied with her (maternal) place
outside the system, her immanence is tautologically frozen and can never
be transcended. For Brossard and many other feminist writers, it is time to
pass through the mirror into an-other economy.

The lesbian writer, by reason of her anomalous relation to (male) culture, is peculiarly suited, pre-scripted to create a desiring subject/subject of
desire. This is a tricky claim and a calculated risk. Brossard does not
disqualify (heterosexual) woman-as-creator, but any woman who identifies
with men labors under a terrific historical burden of male fantasy. (Of
course there is no escaping the fathers [of texts, of theory] or the sons, with
which even lesbian mothers may have to reckon.) The Brossardian text
takes desire and pleasure, or in other words writing, as its point of departure. Conflating *emotion and thought* ("the thought of emotion/the emotion
of thought"), as well as *language and desire* (words are an irreducible source
of pleasure), Brossard eroticizes the body—the text's body and the body's
text. She focuses on the lesbian-as-desiring-subject of the imaginary-as-
semantic-field. The figure of the lesbian is at once an object of desire, and
a "double" through which the passion (for/in writing) can be channeled.
Two key images suggest the interplay involved in this process: the cortex
(corps/texte or body/text) and the spiral. These figures encode not only
lesbian experience and identity, by which are meant the stories we construct in order to found an ontological presence in the world, but also the
movement of lesbian memory.

PICTURE THEORY

Brossard's favorite terms and creative strategies play in the spaces between referentiality, desire, thought, and writing. "Picture theory" is a
polysemic term in the Brossardian lexicon that refers to a version of (lesbian) reality that is at once morphogenetically (to return to Michèle Causse's
term) ec-static and "perfectly readable." A piece entitled "Intercepting

Reality" reflects on how writing and thought are organized. Writing links the visible and invisible, and gives form to evidence (LA 144). If language structures reality, then transformation, which would occur in and through language, is possible (144). The truly seductive texts are the ones that alter the way we see our lives, "the sense we have learned by heart" (146). Thought is slowed down through writing, Brossard says; time and space merge so that thought itself is spatialized: here reality can be intercepted. Writing introduces a state of weightlessness; when we reenter gravity we remember what it felt like to be free of normal sensations, ambivalence, and contradiction. We become "aerial." In this movement in and out of the earth's field of force, words become fictional and have "a strangeness that fascinates us" (145): "Charged with that memory, words give us the sensational sensation of a sense" (145).

The Brossardian text depends on sensual/erotic wordplay to displace meanings that inhibit imagining for the woman/lesbian subject. While psychoanalysis, with its theory of the return of the repressed and displacements of desire, provides ample ground for this practice, more immediate sources are the local writing scene in Quebec in the seventies and the texts of Roland Barthes, especially *Le Plaisir du texte* (*The Pleasure of the Text*, 1973), and *A Lover's Discourse* (1977). The inscription of sexual pleasure was a primary agenda of the new writing in Quebec, to liberate the social text from centuries of repression, most often attributed to the Roman Catholic church. For Barthes, textual "jouissance" is analogous to sexual pleasure, but does not reproduce it "literally" (*Plaisir* 88). Brossard herself never hesitates to blur the differences between textual and sexual arousal. Incantatory modulations of the words as material embodiments of sound produce a textual erotics of the lesbian body. The many figural pleasures of the text evoke the multiple surfaces of the body, making love through/to the text, the author/reader turn (each other) on: the act of writing (reading) was never so physical.

Brossard has taken it upon herself to write this text, not so much any longer for the sake of the scandal, nor certainly to divide the "castrated" subject, but to give the lesbian subject (of writing) back (to) her body. She would agree with Barthes that the "atopia" of the pleasurable text (*Plaisir* 39) can provoke useful dislocations of the canonical structures of the language (lexical and syntactical), in order to transform the very material of language (*Plaisir* 51). "As soon as I name I am named," writes Barthes, which initiates a war of fictions, of sociolects (*Plaisir* 50–51). The artful cultivation of "jouissance" in the text can destroy categories and references (gender/genre) (*Plaisir* 51), and fracture the language and the culture (*Plaisir* 82). We recall Brossard's double purpose: to eliminate phallocentrism from the language which is her medium of (self-)knowledge and creation, and to incite the lesbian subject to articulate her desire in new ways: "(among women, memory comes back like consciousness//open me, tonight, it's all about our mouths and our arms, and since it's all about us//open me)" (*Lovhers* 58).

"Writing aloud," as Barthes puts it, is a good way to qualify Brossard's praxis: her "voice" has exceptional power to set words in motion, sliding, gliding in unedited patterns. What "jouissance" seeks in the text are "pulsional incidents, a language that is covered in skin, in which you can hear the patina of consonants, the voluptuousness of vowels" (*Plaisir* 104–05). Whether she is writing theory, fiction, or poetry, or a blend of the three in "fiction-theory," Brossard inscribes a sensual excitement in the text by wordplay, soundplay, syntactical inversion and reversal, and other manipulations that call attention to the surface (skin, screen) of the text. The text and the body write each other; signifiers function in differential equations that locate the continuously transformed curves (velocity) of the lesbian body whose pan-eroticism refigures meaning in/of the text. The reader hears the rhythms and sounds of the language resonating in her ears as the syllables pulse through her blood and nerve circuits.

so sensitive when the skin lends itself and when we are gifted for certain sparse words in bed that mouths give up at dayfall——successively it is crossed by a dream, entwined women, in the least detail branches out and compromises itself——some appeasement, the echo deferred, dispersal, the night declines its relays. to explore: the ultimate intimate elsewhere. (*Lovhers* 97)

Brossard plays with rhetorical devices between outside and inside, between sensual surfaces, emotion and thought. Stressing out grammar and syntax, she spins her texts and the reader's perceptions out of (conventional) control in order to displace traditional rules and patterns, to set uncanny processes in motion and make radically altered generic and sexual/textual schema possible. This is her "ultimate intimate elsewhere":

so transform me, she said
into a watercolour in the bed
like a recent orbit
the curtains, the emotion

tonight we are going to the *Sahara*

(Lovhers 72)

Intertextual allusions turn the "regard to us," (101) to memory, while "picture theory" in a material sense (visual images and graphesis) introduces further dimensions into the texts. Photographs and drawings in *Lovhers* move the poetry into other planes. In *The Mauve Desert* Brossard collects the images for an inner dossier of "the long man" whose shadow haunts the work, on whom we must keep a portfolio if we are to survive. The author of *a book* continues to emphasize the process and product of her writing with a witty reconstruction of the "book" in her latest fiction as in "picture theory" opening up a newly structured space for encoding lesbian experience.

A PRACTICE OF READING

Reading: on the one hand Brossard provides a critical analysis of the texts of Western culture for their founding ideologies, especially for locating the origin of Woman in the Mother. On the other hand she gives us a joyful word-to-word immersion in the lesbian intertext, interstices that nourish our sense of "self." The first text of the lesbian trilogy (1977–80), *These Our Mothers or the Disintegrating Chapter,* was the most painful and difficult to write (Discussion with author, Paris 1988). It is a work of dispossession and self-reclamation. In French the title refers to the mother (mère), the sea (mer), bitterness (amèr), and a host of correlated notions. As Barbara Godard notes in her preface to the translation, Brossard removes the silent (feminine) "e" from the title to suggest a silence or an absence, or to move toward a neutral grammar, a purpose likewise served by adding an extra "e" to supposedly generic terms in order to feminize (contra-dict the concealed masculinity in) them (*These Our Mothers* 7). Two years earlier, in the first feminist issue (edited by Brossard) of the important review *La Barre du jour* entitled "Women and Language" (1975), she had devoted a whole article to "The Mutating Mute E" (Forsyth 161–62).

The subtitle of the work, "The Disintegrating Chapter," directs attention to the institution of motherhood in Western culture, which she examines, as does Adrienne Rich, in *Of Woman Born* (1976), for socioeconomic and political ideology. Their projects are complementary, Brossard eschewing the historical to work on two points Rich mentions but does not pursue, first the assertion that "poetry was where [she] lived as no-one's mother," and second, her question what, then, "do we do with our lives?" (Rich 31, 281). Brossard begins with a declaration of lese-motherhood: "I have killed the womb" (15). She then designs new sets of relationships, "working so we may lose the convulsive habit of initiating girls to the male like a current practice of lobotomy" (109). As Louise Dupré notes in her preface to the new French-language edition, key terms have to be reworked, their surface meanings evacuated to provide the woman writer access to the symbolic, words like "difference," "eye," "figure/face," and "fiction" (12). Brossard's proclaimed purpose in writing this "fiction-theory" is to protect the bodies of her lover and her daughter, to dis-cover in them a species, a center (19). Patriarchal representations have to be defused as one explodes a bomb or war machine so it will not go off accidentally. The writer must free herself from the internment of the womb. The origin (origyne) is relocated in the alphabet (19). But the process is endlessly complex and discouraging: "there is always one body too many in her life," mother, child, the same (21).

"If it were not lesbian, this text would have no sense [direction]" (22). The text is at once womb, matter, and production. The narrator must "kill the biologic mother" in order to "explode fiction, ideology," substituting the "word for word" for the "body to body" (29). Negotiating between the imaginary and the symbolic requires a deconditioning process that confronts metaphor and symbol directly (22). It means rewriting the whole script: in the last decade many fine feminist minds have addressed the sometimes bitter relationship of the daughter to the mother and vice-versa as they are inscribed in patriarchy. The "symbolic" mother in Brossard's text is inaccessible for reproduction; Brossard moves her in a space of desire which blots out history, cancels the fictions of "women in heat" and beautiful schizophrenics (23). Brossard is careful to reground her vision in the materiality of a lesbian mother's life in this text, a preoccupation uncommon in a work that eschews "ordinary reality." Giving birth to oneself is difficult enough; to prepare a symbolic ground to receive new mother-daughter, "daughter/mother" figuration—beyond heterosociality, marriage, and the (patriarchal) family—is not only difficult but dangerous and solitary. The narrator is suddenly seized with anxiety (rare in Brossard's oeuvre): "The silence here is unbearable. Everything gravitates around a senseless grammar. I killed the womb too soon" (32). Playing with the polysemic possibilities of the word "fille" in French, the lesbian dream comes to her rescue. "Between women we can liquidate the insanity"; the daughters-mothers in a multiple prism, public, fantastic, "stretch their arms like sexual interventions in the political pages of daily reality" (35). The lesbian-mother figure returns in *The Mauve Desert* in which two expectant women spend an ecstatic night in each other's arms, invoking their future daughters in a revised scenario of lesbian (partheno)genesis. The daughters will later seek each other as they near the threshold of maturity in order to explore with their young bodies and minds new parameters of response-ability.

The lesbian mother "inscribes the final contradiction" (44). She proposes the "reverse path from object to subject" so that she will no longer have to live "deferred" (45). Using the term in a non-Derridean sense, Brossard does not mean to return to a metaphysics of presence and/or a univocal subject, but rather to permit heterogeneity and polyvocality. The sociolect that recognizes only phallic mothers and patriarchal daughters is thus attacked from (at least) two angles, by direct provocation or taking (political) positions "in the old way," and by textual operations that make new spaces, imagining, theory, and fiction possible. Difference and derivation are introduced in order to tease out, for the benefit of a revised grammar (field) of generational relations among women, all of the generic possibilities of the terms. In so doing, Brossard moves from the reductive means by which women have been encouraged to measure themselves to a higher mathematics of differential equations. One must refuse the difference generated in the phallic "ideological *laboratory*" (43), a term Brossard writes in French without the final *mute* "e," to show, as Godard observes, the absence of women from this scene of investigation (7).[3] The lesbian lovers negotiate an altered relationship with each other in terms of mothering and daughtering: a "luminous specter," they are "projected against each other like a polysemic dream" (45). Before the mirror, difference is an illusion that cuts the narrator in two; difference is the remainder after the operation of subtraction (46). In the fissure, the breach, an explosion converts mauve to red (48): a new kind of theory-fiction (the book the poet is writing), will exorcise, re-inscribe difference. Resistance, "putting an end to the social contract" (52): in the long term the landscape is modified, takes on an-other form. "To write *I am a woman* is full of consequences" (53).

A PRACTICE OF WRITING

"To write *I am a woman* is full of consequences"[4] is Brossard's signature: each time it cycles back into her writing like a comet of measureless magnetic force, its sonorous qualities generate new energy and signifying potential. Like Adriennne Rich's *Of Woman Born, These Our Mothers* has lost none of its force in more than a decade.[5] Brossard joins daughter and mother with the third term, *lesbian,* in a strategy that precludes oppositional logic and eludes reification. The movement from the fictional to the political via the symbolic territory of writing and the material reality of caring for a small child and a lover leads Brossard to "unpack" the proscriptions, descriptions, and inscriptions that are collected under the term *representation,* tracing on the page patriarchal distortions that adhere to her skin. The next two parts of the lesbian trilogy, published the same year (1980), revise and complement the project.

In "Kind Skin My Mind," Brossard defines the lesbian as an "intuition of the most daring lucidity" (*AL* 121). She represents "a mental energy, . . . a threatening reality for *reality,* . . . the impossible reality realized, which incarnates all *fiction,* chanting and enchanting what we are or would like to be" (*AL* 121). This is the rationale for the writing program pursued in *Surfaces of Meaning* under the aegis of three personae: Adrienne, Gertrude, and Yolande, whose patronyms (Rich, Stein, and Villemaire) are erased. The names reaffirm Brossard's contention that "the lesbian creates space and time. She is a calendar, she might be a date, but most of all *she is your memory*" (*AL* 122).

The figure of the spiral, deriving from the form of the chambered nautilus and ancient inscriptions of the female, is updated in *Surfaces of Meaning* to accord with the temporal and spatial models of a new physics. The spiral suggests recollection, a re-gathering of energy ("recueillement") (14): "The spiral turns on itself and produces delirium. Then one can hear sound waves that are inaudible in normal reality time" (15). Delirium refers both to the peak (spire) and to the (radical) root (17). The *radical* is always understood in Brossard's work as a root, a referent, subtext, or pretext, an undertone, a primary source of meaning. The term *lesbian* collects analogous orienting power: "the lesbian is . . . the centre of a captivating *image* which any woman can claim for herself" (*AL* 121). The "any" woman here is likewise "every" woman, as in Adrienne Rich's "lesbian continuum."[6] The message is political in the sense that if we do not exercise our choices we lose them: "A lesbian is radical or she is not a lesbian. A lesbian who does not reinvent the [world] is a lesbian in the process of disappearing" (*AL* 122).

Surfaces of Meaning refigures outside and inside which oppose reality and subjectivity, daily life and fiction, social programming and desire, evidence and ecstasy, the dark night of patriarchal history and the luminous certainty of lesbian memory. The spiral indicates a new process has been set in motion, which Brossard calls the "thought of emotion and emotion of thought" (*LA* 54). This is what awaits the reader when she lifts the edge of the down comforter (*Surfaces* 51–53), when she peeks under the corner of the page, when she recognizes that a book is black marks on a white page. Writing is a spiral, a helix, an "uncertain prose of the avid body" (19). Linear models with their "just median" (good sense) give way to figures that "take on any allure," and where "anything can happen" (22). This is an "unthinkable geometry: the ardent form," in which "emotion moves from spire to spire," (23) in-spiring unimagined practices of writing. The writer imagines that there is "a center in the center of words, an inside you note like an aspect of reality" (32). The short section of *Surfaces of Meaning* entitled "Celebrations" explores what it means for the (lesbian) writing subject to enter the spiral, what it does to words that carry meanings and to the structures of language. But as it moves into the final section, "The Traces of the Manifest," the reader resurfaces on a disconcerting image of women bending their wills to common expectations (37). What are surfaces of meaning "in the face of the reality of the bent backs of women" (37)?

In exposing the (phallocentric) oppression that names us, one can exorcise its surface meaning, manifest traces, and apparent sense (47). The writer is privileged precisely because she knows the operations of language and thought, and she can trick them. She can make both reality and fiction work for her.

I often stop to think about these mechanisms, derivation: free of my moorings. Then I tend to think of myself reading *in the deferred,* simply becauuse there are so many words to hold me captive. That provokes my agitation in the holes of memory, *the holes are white or black I say that the hole is luminous and that the ties are wound in its nerve center, caused by the intensity of the apparition the exuberance of the metaphors the discharge the derivation: the déjà vu, the unedited, the respiratory tissue, the usury of delirium.* (*Surfaces* 50)

The mechanisms of the spiral—slippages, a clandestine fire, nights of brilliance, ellipses, the instinct and the memory of movement, the imagination and the recollection of the lesbian body (*Surfaces* 46–47)—can rupture the feeling/self of female social conditioning. What a pleasure when they begin to function, provoking writing, reading! (51) The process consists of defusing "daily reality" by "putting the evidence out of condition to harm" (54). Lesbians know ordinary reality can be a matter of life and death, as we see in *The Mauve Desert*. The feminist dictum, the private is political, is at once liberating and terrifying. The "process" is "what stands out in the dark, that sort of anguish they wanted to evacuate in speaking of the text, *but at the source of the text is the skin* the intention the chest and then *finally the temples*" (54).

Brossard describes her resistance to the anecdotal as a refusal of the dailiness of assimilated roles that distance any hint of excess. Realism is a permanent temptation for the artist since "the ellipsis that avoids it seeks it more avidly than ever" (58) in an enactment of the law of the eternal return or the return of the repressed (Freud, Lacan). "Writing," she says, "is an insurmountable fiction," just as (in reality) "an insurmountable fiction sends us right back to writing" (61). The latter refers to "a certain appearance of truth in the practice of daily life" (61). What this daily reality cannot account for (even proscribes) is an enactment of desire, which, as we know from psychoanalysis, which Brossard (like Wittig) rejects, escapes or exceeds representation. How then can the spiral be inscribed? Brossard weaves together "possibilities among words, gestures, my desire that inhabits the city . . . the turning of a life." The body is the final limit of fiction and reality (61).

Understanding full well the difficulty of negotiating among reality, fiction, and the spiral, the writer continues to interrogate the connections— between New York and Montreal, between characters, between summer and autumn, tracing changes in the allure of the city, and syntheses of reality (68). She imagines writing with "a structure of fire" on days when desire crosses from one zone to another (74). The physical condensation of this desire forces her thought to integrate the shock waves and the silences that traverse the body (74). As she approaches the end of her book she senses "something plausible has filtered in, a legitimate form of reality" (75). At the foot of the cliff, up against it, fiction devours history and vice-versa, consuming the apparent meaning, leaving the fire. The surface of the story is torn apart; fiction sleeps in its surface hole, leaving the fire, the cliff. Like the writer, the reader is left with versions (75–76), with a reading deferring and deferred.

A PRACTICE OF LOVE

The third book in the trilogy, *Lovhers* (1980), is an attempt to inscribe a lesbian reading/writing of "a lover's discourse" (Barthes). Here Brossard transforms lesbian desire into emotion, into thought, into words, into memory, into an "aerial" vision of the future, into an "essentielle":

women with curves of fire and eiderdown
fresh-skinned—essential surface
you float within my page she said
and the four dimensional woman is inscribed
in the space between the moon and (fire belt)
of the discovery and combats that the echo
you persevere, fervour flaming.

(*Lovhers* 68)

The French title alludes to Wittig and Zeig's *Lesbian Peoples: Material for a Dictionary,* in a continuing effort on Brossard's part to highlight the intertext, to re-collect lesbian memory. The lov(h)ers are two women, an "I" and a "you," facing a text, their text, to read and to write (it) (them) together (ensemble), in a semblance, resemblance. The book is a record, a trajectory, of knowing an/other woman; their eyes "open," in Michèle Causse's terms, "upon strange correspondences" (*Amantes* 11). What corresponds is the *corps/texte,* the cortex (a term Brossard uses continuously since her article "Le Cortex exubérant" in *La Barre du jour,* 44 [1974]). The writer hopes to analyze, or rather reproduce, the "rapture" *(ravisse-ment),* which, like the French word, conceals its root (rapt, rape, *ravir*), and recalls "rupture." *Rapture* is a "theory of reality," Brossard declares; it is a "mental experience in which fragments and delirium translate a practice of great e-motion" (*Amantes* 11).

"I don't stop reading/unreading/delirium": this polysemic refrain (*Amantes* 11–12) leads into the first section of the book. Here is another image of the spiral, and the title: "(4): Lovhers/Write." It is not clear at first what the "4" represents, perhaps merely a number rather than a letter, and that it is not the number two, a sign for the heterosexual couple. Later we discover the "woman in four dimensions" (57), and see that like Mary Daly's "cerebral spinning" of Brossard's epigraph, the figure of woman in this book of poetry is an invitation to move into new zones in which the passion for reading, writing, and the female body can no longer be held apart. As I have noted elsewhere, lesbian love is a discourse that disrupts or radically interrogates all of the authorizing codes of our culture.[7] The potential for a truly well conceived and innovative book on lesbian love to disseminate a radically revised system of perception and enunciation is enormous. Further, as Barthes observed, love is our most occulted discourse (*A Lover's Discourse* 5), and those who have attempted to tell its story have written untenable fictions. In Brossard's text, reading, unreading, delirium, and ex-citation work together. "Excitement" puts "reality in peril"; as an "invitation to knowledge," it integrates sense and the senses (*Amantes* 12).

In *Lovhers* the practices of reading, writing, and love converge. "I do not stop reading," writes the poet, "excitation: what incites me unedited in my skin" (13). This is June, the month of (love) fever, and of voyages to distant and often exotic points of discovery. Barbara Godard suggests that a reading of *Lovhers* with Adrienne Rich's *Twenty-one Love Poems*, likewise set in New York, and from which Brossard quotes a key erotic passage, can "increase the connotative resonances" of Brossard's text (*Lovhers* 9). However, Brossard cites a whole series of writers as she spins out her own words. In particular, she emphasizes the text of Djuna Barnes's *Nightwood*, which elicits the passion of a new love affair. A writing project that engages her lover preoccupies the narrator as well, stimulating meditation on the movement between word and thought, what kind of look the lover has on her face as she is working on this problem, as she enunciates the theory, theorizes the play, experiences the emotion of the process (of thought and language). "I realize to what point our fictions cross paths," the narrator observes (17). Reading her lover, she tries to (dis)place herself in her lover's words, "to see them from all angles, to find zones of welcome in them: m'y lover, my love" (18). For the poet, decoding and recoding are complex operations, and her lover's writing gives her little help. Her lover lists her own name among the references in her paper, which amazes the poet, who must inscribe the number (4) before lovers (fem.), and states that she can "only proceed by initials" (19). So, she says, "Imagine a bit what *fiction* could mean under these circumstances, an excess of realism forced to conceal itself behind a screen of skin: it's the tension that every practice of emotion requires" (19).

One of the puzzles the poet tries to untangle is the dynamic of the immersion/submersion of reading and writing. Referring to a writer who became hopelessly locked into his work like his own hell, and who could only speak of writing "under the volcano" (20), she says: "It's the worst thing that can happen to me. It has happened to me. Since then I don't stop reading to come back to the surface, to find my surfaces. That must be why I am obsessed with the apparent meaning." But she warns us not to confuse this with a confession, although she might be confiding something, even writing a real letter. "Y. V. said it clearly in *The Great She-Bear:* 'This text was already written before it happened to me' " (20). The writer's pen is like a powerful microscope, studying in "cross-section" the point of inter-section between a collective history and personal history (even unrecorded). The same is true for the place where any fictions cross paths, for example the poet's self-narration and that of her lover. Reading her lover is what really excites her, "the project of the text and the text of the project are accomplished to the taste of words, to the taste of a kiss" (21).

The relationship between the two women translates as the coherence between what each of them is writing (21). Reading teases out the unedited in their skin (13); "lesbians of writing" never stop reading. They must recover the dailiness of fictions: mouths, thighs, fever. *Dailiness* and *fiction* are ambivalent terms in the Brossardian lexicon: "fiction-theory" is what mediates between them and establishes a conceptual framework for the rapport between the lesbian body and the material world. The body is, in fact, a "place of knowing" in the text (Spivak 261). Similarly, "picture theory," a polysemic term used first in this text, "tells the in-tension of the tongues" (28). As the (4) lovers concentrate, focus their at-tention, thought surfaces in all the senses (28). Obsessively they read mouths, texts, disman-tling power, which returns like a wave of vertigo (30–31).

Picture theory (26–28) blends metaphor with a "tableau of reality" ("En-tretien" 178). The grammatical intervention of a feminine plural introduces the unthought/unedited; language (fem.) becomes a spectacle of what we cannot imagine as such, in the feminine (178). The lesbian subject literally cannot trust her eyes; reality has to be reconceptualized. The sea, the island, surface meanings, women's bodies intersect with the body of the text; the poet keeps reading: "the mental space of the word women in ink calls forth the unedited in myths . . . turning forms of ease in the imag-inary" (*Amantes* 38). The "open veins of biographies" lead through words, symbols, memory, water, chemistry, to the *"integral . . . my woman,* so that no cliché can separate us" (40–41).

An/other sort of graphesis, a "bio-graphy of fire" can produce an identity of rapture (38) *(ravissement),* suggesting what has been seized back, rav-ished, and the ultimate pleasure, which is an altered state of *(lesbian)* consciousness. The term "integral" disseminates images of lesbians and lovers in whom the body and the text are fully integrated. Although they never forget that skin, the skin of combat, is at the origin (39), they are women with "aerial roots" who exist in new dimensions, the fourth dimension projected here. Among women, Brossard states, memory returns like a conscience (47). From memory we choose what incites us to work ("ce qui ouvre et oeuvre") (48).

Memory is dual for the narrator, and the poet must (become her) double to evoke a memory as if she were writing harmony (48). As Monique Wittig declared (in *Les Guérillères*), she must either re-member or invent. The poet re-places her lover by wearing her perfume; like ink and the silk route, the odor of intimacy (with women) produces visions. Memories may be surfaces or depths; they bring a consciousness of space, a space of the imaginary for women (49). But not all memories are of love; some memories are of torture—women have been tortured as a text or a style can be tortured, and sometimes memory falters (48–51). A failure of memory projects the body into tumult and paradox (50).

The mirror and the window recall the generic meaning of "theory" as (visual) speculation, providing a sense of perspective (like the graphics and photos included in the text). Here, with the "harmony and precision of grafitti in our eyes," we approach the Barbizon Hotel for Women where we encounter the four-dimensional woman, with "aerial roots." A "converging, cyclical tenderness" (58) shows women merging in an "ex/centric passion" (60). The poet notes: "I have succumbed to all the visions—delirious around all the figures, aerial in the use of glass and verb" (67). Writing is a polysemic statement of love that fuses a particular historical moment and mythologies (54).

Brossard's "aerial woman" or woman with "aerial roots" is "clear vision" which dislocates (patriarchal) images and fiction: loving gestures of women and memory suddenly produce "daughters of utopia . . . in italics," women "deploying their vertigo . . . dazzled, . . . [a] ritual slow-motion of love, . . . tempted by the gravity of ecstasy" (70–71). The term *aerial* moves the text beyond linearity. The poet privileges "echo, return, repetition" because of "the vitality of cycles: our images" (72). Since a prescriptive silence veils lesbian memory, analyzed by Marie-Jo Bonnet (in *Un Choix sans équivoque* [*An Unequivocal Choice*]), the poet is under great pressure to reclaim inter-texts, to record every temptation, to quote the whole thing (73).

In *These Our Mothers* Brossard noted that she read the differences on the body of her lover as a "differential equation." Like other major orienting figures in her work (cortex, spiral, aerial, integral, island, skin, horizon), this one indicates the conceptual strength and intellectual audacity of her work. She proceeds like a scientist and an explorer, insisting on precision, and on figures for the twentieth and twenty-first centuries that stimulate us to imagine and think in new modes ("Entretien" 195): "Every vision is a mathematics of imaginary space" (78).

Vertigo occurs when the woman subject perceives that rather than turning, "the world files by her in a straight line according to patriarchal tradition" (*Amantes* 82). By contrast, her vision is "full of reflections, . . . a version of existence which takes a displacement of the horizon for granted" (*Lovhers,* 88). The "essentielle," here, is an abstraction of the potential for woman to start existing according to her own desire (87). Without such a model we cannot create anything new. "Spiral 2" furthers Monique Wittig's project of (re)writing the lesbian body: "spatial, initial, irrigate the inside of the tissues, the skin rises up, i am seeking completion————to continue in acts of drifting and of the visible, the tensions present in certain inscriptions when emotion anticipates in such a way that roots are tangled . . . the setting to work of ultimate possibles" (*Lovhers* 91). The complex phrase in which one concept is thrown against another is an effort to precipitate new meaning through a synchronicity that attempts to hold multiple dimensions before the mind's eye (eschewing linearity). Likewise, the poet begins *in medias res* and ends with syntactical incompletion in order to undermine the obsessive grammaticality of traditional discourse. For example, "spiral 3":

it's in space: figure and i add landscape / everything is inverted / i give myself up to the recommencement of the act face to face with language as in the beginning of the inversion of identities. to concentrate myself upon the essential agitation or myself dispersed like multiple connections touching my whole surface, the limits. to persist so memory, after that. (*Lovhers* 92)

Identities are overthrown, figures are inverted. We abandon ourselves to new beginnings, multiple liaisons, and memory (89).

Turning on itself, propelling us toward unsuspected sites, the spiral connects us with our roots, the radical past, and the energy of the present. The lesbian body inaugurates a new cycle (90). We are initiated to lightning, ellipsis, gender, night, the city, as we are lulled by the unthought of the poem. The unthought recalls Brossard's concern with paradox and enigmas, re-joining signs which maintain life, distance one from it, as bodies double in alarm and "consent to awaken" (93). Night, a sign for patriarchal reality, provokes visions and discernment. The narrator's lover gives her alternate insights, "intense reality" or "shadowy integrity," so that although she comes from "the most distant place" she comes "to take a place" (95).

"Sleep" concludes with a program that the book has almost brought to completion: "to explore: the ultimate intimate elsewhere" (96). "Excess" begins with the "intention that unties the vocal cords of childhood in the feminine . . . she pushes reflection to the limit, at the bottom very doubles: with" (the last two terms encoding the lesbian) (99). The overdetermination of *excess* leads to the source, which is memory: a "real duration because history has its reasons" (102). *Jouissance* (fem.) is contrasted with politics (masc.), "the silence of bodies distended by hunger, brutalized by fire, dogs, torture" (100).

The final section of the book is "My Continent," with "my" written in the feminine. It is "a space and a hypothesis" (105) which grants the lesbian existence of "radical urban women." Although she qualifies the city as homo/ideologic, there is a "particular taste of civilization" (81) in the city, where people think ("Entretien" 184). The city (New York) is thus both enabling for women since it focuses so many cultural signals and memories, and disabling in that the signs are often alien. Thus we "walk in the abstract . . . overexposed," in the city (62), but memory tips the balance: "a tongue that has visions it is important to retain" (64). Further, Brossard locates the scene of writing in the city (Montreal). Certain vibrations, a subterranean "avalanche," are audible only to women (81). The toll taken on the lives of women who lack their "sack of provisions" gives one a sense of vertigo when the city begins to turn on itself, and calls forth a "taste for the sea" (81). The "continent" is at once the city and an aerian, atopic space to which she would give further consistency in later projects, a locus in which the forces are redrawn, so that the "sea goes to the city" (107). It is the "multiple continent" of those (lesbian writers) who have "signed," given the rest of us a sign (108).

Spaces in *Lovhers* (Montreal, the sea, New York's Barbizon Hotel for Women, the utopian time/space of the "vision" sequences) are not separable. Like interlocking modes of perceiving, feeling, and thinking, they imply each other, as the desiring body and the text write each other. *Nightwood* leads the poet to locate an erotics of reading / a reading of erotics that are inseparable, and equally implicating the love of writing / the writing of love. For Brossard this can be imagined only in relation to lesbian experience which she illuminates by bending her thought to merge with the words of/for her body; this is the "white center" in/to which she collects her poetry. The term "lesbian" casts a particular brilliance, light playing a special role in all the works.

> my continent, I want to speak of the radical effect
> of light in broad daylight
> today, I held you close,
> beloved of all civilization, of all
> texture, of all geometry and of flames,
> delirious as one writes: and
> my body is enraptured.

(*Lovhers*) 109)

Although urban lesbians lead a problematic existence, the light prevails: when the city becomes too dreary there is always the sea, the island to reincite and reinspire.

As feminists, Brossard declares, we have to confront "ceaselessly the inner necessity that incites us to exorcise the nightmares, to trace the dream and utopia" ("L'Angle" 25). Her pivotal role in elaborating the new Québécois "genre" of "fiction-theory" within the larger field of postmodern writing has permitted a unique inscription of lesbian-feminist subjectivity. "Women writers practicing [fiction-theory] have an acute consciousness of the work of language," observes France Théoret. "In the most probing texts, words send us back to words, and theory is signaled in the interstices" (148). Words from the dictionary are reoriented because "to change the words is to change the look of things" (148–49). Théoret says we can "think that utopia has been realized, a utopia without other promise than the imaginary which has become visible in language" (149). "Fiction-theory" and "writing in the feminine" (as compared with "écriture féminine") establish a differential rapport with the referent, with the real (149).[8] According to Brossard, the bottom line for the feminist writer, who must find creative means to express her sense and her dignity, is her ability to concentrate, block out, abstract from the reality that oppresses her and distracts her from her work ("L'Angle" 23–25).

Like feminist theorists who call for revised models of discursive production and social construction,[9] the works of Nicole Brossard are radical in the ways they operate on the symbolic system we call language, which systematically silences women and other oppressed groups. She affords her reader a new relationship to the figural potential of the imagination, to the body and/of the text, and a utopian vision that would totally re-as-sign our "being" in the world. Her works re-write all social constructions, including subjectivity, sexuality, and gender. Only in such a radically redesigned space can the lesbian imagination find freedom. The political threat/accomplishment of Brossard's desiring writing permanently unsettles what Linda Kauffman calls the "text's paternity, lineage, genealogy, genre" (23), helping to destroy the ideologies of authorship and mimesis. As the mute "e" and the "barred" lesbian/female subject exchange the castrated space of erasure for a new horizon of desire, we are enraptured by the mauve promise of a new dawn.

A HOLOGRAM OF DESIRE

For Brossard, there are words that seek us out just as we are searching for them. Certain words have an irreducible aura; they set off a chain reaction. Like the body, we cannot circumvent them. "Lesbian" becomes a "hologram of desire," where reading and writing, memory and utopia are fused in a creative symmetry ("Memory"), playing in the neural pathways of our minds. Brossard's latest writing insists on a double momentum of the body ("anterior and virtual") and a dual function accorded the sounds of the language (a "distinct pronunciation" and "sonorous form" of desire of/for her). Concentrating to maintain our equilibrium as we follow the complex steps of this lesbian *tango,* we surrender totally *[éperdument]* to an unedited music as we follow the voice in the text that inscribes it.[10] "The reality is rounded out" ("Eperdument" 29). At the outer limits of signs, we read, "the tongue turns without respite to the unthought"; the words dance and the knots of memory come untied (30–31). "Deep in the brain the image comes alive" and makes its way into the vocabulary (32). Charged with emotion the image tells us that beyond the monsters and crumpled paper we can write of "cities, mirrors and the absolute" (33). We merge with the image that gently replaces the subject. The fever Brossard describes is contagious, and we too desire such an image (of writing/ reality/ ourselves) as in "a spiral of love" (33). Since her journey as an artist and her interventions as a radical lesbian feminist are far from complete, we expect her "virtual" woman and differential equations to lead to many more discoveries. The *Mauve Desert,* we find, opens on to a mauve horizon.

NOTES

All decisions regarding translation are my own. In particular, working from the French texts, I have chosen on occasion to use my own readings rather than published English translations of Brossard's work. Most often, my intention is to provide a reading that is as close to the original French as possible—some may say too literal—in order to honor Brossard's choice of words. The literary translator must attend to other considerations of tone, rhythm, style, and diction in the English text.

1. Brossard rewrites or overwrites the Freudian "dark continent" of female desire. On the figure of the island, see also Shaktini's chapter on Wittig in this collection.
2. I will cite *La Lettre aérienne* [*LA*] when the translations are mine, and refer to *The Aerial Letter* [*AL*] when I use Wildeman's translation. Other translations are mine unless otherwise noted.
3. Brossard substitutes "laboratoir" for "laboratoire."
4. "Ecrire *je suis une femme* est plein de conséquences."
5. The "differential" analyses of Rich and Brossard are of essential significance to lesbian/feminist readers, and counterbalance the solidly psychoanalytical and increasingly Christian work of Julia Kristeva, as well as practitioners of "écriture féminine" like Hélène Cixous and Luce Irigaray whose polemic may slip into essentialism by blurring the lines between the biologic and the imaginary, and who at the very least reprivilege the "maternal" as it is elaborated by psychoanalysis.
6. Adrienne Rich used the term "lesbian continuum" in "Compulsory Heterosexuality and Lesbian Existence," collected in *Blood, Bread and Poetry*. See 51ff. and the "Afterword," 68–75.
7. The essay, "Writing against Writing and Other Disruptions in Recent French Lesbian Texts," appears in the volume edited by Linda Kauffman entitled *Feminism and Institutions* (Oxford: Blackwell, 1989), 211–39.
8. What the Québécoises call "écriture au féminin" is postmodern feminist writing, whereas "écriture féminine," practiced in France, derives from the insights of psychoanalysis.
9. In particular the linguist Claire Michard, and the social psychologist Celia Kitzinger have called for totally revised theoretical models of discursive production (Michard *passim*) and social construction (Kitzinger 178–98) in order to provide a space for women and for lesbians in language, discourse, and society. In comparison with such a revolutionary program, the revisions of a nonsexist lexicon may accord women more respect and autonomy but leave underlying ideology unchallenged. Similarly, as Kitzinger argues, the work of social scientists on homophobia and a positive self-image for "gay" women, which promote the rights of the individual to personal fulfillment, are symptomatic rather than systemic solutions, and as such nonthreatening to the dominant discourses of a liberal-humanist capitalist society.

10. The tango is for Brossard a figure of (lesbian) desire, and her favorite dance form.

WORKS CITED

Barthes, Roland. *Fragments d'un discours amoureux*. Paris: Seuil, 1977. Trans. Richard Howard. *A Lover's Discourse: Fragments*. New York: Hill and Wang, 1978.

———. *Le Plaisir du texte*. Paris: Seuil, 1973.

Bonnet, Marie-Jo. *Un Choix sans équivoque: recherches historiques sur les relations amoureuses entres les femmes XVIe–XXe siècle*. Paris: Denoël, 1981.

Brossard, Nicole. "Access to Writing: Ritual of the Written Word." Trans. Marian St. Onge and Monique Fol. *Trivia* 8 (1987): 8–14.

———. *Amantes*. Montreal: Les Quinze, 1980. Trans. Barbara Godard (*Lovhers*). Montreal: Guernica, 1986.

———. "L'Angle tramé du désir." In *La Théorie un dimanche*. Montreal: Rémue-ménage, 1988, 13–26.

———. *A Book*. Trans. Larry Shouldice. Toronto: Coach House, 1976.

———. "Le Cortex exubérant." *La Barre du jour* 44 (1974): 3–10.

———. *Le Désert mauve*. Montreal: L'Hexagone, 1987.

———. "Entretien avec Nicole Brossard sur *picture theory*." *La Nouvelle barre du jour* 118–19 (1982): 177–201.

———. "Eperdument." *La Théorie un dimanche*. Montreal: Rémue-ménage, 1988, 27–33.

———. *French Kiss*. Trans. Patricia Claxton. Toronto: Coach House, 1986.

———. *La Lettre aérienne*. Montreal: Rémue-ménage, 1985. Trans. Marlene Wildeman (*The Aerial Letter*). Toronto: Women's Press, 1988.

———. "Memory: Hologram of Desire." *Trivia* 13 (Fall 1988): 42–47.

———. *Picture Theory*. Montreal: Nouvelle Optique, 1982.

———. *Le Sens apparent*. Paris: Flammarion, 1980.

———. *These Our Mothers or the Disintegrating Chapter*. Trans. Barbara Godard. Toronto: Coach House, 1983.

Causse, Michèle. "Sub-in-vertere." *Traces: écriture de Nicole Brossard. La Nouvelle barre du jour* 118–19 (1982): 147–49.

Forsyth, Louise. "Beyond the Myths and Fictions of Traditionalism and Nationalism: The Political in the Work of Nicole Brossard." In *Traditionalism, Nationalism, and Feminism: Women Writers of Quebec*. Ed. Paula Gilbert Lewis. Westport, Conn.: Greenwood, 1985, 157–72.

Godard, Barbara. " 'Je est un autre': Nicole Brossard au Canada anglais." *La Nouvelle barre du jour* 118–19 (1982): 150–55.

Kauffman, Linda. *Discourses of Desire: Gender, Genre and Epistolary Fictions*. Ithaca: Cornell University Press, 1986.

Kitzinger, Celia. *The Social Construction of Lesbianism*. London: Sage, 1987.

Lacan, Jacques. *Encore (Le Séminaire: livre XX)*. Paris: Seuil, 1975.

Marini, Marcelle. "Marguerite Duras: une nouvelle écriture du politique." *Il Confronto Letterario*. Quaderni des dipartimento de lingue e letterature straniere moderne dell' università di Pavia. Supplemento al n. 8 (n.d.), 35–50.

Meese, Elizabeth A. *Crossing the Double-Cross: The Practice of Feminist Criticism*. Chapel Hill: University of North Carolina Press, 1986.

Michard, Claire. "Some Socio-enunciative Characteristics of Scientific Texts Concerning the Sexes." In *The Nature of the Right: A Feminist Analysis of Order Patterns*. Amsterdam: Benjamins, 1988, 27–59.

Nepveu, Pierre. "Nicole Brossard: Notes sur une écologie." *La Nouvelle barre du jour* 118–19 (1982): 139–44.

Rich, Adrienne. *Of Woman Born: Motherhood as Experience and Institution*. New York: Norton, 1976.

Rosenfeld, Marthe. "The Development of a Lesbian Sensibility in the Work of Jovette Marchessault and Nicole Brossard." In *Traditionalism, Nationalism and Feminism: Women Writers of Quebec* Ed. Paula Gilbert Lewis. Westport, Conn.: Greenwood, 1985, 227–39.

Spivak, Gayatri Chakravarty. *In Other Worlds: Essays in Cultural Politics*. New York: Methuen, 1987.

Théoret, France. *Entre raison et deraison*. Montreal: Herbes Rouges, 1987.

Wittig, Monique. *Les Guérillères*. Paris: Minuit, 1969.

Wittig, Monique, and Sande Zeig. *Lesbian Peoples: Material for a Dictionary*. New York: Avon, 1978.

TWENTY

Myth and Community in Recent Lesbian Autobiographical Fiction

Yvonne M. Klein

In an essay published in 1983, Bonnie Zimmerman reviewed a group of lesbian novels in which the protagonists undertook an educational journey through the patriarchal landscape toward a lesbian nation. Zimmerman noted that, in contrast to earlier, comparable lesbian fiction, which frequently ended in the defeat of the protagonist's lesbianism, so that she ends either by committing suicide or getting married later, "feminist" novels tend to launch the narrator toward a new vision of lesbian community "apart from patriarchy, in which female powers can be integrated, in which there are no limitations or compromises, in which the patriarchal, heterosexist world exacts no price" (257). Zimmerman correctly attributes this shift in direction to a new feminist and lesbian consciousness which permits the lesbian to locate herself, perhaps for the first time in this century, at the center of her own experience, to move in from the marginality of "queerness" to the imaginative reality of a lesbian nation.

But in the years since these hopeful novels first appeared, there has occurred a considerable change in the objective political circumstances which, to a greater or lesser extent, originally shaped their vision. The prospect of an ever-expanding army of lovers has contracted and the notion of establishing a literal lesbian nation, alternative to and competitive with patriarchy, is all but dead. The expansive autobiographical lesbian novels of the seventies have something of a hollow ring when read in Thatcher's Britain, Bush's America, or Mulroney's Canada, but this by no means implies that a return to the narrow strictures of the "prefeminist" period is either forced or imminent. A significant and impressive group of novels has emerged, novels which fall clearly into the type of the lesbian novel of formation, but which resolve themselves neither in defeat nor in a triumphant and irrevocable departure from patriarchy. Though all are unmistakably feminist and unreservedly lesbian, their endings are, to a greater or lesser degree, occluded. Rather than projecting forward a vision of a new community of living Amazons, they reach back to reinvent a mythic history of female power out of the shards and scraps of their childhood and their culture. None of these novels returns to the prefeminist resolution which granted a greater validity to the heterosexual world than to the narrator's own sense of self or sexual identity. Nonetheless, neither do they dismiss that world as irrelevant or altogether lacking in value. The territory held in these works has no literal extension in a political or social reality. It escapes futility less through reference to a larger social context than to a transcendent spiritual one.

The writers considered in this chapter (Barbara Deming, Audre Lorde, Jeanette Winterson, and Jovette Marchessault) represent about as diverse a set of social backgrounds as might be imagined within Western industrialism. Nevertheless, their accounts of growing up lesbian bear striking similarities to one another. Their novels concern the narrators' struggles to foster and maintain an emergent lesbian consciousness against an unyielding, hostile, or uncomprehending heterosexual surrounding which, if it can recognize the narrator at all, sees her as grotesquely deviant. These works occupy a position somewhere between autobiography and novel. She whose life is the substance of the narrative travels under her own name through a world populated with pseudonymous characters whose names have been changed, frequently to protect their guilt and complicity in repression and denial or the author from a lawsuit. Thus only the narrator stands in front of the reader as her true self; those around her can be, and are, remade to suit the needs of the narrative.[1] In this regard, the lesbian narrators, as Marilyn R. Farwell observes in her discussion of the lesbian imagination, enter "into a relation of exchanged honesty and trust" with the reader, and "the writing of the text becomes an act which affirms self in community with others" (118).

If the writing of the text affirms community, the books themselves detail the search for it, a search which is not always rewarded in a strictly literal way. In Deming's A Humming Under My Feet, the narrator, Bobbie, sets off on a journey which is in fact a flight from a situation which has become too painful to be borne. She leaves behind a lover of eight years who has married her brother and is pregnant with his child. The Korean War has just begun, and another brother is in the army. The heterosexual world of marriage and war seems more real to Bobbie than her own life and, indeed, she contemplates marriage herself as a way of becoming more real to herself and to her women lovers, all of whom seem destined to leave her for men. She is told that people do marry, but what of those who don't or won't? Are they less or other than people? She has not availed herself of the support to be found in the lesbian community that existed in the 1950s. Aside from her lovers, her friends, with the exception of a few gay men, all appear straight, and when by chance she comes across a woman who might not be, neither reveals herself to the other. She has avoided lesbian bars, "having found it easier to hold onto my pride by not having such visits. Easier to repress society's views of us" (58). When she does visit a Paris gay bar, she discovers, with a shock, that she is as unrecognized there as she is at large. Although this book is exceptional in the group under discussion, in that it records events which occurred when the author was past thirty, psychologically she is in the same condition of becoming as the adolescents of the other novels.

In Lorde's *Zami*, the narrator seems never to have wistfully imagined permanent residence in the "real world," since entrance into that world was never a likely option. Legally blind, a black child in a white school, a poet in a practical family, Audre begins "outside" and learns very early that the route to survival lies in finding a community of outsiders to sustain her. If in *Humming* it is homophobia which renders Bobbie invisible in her full identity, in *Zami* it is racism. Traveling in liberal white circles which pride themselves on color blindness and so cannot see their own racism, Audre cannot name the barrier between herself and her white friends even to herself: "It was in high school that I came to believe that I was different from my white classmates, not because I was Black, but because I was me" (82). But her lesbianism does prevent her full acceptance into black society, even if it does not bar her participation in bohemia:

Like when your Black sisters on the job think you're crazy and collect money between themselves to buy you a hot comb and straightening iron on their lunch hour and stick it anonymously into your locker in the staff room, so that later when you come down for a coffee break and open your locker the damn things fall out on the floor with a clatter and all ninety-percent of your library co-workers who are very white want to know what it's all about. (181)

Audre must find a way of bringing her two worlds together and of being her real self in each.

For Bobbie and Audre, their situation as outsider is a source of pain; to Jeanette, in Winterson's *Oranges Are Not the Only Fruit*, it is a source of strength. Adopted as an infant into a family of Plymouth Brethren, she grows up in a subsociety, almost exclusively female, which is itself outside the dominant culture. Her mother's radio is tuned to the World Missionary Service, not the nine o'clock news; Jeanette's history and zoology lessons are drawn from the Old Testament. Her mother, who seems quite mad to the neighbors, succeeds, by sheer force of conviction, in creating a female world of power where men are treated as awkward conveniences inside a rigid patriarchal framework. It is a world which arms Jeanette in a quite remarkable way. Faced with the contradictions between home and the social norms enforced by school, most children lose confidence in themselves and seek to invent for themselves a more socially acceptable self. The distance between what Jeanette believes and how the rest of the world lives is larger than usual, but she does not falter: "[E]veryone at school avoided me. If it had not been for the conviction that I was right, I might have been very sad. As it was, I just forgot about it" (43). When troubled by the contradiction between the "daily world" and her own and her mother's eschatological vision, she subsumes the quotidian world into her own myth, a conflation of biblical and ordinary fact:

One day, I learned that Tetrahedron is a mathematical shape that can be formed by stretching an elastic band over a series of nails.
But Tetrahedron is an emperor . . .
The emperor Tetrahedron lived in a palace made absolutely from elastic bands. To the right, cunning fountains shot elastic jets, subtle as silk, to the left, ten minstrels played day and night on elastic lutes.

She goes on to embellish the tale, concluding with a moral. Walking around his elastic theater, the emperor learns that "no emotion is the final one" (49).

But no matter how far biblical myth may be bent and stretched to accommodate the desire for a new imaginative reality, there is a point beyond which it cannot be reshaped and the structure snaps. Neither Jeanette's mother nor her church can accommodate her lesbianism; her mother collapses at the prospect of "Unnatural Passions" and publicly concedes that St. Paul was right in restraining women in the church, leaving Jeanette bereft of her faith in her mother's loyalty to her against male power. "It was," she says, "her weakness for the ministry that had done it. . . . I knew my mother hoped I would blame myself, but I didn't. I knew where the blame lay. If there's such a thing as spiritual adultery, my mother was a whore" (134).

From the very beginning of Marchessault's "A Lesbian Chronicle," the narrator situates herself even further outside as she denominates herself the "little extra-terrestrial lesbian," exiled from Paradise in the medieval Quebec of the 1950s. She has been born with a "hard knot of resistance" (34), inherited from her foremothers, a resistance which the patriarchal Catholic church does its (literal) damndest to dissolve. She has no allies in her struggle: her family is in league with the Church; all the other women she knows seem entranced by male power. But she is protected by language, by what she terms her "etymological intuition," achieved in a garage at the age of six. She asks her uncle the name of the little knob he pulls when he starts the Ford and is told it is the choke. "It regulates the gas," he says. "In French, people sometimes call it *l'étrangleur*—the strangler" (36). That two mutually incomprehensible words for the same thing exist reveals the source of the puzzling duality she has observed in her cousin who, by day, submerged in the glorious Ontario summer, is free, inventive, and joyous, but who turns into the night cousin, dull, subdued, and inarticulate, when her boyfriend appears. The lesson is not lost on Jovette: if she will live, she must get possession of the language, make it her own, so that her words "may break down the separation between women. Power and oppression must someday come to terms with this book" (58). Like Jeanette, Marchessault bends and stretches the language of the myth into which she has been born to make it conform to her visionary needs, but in her hands, it does not snap because, opposing and enriching it, is a memory of another language and another myth from the millennia before the patriarchal God— the memory of the Mother.

It is this memory which connects these four books, based though they are on widely different life experiences—their collective reliance on the power of myth to heal, to relieve the sense of isolation and futility conse- quent on the outsider's position. Alicia Ostriker, in discussing the place of myth in women's poetry, calls the process "revisionist mythmaking," and says that the revised myths are

corrections; they are representations of what women find divine and demonic in themselves; they are retrieved images of what women have collectively and histori- cally suffered; in some cases they are instructions for survival. (215)

Certainly the myths in these books perform many of these functions, but Judy Grahn's term, *mythic realism*, seems better able to describe the partic- ular quality of these very lesbian myths. The myths in these works are not revised or reinterpreted versions of phallocentric icons or merely signposts to survival; they are survival itself. The myths invoked here are powerful in and of themselves, not just as a means of re/viewing the world, but as unanticipated, even unsought, empowerment. In the simplest instance, when, at the climax of her story, Bobbie makes contact with the truncated goddess figure in the field at Epidauros, she does so with no *conscious* awareness of the matriarchal past. Nevertheless, it is Bobbie who resembles the speechless, broken, alienated Orpheus of Muriel Rukeyser's visionary encounter and the goddess, headless, limbless though she is, who heals. Kneeling, holding the "shining, ancient breasts," Bobbie can at last say:

"I am the self that I am. I affirm it. . . . Yes I am. And I will not be robbed of my sex. And I will not be shamed." The stone breasts were cool under my hands, with the coolness of water found at a spring, life-giving. I felt the spirit of the stone enter my hands with this coolness and enter my soul. I sang (without any sound): "Yes. It is the truth about me and so I will live it." (252)

In *Zami,* it is no marble goddess which empowers, but a real-life incarnation of the female poet warrior goddess Afrekete/Kitty, met casually at a party in Queens, who teaches Audre "roots, new definitions of our women's bodies—definitions for which I had only been in training to learn before" (250). It is the magic power of Afrekete, experienced while making love to Kitty on a rooftop in New York, which makes possible a necessary transformation:

Afrekete, Afrekete ride me to the crossroads where we shall sleep, coated in women's power. The sound of our bodies meeting is the prayer of all strangers and sisters, that the discarded evil, abandoned at all crossroads, will not follow us upon our journeys. (252)

Thus it is that Audre at last discovers the latitudes of Carriacou, the lost lesbian paradise and source of her own mother's power, though it is no longer home. And so too can she begin to incarnate herself as Afrekete, "the mischievous linguist, trickster, best beloved, whom we must all become" (255).

As they touch and are touched by prepatriarchal goddess figures, Bobbie and Audre tap into a source of creative energy unavailable to Jeanette as long as she remains within the mythic structure of the Judaeo-Christian Bible. When she falls in love with a young woman, she discovers that the inelasticity of the Church will not permit her to follow what she had believed to be her destiny, to be a prophet of the Lord, and at the same time retain herself. No biblical model exists to sustain her. An ambiguously sexed demon attempts to encourage her, remarking that it is here "to keep you in one piece; if you ignore us, you're quite likely to end up in two pieces, or lots of pieces . . ." and leaves her with a token, a tough brown pebble (rather like Jovette's "hard knot of resistance") to remind her of who she is (34). It is not quite enough. Jeanette ransacks romantic myth for a story to replace what she has lost. But neither fairy tale nor romantic legend leads her anywhere save to a resigned acceptance of her lot. Toward the end of the book, she still misses God and the absolute dependability of that presence in her life:

[V]ery human relationships will match up to it. I have an idea that one day it might be possible, I thought once it had become possible, and that glimpse has set me wandering, trying to find the balance between earth and sky. (176)

Jovette, in "Lesbian Chronicle," also discovers the limitations of Christian myth. Though she dances to the tune of her religious instructors, the dance remains stubbornly her own, outwardly obedient but ineffably un-Catholic. But this is not an accommodation she can maintain forever. She feels her sanity beginning to crumble. Exiled from birth in the "Land of Perpetual Sacrifice," confined to the futile circlings of the "herd of women" who are confined and controlled by the cowboys of Church and State, she glimpses her potential escape one day in a group of distant women "walking in a different direction . . . [who] moved more slowly, descendants of a past I did not know" (66). Painfully, slowly, she works her way toward them and, in their healing presence, recovers her true self:

Such a blossoming sensation in my tree-body, in the branches of my arms, the roots of my legs, the flowers of my fingers, the leaves of my hair, the dewdrops of my mouth, and the stars of my imagination! I was born. The divine infant was born, for herself alone. . . . I met other women to whom the same thing was happening. I became happy, even mad with joy. (68)

If this were the book's final statement, "A Lesbian Chronicle" would duplicate the direction toward a larger lesbian community noticed by Zimmerman in the novels of the 1970s. But this is not quite the end. Despite the triumphant exorcism of the patriarchal religious past and its replacement by the organic metaphor of matriarchal myth, Jovette remains oddly isolated at the conclusion. She cannot return to share her new being with the women of her previous life, since patriarchy has control of the lines of communication. In a concluding passage, she has planted herself firmly at the roots of the living tree of matriarchal memory, the tree called "Mother-in-flower," rapt in the ecstatic contemplation of the "living night in her new land" (Note 70), but it is a land seemingly populated by just herself and perhaps a lover. In the absence of community, consciousness of a sustaining mythic inheritance must suffice.

The lesbian novels of the early seventies presumed that the narrator's joyful coming to a full and confident lesbian identity would necessarily be followed by a movement into an expanding lesbian community which, though it might exist within the parameters of patriarchal society, could ignore and even in the end replace it. These more recent novels appear to mark a retreat from this political optimism. The narrators of these works all remain, to a certain extent, "outside," though they no longer view themselves as marginal or deviant. For Deming and Lorde, the absence of an evident, confident, available lesbian community might be attributed to the fact that the events described took place in the 1950s, before the advent of a new lesbian consciousness, but Winterson and Marchessault are dealing with recent events. It would appear that the failure of the immediate prospect of a lesbian nation has required lesbian writers to seek another means of confirming the legitimacy and centrality of their own experience. If it cannot be found in a wider social and political association, it may be discovered within a self which has retrieved its connection with a mythical matriarchal past more abiding and more fundamental than any passing political context. All of these works, then, in the evocation of a timeless mythic continuity, find means to celebrate and affirm a lesbian self and provide at least a signpost, its finger pointing in a direction past despair.

NOTES

1. For the sake of clarity, the authors will be referred to by their last names, the narrators by their first.

WORKS CITED

Deming, Barbara. *A Humming Under My Feet: A Book of Travail*. London: Women's Press, 1985.
Farwell, Marilyn R. "Toward a Definition of the Lesbian Literary Imagination." *Signs* (1988): 100–118.

Grahn, Judy. *The Highest Apple: Sappho and the Lesbian Poetic Tradition*. San Francisco: Spinsters/Aunt Lute, 1985.

Lorde, Audre. *Zami: A New Spelling of My Name*. Trumansburg, N.Y.: Crossing Press, 1982.

Marchessault, Jovette. "A Lesbian Chronicle." In *Lesbian Triptych*. Trans. Yvonne M. Klein. Toronto: Women's Press, 1985.

Ostriker, Alicia Suskin. *Stealing the Language: The Emergence of Women's Poetry in America*. Boston: Beacon, 1986.

Rukeyser, Muriel. "The Poem as Mask." In her *Collected Poems*. New York: McGraw, 1978.

Winterson, Jeanette. *Oranges Are Not the Only Fruit*. New York: Atlantic Monthly Press, 1988.

Zimmerman, Bonnie. "Exiting from Patriarchy: The Lesbian Novel of Development." In *The Voyage In: Fictions of Female Development*. Ed. Elizabeth Abel, Marianne Hirsch, and Elizabeth Langland. Hanover N.H.: Univ. Press of New England, 1983, 244–57.

TWENTY-ONE

The Journey Back to Female Roots: A Laguna Pueblo Model

Annette Van Dyke

Paula Gunn Allen is a mixed-blood Native American lesbian who says she is Laguna Pueblo/Sioux/Lebanese-American and that she "writes out of a Laguna Indian woman's perspective" (Allen, *Sacred Hoop: Recovering* 6). Allen continues her cultural tradition in her novel by using it in the same way in which the traditional arts have always functioned for the Laguna Pueblo. She has extended traditional storytelling into the modern form of the novel by weaving in the tribal history, cultural traditions, and mythology[1] of the Laguna Pueblo to create a form of curing ceremony for her readers.

Allen published her novel *The Woman Who Owned the Shadows*, in 1983. She has many scholarly articles and chapbooks of poetry, and she has edited *Studies in American Indian Literature* (1983). A major book of poetry, *Shadow Country,* was published in 1982; her new book of poetry is entitled *Wyrds,* and a novel, *Raven's Road,* is in progress.

Underlying American Indian literature are cultural assumptions and a worldview which contrast sharply with those underlying most non-Indian literature (Allen, "Symbol and Structure" 267–70). To understand how Allen uses her cultural tradition in her novel, it is best to know something about the culture from which she comes. The Pueblo worldview, like that of other tribal cultures, is based on the concept that all things inanimate and animate are related and are part of the whole. Plants, animals, rocks, and people are in a reciprocal relationship, and people must carry on rituals, prayers, and offerings to keep things in balance in that reciprocal relationship. To the Pueblo, who have kept their worldview essentially intact, life is sacred and everything including the arts contributes to "light, life, well-being" (Parsons xi). The task of the individual is to contribute to the well-being of the group and keep the shifting balances in harmony.

Since the invasion of white men bringing a worldview which separates spirit and body, inanimate and animate, ceremonies are even more important to keep the relationships between all things in balance. The ultimate expression of this lack of balance is the development and use of the atomic bomb which another Laguna writer, Leslie Marmon Silko, documents in her novel, *Ceremony*. In this sense, lack of balance affects not only the individual but the whole of civilization. A worldview which separates spirit and body, inanimate from animate lacks respect for other parts of creation and fails to see the interrelatedness of all things—one's place in the web of being. The Euro-American worldview elevates one part of creation above others: humans over plants, animals, and earth; and mind/spirit over the physical. This leads ultimately to a lack of balance.

For the Laguna, geographic place is intricately tied into understanding one's place in the web of being, a special tie to the land. Balance cannot be achieved without a "knowing" related to continuity in a certain place. That place is important in Laguna culture is not surprising because the Pueblo are part of a cotinuum of inhabitation of the area from southern Utah and Colorado to northern Mexico since 10,000 B.C. The ancestors of the Pueblo occupied the four corners area, the spot where the states of Colorado, Utah, Arizona, and New Mexico intersect, and the Lagunas themselves have occupied their present area since about the thirteenth century (Momaday 50–54 and Dosier 31–34).[2]

In contrast to the Laguna way of harmony with the environment, critic Reyes Garcia points out that the Euro-American way of shaping and controlling the environment "deprive[s] all lives, most of all their own, of substance." He feels that without our being able to "respond to the fertile meaning places hold, . . . our pulsing lives here will stop and Earth will come to an end, its radioactive memory locked in 'witchery's final ceremonial sand painting' " (46). Allen explores this theme in her novel *Raven's Road,* when she refers to the possible rebirth of Sun Woman as part of the atomic testing going on in the desert. As the main character watches the rising mushroom cloud, she saw "the old woman or great white bear or sun maiden or sun shield. . . . In her memory's eye she could see that the visual was of an old woman's face huge as the sky . . ." (58). Allen points out that Euro-Americans have no respect for the forces of the environment with which they tamper because they believe that they control everything. The delicate balances have been disrupted, and we must work to recover them. One way of righting the balance is by storytelling.

For the Lagunas, storytelling often functions as a ceremony for curing.

Allen continues in this tradition—her novel is an offering to balance the world and enact healing rituals for herself and others. In an essay Allen says: "At base, every story, every song, every ceremony, tells the Indian he [sic] is part of a living whole, and that all parts of the whole are related to one another by virtue of their participation in the whole of being." ("Sacred Hoop: A Contemporary" 117). She says that when the Europeans came in the fifteenth century, "the fragile web of identity that long held tribal people secure has gradually been weakened and torn. But the oral tradition has prevented the compete destruction of the web, the ultimate disruption of tribal ways" (Sacred Hoop: Recovering 45). Through "the women who speak and work and write," the oral tradition continues now in English and helps to mend the web (Sacred Hoop: Recovering 50). In an interview, Allen has said that her novel is a "medicine novel" or a "ritual handbook" meant to "get inside" the reader's head.

Allen's novel, then, can be seen as a kind of curing ceremony—a ceremony to insure survival and create new life. In a recent essay in Sinister Wisdom, Allen argues that feminists need to know about American Indian societies which are "recent social models from which its [feminism's] dream descends and to which its adherents can look for models" to reclaim the lost heritage of what she calls "gynarchial societies" ("Who is Your Mother?" 39). Allen continues:

We as feminists must be aware of our history on this continent. We need to recognize the same forces that devastated the gynarchies of Britain and the Continent also devastated the ancient African civilizations. . . . I am convinced that those wars have always been about the imposition of uncontested patriarchal civilization over the wholistic, pacifistic and spirit-based gynarchies they supplant, and to this end the wars . . . have not been . . . waged over the land and its resources, but more, they have been fought within the bodies, minds, and hearts of the people of the earth. This is, I think, the reason traditionalists say we must remember our origins, our cultures, our histories and our mothers and grandmothers, for without that memory, which implies continuance . . . we are doomed to extinction. (39–40)

Because Indian values and culture have informed generations of Euro-Americans from the beginning of their emigration to America, and the Indian vision of a free and equal society has been the same as that of radical thinkers throughout history (Allen, "Who" 41–44), to recover the Indian values is to recover our own most radical values. Therefore, as we trace the journey of the main character in Allen's novel, we trace a model for our own.

Allen's novel, *The Woman Who Owned the Shadows,* is about a journey to healing—a journey back to the female center. At the beginning of the novel, the central character, Ephanie Atencio, is a half-breed who has lost the sense of who she is; she is isolated and fragmented as a human being, belonging neither to the Pueblo community nor to the non-Indian community. Ephanie has a fragmented self from an inner war. As a half-breed Guadalupe[3] woman, Ephanie is caught in the erosion of the traditional place of honor and respect in which a Guadalupe woman is held by her tribe and in the stereotyped and patriarchal view from which she is viewed by non-Indians. She is surrounded by forces which work to destroy whatever link she has to the traditional culture in which the women were central figures. The reader follows her struggle to regain her sanity as she sorts out her childhood and her tribal beliefs and connections, marries a second-generation Japanese-American man, and deals with the death of one of their twins. She joins a consciousness-raising group, goes to a psychiatrist, studies the old traditions, and tries to commit suicide, but it is only when she is able to synthesize what she has learned from all of this, see its connection to her tribal traditions, and reaffirm the importance of the female, especially the importance of the "amazon tradition,"[4] that she is healed.

The Laguna society to which Allen's mother and maternal grandmother belonged and in which she places her character was matrilineal (descent recognized through the female line) and matrilocal (ownership of houses held by women). Allen says her "mother's Laguna people are Keres Indian, reputed to be the last extreme mother-right people on earth"[5] (*Sacred Hoop: Recovering* 48). Women also controlled and cared for the ceremonial objects (Parsons 182, 192–93, 888–89) and the power to conduct ceremonies came from both men and women (Allen interview). According to Allen, one of the problems with Christianity is that it attempts to use "male power" only. Women also owned the crops while men did the farming. The primary deities were Thought Woman (Tsitstinako) and her sisters, Corn Woman (Iyatiku), and Sun Woman (Nautsityi). For Allen, "womanness . . . is preponderant; it is the source of human male and human female, the giver and bestower of life, ritual, afterlife, social power, and all that is sacred" ("Where I Come From" 17). Because the Laguna society in which Allen places her characters has lost this central importance of the female, both the Laguna and Euro-American society need balancing. The old stories are not effective in acting as curing ceremonies because they do not account for the influence of Euro-American culture.

Allen's main character in *The Woman Who Owned the Shadows* illustrates the isolation and fragmentation which occur if individuals pull away or are left out of the community and their experience or "story" cannot be seen as part of the whole. As a mixed-breed person who lives apart, Ephanie is unable to fit into the old ways; there are no stories for her experiences. Only when she makes sense of the old stories by seeing the continuities in them and how she fits into those continuities can she be healed, for the Laguna believe that everything that has happened will happen again only in a different form. Her journey to healing is primarily an isolated one,[6] an interior journey. She puzzles over the old stories, searching for answers, looking for the patterns until, one day, she understands their continuity— how they fit together:

She understood the combinations and recombinations that had so puzzled her. . . . First there was Sussinstinaku, Thinking Woman, then there was She and two more: Uretsete and Naotsete. Then Uretsete became known as the father, Utset, because Naotsete had become pregnant and a mother, because the Christians would not understand and killed what they did not know. And Iyatiku was the name Uretsete was known by . . . and so the combinations went on, forming, dissolving, doubling, splitting. . . . All of the stories informed those patterns, laid down long before time, so far. (207–8)

An important role of the storyteller, then, is to tell the story according to the requirements of the listeners. Therefore, the story must be adapted to the particular audience. Leslie Marmon Silko, another Laguna writer, reminds us in an essay that "Storytelling always includes the audience and the listeners, and in fact, a great deal of the story is believed to be inside the listener and the storyteller's role is to draw the story out of the listeners" ("Language" 57).

Having identified her readers as needing stories to make sense out of today's complicated world and yet connect to the important "stories" or values of the past, Allen tells a modern story calculated to do this. She begins with the Laguna creation myth which opens with a female creator spirit, Tsitstinako or Thought Woman. She is also identified as Spider Woman in some versions of the myth. She creates two sisters, Iyatiku and Nautsityi, who with various animal helpers bring the people from the four worlds of the underworld. They emerge at Shipap. Iyatiku or Corn Woman becomes the mother of the Indians while Nautsityi or Sun Woman becomes the mother of the others.[7] In her function as a storyteller in the Laguna tradition, then, Allen evokes Thought Woman at the beginning of her novel. Allen's prologue recounts the creation story, and she dedicates the novel to her "great grandmother, Meta Atseye Gunn./To Naiya Iyatiku./ And to Spider Grandmother, Thought Woman,/ who thinks the stories I write down" (iii).

By dedicating her novel to Thought Woman, from whose intelligence all life comes, Allen celebrates and honors her as the supreme storyteller. Through the novel, Allen shows Thought Woman/Spider Woman the love and respect she deserves, and in turn she will give her blessing. "After her," as a line in one of Allen's poems goes, the poet "mend[s] the tear with string"—the poet, following the Creator's example, attempts to weave together the stories to affect healing for the people ("Grandmother" 126).[8] Allen places her novel in the context of the Laguna tradition and signifies that she is honoring Spider Grandmother while taking part in the Grand-mother's thinking by telling a story for the people which will bring old and new experiences together in a coherent whole. In an essay, Allen says such activity attempts "to bring the isolated self into harmony and balance" with the reality celebrated in legends, sacred stories, songs, and ceremonies and "to actualize in language, those truths of being and experience that give to humanity its greatest significance and dignity" ("Sacred Hoop: A Contem-porary" 113).

In Laguna mythology, there is a story about how Thought Woman's sisters, who have been given the task of naming and giving "human form to the spirit which was the people" (Allen, *Woman* 148), quarrel and separate. The quarrel and subsequent separation seem to be the prototype for much of the evil in the world. The result in the modern stories is that the children of the two sisters (whites, Asians, Indians, Africans, etc.) have forgotten that they are related and have forgotten as well that they are related to things inanimate and animate. Most of the descendants of the two sisters have forgotten that people must carry on rituals to keep things in balance. This forgetting leads to separation from the land, to drought, to war, to division of the self.

This is what happens to Allen's main character, Ephanie. In Allen's novel, the quarrel and subsequent separation of Corn Woman and Sun Woman form the central mythic antagonism. In the novel, the sisters are called "double women," (2) and the modern conflict is that Ephanie is separated from herself—she is herself a double woman comprised of war-ring parts: "She wished she could tear out the monstrous other in her, reveal or find the one within that matched her, loving, passionate, wild and throbbing . . ." (132).

Ephanie has lost her connection to the Guadalupe community and the traditions which sustain them. As a mixed-breed, Ephanie is caught between cultures—accepted neither as Guadalupe nor as white. In her torment to discover who she is, Ephanie says:

One thing she could not go back to, though she had tried symbolically, in dreams, in books, was the old heathen tradition. She had never been to a masked dance. She had not been allowed. Even her mother had not been there since she was a small child, taken by Grandma Sylvia, Shimanna, across the spaces between one village and the next, around the lake that was no longer there, to the square to see the katsinas, the gods, enter and bowing, stepping, dance, the spruce collars dipping and swaying gravely with their steps.

"I never saw them," she said quiet, wistful, "because they left, and left me out."

When Sylvia left, when Ephanie's mother grew up and married out as well, those doors had closed. (148)

Besides her difficulties with her Guadalupe heritage, Ephanie also has difficulty meeting the non-Indians' stereotyped expectations of her. They expected her to be an "Indian maiden" who was "noble, . . . wise, . . . and exotic" (66–67), when, in fact, she was just like other women who had gone to college and had been involved in political activities. They just made her feel as if she didn't belong.

In the novel, the division of the self in the main character has to do with her separation from the earth which is seen as the Mother. Allen says in an essay that the essential nature of femininity is associated "with the creative power of thought," thought of the kind which produces "mountains, lakes, creatures and philosophical/sociological systems." She warns, however, that "it is not in the mind of the Pueblo to simply equate in primitive modes earth-bearing-grain with woman-bearing-child" ("The Feminine," 130–131). Allen's use of the Laguna view toward the land, its femaleness, and its spirituality underlies her work:

The land: a vast, intense, spirit woman, whose craggy fastnesses, deep dry waterways, miles and miles of forest and wilderness, reaches upon reaches of mesas, 40,000 deep skies where thunderheads of frightening force and awesome majesty sail ponderously, give me my primary understanding of womanness, of gender in its female sensibility. ("Where I Come From" 16)

Ephanie experiences this division from self, from the land, the Mother, as her cutting "herself off from the sweet spring of her own being" (*Woman*

203) because she is a woman from a traditionally female-centered culture. Like the Creator sisters of the ancient story who compliment one another as they go about their tasks, Ephanie has a best friend as she grows up in Guadalupe—a Chicanà named Elena. "They were so close they were like twins: Because Elena's gold-tinged hair looked dark in the photograph's light, no one could say which was Elena, which Ephanie. With each other they were each one doubled. They were thus complete" (22).

However, when they are nine, the nuns find out they have been "playing . . . between each other's legs" (13) and warn them of the seriousness of their offense. When the nuns tell Elena's mother, Elena has to tell Ephanie that they cannot see each other anymore:

Ephanie sat. Stunned. Mind empty. Stomach a cold cold stone. The hot sun blazed on her head. She felt sick. She felt herself shrinking within. Understood, wordlessly, exactly what Elena was saying. How she could understand what Ephanie had not understood. That they were becoming lovers. That they were in love. That their loving had to stop. To end. That she was falling. Had fallen. Would not recover from the fall, smashing the rocks. That they were in her, not on the ground. (30)

Later at the convent school, Ephanie watches as two nuns fall in love and are joyous in each other's presence in an otherwise joyless and somber place. However, when one of the nuns is sent away, the somberness returns and the girls lament the loss of love and happiness. Step by step, Ephanie learns to distrust herself and her love for other women.

When she is twelve, Ephanie falls from a tree when she is challenged by her cousin Stephen to jump from a rope. She slips and ends up with two broken ribs and a punctured lung which collapses. She feels she has been tricked and betrayed by Stephen and like the loss of her relationship with Elena, this "fall" causes her much pain, both psychically and physically. "After she fell the sun went out. . . . [She] learned to prance and priss, and did not notice the change, the fear behind it. The rage. And did not ever say aloud, not even in her own mind, what it was all about" (203). The tree from which she falls becomes the symbol of her "drought of the spirit." It was "lying, against the ground, split in two" (132)—"dying, all filthy and rotting and dying" (133).

Ephanie begins to put all of her energy into becoming a "lady." Here the Catholicism combines with other pressures to force her to be "alien" to herself. Her Catholic school experience tries to train her to be the Euro-American ideal of womanhood:

Long, empty, polished corridors. Silent white faces of women whose whole heads and bodies were encased in black heavy fabric. Whose rosaries hanging dark and heavy down their legs clinked with every quiet step they took. Of those white faces, almost always unsmiling. Of those white hands that never touched a child. Of those white faces smiling, tight and stiff, as though that simple expression caused great pain. Who said she must pray. Must ask to be forgiven. . . . Must remember to sit quietly at the table. And never ask for more. Who must eat when told, sleep when told, wake when told, play when told, work when told, study when told, piss when told, shit when told, and must never never use too much paper to wipe her butt. Her tiny child's butt. (154)

Part of herself is at war with the other, trying to kill that loving part which had transgressed in Euro-American culture: "She felt rise within her words and pictures, understandings and interpretations that were not hers, not her, alien, monstrous, other than her, in her, that wanted her dead, wanted her to kill, to destroy whatever was of meaning or comfort to her . . ." (132).

Ephanie has learned to doubt herself and her love for other women. She "abandons" herself—she never again believes in herself: "I was going to be a hero, before I got sidetracked, she thought. I was going to be full of life and action. I wasn't going to be the one who lived alone, afraid of the world. Elena and I, we were going to do brave things in our lives. And we were going to do them together" (209).

Of lesbianism in traditional Indian cultures, Allen says that because young men and women were often separated from the large group for extended periods, same-sex relationships "were probably common" (Sacred Hoop: Recovering 256). However, besides this opportunity, there were also those women whose orientation toward other women was a matter of "Spirit direction" (257). In the case of the Lakota (Sioux—part of Allen's heritage), such a woman would have dreamed of "Double Woman," and from then on, she would be a skilled craftsperson, doing both women's and men's work. According to a Lakota account, a "Double Woman dreamer" could act "like a crazy woman"—"deceptively," promiscuously, and such women are known to "cause all men who stand near them to become possessed" ("Double Woman" in Roscoe 88). This account points out the power and special burden that was considered to accompany this kind of dream—a power that was highly respected by the Lakota—and it also mentions a ritual that two women who were "Double Woman Dreamers" might carry out to "become united by the power of the Deity" (Allen Sacred Hoop: Recovering 258). The Lakotas would have considered a woman who dreamed of the moon spirit, Double Woman, to be a sacred person or *wakan*. According to Allen, such a woman would have been a "medicine woman in a special sense. She probably was a participant in the Spirit . . . of an Entity or a Deity who was particularly close to earth during the Goddess period . . ." (257). Allen goes on to say that "essentially a woman's spiritual way is dependent on the kind of power she possesses, the kind of Spirit to whom she is attached, and the tribe to which she belongs. She is required to follow the lead of Spirits and to carry out the tasks they assign her" (257). However, as Walter Williams notes, "It is common for people to claim reluctance to fulfill their spiritual duty no matter what vision appears to them. Becoming any kind of sacred person involves taking on various social responsibilities and burdens" (29).

It is also true that by "interpreting the result of the vision as being the work of a spirit, the vision quest frees the person from feeling responsibility for his [or her] transformation" (Williams 29). Allen describes this belief in a transforming spirit in *Raven's Road*. The protagonist, Allie Hawker, recalls her initiation into lesbian sex by her female army captain:

She stood, drawing Allie to her until their breasts touched, until their breasts fell into the softness of each other. Then slowly, deliberately, the captain kissed Allie, and that was all there was to it, and just like, swiftly and silently as a deer pauses a moment then vanishes into the bush, Allie was taken by that twilight world, made a citizen of it, an outcast who forever would belong to wilderness, and there would be at home.

They had stories about it, the Indian people. Some of them, not her tribe, but her friends, had told her about Deer Woman, how she would come to a dance, so beautiful, so enchanting. She would choose you to dance with, circling the drum slowly, circling, circling, in the light that blazed darkly from the tall fires that ringed the dance ground; she would dance with you, her elbow just touching yours, her shawl spread carefully around her shoulders and arms, held with breathtaking perfect precision over her cocked right arm, torso making just the right sideward bow, tiny steps perfect in their knowing of the drum. She would dance you, dance into you, holding your gaze with her eyes, for if your eyes looked down at her feet you would see her hooves and the spell would be broken. And after a time she would incline her head, say, perhaps, come, and you would follow. Away from the fire and the dancing, into the brush, into the night. And you would not return, or if you did, it would be as somebody else. (Quoted in Roscoe 144–45)

In *The Woman Who Owned the Shadows*, Ephanie has not followed her spiritual way. As a child she had had a strong sense of herself as brave and free, which she had given up as an adolescent. However, the spirits did not give up on her that easily and later, when she is an adult, her friend Teresa tells her that "the spirits" are trying to tell her "something important." Again she tries to avoid hearing their message. Finally, they tell her to investigate "some trouble that has been going on for a long time" (62). It is the vision of herself rejecting the role which the spirits had given her that she finally remembers. However, before she begins to understand what has happened, she listens to her warring self and tries to hang herself. According to Williams, for one who resisted her spiritual duty, this action is not particularly unusual. Williams tells a story of a Lakota boy in the 1880s "who tried to resist following his vision from Double Woman" (30). After his rebellion, the boy committed suicide.

Ephanie, however, hanging from a ceiling pipe, is able to cut herself loose, and this subsequent third fall jars her from her death wish into an understanding and an appreciation of life:

After she had begun to weep, quietly, with relief, with sorrow, with comprehension. Of what had driven her. The grief, the unbearable anguish, the loneliness. The rage. She realized how grateful she was. For air. For life. For pain. Even for the throbbing pain in her throat. (164)

This fall duplicates the fall of Sky Woman (a Seneca-origin myth and the title of a section in Allen's book), who with the help of some animals turned what should have been a fall to her death into life, populating a new world. In Ephanie's case, the fall begins a process of healing and reclaiming what is hers. She must separate the truth from the lies—see how her life could be made one again. Ephanie must see how the Catholicism had acted to reinforce the Euro-American values about gender and sexuality. Euro-American society holds that there are only two genders—male and female; however, many traditional Native American societies offered another alternative for both men and women—a position with "a clearly recognized and accepted social status, often based on a secure place in the tribal mythology" (Williams 2). In the Lakota tradition, for example, one of the Creator sisters was changed to a male so that the Christians could understand how the Creators could give birth to the people. Ephanie must see that her traditional culture would have seen her desire to live with and love women as a spiritual calling. They would have urged her to use the special powers she would have been given by her acceptance of her spiritual duty for the good of the tribe and her clan.

Allen's *The Woman Who Owned the Shadows* is patterned into sections in which the contemporary story parallels the mythic accounts at the beginning of each section. Part II, for instance, begins with a Prologue entitled, "Rite of Exorcism: (The Spruce Dress)" which promises that Ephanie will recover. In the Prologue, the spirits join the patient, aiding her with their power: "She dwells with me." The patient with their help becomes "one who slays alien gods," thereby "sweeping away the sickness" (51–52) until she can accept the gifts of the gods. In the contemporary story, part of Ephanie's healing comes when she recovers her own vision of herself, accepting her strong connection to the ancient tribal power of the sisterhood of the medicine women:

And she understood. For those women, so long lost to her, who she had longed and wept for, unknowing, were the double women, the women who never married, who held power like the Clanuncle, like the power of the priests, the medicine men. Who were not mothers, but who were sisters, born of the same mind, the same spirit. They called each other sister. They were called Grandmother by those who called on them for aid, for knowledge, for comfort, for care. (211)

Ephanie comes to understand how "spirit, creatures and land can occupy a unified whole" (Allen, *Sacred Hoop: Recovering* 124). According to Williams, the role of the man or woman who took on qualities of the other sex, was to act as a mediator not only "between the sexes but between the psychic and the physical—between the spirit and the flesh. . . . They have double vision, with the ability to see more clearly than a single gender perspective can provide" (41–42). But this gift of the spirits was also a burden as Ephanie comes to realize. If her understanding is doubled, in times of trouble there is also double pain and the task of healing:

The curse laid upon her flesh was her gift as well. She knew that with certainty. That she was always, unendingly, aware of the pain. Of the people. Of the air. Of the water. Of the beasts and the birds. She could not escape that knowledge. In every eye, in every mind, the pain lay, blossoming in bewilderment, in blood. They never knew why they suffered. Nor did she. . . . And they also understood the gift, the curse, some of them. . . . They thought she could make them well. (185)

As her room fills with the spirits of the Grandmothers, she is able to join them in their dance and listen to their message. They tell her that "there are no curses. There are only descriptions of what creations there will be" (212). A spirit woman shows Ephanie her destiny—how she fits into the Double Woman pattern:

"It is the sign and the order of the power that informs this life and leads back to Shipap. Two face outward, two inward, the sign of doubling, of order and balance, of the two, the twins, the doubleminded world in which you have lived," she chanted. (207)

Ephanie is told to pass the story—the information—on to the Euro-American woman, Teresa, "the one who waits" (210), and presumably on to us, the readers. By accepting her spiritual duty, Ephanie is healed and the story is complete.

By allowing the reader to participate in the curing ceremony of the novel by following the main character in her own restoration of balance, Allen seeks to restore balance to the community-at-large. Through this the reader is reminded of the power of storytelling and the responsibility of each human to the community. Further, if, as Judy Grahn says in her comment on the back cover, "you come with an honest heart," the novel enables the non-Indian reader to begin to see from a non-Euro-American perspective. To begin to change the Euro-American vision of disconnectedness to one of connectedness would be a "curing" indeed. As Williams notes, a most important function of a curing is a "healing of the mind" (34). Although the novel ends with Ephanie's understanding of her connection to her heritage and although the reader does not see how it will affect her life, Allen's novel is also an important offering to Native American lesbians. She has shown a connection that present-day lesbians might make to a special spiritual heritage and role which such women played in Native American cultures. As Allen says, "It all has to do with spirit, with restoring an awareness of our spirituality as gay people" (quoted in Williams 251).

More generally in the novel, the healing of the main character occurs when she is able to reconnect with the female principle which is exemplified in Thought Woman and her sisters and consists particularly of life and strength—she recovers the ancient qualities of woman who was seen as "strong and powerful," balancing the ancient qualities of man who was seen as having "transient or transitory" qualities (Allen, "Where I Come From" 17). This balancing of qualities where "woman-ness is not of less value than man-ness" (17) allows both the individual and tribe to continue and prosper. The telling of the story allows the listeners/readers to visualize how their experiences fit into the great web of being, the patterns of life. The story and the experiences become one, leading to harmony and healing. By using this journey as a model, we can begin to see how to reclaim our female deities and "the wholistic, pacifistic and spirit-based" (Allen, "Who Is Your Mother?" 39) principles of our grandmothers in order to bring together mind/spirit and body, inanimate and animate, to insure continuance of the earth as well as the individual.

NOTES

1. I follow Malinowski's definition of mythology as "the sacred tradition of a society . . . a body of narratives woven into their culture, dictating their belief, defining their ritual, acting as the chart of their social order and the pattern of their moral behavior" (249).
2. The actual dates for the founding of Laguna are controversial. Many scholars say that it was founded after the Pueblo rebellion against the Spanish in 1680. This time period seems to be selected because Governor Don Pedro Rodriguez Cubero visited the pueblo and named it San Jose de la Laguna in 1669. For instance, see Parsons, 888, and Eggan, 253, for discussions of Laguna's founding. However, Florence Hawley Ellis makes a good argument for its founding being in the thirteenth century (45–46).
3. Allen says that "the goddess who appeared to the Indian Juan Diego in 1659 and who is known as Our Lady of Guadalupe" is represented much like the Laguna concept of the goddess, Iyatiku (Corn Woman or Earth Woman). See Allen, *Sacred Hoop: Recovering*, 26. I believe she is using Guadalupe as symbolically equivalent to Laguna, and in this context, the use also puts more emphasis on the femaleness of the culture Allen is describing.
4. In his book, *The Spirit and the Flesh: Sexual Diversity in American Indian Culture*, Walter Williams describes the Native American women who take on an essentially male social role in their respective cultures as "amazons," for lack of a better term (11).
5. Keres is a language which many of the Pueblo peoples speak, but as other Pueblo peoples belong to other language groups, people from different villages often have difficulty understanding one another. See Dosier, 37 and Parsons, 10–11. Allen is making the point that only the Keres-speaking group is considered to be a "mother-right" people.
6. Because Ephanie is essentially without community, there is also some reference in the novel to her being a "witch," a designation given to those who were seen as causing harm—often someone outside the group.
7. The previous displayed quotation from Allen about the sisters points out some of the problems encountered in looking at the different mythological accounts in the ethnographies where the names have different spellings and change frequently. There are even differences between the versions which Leslie Marmon Silko and Allen use in their novels. Silko uses Nau'ts'ity'i and I'tcts'i-ty'i as the names of the two sisters with Nau'ts'ity'i as the mother of the Indians and I'tcts'ity'i as the mother of the others. Allen uses Iyatiku as mother of the

Indians and Naotsete as the mother of the others. See also Allen's discussion in *Sacred Hoop: Recovering,* 20.

8. See also Scarberry, 106–7, for a discussion of the poem.

WORKS CITED

Allen, Paula Gunn. "The Feminine Landscape of Leslie Marmon Silko's *Ceremony.*" In *Studies in American Indian Literature: Critical Essays and Course Designs,* New York: MLA, 1984, 127–33.

———. "From Raven's Road." In *The New Native American Novel, Works in Progress.* Ed. Mary Dougherty Bartlett, Albuquerque: Univ. of New Mexico Press, 1986.

———. "Grandmother." In *The Third Woman: Minority Women Writers of the United States.* Ed. Dexter Fisher. Boston: Houghton, 1980, 126.

———. Personal Interview. 20 June 1985.

———. "The Sacred Hoop: A Contemporary Indian Perspective on American Indian Literature." In *Literature of the American Indians: Views and Interpretations.* Ed. Abraham Chapman. New York: NAL, 1975, 111–35.

———. *The Sacred Hoop: Recovering the Feminine American Indian Tradition.* Boston: Beacon, 1986.

———. "Symbol and Structure in Native American Literature: Some Basic Considerations." *College Composition and Communication* 24 (1973): 267–70.

———. "Where I Come From God is a Grandmother." *Sojourner: The Women's Forum* (August 1988): 16–18.

———. "Who Is Your Mother? Red Roots of White Feminism." *Sinister Wisdom* 25 (1984): 34–46.

———. *The Woman Who Owned the Shadows.* San Francisco: Spinsters, Ink, 1983.

———. *Wyrds.* San Francisco: Taurean Horn, 1987.

Dosier, Edward P. *The Pueblo Indians of North America.* New York: Holt, 1970.

Eggan, Fred. *Special Organization of the Western Pueblos.* 1950. Rpt. Chicago: Univ. of Chicago Press, 1963.

Garcia, Reyes. "Senses of Place in *Ceremony,*" *MELUS* 10, no. 4 (1983): 46.

Hawley, Florence. "Anthropology of Laguna Pueblo Land Claims." In *Pueblo Indians.* Ed. David Agree Horr. Vol 3. New York: Garland, 1974. 45–46.

Malinowski, Bronislaw. *Sex, Culture, and Myth.* New York: Harcourt, 1962.

Momaday, N. Scott. "I Am Alive." In *The World of the American Indian.* Ed. Jules B. Billard. Washington, D.C.: National Geographic, 1979, 50–54.

Parsons, Elsie Clews. *Pueblo Indian Religion.* Chicago: Univ. of Chicago Press, 1939.

Roscoe, Will, Coordinating Editor. *Living the Spirit: A Gay American Indian Anthology.* New York: St. Martin's, 1988.

Scarberry, Susan J. "Grandmother Spider's Lifeline." In *Studies in American Indian*

Literature: Critical Essays and Course Designs. Ed. Paula Gunn Allen. New York: MLA, 1983. 100–107.

Silko, Leslie Marmon. *Ceremony*. New York: NAL, 1978.

———. "Language and Literature from a Pueblo Perspective." In *English Literature: Opening Up the Canon*. Ed. Leslie A. Fiedler and Houston A. Baker, Jr. Selected papers from the English Institute, New Series, No. 4. Baltimore: The Johns Hopkins University Press, 1981, 55–64.

Williams, Walter L. *The Spirit and the Flesh: Sexual Diversity in American Indian Culture*. Boston: Beacon, 1986.

TWENTY-TWO

Core of the Apple: Mother-Daughter Fusion/Separation in Three Recent Lesbian Plays

Rosemary Curb

Mother Hera kept the magic apple garden in the west, where the Tree of Life was guarded by her sacred serpent. . . . [T]he Great Goddess [was] offering life to her worshippers in the form of an apple. . . . Hidden in the apple's core was the magic pentacle, or sign of Kore. Just as Kore the virgin was hidden in the Mother Earth (Demeter) and represents the World Soul, so her pentacle was hidden in the apple.
— Barbara G. Walker, *Woman's Encyclopedia of Myths and Secrets*

Long after I had announced my lesbian identity in a very public way, I asked my mother how long she had known that I was a lesbian. Initially I was shocked by her answer. Later I thought, "But of course!" She said, "I always knew." Always? *In utero?* Did the obstetrical nurse deposit me into my mother's bed-jacketed arms wrapped in a lavender blanket? Did she say (deadpan as in a cartoon I've seen duplicated frequently): "It's a lesbian!"?

However far back in our lives our mothers "know," actually coming out to one's mother and mutually acknowledging the "L" word is the ultimate Big Scene for most lesbians. No wonder many recent lesbian plays feature this traumatic moment and its repercussions. Why do lesbian daughters fear that coming out will bring rejection and abandonment from their mothers? Why do mothers fear and despise their daughters' lesbianism?

Maiden goddess Kore nestles in the heart/core of the apple mother (Demeter, Ceres, Gaia, all versions of the Earth Mother), just as the lesbian daughter lies in the heart of the maternal labyrinth, untainted by heterosexual invasion or bondage to a husband's patrilineal family. Unlike the heterosexual daughter, the lesbian retains or reclaims the integrity of Kore, who pays no homage to male domination or ownership of her body.

355

The lesbian body/self belongs to her self and to women, as the magic pentacle at the core belongs to the uncored apple.

In *Of Woman Born: Motherhood as Experience and Institution,* Adrienne Rich notes the intimacy of the bond:

This cathexis between mother and daughter—essential, distorted, misused—is the great unwritten story. Probably there is nothing in human nature more resonant with charges than the flow of energy between two biologically alike bodies, one of which has lain in amniotic bliss inside the other, one of which has labored to give birth to the other. The materials are here for the deepest mutuality and the most painful estrangement. . . . Yet this relationship has been minimized and trivialized in the annals of patriarchy. . . . Like intense relationships between women in general, the relationship between mother and daughter has been profoundly threatening to men. (226–27)

According to Rich, the root of much mother-daughter conflict, regardless of sexuality or cultural difference, comes from men's fears of women's bonds and the consequent patriarchal control of the institution of motherhood.

Healthy mother-daughter bonding might, however, become frozen as unhealthy fusion, whether or not the daughter is lesbian. Both mother and daughter grow anxious and fearful about separation. Most psychoanalytic explorations of these separation anxieties assume that both mothers and daughters are heterosexual. Heterosexual daughters, however, are more likely to experience rites of passage which facilitate separation from mothers in socially sanctioned ways. For example, the fusion of mother and daughter is broken when they imagine themselves competing for male attention. When the daughter marries a man and begins a new family, she is considered fully adult—individuated and separate from her mother. The lesbian daughter, on the other hand, has no such clear-cut rite of separation.

Nancy Chodorow postulates that mothering "reproduces" itself generation after generation, since girls learn from their mothers how to mother, just as boys learn to be independent and autonomous: "Women, as mothers, produce daughters with mothering capacities and the desire to mother. These capacities and needs are built into and grow out of the mother-daughter relationship itself" (7).

Lesbian critics, such as Adrienne Rich ("Compulsory Heterosexuality" 23–75) and Pauline Bart (150), have demonstrated the heterosexism implicit in Chodorow's assumption of the universality of the heteronuclear family. Nevertheless, Chodorow's model of the post-Oedipal gender personality development for girls helps to explain the separation anxiety which lesbian daughters in the plays described here experience in disclosing their identities to their mothers. Furthermore, lesbian daughters, whether or not they are biological mothers, are socialized to develop mothering capacities, which may be directed toward their lovers or mothers as well as children.

In the three plays discussed below, heterosexual mothers and lesbian daughters experience terror akin to a fear of annihilation as they separate. The daughters' ambivalent acceptance of their lesbianism and the mothers' homophobia and guilt obsessions fray the mutually nurturing bonds and intensify anxieties. Both mothers and daughters have weak ego boundaries for reasons discussed below in the analyses of the plays. Daughters may be unwilling to let go of the mothers' caretaking for fear of their own lack of independent strength and autonomy. Sometimes they transfer a dependence and need to be nurtured on to their lovers. Mothers, on the other hand, may perceive their daughters' "coming out" as a rebellious phase calculated to cause family turmoil and social embarrassment. Mothers may also experience panic at the prospect of losing their daughters entirely. Both mothers and daughters may perceive one another as extensions of self. Whatever the cause of the fusion or anxiety, mother-daughter separation in the plays discussed below produces profound pain.

Beyond psychological similarities, cultural differences, especially race and class differences, make the coming-out experience which initiates separation unique in each of the plays. In *Ruby Christmas* by Sarah Dreher, a college-educated daughter in her mid-thirties returns to her small-town, middle-class WASP family after having announced her sexual identity to a rigid and resistant mother. The mother makes her all-embracing disapproval of everything from her daughter's sexuality to her daughter's rejection of a professional career brutally clear. In *Going to Seed* by Nancy Rawles, the lesbian daughter rejects her mother's black working-class aspirations and leaves for a predominantly white college and a career as a writer. In *The Lunch* by Michelle Gabow, the lesbian daughter of a Jewish working-class family also rejects her mother's apparent values, while actually living out her mother's never-realized artistic aspirations.

Certain questions may facilitate our analyses of separation anxieties in the plays. How is the daughter's self-worth and ability to separate from her mother affected when the mother responds with disgust or denial to the announcement of her daughter's lesbianism? How do mothers and lovers compete for the daughter's attention and affection? How does the daughter's fear of hurting those she cares about create conflicting loyalties? How does food serve as an emblem of mothering—the core drawing nourishment from the apple, the daughter eating and drinking the body of the mother as communion sacrament?

In *Ruby Christmas* by Sarah Dreher,[1] lesbian daughter Bronwen comes home for the double celebration of Christmas and her parents' fortieth wedding anniversary. Harriet, her mother, listens without protest to the harsh judgments of her neighbor and nemesis, Charlotte, wife of her husband's boss and manipulator of the town's social life and mores. All her married life in Mason, Pennsylvania, Harriet has fabricated a tissue of lies in order to placate the disapproving Charlotte, who plays a negative maternal role in Harriet's life. The town name suggests the clamped-down repressions of life in a middle-class, tight-lidded glass jar. Harriet tries unsuccessfully to force Bronwen to put on a dress and a facade of docile amiability for Charlotte.

To her lover Kelley, Bronwen asserts her "right to be there" for her mother's anniversary, "one of the most important events in her life" (151). Nevertheless, Bronwen feels the paralysis of parental disapproval for her way of life: she has relinquished her position as a research oceanographer to become a lobster trapper for Kelley's Restaurant. She clings to a fantasy past, telling both Kelley and sister-in-law Lorraine: "I was my mother's daughter" (160). Reminiscing about past intimacy (remembering tricks her mother and she played on her father at the dinner table or jokes they whispered to each other in church) feels safer for Bronwen than the present confrontation. She fondly recalls falling asleep on the porch glider on summer evenings to the consoling sound of her mother's voice chatting amiably with another woman.

Harriet also grieves for the lost bond with her daughter which she tries to awaken by showing Bronwen's baby pictures to Kelley and remembering her terror when Bronwen disappeared one day at the beach. At present, however, mother and daughter bait each other with mutual insecurities and hostilities. When Harriet snaps, "I don't know what I did to make you hate me," Bronwen replies, "I know what *I* did to make you hate *me*. I'm a lesbian" (162). Both grieve and challenge the other to defend her life and her values.

In her unpublished master's thesis, Jill Dolan notes, "The lesbian breaks the rules by refusing to submit to her heterosexual training in the family" (22). Using the terminology in *Bound by Love* by Paula Webster and Lucy Gilbert, Dolan demonstrates that the lesbian daughter refuses to be the

Good Girl or mother's helper as well as the Princess, who aligns herself with the father's authority, and falls uncomfortably, therefore, into the category of Bad Girl. Bronwen's uneasy separation from her mother leaves her yearning for a nostalgic Good Girl past, which may never have existed but which is certainly lost forever to her.

Aware of Bronwen's self-destroying anguish, Kelley confides to Harriet, "She needs your approval terribly. . . . You're very much alike. She loves you. She didn't come here to hurt you. She came to please you" (156). Playing the Bad Girl, Bronwen taunts her mother: "Why don't you trade me in on a new model?" (156) She believes that her mother never wanted her to grow up and out of her control. Bronwen tells Kelley:

You know, when I was a little kid, she'd pick me up and swing me around and sit me down on the counter in the kitchen while she cooked. She'd look over at me, and there'd be such . . . joy in that look. But something changed over the years. It wasn't anything I did. Something changed in her. One day I caught her watching me. The way she stared . . . it was as though she . . . wanted to kill me. (158)

It is also likely that Harriet is trying to kill the Bad Girl in herself through her disapproval of Bronwen.

Luise Eichenbaum and Susie Orbach provide some insight into Harriet's ambivalence. They identify three major aspects of the mother-daughter interaction: (1) the mother identifies with her daughter because of their shared gender and feels as if she is "reproducing herself" (40); (2) she projects onto the daughter feelings she has about herself, "seeing her daughter not as a separate person but as an extension of herself" (41); and (3) she "unconsciously acts toward her infant daughter in the same way she acts internally toward the little-girl part of herself" (44). Over the years, Harriet has responded to Bronwen with contradictory feelings arising out of her own confusion about having needs. She vacillates wildly between tenderness and nurturing on one hand and punishment and deprivation on the other. What Harriet seeks to kill in Bronwen is her own needy "little girl" self. Dimly regretting her own emotional deprivation, she resents Bronwen's perceived freedom.

At a similar but more positive point of recognition in an autobiographical story in *Different Daughters: A Book by Mothers of Lesbians*, Reva Tow marvels at the wider multicultural horizons and racially mixed experiences of her lesbian daughter: "I felt twinges of envy. How narrow my corridor of life compared to Nat's. I did have three close friends, but their lives were much the same as mine. We never ventured out of our white middle-class world. It had never occurred to me to go beyond the familiar boundaries" (Rafkin 42). With less insight than Reva Tow, Harriet seems paralyzed within her narrow confines.

In *Ruby Christmas* Bronwen learns that the only way to win Harriet's approval is to stifle or hide her emotional cravings, disappointments, angers, and anything that separates her from her mother. So painful is her mother's rejection, that Bronwen contemplates regressing to a younger, more acceptable self in order to win maternal approval:

She used to love me. . . . I was her little girl. Is that what she wants me to be, Kelley? Her little girl? Because if that's what she wants, that's what I'll be. Why the hell won't she touch me? (185)

Ironically it was Bronwen's uncomfortable separation from her mother that led to her coming out: "I never should have told her the truth about me. But I hated lying and pretending and making up imaginary boyfriends. It made me feel so far away from her" (184). However, the daughter's attempt to diminish the distance created by dishonesty provokes the even greater distance of homophobia: "She looked at me, put her cup down, walked to the sink, and threw up" (185).

Despite Harriet's nonaffirming, even horrified responses created by her rigid homophobia, the play offers glimpses of earlier efforts to provide her daughter with a more independent life than her own. Charlotte snaps, "You indulge that girl, Harriet. You always have. Your mistake was in sending her to college. Lanse always says education ruins a woman" (142). Harriet hoped, however, that escape from Mason might liberate her daughter.

The town itself seems lethal. Kelley notices that the trees lining the streets of Mason have the limbs cut off so that they are only trunks and twigs: "If they do that to their trees, what do they do to their children?" (151) Harriet's foil and confidante, Adele, who has moved from Mason, calls the town a Vampire. In fact, blaming the town for her painful separation saves Bronwen from directly confronting her mother's rejection.

Although Harriet does not change any attitudes from the beginning to the end of the play, she accepts responsibility for her reversal of fortune and catastrophe: final severing of all bonds with her daughter. Long before the play opens she has chosen the conservative values of the town and the stability of her marriage to a selfish and demanding husband above her daughter's needs. Although Bronwen had a childhood surrounded by material comforts, Harriet describes her own childhood of poverty as explanation for having sold herself to the town's leading capitalist family.

Jean Shinoda Bolen describes the destructive Demeter type of mother as withholding approval the more independent her daughter grows: "She experiences the child's growing autonomy as an emotional loss for herself" (176). When Bronwen leaves, she sadly asks her friend Adele, "I'm never going to see her again, am I? She was the joy of my life, once. . . . I gave her everything I never had, and she didn't want it" (188–89). At the end Harriet experiences the final tragic recognition of her self-chosen fate.

Ruby Christmas offers balm to heal the wounds of the separation for the lesbian daughter facing maternal rejection. In an afterword, Sarah Dreher dedicates the admittedly autobiographical play to her mother's memory, noting that although she never acknowledged her lesbianism to her mother and thus avoided the fight that would have resulted in permanent separation, she watched her mother gradually change "into the angry, insecure, brittle Harriet of the play" (191).

Going to Seed by Nancy Rawles,[2] presents a more optimistic outcome for the mother-daughter struggle to separate and to establish healthy boundaries based on consciousness of difference and mutual respect. Three generations of an all-female, working-class black family meet in Vivian's small apartment in an inner-city Los Angeles neighborhood overrun with street thugs. Most of the play's activity takes place in the vicinity of the dining table in celebration of family meals: Easter breakfast in Act I, Easter dinner in Act II, and a birthday celebration with cake for Vivian in Act III.

The play opens with a fantasy meal representing Vivian's feelings about her daughters' treatment of her. She comes home weary from her job as supermarket checker, plops a pizza on the table, and invites her two daughters to the table. She begins saying grace when the twenty-nine-year-old daughter, Paula, home for Easter from a failed marriage and a boring job in Chicago, dances in, wearing a swimsuit and carrying a blaring radio. She pays no attention to Vivian as she flips through the newspaper looking for an apartment and a job. Twenty-one-year-old Angela dashes in, puts her typewriter on the table and continues typing, also paying no attention to her mother. All Vivian's attempts to reach her fail, until Angela grabs a piece of pizza and heads for the door saying, "This is great. I know I'll never find cooking as good as yours" (7), oblivious to the fact that her mother has not baked the pizza but spent her hard-earned money in order to please and nurture her daughter. Vivian plays out her separation anxiety: "You're just going to walk off and leave me here? . . . But who's going to take care of me while you're gone? . . . You'd leave your mother hostage to a street gang while you run off to some college?" (8) Vivian has been so fused to her daughter that Angela's departure feels to her like an amputation.

Toward the end of the play, Vivian's mother, Irene, comments, "It's like Angela gave life to you and not the other way around" (60a). Later in the play we learn that when Vivian became pregnant with her second child, her husband, Floyd, left her because he didn't want any more babies to take care of. "He wanted a mother," Vivian flatly states (60b). Since Angela's birth Vivian has had a close, symbiotic, almost fused bond with her daughter. Since her daughters have grown and moved away, Vivian has been raising a pitiful little garden reminiscent of the spindly plant which symbolizes the optimism of Lena Younger in Lorraine Hansberry's A *Raisin in the Sun*. Vivian compares mothering to gardening. In her tiny garden plants can barely survive. All of Angela's life, her mother has struggled with limited means and opportunities. In a racist and sexist culture, the pinnacle of achievement for her is being "Checker of the Month" and having her photograph displayed in front of the manager's booth. When she asks Angela what college can teach her that her mother cannot, Angela reminds her that she's not "accredited"—neither in society at large which devalues an aging working-class black woman nor in the world of Angela's ambition.

Musing on Angela's lesbianism, Vivian can't understand how the daughter to whom she has always felt connected can be so unlike her mother:

She was *my* child. Paula was somebody else's too. But Angela was all mine. I wanted her to be strong. I wanted her to be brave, independent. Lord knows I took care with that child. I just don't understand it. Most things, you plant them, and they come up straight. (99)

Vivian's word *straight* operates in several ways. Vivian fears her daughter's deviance, which she considers unhealthy and socially crippling.

Both mother and daughter fail to be what the other seeks in the mirror of mother-daughter fused bonding. Instead, they reflect each other's inadequacies. Angela's separation anxiety builds to a climax with her fear of rejection by Vivian when she tells her she is a lesbian. Because she has always felt fused to her mother, Angela has what Chodorow describes as weak ego boundaries: "From the retention of preoedipal attachments to their mother, growing girls come to define and experience themselves as continuous with others; their experience of self contains more flexible or permeable ego boundaries" (169). Flexible ego boundaries may enable the lesbian daughter to experience empathy or compassion more deeply, but may also complicate her struggle for independence and separation from her mother.

Furthermore, Angela's anxiety in anticipation of her mother's possible rejection separates her from her lover, Michelle, who is jealous of Angela's attachment to her mother. Ironically Angela's lover entered her life in the role of "mother." Michelle hosts a satiric phone-in radio show called "Your Mother" on which she dishes out "good mother" advice and "bad mother" insults to people who phone in. One night before the play opens, Angela has phoned in for advice about her mother. At the time the play opens, Angela has been living with Michelle for about a year but has fled, following a quarrel, to her mother's apartment. Thus Angela vacillates in her need for nurturing between her lover and her mother, failing to establish healthy boundaries with either of them. At the point of crisis depicted in the play, Michelle is losing patience with Angela's confusion about her sexual identity:

What are you waiting for? Your mother's approval? . . . All year long your mother's been crying over our bed. . . . My mother didn't want me. She told me so. My hope of being loved by her died before she did. But I still *wanted* it. I still fantasized that, in a crunch, with the whole world against me, she would stand by me. Just because I was hers. (38–39)

Michelle illustrates that it is possible to survive a mother's rejection.

In agony about her rift with Michelle, Angela comes out to her sister, Paula, who attempts to deny Angela's lesbianism by reminding her that as a journalist she has a habit of siding with every oppressed group, as if she didn't belong to enough outsider categories already: "You always like to take things one step further. Being a Black person isolates you. Being a woman imprisons you. But being gay makes you a leper. So, why just be unpopular when you can be booed off the stage? Go for the gusto!" (62) Despite Paula's warnings to keep her lesbian identity hidden, Angela tells Vivian for the same reason Bronwen does—the need for honesty to break down the barrier: "It's like I'm lying to her all the time. The person who comes home is not really me" (64–65). Vivian responds to the revelation by withdrawing to her garden, especially when Michelle arrives for Easter Sunday dinner.

Refusing to accept her daughter's lover, Vivian indulges in feeling sorry for herself because she believes that her mother, daughters, and, worst of all, her daughter's lover are taking her for granted. Michelle's enthusiasm for Vivian's yams, which she has never eaten before, momentarily wins Vivian. But after dinner Vivian vehemently rejects her lesbian daughter:

VIVIAN: I want you to leave.
ANGELA: I'm not leaving.
VIVIAN: This is *my* house! Why did you come here?
ANGELA: Because I belong here. This is *home* for me.
VIVIAN: *You haven't been home all year!* I waited for you. I waited for you to call or write. You didn't make a move. I don't care *where* you are, *what* you are doing. And, then, you show up at my door, and I'm supposed to be happy to see you?
ANGELA: "I don't want any of *that* in my house." Now, how am I supposed to interpret that? What am I supposed to do? Keep coming home to this rejection? You treat me like a stranger.
VIVIAN: You *are* a stranger! I don't know *who* you are. Angela isn't this way.
ANGELA: Angela's changed, Mama. Angela's grown up. Angela belongs to herself now.
VIVIAN: *Not in her mother's house!* (92–93)

Vivian's desperate need to have her values win over her daughter's echoes a similar clash of values between Mama and Beneatha in A *Raisin in the Sun,* when Mama forces Beneatha to say, "In my mother's house there is still God" (39).

In the short third act, both Paula and her grandmother try to mend the rift between Angela and Vivian by pointing to the obvious truth of the intensity of love between mother and daughter. Vivian's acceptance of Angela also echoes Lena Younger's acceptance of her children, Beneatha and Walter Lee in A *Raisin in the Sun.* Vivian states, "You are my *children.* If I didn't love you, then who else would? But you can't look to children for support, Angela"(102a). After Angela moves back in with Michelle, Vivian phones Michelle on "Your Mother" for advice, widening the circle of nurturing. Vivian can embrace the motherless Michelle, who plays "Mother" to the anonymous radio world.

In an earlier one-act version of *Going to Seed,* entitled "Angela" and featured in the 1985 Broadcloth series of At the Foot of the Mountain Theater in Minneapolis, Angela sends her mother a copy of her coming-out editorial in the college newspaper. Lesbians who write or who are in the public eye may announce their lesbianism to parents through the media. The support and/or fury of the whole world can perhaps buffer the anticipated maternal explosion. In Rafkin's *Different Daughters,* an actual working-class, heterosexual black mother of a prominent lesbian daughter tells a story with circumstances similar to the ones created by Rawles. The daughter announced on a television news report that her lesbianism was a factor in the discrimination suit she was fighting. Rheba Fontenot, the mother, said, "I felt betrayed. I felt anger. I felt embarrassment" (Rafkin 82–84).

Before Vivian can assess her own feelings of anger and betrayal or determine whether she thinks Angela is going through a rebellious phase or was led into lesbianism by Girl Scouts, a gang of homophobic fraternity boys attack and rape Angela. In the face of external violence, Michelle and Vivian rally together to support Angela. They admit to each other that Angela's love for each of them is good for her. Vivian recalls how happy Angela was when she first found Michelle, even though it broke Vivian's heart to think of Angela moving away from her. Vivian avenges her daughter's attack with Demeter-like fury by throwing blood on the doorposts of fraternity houses. When campus police try to remove her, she pelts them with radishes from her garden. At a rally she speaks to two thousand people: "They say *I* should be shamed because my daughter loves a woman. I should be shamed to love my daughter. Well, I'm not shamed. I love my daughter. And they going to pay for what they did to her" (54–55).

In both versions Vivian's homophobia and separation anxiety are transformed into pride and strengthened maternal love. Vivian comes to accept her daughter's lesbianism and her lover. Angela comes to a fresh appreciation of her mother as a strong and separate person. She recognizes that she does not have to take care of her mother nor does she need to make her lover a substitute mother.

The Lunch by Michelle Gabow[3] also weaves realistic scenes into a ritual meal. In the central narrative, Leah, a middle-aged mother, and Rachael, her adult daughter, are having lunch in Gimbels' basement. Mother and daughter are named for the biblical sisters married to Jacob, legendary patriarch of the twelve tribes of Israel. Shadow or "dybbuk" characters named Leye and Rachel play waitresses and act out past scenes in Leah's and Rachael's lives. Giving mother and daughter the names of biblical sisters suggests that under patriarchy all women suffer as comrades and sisters. The hierarchical power of mother over daughter separates women.

In *The Lunch* two generations suffer from separation anxiety. The play opens with the grandmother's funeral, a fantasy sequence in which Leah forces Rachael to look at her grandmother's body in the coffin. In the third act Rachael recalls looking at her grandmother, Buby Gold, in the open casket: "I saw nothing but a green skinned body, a lifeless face made up like a doll when she never wore a drop, and bobbed hair instead of a long braid that once haloed the top of her head" (61). The plays closes with Leah begging her dead mother: "Momma, don't leave. I'm not ready yet. It's too short. Please stay. I have so much to tell you." The ghost of Buby Gold replies, "My Lenilah, it's time to let go now. Let me have my freedom" (78). Considering how difficult Leah finds it to let her mother leave her, we can imagine that her relationship with her adult daughter will manifest similar fusion.

In an opening fantasy Leah calls out to Rachael to rescue her from drowning. At first Rachael cannot see her mother; then when she sees her she says she's scared: "You never taught me to swim" (3). In this case, swimming is a metaphor for living. The mother is asking the daughter to save her life, to give her life, to be dragged down by the weight of the mother's need. But the daughter protests that the mother never taught her how to survive because she never really acknowledged the daughter as a separate person. Leah obviously never learned to swim herself, since she got married when she was just beginning to discover who she was and what talents she had.

Leah's fears of aging intensify her fears of separating from her dead mother. "I'm an old lady orphan," Leah tells Rachael and calls herself "a tower of strength" at the time of Buby's death, making all the funeral arrangements, even though her three brothers had always called her "meshugeneh" (crazy). "When it comes down to it, the girl does all the work; there's nothing like a daughter" (60). Her statement is not only a warning to Rachael but her own hope that she did not fail her mother. In her grief Leah remembers her mother taking her to dance contests once a month at the synagogue and her joy at her daughter's victory: "I remember your Buby's face when I ran up and kissed her with my trophy. It was the first and only time I ever saw pride in her eyes for me. You know she always tried to discourage me about being professional, but I remember that day and her eyes" (61). Nevertheless Buby discouraged her daughter's other physical adventures, such as forbidding her to ride her brother's motorcycle. Like Rachael, Leah also had artistic and professional ambitions which separated her from her mother's domestic bondage. Leah remembers hiding a book of Van Gogh paintings, which her sister had sent her when Rachael was a child, in the bottom of the bathroom clothes hamper.

Dramatis personae are listed as *Menu,* suggesting that mothers and daughters not only feed one another but also feed off the other in real and symbolic ways. Jane Gallop refers to a sixteen-page monograph by Luce Irigary, *Et l'une ne bouge pas sans l'autre,* in which the title ("And one cannot move without the other") evokes "paralysis and the impossibility of separation" of the daughter from the mother because of the daughter's drawing her essential sustenance from the mother: "The oral relation ought to be one in which the daughter absorbs (from) the mother. Yet that transaction is confused with the mother's absorbing the daughter, since the difference between the two is not stable and since absorption is precisely a process which undermines boundary distinctions" (114).

In Jewish culture, food is significant and essential because it represents familial love. Nevertheless, perhaps out of a fear of provoking the violence of the past, Leah meets her daughter in public rather than at home. Rachael asks, "Mom, why do you suppose we always go to restaurants to talk? I mean why can't we have these lunches at home? What are we afraid of . . . a lunch with my mother?" (10) Both fear rejection by the other leading to a final terrifying separation.

In the first scene Rachael also frets that her appearance gives her lesbianism away: "What possessed me to get a haircut now? It's soooo butch. And where are those goddam enamel earrings when I need them?" (12) Much to Rachael's surprise, Leah approves her haircut and, by symbolic extension, her daughter's lesbian body, despite Rachael's terror and avoidance. Leah slyly states, "I may know more about *you* than *you* think" (21).

Rachael reveals her own homophobia and fear of rejection, voicing fears similar to those expressed by Bronwen and Angela: "Believe me, I wanted to tell you. You can't imagine how sick I am of lying. But to tell the truth, I thought you would have a real live, large nervous breakdown, and I didn't know if I could handle that right now" (21). Conscious of protecting her mother's feelings, Rachael fails to recognize that she is also deferring her mother's anticipated disapproval.

Carol Gilligan has noted that girls and women are more apt to consider the context of choices, relationships involved, and who might get hurt when they make moral decisions. They are more constrained by the complexities of choices. "Sensitivity to the needs of others and the assumption of responsibility for taking care lead women to attend to voices other than their own and to include in their judgment other points of view" (16). Both Angela and Rachael defer coming out in order to avoid causing their mothers pain. Taking care of their mothers—that is "mothering" them—also defers the pain of separation. Daughters may take on the role of educating their mothers about feminism—Angela through her newspaper articles and Rachael through her painting. Many of the mothers whose statements appear in Rafkin's *Different Daughters: A Book by Mothers of Lesbians* report attending conferences on feminism and gay rights with their daughters.

Despite her struggle against homophobia, Leah offers clichéd responses. She regrets not having grandchildren, and she quips, "I really don't understand—you don't look like (PAUSE) that" (22). This ironically parallels "You don't look Jewish," the punchline of a self-hating, anti-Jewish joke Leah later tells her dead mother, standing over her grave.

In the second act, the Dessert, Leah asks Rachael about her recent painting. Rachael replies that she couldn't bring it because she feels "unfinished" about her painting and herself. Leah says, "That's the way I feel about my children" (37), acknowledging that Rachael's paintings are like children. Rachael imagines showing her mother her symbolic painting: "Two rocks facing each other and an abyss for a table. An abyss. There's so much to discover. The rocks are the shape of a woman's body. The abyss, the womb. But Mom, which one of us is birthing?" (10) Revealing her dark secret self to her mother, Rachael is revealing her lesbianism. She suggests that the mothering and birthing go both ways. Not only does Rachael nurture the mother, but she gives birth to ideas and images in her painting: "But Mom, in that abyss, I found color. Rainbows on color. And a mauve came out and swept my body. It was warm and dewy. It enveloped me or was it you? Who is the abyss birthing?" (11).

Recognizing their mutual mirroring provokes matrophobia, that is, according to Adrienne Rich, "the fear . . . not of one's mother or of motherhood but of *becoming one's mother*" (*Of Woman Born* 237). Conversely the mother may fear becoming her daughter—that is, "filiaphobia." Symptomatic of her filiaphobia, Leah absently asks, "Can a mother catch a daughter's disease?" (45). She means, of course, Rachael's lesbianism. Oddly enough, Leah connects her question with a memory of her first period and Buby slapping her in the face saying, "It's tradition, mein Leah. It's tradition" (43). In Jewish women's tradition, the slap which brings color to the cheeks reminds the daughter to get ready to face womanhood. Is a daughter's coming to maturity symbolic of her loss of innocence and share in Eve's curse? Does the mother indirectly pass on the father's horror and hatred of the power of women's blood? Has the daughter now become the sexual competitor of the mother?

To see the deepest secrets of the daughter requires the mother to recognize those qualities in herself. The mother must accept the daughter in herself and herself in the daughter. If the daughter is a lesbian and the mother is homophobic, such recognition is horrifying to the mother, and the mother's horror arouses both separation anxiety in the daughter as well as self-hatred.

Cross-culturally, mothers may separate from daughters as token torturers of daughters, passing on patriarchal rules and physical bondage. For example, Mary Daly describes such institutionalized violence against women as Chinese foot-binding and African clitoridectomy, in addition to daily violence against women in Western culture. Jill Dolan notes that lesbian theater redefines family boundaries:

Mother and daughter embrace through the bars of patriarchal authority that imprisons them both. The rule of the man's world always mediates between them: from mother to daughter, from daughter to her own daughter. Lesbianism can be seen as rejection of the traditional, nuclear family paradigm that has fostered this relationship. ("Toward" 20)

Rachael asserts that her creative process is nurtured by her lesbian identity. "It's bound to come out in my paintings," she tells Leah, who mutters under her breath, "My enemies should live so long" (37). Rachael fears disclosing herself through her art in much the same way that she fears being a social embarrassment to her mother. Nevertheless, Rachael criticizes her mother for speaking Yiddish because Rachael doesn't understand it. Just as Leah considers Rachael's flaunting of lesbian culture an embarrassment, so does Rachael reject her mother's Yiddish speech because it embarrasses her.

Leah must uncover the darkest secrets, her own rage and violence toward Rachael, in order to heal the wounds between them and to separate as adults from each other. Only through the distancing of children's games can the abused Rachael acknowledge her fear:

A mother and a daughter had a fight
The mother punched the daughter right in the nose

What color was her blood?
Purple. . . . P-U-R-P-L-E, Purple."

(5)

In the third act titled "The Check," Rachael, playing her adolescent self, acts out with dybbuk Leye, playing Leah as a young mother, what was apparently a frequent ritual with her mother. Leye as Leah screams woman-hating, Jew-hating, self-hating threats of violence and dismemberment at her fleeing daughter. "Don't run away from me, young lady! You made me pay for those goddam painting lessons, so you better get your Jewish ass in here and paint. . . . If you make me go and get you, so help me God I'll kill you for the whole neighborhood to see" (49). Playing herself as young mother, Leah seeks her mother's advice and consolation on the telephone: "Mom, I'm scared. I hit Rachael. . . . There are bruises . . . I can't be a balabustra. I don't know how to be a good mother. . . . Either she's going to send me to the nut house or I'll kill her" (50). Buby Gold offers Leah no help for the terror she feels in the face of her violent desires and actions. She tells Leah, "Be happy" (50). By denying her daughter's cry for help, Buby Gold perpetuates and condones the violence of child abuse.

Adrienne Rich calls mothers' actual violence and violent fantasies against their children, especially daughters, "the heart of maternal darkness" (*Of Woman Born* 260–86). When a mother actually kills her children and her shocking and "unnatural" crime is splashed across the headlines, such a woman becomes a scapegoat. Through her negative example, other mothers learn to repress violence, rather than to recognize the disease as the institution of motherhood itself and not one woman's bizarre aberration. "The scapegoat is also an escape valve: through her the blind passions and the blind raging waters of a suppressed knowledge are permitted to churn their way so that they need not emerge in less extreme situations as lucid rebellion" (283).

Leah cannot see her violence in its political context because, like other women, who act out their violence against the oppressions which stifle and constrain them on those closest and most vulnerable, she perceives her situation as an individual problem for which she is to blame. Making women scapegoats prevents us from seeing that the social construction of motherhood under patriarchy as perpetually self sacrificing creates such repression and bottled up fury in women that it is amazing that more women don't kill their children.

On the other hand, as a corollary to her matrophobia, Rachael fears developing all the diseases in her matrilineage. Since her mother had cancer and her grandmother died of it (all the while denying its existence or that she was dying), Rachael fears that every lump or sore she develops is the first sign of cancer. Mostly she fears becoming "meshugeneh" (crazy) like Buby Gold and Leah. Not allowing anyone to come too close to her shields her, she thinks, from facing these deepest terrors.

The dybbuk selves dramatize Rachael's ambivalence regarding sexual and emotional intimacy with her lover, Donna. Leye as Donna says, "You always push me away when I need you. . . . You hide. You're hiding right now. . . . Let me closer. I won't hurt" (55). But Rachel as Rachael screams, "Get the hell away from me!" Having the same shadow selves play Rachael in relation to her mother and to her lover demonstrates that Rachael's fear of intimacy is actually fear of her mother and herself and her mother's potential violence as well as fear of her own submerged and vengeful rage against her mother. The child self in Rachael still fears that her mother may actually kill her as threatened. The adult Rachael has internalized the woman-hating culture. She believes that her mother's hatred and hostility have ample justification and that as daughter mirroring mother she is responsible for her mother's rage and deserves to be hurt.

Thus mother and daughter are locked in murderous bondage, blaming themselves and each other for the effects of an institution neither of them created. They dance their bondage to Leah's poem:

If I had my way
There would have been no children . . .
I hit hard.
Your whining came into my sleep,
even my sleep.
I tied your legs that danced
in our neighbor's houses by day
and on my body at night.
In the day I shut your mouth good.
But your body danced in my dreams.
Your flailing bruised arms choking
even my dreams
that were silent wails of the heart
for us,
my Rachael,
for us.
If I'd had my way

I would have had no children.
But you had your way and had your way, and had your way,
and had your way, and had your way.

(67)

Leah resents her lesbian daughter's rule-breaking, her independence, her creativity, her joy and desire in her body through dance. Rachael's parallel dance/poem reveals herself as "private Rachael/ waiting for the slap to come,/ and come, and come" (68). Leah's repetition "and had your way" parallels Rachael's repetition "and come." Such repeated phrases reveal that both mother and daughter perceive themselves as powerless. Using the theories of Jean Baker Miller, Coppélia Kahn analyzes "the false idealization of the selfless altruistic mother" (78).

The Lunch concludes with Rachael, Leah, and Buby Gold offering each other tentative affirmations. Leah says, "I'm proud of you—of all of it you know" (76). Rachael concedes that her mother has probably had her own share of closets. The play ends on a note of hesitant forgiveness.

Each of the three plays resolves the mother-daughter fusion with a reassertion of the need to separate. All three daughters have actually moved out of the maternal home before the plays open. The plays dramatize the daughters' homecoming. In the case of *The Lunch,* the mother ironically finds it safer not to meet her daughter in the memory-laden home. In contrast to the black and Jewish mothers, the white mother in *Ruby Christmas* does not offer to feed her daughter anything but alcohol, the socially acceptable tranquilizer of middle-class family rituals. Although neither Vivian nor Leah spends time cooking, they both urge their daughters to eat the food they buy for them as symbolic extensions of the mothers' bodies. As in many modern American plays, eating and drinking rituals frame family combat.

Ruby Christmas maintains the linear and chronological Ibsen style of fourth-wall, realistic domestic tragedy. Dreher follows the tradition of American realism created by Lillian Hellman and Arthur Miller. For lesbian audiences, Jane Chambers popularized domestic problem plays with lesbian content in the 1970s. Since the death of Jane Chambers, Sarah Dreher has been the primary lesbian playwright of Ibsenesque social problem plays centered in domestic conflict. The conflict in *Ruby Christmas,* for example, is caused by sexism and homophobia. Some of the problems discussed are fear and hatred of homosexuals and homosexuality, lack of education and self-determination for women, and negative constraints caused by conformity to feminine gender stereotypes. Although the play ends in catastrophe with little catharsis, viewers and readers probably consider the destroyed relationship between Harriet and Bronwen, as well as their mutual diminished feelings of self-worth and increased feelings of helplessness and hopelessness, as personal problems amenable to individual solutions. Only viewers with feminist consciousness will see the political context of the choices available to both mother and daughter.

The other two plays use nonrealistic sequences in order to present the psychic and dream life of characters and the interplay of memories and fantasies embedded in a decipherable linear narrative. Vivian's opening dream in *Going to Seed* dramatizes her feelings of rejection by her daughters. Angela's dream of meeting her mother, grandmother, and sister at Venice Beach (California) dramatizes her wish fulfillment for each of them to be autonomous, creative, independent, and happy. The frequent sounds of the "Your Mother" radio show in the family apartment illustrate Angela's divided loyalties between mother and lover.

The Lunch embeds creativity and play through childhood games, biblical stories, and long-standing repeated arguments within the ritual of lunch at a restaurant. Rachael's morning ritual of greeting the painting in progress and the ego-tripping superwoman fantasy message on her answering machine dramatize her daily hopes and fears. Ritual violence demonstrates the power dialectic from mother to daughter: Buby Gold's giving Leah the ritual slap when Leah's menses begin becomes transformed in the next generation to Leah beating Rachael so brutally that she is covered with bruises. Surrounding the contemporary lunch games are the biblical rituals of the sisters and wives of Jacob. The nonrealistic sequences—fantasies, dreams, rituals—reinforce the collectivity of the individual struggles portrayed.

Adrienne Rich asks that "the institution of motherhood . . . be destroyed" (*Of Woman Born* 286) in order for women's bonding to flourish. Following Rich's admonition, current lesbian theorists note the oppressive erasure of lesbian identity, not to mention class and race difference, in the overuse of the motherhood paradigm in feminist critiques of patriarchy. Jeffner Allen states: "Motherhood is dangerous to women because it continues the structure within which females must be women and mothers and, conversely, because it denies to females the creation of a subjectivity and world that is open and free" (315).

Jill Dolan considers focus on mother-daughter relationships in cultural feminist theater to be unfortunate (*Spectator* 86). She critiques its absence of explicit lesbian desire. In an article on "woman-conscious drama" I state, "An erotic charge pulses through women's collective self-consciousness. In the mirror of play we see and show sister, mother, daughter, lover, self" (316). Such focus on female bonding, according to Dolan, "remains defined by the ideology of sexual difference" and therefore fails to critique the representation of gender itself (*Spectator* 99). There is ample room for debate about which theatrical forms best serve feminist political ends. Meanwhile, the representation of the mother-daughter bond remains the central paradigm of feminist drama in the United States of the past two decades.

To return to my opening image, I recommend the goddess Kore as patron of young lesbian daughters. According to Barbara G. Walker, Kore is "Holy Virgin, inner soul of Mother Earth (Demeter); a name so widespread, that it must have been one of the earliest designations of the World Shakti or female spirit of the universe" (514). Kore is confused with and in later myths identified with Persephone, who was Queen of the Underworld long before the story of abduction and rape by Hades. The Eleusinian Mysteries celebrated the Triple Goddess as three points of a turning triangle: maiden, mother, crone (786). Incidentally, both *Going to Seed* and *The Lunch* represent the Triple Goddess by three generations of women, in which the lesbian daughter remains the perpetual maiden.

How did power slip from mothers in these prehistoric, life-affirming, woman-centered cultures? Azizah al-Hibri postulates that male fear of death led to male ownership of children as a hedge against mortality once the male role in reproduction was understood (82–86). Eva Feder Kittay considers that male "womb envy" led to a systematic separation of generative and nurturing activities and a devaluation of everything female in opposition to masculine physical dominance (105–13). For the last several thousand years under patriarchy, as evidenced in history, art, and literature, motherhood has enslaved women so that women's maturity serves to perpetuate patriarchy.

Mothers and daughters can never be entirely separated. The healthier the separation of mother and daughter, the more likely the lesbian daughter can form loving bonds with other women. Lovers can never replace the mother but always shadow her in some fashion. In healthy lesbian relationships both women mother the other out of the strength of their love rather than the weakness of mutually unfulfilled needs.

The seed buried in the magic pentacle at the apple's core "remembers" the living tree of mother-right. The lesbian daughter embodies the matri-lineage of the magic apple garden of no-man's-land far more than her heterosexual sisters who are given by fathers to husbands in the bonds of matrimony. It matters little that most lesbians do not have biological daughters, since all women can claim genetic memory of that time before fathers claimed power over women. Re-membering ancient sacred bonds might free both daughters and mothers to separate freely and lovingly.

NOTES

1. Sarah Dreher, a practicing clinical psychologist living in Amherst, Massachusetts, is best known to lesbian readers as the author of the Stoner McTavish mystery and adventure novels. Her play *8 × 10 Glossy* was recognized by the Alliance for Gay and Lesbian Artists in the Entertainment Industry for "responsible portrayal of lesbian characters and issues." That play and *Ruby Christmas,* both of which have been produced several times, are published in *Places, Please! The First Anthology of Lesbian Plays,* edited by Kate McDermott. In 1988 New Victoria published five new plays under the title *Lesbian Stages.*

2. Nancy Rawles has written and produced several plays in addition to the two discussed in this chapter. *Nothing But a Lie* was produced at a community theater in Chicago in 1987. *Going to Seed* was produced at Rhinoceros Theatre in San Francisco in 1988.

3. Michelle Gabow, originally from Philadelphia but currently living in Jamaica Plain, Massachusetts, has been writing and acting in the Boston area for fifteen years. *The Lunch,* her second play, was produced in Jamaica Plain in 1988. Her new comic drama, *The Knock Knock Joke,* which explores grieving, and *The Queen of Swords,* a video play about a homeless poet, are being produced by the Women's Theatre Project and Wisebird Productions. As a commitment to searching out powerful voices which often go unheard, Michelle teaches creative writing to women and street kids. She sees community theater drawing both professional and nonprofessional actors to create productive, lesbian, and culturally diverse productions. In a personal letter to me, she states, "Writing is always a celebration of my roots as a Jewish woman and all the many wandering souls travelling inside me, crazy to come out" (15 February 1989).

WORKS CITED

Allen, Jeffner. *Lesbian Philosophy.* Palo Alto, Calif.: Institute of Lesbian Studies, 1986.
Bart, Pauline. "Review of Chodorow's *The Reproduction of Mothering.*" In *Mothering:*

Essays in Feminist Theory. Ed. Joyce Trebilcot. Totowa, N.J.: Rowman & Allenheld, 1983. 147–52.

Bolen, Jean Shinoda. *Goddesses in Everywoman: A New Psychology of Women.* New York: Harper, 1984.

Chodorow, Nancy. *The Reproduction of Mothering: Psychoanalysis and the Sociology of Gender.* Berkeley: Univ. of California Press, 1978.

Curb, Rosemary. "Re/cognition, Re/presentation, Re/creation in Woman-Conscious Drama: The Seer, the Seen, the Scene, the Obscene." *Theatre Journal* 37 (1985): 302–16.

Dolan, Jill. *The Feminist Spectator as Critic.* Ann Arbor: UMI, 1988.

———. "Toward a Critical Methodology of Lesbian Feminist Theatre." Master's Thesis. New York University, 1983.

Dreher, Sarah. *Lesbian Stages.* Norwich, Vt.: New Victoria, 1988.

———. *Ruby Christmas.* In *Places, Please! The First Anthology of Lesbian Plays.* Ed. Kate McDermott. San Francisco: Spinsters/Aunt Lute, 1985. 137–91.

Eichenbaum, Luise, and Susie Orbach. *Understanding Women: A Feminist Psychoanalytic Approach.* New York: Basic, 1983.

Gabow, Michelle A. *The Lunch.* Unpublished script, 1983.

Gallop, Jane. *The Daughter's Seduction: Feminism and Psychoanalysis.* Ithaca: Cornell Univ. Press, 1982.

Gilligan, Carol. *In a Different Voice: Psychological Theory and Women's Development.* Cambridge: Harvard Univ. Press, 1982.

Hansberry, Lorraine. *A Raisin in the Sun.* New York: Signet, 1958.

al Hibri, Azizah. "Reproduction, Mothering, and the Origins of Patriarchy." In *Mothering: Essays in Feminist Theory.* Ed. Joyce Trebilcot. Totowa, N.J.: Rowman & Allenheld, 1983. 81–93.

Kahn, Coppélia. "The Hand That Rocks the Cradle: Recent Gender Theories and Their Implications." In *The (M)other Tongue: Essays in Feminist Psychoanalytic Theory.* Ed. Shirley Nelson Garner et al. Ithaca: Cornell Univ. Press, 1985. 72–88.

Kittay, Eva Feder. "Womb Envy: An Explanatory Concept." In *Mothering: Essays in Feminist Theory.* Ed. Joyce Trebilcot. Totowa, N.J.: Rowman & Allenheld, 1983, 94–128.

Rafkin, Louise, ed. *Different Daughters: A Book by Mothers of Lesbians.* San Francisco: Cleis, 1987.

Rawles, Nancy. *Angela.* Unpublished script, 1983.

———. *Going to Seed.* Unpublished script, 1984.

Rich, Adrienne. "Compulsory Heterosexuality and Lesbian Existence." *Signs* 5 (1980), 631–60.

———. *Of Woman Born: Motherhood as Experience and Institution.* New York: Bantam, 1976.

Walker, Barbara G. *The Women's Encyclopedia of Myths and Secrets.* New York: Harper, 1983.

376   ROSEMARY CURB

Afterword: Lesbian Studies in the 1990s

Catharine R. Stimpson

In 1923, Gertrude Stein wrote *A List,* one of her sly, incorrigible plays. Together, two women characters, Martha and Mabel, murmur:

Susan Mabel Martha and Susan, Mabel and Martha and a father. There was no sinking there, there where there was no placid carrier.

Despite the presence of a nameless father, the women combine and recombine. Despite the absence of a placid carrier, these units and unities seem to swim. At least, they refuse to sink.

About a year later, Ma Rainey, born Gertrude Pridgett, recorded one of her pungent, defiant, knowing songs, "Shave 'Em Dry Blues." In the fourth stanza, she announces that "State Street women" are "wearing brogan shoes." On the record, the sixth stanza may be unclear, but the lead sheet reads:

Some women got big feet like a man.[1]

Gertrude Stein and Gertrude Pridgett, Martha and Mabel and Susan, State Street women—together they represent careers to be noted, characters to be contextualized, stanzas to be scanned. All are gifts and challenges to lesbian studies, an enterprise that explores the history and meaning of sexual difference in general and of lesbianism in particular, that invaluable way of being in, with, and against the world.

During the 1970s gay and lesbian caucuses were formed in the academic disciplines. But as a self-conscious interdisciplinary educational movement, lesbian studies probably begins in the United States in 1977 with the founding of the lesbian caucus of the National Women Studies Association. Since then, it has grown nationally and internationally.[2] Outside of the United States, the Netherlands has been unusually supportive. Helping to make the lesbian caucus possible in 1977 were at least three preceding activities that bordered on and overlapped with one another. They were:

1. Feminist and lesbian feminist theory. In 1949, in the original, French edition of *The Second Sex*, Simone de Beauvoir, after brooding about the viriloid woman, had represented lesbianism as a dignified existential *choice*, a mode of action in a given situation. Nearly twenty years later, lesbian feminist theory began to grow. In 1968, for example, Anne Koedt, in "The Myth of the Vaginal Orgasm," had located female sexual pleasure, not in the vagina, but in the clitoris. Women could have sexual pleasure without the male sexual organ. Because of this, the clitoral orgasm threatened heterosexual institutions. Lesbian sexuality was proof and symbol of such gratifications and such threats. In 1972, to give two other examples, Sidney Abbott and Barbara Love published *Sappho Was A Right-On Woman*; Del Martin and Phyllis Lyon *Lesbian/Woman*. Both justified lesbian activism and rights.

2. Academic scholarship about women, gender, and homosexuality, a review and reconstruction of every academic discipline to eliminate old errors and to provide deeper, more accurate readings of reality. In 1974, both Dolores Klaich's *Woman Plus Woman: Attitudes Toward Lesbianism* and the first issue of *The Journal of Homosexuality* appeared. Klaich may have been speaking to a general audience; *The Journal* to "rigorous" empirical researchers, clinicians, and "helping professionals." In varying degrees, both demonstrated that bias had marred earlier representations of homosexuality. In 1975, Carroll Smith-Rosenberg published "The Female World of Love and Ritual." Immensely influential, the essay presented and analyzed loving friendships between nineteenth-century women. It also argued against binary thinking about sexuality, against polarizing "the normal and the abnormal," the heterosexual and the homosexual. Smith-Rosenberg suggested that instead:

we view sexual and emotional impulses as part of a continuum or spectrum of affect gradations strongly affected by cultural norms and arrangements, a continuum influenced in part by observed and thus learned behavior. (28–29)

Among other pioneering texts were Jonathan Katz's 1976 *Gay American History*, a massive collection of documents, and Barbara Smith's 1977 "Toward a Black Feminist Criticism," which probed the tensions and connections among blacks, feminism, lesbianism, literature, and literary criticism.

3. Independent research and thinking. Like women's studies, lesbian

studies has been and is as dependent on work outside of the academy as literature is on language. Lesbians of all ages, races, and occupations have served as independent scholars. They have cruised the libraries in search of their past and that of their communities. They have kept card files, swapped information, published their own books and journals, written, spoken, and remembered. They have passionately engaged in this work, not for money, not for fame, but for the sustenance of the soul. In 1956, for example, Jeannette H. Foster brought out *Sex Variant Women in Literature* through Vantage Press, which some might rudely call a vanity press. She traces the genesis of the book to an incident when she was a naive college student watching a student council handle a "morals case" in a college dormitory. She found it all incomprehensible. She spent the next twenty-one years on an "extended search" for knowledge about female homosexuality in order to dispel her own perplexed ignorance (iii–iv).

During the 1980s, lesbian studies was to establish itself. It created its own institutions (archives and libraries, symposia and conferences, articles and books, classes and academic programs) and become a part of existing ones. So doing, lesbian studies extended women's studies, which might otherwise collapse into an interrogation of heterosexuality, and balanced gay studies, which might otherwise collapse into an interrogation of male homosexuality. As lesbian studies become more visible and confident, it could leash the pit bulls of homophobia more firmly. For homophobia, and the understandable homosexual fear of its physical, psychological, and legal violence, seeks to block any serious, sympathetic public discussion of gay and lesbian life.

Most of the essays in *Lesbian Texts and Contexts* sensitively trace what public representations we have of women's relationships in women's writings, whether this literature is "realistic" or "experimental." Not coincidentally, lesbians—Stein, Monique Wittig, Nicole Brossard—have been among the most audacious experimental writers of the twentieth century. For the defiance of sexual norms can provoke a radical freedom from textual norms as well. Simultaneously, the need to signify differences with a new, arduous explicitness compels new, avant-garde writing.

Exulting in the strength of a lesbian presence might have tempted lesbian studies to think monolithically, to cast all lesbians as but one woman. Traveling with a passport from the Lesbian Nation, she is to love other women, even if she suffers for it. Magnificently, women of color led in the correction of the error of blobby monolithic thought. For modern lesbians obviously differ among themselves by race and class, religion and education, region and nation, time and age, ideology and political beliefs. The pages of Audre Lorde, Judy Grahn, or Paula Gunn Allen are hardly xerox copies of each other. Nor are those of Radclyffe Hall and Virginia Woolf. Not all lesbians, moreover, are All-Bright, She's-All-Right Heroines. Natalie Barney, for example, admired fascism.

Forcefully, people also disagreed about the definition of a lesbian, a disagreement that is seeping into the 1990s. Is lesbianism a metaphor? Some of the most audacious thinking in *Lesbian Texts and Contexts* suggests this. For "lesbianism" might signify a critique of heterosexuality; a cry for the abolition of the binary oppositions of modern sexuality; a demand for the release of women's self-named desires; a belief that such release might itself be a sign of a rebellious, subtle, raucous textuality. "Lesbianism" might represent a space in which we shape and reshape our psychosexual identities, in which we are metamorphic creatures.

Or is lesbianism an identity that only some women can claim? If so, is lesbianism a public and an erotic identity? A subgroup's transgressive way of behaving within larger societies as well as within a bedroom? Or, less pervasively, is lesbianism an erotic identity? Or, even less pervasively, a series of erotic acts and gestures? Or, is it a mistake so to conflate lesbianism and eros? As Adrienne Rich argues, is there rather a lesbian continuum? On this continuum

lesbian identity is not tied to a self-conscious identity or even to sexual relations or attractions, but to emotional bonds that emerge between women in a patriarchal society. (Quoted in Brown 528)

The growing sophistication of the history of sexuality during the 1980s made the word "lesbian" more and more problematic. For "lesbian" did not really enter the English language as a sexual term until the nineteenth century. To oversimplify, a code of normative sexuality was then emerging and assuming dominance. Two binary oppositions were to structure the fluid complexities and possibilities of behavior: one between masculinity and femininity as social roles, norms, and metaphors; the other between a good, acceptable heterosexuality in which masculine and feminine mate, with masculinity in control, and a bad, unacceptable homosexual in which men mate with men, women with women. At their worst, these male queers are queens who wear women's pumps and gloves and flounces; these female lesbians are butches who wear men's shoes and ties and jackets.

If this meaning of "lesbian" is so recent, how valid can it be as a name for older patterns of female love, pleasure, and desire? Moreover, how can I so glibly speak of "older patterns of female love, pleasure, and desire"? Am I not imposing my own, 1980s', United States vocabulary on the past? This question is part of a large argument in the history of sexuality between "essentialists" who often see gay and lesbian people as a common theme throughout history, though with important local variations, and "social constructionists." Influenced by Foucault, they "argue that all such sexual categories and identities are socially constructed and historically specific" (Duberman 5). A common notion within lesbian studies is that theories and practices of human sexuality change over time. Culture, not some divinity, not dear old nature, regulates sexuality. Yet, because lesbian studies is spread out widely among essentialists and social constructionists, it is self-divided about the degree to which culture exercises this power. Many would reluctantly abandon the notion of their voice as an echo of Sappho's own—even though they might admit that Sappho's voice is a translation of a translation of a translation of a fragment. Others, however, might be less reluctant. For them, the meaning of a lesbian's "invisible identity" will change. A "lesbian identity" once entailed invisibility because no one wanted to see her. Now a "lesbian identity" might entail invisibility because the lesbian, like some supernatural creature of myth and tale, shows that no identity is stable enough to claim the reassurances of permanent visibility.

Like lesbian studies, *Lesbian Texts and Contexts* is hardly placid. Instead, it kicks out at convention and ignorance. It asks us to give a Gertrude Stein and a Gertrude Pridgett their due. If we do so, we will see the courage of women whom the world has dismissed and the creativity of women whom the world has despised. We will also admire the resolve of lesbian studies to boot up the computers of contemporary writing and thinking in order to list that courage and creativity so widely that it will survive whatever cruelties might still be coming along history's battered, battering ram of a path.

NOTES

1. See Lieb, 160–64, 208–9. See also Garber's essay in Duberman, *Hidden from History: Reclaiming the Gay and Lesbian Past*, 341–42. Garber places Ma Rainey's sexuality in a cultural context. This entire volume is a landmark in gay and lesbian studies.
2. The best account of its rapid development is Cruikshank, *Lesbian Studies:*

Present and Future. See, too, Freedman, Gelpi, Johnson, and Weston, *The Lesbian Issue: Essays from Signs.*

WORKS CITED

Brown, Judith C. "Notes" to "Lesbian Sexuality in Medieval and Early Modern Europe," In *Hidden from History: Reclaiming the Gay and Lesbian Past.* Ed. Martin Bauml Duberman, Martha Vicinus, and George Chauncey, Jr. New York: NAL, 1989, 67–75.

Cruikshank, Margaret. *Lesbian Studies: Present and Future.* Old Westbury, N.Y. Feminist, 1982.

Duberman, Martin Bauml, Martha Vicinus, and George Chauncey, Jr. eds. *Hidden from History: Reclaiming the Gay and Lesbian Past.* New York: NAL, 1989.

Foster, Jeannette H. *Sex Variant Women in Literature.* Tallahassee, Fla.: Naiad, 1985.

Freedman, Estelle B., Barbara C. Gelpi, Susan L. Johnson, and Kathleen M. Weston, eds. *The Lesbian Issue: Essays from Signs.* Chicago: Univ. of Chicago Press, 1985.

Garber, Eric. "A Spectacle in Color: The Lesbian and Gay Subculture of Jazz Age Harlem." In *Hidden from History: Reclaiming the Gay and Lesbian Past.* Ed. Martin Bauml Duberman, Martha Vicinus and George Chauncey, Jr., New York: NAL, 1989. 318–31.

Lieb, Sandra R. *Mother of the Blues: A Study of Ma Rainey.* Amherst, Univ. of Massachusetts Press, 1981.

Smith-Rosenberg, Carroll. "The Female World of Love and Ritual." *Signs* 1 (Autumn 1975): 1–29.

Select Bibliography

The following bibliography has been compiled by the editors with suggestions from some of the contributors. It is intended as a supplement to the individual lists of Works Cited supplied by authors at the end of each chapter. It is also intended as a general bibliography about lesbian literature that will be useful as a reference tool. Therefore, we have repeated some entries found elsewhere in the collection whenever such repetition seemed appropriate. We have also tried to limit the selections to works of literary merit by or about lesbians. Most of the books were in print in 1989, but we also included some particularly noteworthy books that are out of print. The dates refer to the most recent edition we could locate.

Fiction

Allen, Paula Gunn. *The Woman Who Owned the Shadows*. San Francisco: Spinsters, Ink, 1983.

Alther, Lisa. *Other Women*. New York: Signet, 1984.

Arnold, June. *Sister Gin*. New York: Feminist, 1989.

Barnes, Djuna. *Ladies Almanack*. New York: Harper, 1972.

———. *Nightwood*. New York: New Directions, 1961.

Birtha, Becky. *Lover's Choice*. Seattle: Seal, 1987.

Blais, Marie-Claire. *Nights in the Underground: An Exploration of Love*. Trans. Ray Ellenwood. Ontario: Musson, 1979.

Bloch, Alice. *The Law of Return*. Boston: Alyson, 1983.

Boucher, Sandy. *The Notebooks of Leni Clare and Other Short Stories*. Trumansburg, N.Y.: Crossing Press, 1982.

Brady, Maureen. *Folly*. Trumansburg, N.Y.: Crossing Press, 1982.

———. *Give Me Your Good Ear*. Argyle, N.Y.: Spinsters, 1979.

———. *The Question She Put to Herself*. Freedom, Calif.: Crossing Press, 1986.

Brant, Beth [Degonwadont]. *Mohawk Trail*. Ithaca: Firebrand, 1985.

Brantenberg, Gerd. *Egalia's Daughters: A Satire of the Sexes*. Seattle: Seal, 1985.

———. *What Comes Naturally*. London: Women's Press, 1986.

Brown, Rita Mae. *Rubyfruit Jungle*. New York: Bantam, 1988.

———. *Six of One*. New York: Bantam, 1988.

———. *Southern Discomfort*. New York: Bantam, 1988.

————. *Sudden Death*. New York: Bantam, 1988.

Burford, Barbara. *The Threshing Floor*. Ithaca: Firebrand, 1987.

Burton, Gabrielle. *Heartbreak Hotel*. New York: Penguin, 1988.

Charnas, Suzy McKee. *Motherlines*. New York: Putnam, 1978.

Chernin, Kim. *The Flame Bearers*. New York: Perennial, 1987.

Cixous, Hélène. *Angst*. New York: Riverun, 1985.

Cliff, Michelle. *The Land of Look Behind: Prose and Poetry*. Ithaca: Firebrand, 1985.

DeLynn, Jane. *In Thrall*. New York: Potter, 1982.

————. *Some Do*. New York: Pocket, 1978.

Dworkin, Andrea. *Ice and Fire*. New York: Weidenfeld, 1986.

————. *The New Womans Broken Heart*. Palo Alto, Calif.: Frog in the Well, 1980.

Forrest, Katherine V. *Murder at the Nightwood Bar*. Tallahassee, Fla.: Naiad, 1987.

Galford, Ellen. *The Fires of Bride*. Ithaca: Firebrand, 1988.

————. *Moll Cutpurse*. Ithaca: Firebrand, 1985.

Gearhart, Sally Miller. *The Wanderground*. Boston: Alyson, 1984.

Gilman, Charlotte Perkins. *Herland*. New York: Pantheon, 1979.

Grumbach, Doris. *The Ladies*. New York: Fawcett Crest, 1984.

Hall, Radclyffe. *The Well of Loneliness*. New York: Avon, 1980.

Hanscombe, Gillian E. *Between Friends*. Boston: Alyson, 1982.

Harris, Bertha. *Confessions of Cherubino*. New York: Harcourt, 1972.

————. *Lover*. Plainfield, Vt.: Daughters, 1976.

H. D. *HERmione*. New York: New Directions: 1981.

Leduc, Violette. *Thérèse and Isabelle*. Trans. Derek Coltman. New York: Farrar, 1967.

Livia, Anna. *Accommodation Offered*. London: Women's Press, 1985.

————. *Bulldozer Rising*. London: Onlywomen, 1988.

————. *Relatively Norma*. London: Onlywomen, 1987.

Lynch, Lee. *Amazon Trail*. Tallahassee, Fla.: Naiad, 1988.

————. *Dusty's Queen of Hearts Diner*. Tallahassee, Fla.: Naiad, 1987.

————. *Home in Your Hands*. Tallahassee, Fla.: Naiad, 1986.

————. *Old Dyke Tales*. Tallahassee, Fla.: Naiad, 1988.

————. *The Swashbuckler*. Tallahassee, Fla.: Naiad, 1988.

McDaniel, Judith. *Winter Passages*. San Francisco: Spinsters, 1984.

Marchessault, Jovette. *Lesbian Triptych*. Trans. Yvonne. M. Klein. Toronto: Women's Press, 1985.

————. *Like a Child of the Earth*. Trans. Yvonne M. Klein. Vancouver: Talonbooks, 1988.

Miller, Isabel. *Patience and Sarah*. New York: Fawcett Crest, 1985.

Miner, Valerie. *All Good Women*. Freedom, Calif.: Crossing Press, 1987.

————. *Blood Sisters: An Examination of Conscience*. New York: St. Martin's, 1982.

————. *Movement, A Novel in Stories*. Trumansburg, N.Y.: Crossing Press, 1982.

————. *Winter's Edge*. Trumansburg, N.Y.: Crossing Press, 1985.

Morgan, Claire [Patricia Highsmith]. *The Price of Salt*. Tallahassee, Fla.: Naiad, 1984.

Naylor, Gloria. *The Women of Brewster Place*. New York: Penguin, 1988.

Newman, Lesléa. *A Letter to Harvey Milk*. Ithaca: Firebrand, 1988.
Richardson, Henry Handel [Ethel Florence Lindesay Richardson]. *The Getting of Wisdom*. New York: Dial, 1981.
Rule, Jane. *The Desert of the Heart*. Tallahassee, Fla.: Naiad, 1985.
————. *Memory Board*. Tallahassee, Fla.: Naiad, 1987.
————. *This Is Not For You*. Tallahassee, Fla.: Naiad, 1982.
Russ, Joanna. *The Female Man*. Boston: Beacon, 1986.
Sarton, May. *Mrs. Stevens Hears the Mermaids Singing*. New York: Norton, 1975.
Shockley, Ann Allen. *Loving Her*. Tallahassee, Fla.: Naiad, 1987.
Silko, Leslie Marmon. *Ceremony*. New York: NAL, 1978.
Stein, Gertrude, *Fernhurst, Q.E.D. and Other Early Writings*. New York: Liveright, 1971.
————. *Selected Writings of Gertrude Stein*. Ed. Carl Van Vechten. New York: Vintage, 1972.
Vivien, Renée. *A Woman Appeared to Me*. Trans. Jeannette H. Foster. Tallahassee, Fla.: Naiad, 1982.
————. *The Woman of the Wolf*. Trans. Karla Jay and Yvonne M. Klein. New York: Gay Presses of New York, 1983.
Walker, Alice. *The Color Purple*. New York: Pocket, 1985.
White, Antonia. *Frost in May*. New York: Dial, 1948.
Wilson, Barbara. *Murder in the Collective*. Seattle: Seal, 1984.
Winterson, Jeanette. *Oranges Are Not the Only Fruit*. New York: Atlantic Monthly Press, 1988.
Wittig, Monique. *Les Guérillères*. Trans. David Le Vay. Boston: Beacon, 1985.
————. *The Lesbian Body*. Trans. David Le Vay. Boston: Beacon, 1986.
————. *The Opoponax*. Trans. Helen Weaver. Plainfield, Vt.: Daughters, 1966.
Woolf, Virginia. *Orlando: A Biography*. New York: Harcourt, 1956.
Youngblood, Shay. *The Big Mama Stories*. Ithaca: Firebrand, 1989.

Anthologies

Adelman, Marcy, Ph.D. *Long Time Passing: Lives of Older Lesbians*. Boston: Alyson, 1986.
Allen, Paula Gunn, ed. and introduction. *Spider Woman's Granddaughters: Traditional Tales and Contemporary Writing by Native American Women*. Boston: Beacon, 1989.
Balka, Christie, and Andy Rose, eds. *Twice Blessed: On Being Lesbian, Gay and Jewish*. Boston: Beacon, 1989.
Beck, Evelyn Torton, ed. *Nice Jewish Girls: A Lesbian Anthology*, rev. and exp. ed. Boston: Beacon, 1989.
Bradshaw, Jan, and Mary Heming, eds. *Girls Next Door*. London: Women's Press, 1986.
Brant, Beth [Degonwadont], ed. *A Gathering of Spirit: A Collection by North American Indian Women*. Ithaca: Firebrand, 1988.

Conlan, Faith, Rachel da Silva, and Barbara Wilson, eds. *The Things That Divide Us*. Seattle: Seal, 1985.

Cruikshank, Margaret, ed. *New Lesbian Writing*. San Francisco: Grey Fox, 1985.

Decarnin, Camilla, Eric Garber, and Lyn Paleo, eds. *Worlds Apart: An Anthology of Lesbian and Gay Science Fiction*. Boston: Alyson, 1988.

Geok-lin Lim, Shirley, and Mayumi Tsutakawa, eds. *The Forbidden Stitch: An Asian American Women's Anthology*. Corvallis, Oreg.: Calyx, 1989.

Gómez, Alma, Cherríe Moraga, and Mariana Romo-Camona, eds. *Cuentos: Stories by Latinas*. New York: Kitchen Table/Women of Color Press, 1983.

Hoagland, Sara Lucia, and Julia Penelope, eds. *For Lesbians Only: A Separatist Anthology*. London: Onlywomen, 1988.

Kagel/Kantrowitz, Melanie, and Irena Klepfisz, eds. *The Tribe of Dina: A Jewish Women's Anthology*. Montpellier, Vt.: Sinister Wisdom, 1986.

Lesbian Writing and Publishing Collective, ed. *Dykeversions: Lesbian Short Fiction*. Toronto: Women's Press, 1986.

Livia, Anna, and Lilian Mohin, eds. *The Pied Piper: Lesbian Feminist Fiction*. London: Onlywomen, 1989.

Mohin, Lilian, and Sheila Schulman, eds. *The Reach and Other Stories*. London: Onlywomen, 1984.

Moraga, Cherríe, and Gloria Anzaldúa. *This Bridge Called My Back: Writings by Radical Women of Color*. New York: Kitchen Table/Women of Color Press, 1983.

Oosthuuizen, Ann, ed. *Stepping Out: Short Stories on Friendship between Women*. New York: Pandora, 1986.

Ramos, Juanita, comp. and ed. *Compañeras: Latina Lesbians (An Anthology)*. New York: Latina Lesbian History Project, 1987.

Silvera, Makeda, ed. *Fireworks: The Best of Fireweed*. Toronto: Women's Press, 1986.

Smith, Barbara, ed. *Home Girls: A Black Feminist Anthology*. New York: Kitchen Table/Women of Color Press, 1983.

Plays

Chambers, Jane. *Last Summer at Bluefish Cove*. New York: JH Press, n.d.

———. *My Blue Heaven*. New York: JH Press, n.d.

Curtin, Kaier. *"We Can Always Call Them Bulgarians": The Emergence of Lesbians and Gay Men on the American Stage*. Boston: Alyson, 1987.

McDermott, Kate. *Places, Please!: The First Anthology of Lesbian Plays*. San Francisco: Spinsters/Aunt Lute, 1985.

Marchessault, Jovette. *Saga of the Wet Hens*. Trans. Linda Gaboriau. Vancouver: Talonbooks, 1983.

Shewey, Don, ed. *Out Front: Contemporary Gay and Lesbian Plays*. New York: Grove, 1988.

Poetry

Allen, Paula Gunn. *Wyrds*. San Francisco: Taurean Horn, 1987.

Barnstone, Willis, trans. *Sappho and the Greek Lyric*. New York: Schocken, 1988.

Bishop, Elizabeth. *The Complete Poems 1927–1979*. New York: Farrar, 1983.

Brossard, Nicole. *The Aerial Letter*. Trans. Marlene Wildeman. Toronto: Women's Press, 1988.

———. *Lovhers*. Trans. Barbara Godard. Montreal: Guernica, 1986.

———. *Sous la langue/Under Tongue*. Montreal: Gynergy, 1987.

Broumas, Olga. *Beginning with O*. New Haven: Yale Univ. Press, 1977.

———. *Pastoral Jazz*. Port Townsend, Wash.: Copper Canyon, 1983.

Brown, Rita Mae. *Poems*. Freedom, Calif.: Crossing Press, 1973.

Clarke, Cheryl. *Living as a Lesbian*. Ithaca: Firebrand, 1986.

———. *Narratives: Poems in the Tradition of Black Women*. 2d ed. New York: Kitchen Table/Women of Color Press, 1983.

Crow, Mary, ed. *Woman Who Has Sprouted Wings: Poems by Contemporary Latin American Women Poets*. 2d ed. Pittsburgh: Latin American Literary Review Press, 1988.

Gomez, Jewelle L. *Flamingoes and Bears*. Jersey City: Grace, 1986.

Grahn, Judy. *The Queen of Swords*. Boston: Beacon, 1987.

———. *The Queen of Wands*. Trumansburg, N.Y.: Crossing Press, 1982.

———. *The Work of a Common Woman: The Collected Poetry of Judy Grahn 1964–1977*. Trumansburg, N.Y.: Crossing Press, 1978.

Hacker, Marilyn. *Love, Death, and the Changing of the Seasons*. New York: Arbor House, 1986.

———. *Taking Notice*. New York: Knopf, 1980.

H. D. [Hilda Doolittle]. *Helen in Egypt*. New York: New Directions, 1961.

Jordan, June. *Living Room*. New York: Thunder's Mouth, 1985.

———. *Passion*. Boston: Beacon, 1980.

Klepfisz, Irene. *Keeper of Accounts*. Watertown, Mass.: Persephone, 1982.

Lapidus, Jacqueline. *Ultimate Conspiracy*. n.p.: Lynx, 1987.

Levertov, Denise. *Light Up the Cave*. New York: New Directions, 1981.

Lorde, Audre. *The Black Unicorn*. New York: Norton, 1978.

———. *Chosen Poems, Old and New*. New York: Norton, 1982.

———. *Our Dead Behind Us*. New York: Norton, 1986.

Newman, Lesléa. *Love Me Like You Mean It*. Santa Cruz: HerBooks, 1987.

Parker, Pat. *Jonestown & Other Madness*. Ithaca: Firebrand, 1985.

Pratt, Minnie Bruce. *We Say We Love Each Other*. San Francisco: Spinsters/Aunt Lute, 1985.

Rich, Adrienne. *The Dream of a Common Language*. New York: Norton, 1978.

———. *The Fact of a Doorframe*. New York: Norton, 1984.

———. *Poems Selected and New 1950–1984*. New York: Norton, 1985.

———. *Your Native Land, Your Life*. New York: Norton, 1986.

Sarton, May. *A Grain of Mustard Seed*. New York: Norton, 1971.

———. *Halfway to Silence*. New York: Norton, 1980.

————. *Letters from Maine*. New York: Norton, 1984.

————. *The Silence Now: New and Collected Earlier Poems*. New York: Norton, 1988.

Biography/Autobiography

Brittain, Vera. *Radclyffe Hall: A Case of Obscenity?* New York: A. S. Barnes, 1968.

Carr, Virginia Spencer. *The Lonely Hunter: A Biography of Carson McCullers*. Garden City, N.Y.: Doubleday, 1975.

Cliff, Michelle. *Claiming an Identity They Taught Me to Despise*. Watertown, Mass.: Persephone, 1980.

Colette. *The Pure and the Impure*. New York: Farrar, 1967.

Deming, Barbara. *A Humming Under My Feet: A Book of Travail*. London: Women's Press, 1985.

DeSalvo, Louise. *Virginia Woolf: The Impact of Childhood Sexual Abuse on Her Life and Work*. Boston: Beacon, 1989.

DeSalvo, Louise, and Michael A. Leaska, eds. *The Letters of Vita Sackville-West to Virginia Woolf*. New York: Quill, 1985.

Dillon, Millicent. *A Little Original Sin: The Life and Work of Jane Bowles*. New York: Holt, 1981.

————. *Out in the World: Selected Letters of Jane Bowles 1935–1970*. Santa Barbara: Black Sparrow, 1985.

Field, Andrew. *Djuna: The Formidable Miss Barnes*. Austin: Univ. of Texas Press, 1985.

————. *Djuna: The Life and Times of Djuna Barnes*. New York: Putnam, 1983.

Fitch, Noel Riley. *Sylvia Beach and the Lost Generation: A History of Literary Paris in the Twenties and Thirties*. New York: Norton, 1983.

Flanner, Janet [Genet]. *Darlinghissima: Letters to a Friend*. Ed. Natalia Danesi Murray. New York: Random, 1985.

————. *Paris Was Yesterday 1925–1939*. New York: Penguin, 1981.

Glendenning, Victoria. *Vita: A Biography of Vita Sackville-West*. New York: Quill, 1983.

Hurston, Zora Neale. *Dust Tracks on a Road: An Autobiography*. Urbana: Univ. of Illinois Press, 1984.

Jay, Karla. *The Amazon and the Page: Natalie Clifford Barney and Renée Vivien*. Bloomington: Indiana Univ. Press, 1988.

Leduc, Violette. *La Bâtarde*. Trans. David Coltman. New York: Farrar, 1965.

————. *Mad in Pursuit*. Trans. Derek Coltman. New York: Farrar, 1970.

Lorde, Audre. *Zami: A New Spelling of My Name*. Trumansburg, N.Y.: Crossing Press, 1982.

Meigs, Mary. *The Box Closet*. Vancouver: Talonbooks, 1987.

————. *Lily Briscoe: A Self-Portrait*. Vancouver: Talonbooks, 1981.

————. *The Medusa Head*. Vancouver: Talonbooks, 1983.

Nicolson, Nigel. *Portrait of a Marriage*. New York: Atheneum, 1973.

O'Brien, Sharon. *Willa Cather: The Emerging Voice*. New York: Ballantine, 1988.

Pougy, Liane de. *My Blue Notebooks*. New York: Harper, 1979.

Sarton, May. *At Seventy*. New York: Norton, 1984.

———. *Journal of a Solitude*. New York: Norton, 1973.

Stein, Gertrude. *The Autobiography of Alice B. Toklas*. New York: Vintage, 1933.

———. *Everybody's Autobiography*. London: Virago, 1985.

Toklas, Alice B. *Staying on Alone: The Letters of Alice B. Toklas*. New York: Liveright, 1973.

———. *What Is Remembered*. San Francisco: North Point, 1985.

Troubridge, Una. *The Life and Death of Radclyffe Hall*. London: Hammond, 1961.

Woolf, Virginia. *The Diaries of Virginia Woolf*. Ed. Anne Olivier Bell. 5 vols. New York: Harcourt, 1977–84.

———. *A Writer's Diary*. New York: Harcourt, 1953.

Essays/Literary Criticism

Allen, Paula Gunn. *The Sacred Hoop: Recovering the Feminine in American Indian Traditions*. Boston: Beacon, 1986.

———, ed. *Studies in American Indian Literature: Critical Essays and Course Designs*. New York: MLA, 1984.

Anzaldúa, Gloria. *Borderlands/La Frontera*. San Francisco: Spinsters/Aunt Lute, 1987.

Ascher, Carol, Louise DeSalvo, and Sara Ruddick, eds. *Between Women: Biographers, Novelists, Critics, Teachers and Artists Write about Their Work on Women*. Boston: Beacon, 1984.

Bennett, Paula. *Emily Dickinson*. London: Harvester, 1990.

———. *My Life a Loaded Gun: Female Creativity and Feminist Poetics*. Boston: Beacon, 1986.

Benstock, Shari. "Paris Lesbianism and the Politics of Reaction, 1900–1940." In *Hidden from History: Reclaiming the Gay and Lesbian Past*. Ed. Martin Bauml Duberman, Martha Vicinus, and George Chauncey, Jr. New York: NAL, 1989. 332–346.

———. "Portrait of the Artist's Wife." *Times Literary Supplement*, 30 Sept. 1988, 1065.

———. *Textualizing the Feminine: Essays on the Limits of Genre*. Norman: Univ. of Oklahoma Press, 1990.

———. *Women of the Left Bank: Paris, 1900–1940*. Austin: Univ. of Texas Press, 1986.

Bonnet, Marie-Jo. *Un Choix sans équivoque: recherches historiques sur les relations amoureuses entres les femmes XVIe–XXe siècle*. Paris: Denoël, 1981.

Carruthers, Mary. "The Re-Vision of the Muse: Adrienne Rich, Audre Lorde, Judy Grahn, Olga Broumas." *Hudson Review* 36 (1983): 293–322.

Causse, Michèle. "L'Interloquée." *Trivia* 13 (1988): 79–90.

Chessman, Harriet Scott. *The Public Is Invited to Dance: Representation, the Body, and Dialogue in Gertrude Stein*. Stanford: Stanford Univ. Press, 1989.

Christian, Barbara. *Black Feminist Criticism: Perspectives on Black Women Writers.* New York: Pergamon, 1985.

Cixous, Hélène, and Catherine Clement. *The Newly Born Woman.* Trans. Betsy Wing. Minneapolis: Univ. of Minnesota Press, 1986.

Cook, Blanche Wiesen. " 'Women Alone Stir My Imagination': Lesbianism and the Cultural Tradition." *Signs* 4 (1979): 718–39.

Cornwell, Anita. *Black Lesbian in White America.* Tallahassee, Fla.: Naiad, 1983.

Cruikshank, Margaret, ed. *Lesbian Studies: Present and Future.* Old Westbury, N.Y.: Feminist, 1982.

DeKoven, Marianne. *A Different Language: Gertrude Stein's Experimental Language.* Madison: Univ. of Wisconsin Press, 1983.

Derrida, Jacques. *Dissemination.* Trans. Barbara Johnson. Chicago: Univ. of Chicago Press, 1981.

———. *Margins of Philosophy.* Trans. Alan Bass. Chicago: Univ. of Chicago Press, 1982.

Dijkstra, Bram. *Idols of Perversity: Fantasies of Feminine Evil in Fin-de-Siècle Culture.* New York: Oxford Univ. Press, 1986.

Evans, Martha Noel. *Masks of Tradition: Women and the Politics of Writing in Twentieth-Century France.* Ithaca: Cornell Univ. Press, 1987.

Farwell, Marilyn R. "Toward a Definition of the Lesbian Literary Imagination." *Signs* 14 (1988): 100–18.

Fetterley, Judith. *The Resisting Reader.* Bloomington: Indiana Univ. Press, 1978.

Friedman, Susan Stanford. "Women's Autobiographical Selves: Theory and Practice." In *The Private Self.* Ed. Shari Benstock, Chapel Hill: Univ. of North Carolina Press, 1988. 34–62.

Friedman, Susan Stanford, and Rachel Blau DuPlessis. " 'I Had Two Loves Separate': The Sexualities of H. D.'s *Her.*" *Montemora* 8 (1981): 7–30.

Gilbert, Sandra M. "Tradition and Female Talent." In *The Poetics of Gender.* Ed. Nancy K. Miller. New York: Columbia Univ. Press, 1986.

Gilbert, Sandra M., and Susan Gubar. *The Madwoman in the Attic: The Woman Writer and the Nineteenth-Century Literary Imagination.* New Haven: Yale Univ. Press, 1979.

———. *No Man's Land: The Place of the Woman Writer in the Twentieth Century.* 2 vols. New Haven: Yale Univ. Press, 1988–89.

Grahn, Judy. *The Highest Apple: Sappho and the Lesbian Poetic Tradition.* San Francisco: Spinsters/Aunt Lute, 1985.

———. *Really Reading Gertrude Stein.* Freedom, Calif.: Crossing Press, 1989.

Grier, Barbara, ed. *Lesbiana: Book Reviews from the Ladder, 1966–1972.* Tallahassee, Fla.: Naiad, 1976.

Gubar, Susan. "Sapphistries." *Signs* 10 (1984): 43–62.

Hanscombe, Gillian, and Virginia L. Smyers. *Writing for Their Lives: The Modernist Women, 1910–1940.* Boston: Northeastern Univ. Press, 1987.

Homans, Margaret. " 'Syllables of Velvet': Dickinson, Rossetti, and the Rhetoric of Sexuality." *Feminist Studies* 11 (1985): 569–93.

Irigaray, Luce. *Speculum of the Other Woman*. Trans. Gillian C. Gill. Ithaca: Cornell Univ. Press, 1985.

―――. *This Sex Which Is Not One*. Trans. Catherine Porter. Ithaca: Cornell Univ. Press, 1985.

Jardine, Alice A. *Gynesis: Configurations of Woman and Modernity*. Ithaca: Cornell Univ. Press, 1985.

Jay, Karla, and Allen Young, eds. *Lavender Culture*. New York: Jove, 1978.

Johnston, Jill. *Lesbian Nation: The Feminist Solution*. New York: Simon, 1973.

Kannenstine, Louis F. *The Art of Djuna Barnes: Duality and Damnation*. New York: New York Univ. Press, 1971.

Lacan, Jacques. *Ecrits: A Selection*. Trans. Alan Sheridan. New York: Norton, 1977.

Laity, Cassandra. "H. D.'s Romantic Landscapes: The Sexual Politics of the Garden." *Sagetrieb* 6 (1987): 57–75.

Marcus, Jane. *Art and Anger: Reading Like a Woman*. Columbus: Ohio State Univ. Press, 1988.

―――. *Virginia Woolf and the Languages of Patriarchy*. Bloomington: Indiana Univ. Press, 1987.

Meese, Elizabeth A. *Crossing the Double-Cross: The Practice of Feminist Criticism*. Chapel Hill: Univ. of North Carolina Press, 1986.

Meese, Elizabeth A., and Alice Parker, eds. *The Difference Within: Feminism and Critical Theory*. Amsterdam: Benjamins, 1988.

Millett, Kate. *Sexual Politics*. New York: Ballantine, 1970.

Moers, Ellen. *Literary Women: The Great Writers*. 1976 Rpt. New York: Oxford Univ. Press, 1985.

Newton, Esther. "The Myth of the Mannish Lesbian: Radclyffe Hall and the New Woman." In *Hidden from History: Reclaiming the Gay and Lesbian Past*. Ed. Martin Bauml Duberman, Martha Vicinus, and George Chauncey, Jr. New York: NAL, 1989. 281–93.

O'Brien, Sharon. " 'The Thing Not Named': Willa Cather as a Lesbian Writer." *Signs* 9 (1984): 588–603.

Rich, Adrienne. *Blood, Bread and Poetry: Selected Prose: 1979–1985*. New York: Norton, 1986.

―――. "Compulsory Heterosexuality and Lesbian Existence." *Signs* 5 (1980): 631–60.

―――. *On Lies, Secrets, and Silence: Selected Prose 1966–1978*. New York: Norton, 1979.

Rosenfeld, Marthe. "The Development of a Lesbian Sensibility in the Work of Jovette Marchessault and Nicole Brossard." *Traditionalism, Nationalism and Feminism: Women Writers of Quebec*. Ed. Paula Gilbert Lewis. Westport, Conn.: Greenwood, 1985. 227–39.

Rule, Jane. *Lesbian Images*. Freedom, Calif.: Crossing, 1975.

Segrest, Mab. *My Mama's Dead Squirrel: Lesbian Essays on Southern Culture*. Ithaca: Firebrand, 1985.

Shaktini, Namascar. "Displacing the Phallic Subject: Wittig's Lesbian Writing." *Signs* 8 (1982): 29–44.

Stambolian, George, and Elaine Marks, eds. *Homosexualities and French Literature: Cultural Contexts/Critical Texts.* Ithaca: Cornell Univ. Press, 1979.

Stein, Gertrude. *How to Write.* West Glover: Something Else, 1973.

Stimpson, Catharine R. "Zero Degree Deviancy: The Lesbian Novel in English." In *Writing and Sexual Difference.* Ed. Elizabeth Abel. Chicago: Univ. of Chicago Press, 1982. 243–59.

Walker, Nancy. " 'Wider Than the Sky': Public Presence and the Private Self in Dickinson, James, and Woolf." In *The Private Self: Theory and Practice of Women's Autobiographical Writings.* Ed. Shari Benstock. Chapel Hill: Univ. of North Carolina Press, 1988, 272–303.

Woolf, Virginia. *A Room of One's Own.* New York: Harcourt, 1957.

Zimmerman, Bonnie. "Exiting from Patriarchy: The Lesbian Novel of Development." In *The Voyage In: Fictions of Female Development.* Ed. Elizabeth Abel. Hanover: Univ. Press of New England, 1983. 244–57.

General Lesbian Theory

Abbott, Sidney, and Barbara Love. *Sappho Was a Right-On Woman: A Liberated View of Lesbianism.* New York: Stein & Day, 1972.

Daly, Mary. *Gyn/Ecology: The Metaethics of Radical Feminism.* Boston: Beacon, 1978.

Daly, Mary, and Jane Caputi. *Webster's First New Intergalactic Wickedary of the English Language.* Boston: Beacon, 1987.

Dworkin, Andrea. *Woman Hating.* New York: Dutton, 1974.

Faderman, Lillian. *Surpassing the Love of Men: Romantic Friendship and Love between Women from the Renaissance to the Present.* New York: Morrow, 1981.

Grahn, Judy. *Another Mother Tongue: Gay Words, Gay Worlds.* Boston: Beacon, 1984.

Klaich, Dolores. *Woman Plus Woman: Attitudes toward Lesbianism.* Tallahassee, Fla.: Naiad, 1989.

Wittig, Monique. "The Category of Sex." *Feminist Issues* 2 (1982): 63–68.

———. "The Mark of Gender." *Feminist Issues* 5 (1985): 3–12.

———. "The Straight Mind." *Feminist Issues* 1 (1980): 102–10.

Wittig, Monique, and Sande Zeig. *Lesbian Peoples: Material for a Dictionary.* New York: Avon, 1978.

Bibliographies

Clardy, Andrea Fleck. *Words to the Wise: A Writer's Guide to Feminist and Lesbian Periodicals & Publishers.* 2d ed. Ithaca: Firebrand, 1989.

Foster, Jeannette H. *Sex Variant Women in Literature.* Tallahassee, Fla.: Naiad, 1985.

Grier, Barbara, ed. *The Lesbian in Literature.* 3d ed. Tallahassee, Fla.: Naiad, 1981.

Potter, Clare, comp. and ed. *The Lesbian Periodicals Index*. Tallahassee, Fla.: Naiad, 1986.

Roberts, JR. *Black Lesbians: An Annotated Bibliography*. Tallahassee, Fla.: Naiad, 1981.

Journals

Common Lives, Lesbian Lives. Quarterly. P.O. Box 1553, Iowa City, IA 52244.

Gossip. 3x. Onlywomen Press, 38 Mount Pleasant, London WC1X OAP, United Kingdom.

Heresies. Foundation for the Community of Artists, 280 Broadway, Suite 412, New York, NY 10007.

Lesbian Ethics. 3x. P. O. Box 4723, Albuquerque, NM 87196.

Off Our Backs. Monthly. 2423 18th St. NW, Washington, DC 20009.

Trivia. 3x. P.o. Box 606, North Amherst, MA 01059.